BEING AND VALUE

SUNY Series in
Constructive Postmodern Thought
David Ray Griffin, Editor

BEING AND VALUE

Toward a Constructive Postmodern Metaphysics

FREDERICK FERRÉ

STATE UNIVERSITY OF NEW YORK PRESS

Production by Ruth Fisher
Marketing by Bernadette LaManna

Published by
State University of New York Press, Albany

© 1996 State University of New York

For information, address State University of New York Press,
State University Plaza, Albany, NY 12246

Library of Congress Cataloging-in-Publication Data

Ferré, Frederick.
    Being and value : toward a constructive postmodern metaphysics/
Frederick Ferré.
        p.   cm. — (SUNY series in constructive postmodern thought)
    Includes bibliographical references and index.
        ISBN 0–7914–2755–2 (alk. paper). — ISBN 0–7914–2756–0 (pbk. :
alk. paper)
        1. Metaphysics—History. 2. Metaphysics. 3. Postmodernism.
    I. Title. II. Series.
    BD111.F29 1996
    121'.8—dc20   95-4239
                                                                      CIP

10 9 8 7 6 5 4 3 2 1

To the students of my students

CONTENTS

PREFACE

This book has been a joy to write. I am amazed at how many themes from the breadth of my career in teaching and research have come together here. Just thirty-six years ago, in December 1958, I was finishing my first semester of college teaching by grading final examinations for a course in Modern Metaphysics at Vanderbilt University. I still sense reverberations from that course, taught fresh from my doctoral studies at St. Andrews University, Scotland, where British analytical philosophy and its impact on the great metaphysical issue of God had been my main concern.

Still living in the book are elements drawn from years of teaching at Mount Holyoke College (1959–1962), where my courses included Philo of Alexandria, Augustine, and the Medievals. At Dickinson College (1962–1980), I frequently taught History of Philosophy, from Thales to Nietzsche—a valuable lesson to me in the indispensable importance of the past in understanding the present and anticipating the future. While at Dickinson I cultivated my long-standing interest in the philosophy of science. This too shows in the book. Two sabbatical experiences (1969–1970) were of major influence. At Princeton, I spent a formative year working with Thomas Kuhn in the history of science, with special attention to Nicholas of Cusa, and at Pittsburgh, I enjoyed the stimulation of regular meetings with Adolf Grünbaum, Richard Gale, and Nicholas Rescher on the topic of temporal becoming. My deep disagreement with Grünbaum, whose philosophical deference to the abstract findings of modern mathematical physics irritated me into writing a small corpus of articles (Ferré 1970, 1971, 1972, 1973) and woke me to lasting dissatisfaction with the worldview of Albert Einstein, plays a major role in this book.

Since 1980, my teaching career at the University of Georgia has been intimately interlaced with environmental concerns. Moving to Georgia allowed scholarly and personal interaction with members of Georgia's renowned Institute of Ecology. Ecosystem ecology is vital to my alternative vision of appropriate postmodern science and hints at the proper direction for postmodern theory of reality itself.

Weaving all these strands together—remembering their varied origins but seeing them whole—has been enormously satisfying. Creating these complex intellectual harmonies is of intrinsic value to me, quite apart from any readership consideration. I hope no reader will be offended if I admit that this book, as indeed the whole trilogy of which it is the first volume, is written mainly from a personal yen to draw all this lifetime of thought into a coherent unity. No external pressures required it. Its imperative welled up from within and I gladly obeyed. By this same token, this highly personal project suffers from personal limitations. I wish, for example, that I had a better feel for nonwestern forms of thought, which surely will infuse any truly global postmodern metaphysics. But this I must leave to others.

Though written from personal motives, the book is very much intended for readers. My approach aims to communicate with many types of readers, and I hope they will find satisfactions, too. These imagined readers are not primarily from the present generation of professional philosophers, though I hope they too will be interested. The readers I picture more frequently are my students, particularly the graduate students now standing at the thresholds of their careers. They will participate in the opening generation of twenty-first-century thinkers. As the millennium turns, they will be the ones to introduce and insist on the needed changes in our ways of thinking about reality—and our ways of thinking about thinking and living, too, but those are issues for later volumes. They need not be crusted over with the deposits of modern presumptions. They have been raised in the era of poststructuralism, feminism, liberationism, and environmentalism. Their ideas about reality for the age they will help shape can be fresh constructions.

I hope others, not only the inhabitants of academe, will be among my readers as well. This is my main reason for writing with a minimum of the jargon that too often shields our discipline from outside participation. People from all fields of life are rightly interested in the character of the universe they inhabit. This sort of human curiosity and the attempts to satisfy it have been the basis for the entire saga this book recounts. There is a pervasive (and correct) sense that we have reached an immense turning point where the old will not suffice and the new is not fully formed. Many people now need a chance to view the origin and direction of reality. I hope this volume gives such metaphysically curious people that chance.

My own chance to range mentally over the wide landscapes required for this project and to harvest interests developed over a long career was provided by the University of Georgia in several supportive ways. First, I needed time to reflect and write. This was provided through a research professor faculty position to which I was appointed in 1988. The assignment doubled my opportunity for research activities and halved my normal teaching load. I am grateful, therefore, to former Dean W. Jackson Payne, who nominated me for the special professorship, and to the institution that has since nurtured me with this extraordinary benefit of time. In addition, I needed well-prepared students with whom to interact on the great topics of this book. This was provided by my teaching crucial classes in metaphysics at the precise time I needed to have extensive dialogue with bright and open minds. For two sequential years, these advanced courses enriched and stimulated my planning and writing. I am grateful to the head of the Department of Philosophy, Professor Donald Nute, for this opportuntiy.

Others have helped me as well. I appreciate the friendly criticism and encouragement different parts of this book have received from Professor John B. Cobb, Jr. (Claremont, California) and Professors Betty Jean Craige, Victoria Davion, and Frank B. Golley (University of Georgia). The whole book was finally benefitted by the keen eye and fresh mind of my graduate student, Bethe Segars McRae. These good folk are not responsible for problems that remain, of course, but they have provided useful reality checks when they were requested. My mother, Mrs. Nels F. S. Ferré, has cheerfully performed the much-valued editorial role she perfected on my father's books; and my wife, Barbara, has helped me check the intelligibility of difficult passages by listening to me read them aloud to her in search of tangled syntax (or muddled thought).

David Ray Griffin, colleague, editor of this Series, and friend, deserves my thanks here for having strongly encouraged me to write this book and its two planned sequel volumes for the SUNY Series In Constructive Postmodern Thought. His many criticisms and suggestions helped me avoid a number of needless embarrassments. I am indeed in debt to him in many ways. We have long worked together in various capacities. We both have taken inspiration from the thought of Alfred North Whitehead; and though we have had lively differences over some issues, we have no disagreements (that I know of) about the importance of replacing modern categories of thought with a panexperientialist constructive alternative. It was Griffin who first laid out the highly significant distinctions between "deconstructive" and "constructive" postmodernism, expressed in the Series Introduction and elsewhere (Griffin 1989: 1–7, 29–61). I have enjoyed his companionship on this adventure.

Finally, I wish to thank Mona Freer, my editorial assistant. Her unfailing attention to detail was invaluable, as were her general comments and encouraging reflections on the substance of this book. She is a perfect example of the intelligent nonspecialist reader for whom I hope this book can make a positive difference. She has certainly made a positive difference to the book.

Frederick Ferré
Highlands, North Carolina

ACKNOWLEDGMENT

Thanks are due HarperCollins Publishers for permission to use, with minor amendments, my article, "Auguste Comte," published in *Great Thinkers of the Western World,* edited by Ian McGreal, HarperCollins Publishers, 1992, pp. 348–51.

INTRODUCTION TO SUNY SERIES IN CONSTRUCTIVE POSTMODERN THOUGHT

The rapid spread of the term *postmodern* in recent years witnesses to a growing dissatisfaction with modernity and to an increasing sense that the modern age not only had a beginning but can have an end as well. Whereas the word *modern* was almost always used until quite recently as a word of praise and as a synonym for *contemporary,* a growing sense is now evidenced that we can and should leave modernity behind—in fact, that we *must* if we are to avoid destroying ourselves and most of the life on our planet.

Modernity, rather than being regarded as the norm for human society toward which all history has been aiming and into which all societies should be ushered—forcibly if necessary—is instead increasingly seen as an aberration. A new respect for the wisdom of traditional societies is growing as we realize that they have endured for thousands of years and that, by contrast, the existence of modern society for even another century seems doubtful. Likewise, *modernism* as a worldview is less and less seen as The Final Truth, in comparison with which all divergent worldviews are automatically regarded as "superstitious." The modern worldview is increasingly relativized to the status of one among many, useful for some purposes, inadequate for others.

Although there have been antimodern movements before, beginning perhaps near the outset of the nineteenth century with the Romanticists and the Luddites, the rapidity with which the term postmodern has become widespread in our time suggests that the antimodern sentiment is more extensive and intense than before, and also that it includes the sense that modernity can be successfully overcome only by going beyond, it, not by attempting to return to a premodern form of existence. Insofar as a common element is found in the various ways in which the term is used, *postmodernism* refers to a diffuse sentiment rather than to any common set of doctrines—the sentiment that humanity can and must go beyond the modern.

Beyond connoting this sentiment, the term postmodern is used in a confusing variety of ways, some of them contradictory to others. In artistic and literary circles, for example, postmodernism shares in this general sentiment but also involves a specific reaction against "modernism" in the narrow sense of a movement in artistic-literary circles in the late nineteenth and early twentieth centuries. Postmodern architecture is very different from postmodern literary criticism. In some circles, the term postmodern is used in reference to that potpourri of ideas and systems sometimes called *new age metaphysics,* although many of these ideas and systems are more premodern than postmodern. Even in philosophical and theological circles, the term postmodern refers to two quite different positions, one of which is reflected in this series. Each position seeks to transcend both modernism in the sense of the worldview that has developed out of the seventeenth-century-Galilean-Cartesian-Baconian-Newtonian science, and modernity in the sense of the world order that both conditioned and was conditioned by this worldview. But the two positions seek to transcend the modern in different ways.

Closely related to literary-artistic postmodernism is a philosophical postmodernism inspired variously by pragmatism, physicalism, Ludwig Wittgenstein, Martin Heidegger, and Jacques Derrida and other recent French thinkers. By the use of terms that arise out of particular segments of this movement, it can be called *deconstructive* or *eliminative postmodernism.* It overcomes the modern worldview through an anti-worldview: it deconstructs or eliminates the ingredients necessary for a worldview, such as God, self, purpose, meaning, a real world, and truth as correspondence. While motivated in some cases by the ethical concern to forestall totalitarian systems, this type of postmodern thought issues in relativism, even nihilism. It could also be called *ultramodernism,* in that its eliminations result from carrying modern premises to their logical conclusions.

The postmodernism of this series can, by contrast, be called *constructive* or *revisionary.* It seeks to overcome the modern worldview not by elminating the possibility of worldviews as such, but by constructing a postmodern worldview through a revision of modern premises and traditional concepts. This constructive or revisionary postmodernism involves a new unity of scientific, ethical, aesthetic, and religious intuitions. It rejects not science as such but only that scientism in which the data of the modern natural sciences are alone allowed to contribute to the construction of our worldview.

The constructive activity of this type of postmodern thought is not limited to a revised worldview; it is equally concerned with a postmodern world that will support and be supported by the new worldview. A postmodern world will involve postmodern persons, with a postmodern spirituality, on the one hand, and a postmodern society, ultimately a postmodern global order, on the other. Going beyond the modern world will involve transcending its individualism, anthropocentrism, patriarchy, mechanization, economism, consumerism, nationalism, and militarism. Constructive postmodern thought provides support for the ecology, peace, feminist and other emancipatory movements of our time, while stressing that the inclusive emancipation must be from modernity itself. The term postmodern, however, by contrast with *premodern,* emphasizes that the modern world has produced unparalleled advances that must not be lost in a general revulsion against its negative features.

From the point of view of deconstructive postmodernists, this constructive postmodernism is still hopelessly wedded to outdated concepts, because it wishes to salvage a positive meaning not only for the notions of the human self, historical meaning, and truth as correspondence, which were central to modernity, but also for premodern notions of a divine reality, cosmic meaning, and an enchanted nature. From the point of view of its advocates, however, this revisionary postmodernism is not only more adequate to our experience but also more genuinely postmodern. It does not simply carry the premises of modernity through to their logical conclusions, but criticizes and revises those premises. Through its return to organicism and its acceptance of nonsensory perception, it opens itself to the recovery of truths and values from various forms of premodern thought and practice that had been dogmatically rejected by modernity. This constructive, revisionary postmodernism involves a creative synthesis of modern and premodern truths and values.

This series does not seek to create a movement so much as to help shape and support an already existing movement convinced that modernity can and must be transcended. But those antimodern movements which arose in the past failed to deflect or even retard the onslaught of modernity. What reasons can we have to expect the current movement to be more successful? First, the previous antimodern movements were primarily calls to return to a premodern form of life and thought rather than calls to advance, and the human spirit does not rally to calls to turn back. Second, the previous antimodern movements either rejected modern science, reduced it to a description of mere appearances, or assumed its adequacy in principle; therefore, they could base their calls only on the negative social and spiritual effects of modernity. The current movement draws on natural science itself as a witness against the adequacy of the modern worldview. Third, the present movement has even more evidence that did previous movements of the ways in which modernity and its worldview *are* socially and spiritually destructive. The fourth and probably most decisive difference is that the present movement is based on the awareness that *the continuation of modernity threatens the very survival of life on our planet.* This awareness, combined with the growing knowledge of the interdependence of the modern worldview and the militarism, nuclearism, and ecological devastation of the modern world, is providing an unprecedented impetus for people to see the evidence for a postmodern worldview and to envisage postmodern ways of relating to each other, the rest of nature, and the cosmos as a whole. For these reasons, the failure of the previous antimodern movements says little about the possible success of the current movement.

Advocates of this movement do not hold the naively utopian belief that the success of this movement would bring about a global society of universal and lasting peace, harmony, and happiness, in which all spiritual problems, social conflicts, ecological destruction, and hard choices would vanish. There is, after all, surely a deep truth in the testimony of the world's religions to the presence of a transcultural proclivity to evil deep within the human heart, which no new paradigm, combined with a new economic order, new child-rearing practices, or any other social arrangements, will suddenly eliminate. Furthermore, it has correctly been said that "life is robbery": a strong element of competition is inherent within finite existence, which no social-political-economic-ecological order can overcome. These two truths, especially when contemplated together, should caution us against unrealistic hopes.

However, no such appeal to "universal constants" should reconcile us to the present order, as if this order were thereby uniquely legitimated. The human proclivity to evil in general, and to conflictual competition and ecological destruction in particualr, can be greatly exacerbated or greatly mitigated by a world order and its worldview. Modernity exacerbates it about as much as imaginable. We can therefore envision, without being naively utopian, a far better world order, with a far less dangerous trajectory, than the one we now have.

This series, making no pretense of neutrality, is dedicated to the success of this movement toward a postmodern world.

David Ray Griffin
Series Editor

1

WHAT IS METAPHYSICS?

"Metaphysics" is a miserable word. To many intelligent members of the public it fails to communicate at all; to others seeking occult mysteries it communicates the wrong thing; and to an influential segment of the philosophical community it communicates only a realm of frustration and intellectual bankruptcy. Why stick with it? For many reasons of convenience I would prefer to avoid it. At one point in my teaching career I renamed my metaphysics course Theory of Reality and rechristened my epistemology course Theory of Knowledge to match, in hopes of sidestepping initial confusion and resistance. But almost immediately I had to admit to my students that what we were *really* doing was metaphysics, since most of our texts used the word. My attempted evasion was a failure.

Neither Plato nor the pre-Socratics, powerful metaphysicians that they were, called what they were doing "metaphysics." Even Aristotle, whose great volume by that title saddled posterity—apparently forever—with the term, never used it to refer to what he was doing. Instead he spoke of "First Philosophy," which sounds adequately deep but a good deal less obscure. It was only his editors, by later placing the volume containing his First Philosophy immediately after-the-*Physics* (in Greek, "*Meta-Physika*"), who created the word we love to hate but seem unable to shake.

HOW METAPHYSICAL THEORIES ARE FAMILIAR

Be that as it may, metaphysics is nothing more (nor less) than the theory of reality in general. There have been and are many different such theories, of course,

1

just as there have been and are many different theories about less comprehensive topics. Some are more sophisticated, some less. There should be nothing strange or off-putting about this. Nothing is more familiar than the clash of alternative ways to understand something. What marks metaphysics as unique is that *all* of reality, not just parts of it, is included as its subject matter.

This unlimited comprehensiveness of metaphysical attempts at understanding creates some special logical problems, since, in principle, nothing can be left out. But before we get to those problems, it is important to recognize that theorizing about reality in general shares most of the normal traits of theorizing about anything.

Making a theory is a kind of thinking. As such, it is an activity of beings endowed with mental powers of memory and imagination sufficient to form concepts—which rise at first out of recurrent features recognized within the jumble of immediate experience—and to manipulate them so as to interpret some subject identified as problematic.

All theory has a purpose, a job to do that enforces certain standards on the pain of self defeat. At a minimum, the concepts used need to be put together in ways that avoid cancelling each other out. If the problematic subject is identified as "red," it will be conceptually suicidal to identify it also, at the same time and in all relevant respects, as "not-red." That would be simultaneously to give and to take away, leaving nothing accomplished. Thus, the first functionally grounded requirement of theory—that it maintain the capacity to mean something rather than nothing—is reflected in the standard of *consistency* that theories, simple as well as grand, need to meet.

A second built-in purpose of a theory, to interpret the problematic, to provide a sense of understanding, requires more than simple noncontradiction between its elements. That is a merely negative condition. More positively, if we are to find our way among our ideas, the conceptual elements of our theory must positively hang together so that we can move smoothly without gaps from one element to another. When there is a "hole" in the detective's theory, the police are wise to wait. This stronger functional requirement for theorizing is that of *coherence*. We should be able to reach to the next concept without letting go of our handhold on the last. What this specifically means in practice will differ in different circumstances, but all theory is better (all other things being equal) the closer its concepts fit together.

Concepts are useful to the functions of theorizing, however, only to the extent that they successfully capture important regularities from the given domain where understanding is sought. Note that this observation makes a significant turn in the discussion. Consistency and coherence are what might be called "internal" standards, since they are concerned with the way conceptual elements relate to one another within a theory. But this third standard may be called "external," since it directs attention outward to the *applicability* of the theory to its subject matter. The standard of applicability is minimal. For example, it would be rare (and crazy) to find a theory whose concepts all deal with the refraction of light, being put to use to explain the frequency of divorce among children of the clergy. But applicability is a standard worth noticing, just because it is so fundamental. On the external side it reminds us of what consistency is on the internal side: both are *sine qua non* for the theorizing enterprise. Without consistency, we wind up thinking nothing; without applicability, we find ourselves thinking nothing about the topic of interest.

Just as consistency on the internal side needs supplementing by the more demanding (and more difficult to measure) criterion of coherence, so mere applicability is not enough to measure success in theorizing. It is too easy to satisfy. Much more is needed than merely *some* important data from the problematic domain; in principle, *all* relevant evidence is required if our understanding is to be secure. Gaps in evidence on the external side are as potentially damaging to theoretical success as are holes in coherence on the internal side. This fourth standard is *adequacy*. In principle, it demands evidential completeness. In practice, such perfection in adequacy is no more possible for real-life theorizers than is perfect coherence. But both adequacy and coherence set worthy goals and thus provide useful standards for assessing better or worse as attempted theories approach or fall short of them by greater or lesser extent. A humility-reinforcing way of putting this is that there are, in principle, ways of distinguishing greater from lesser theoretical failures.

The situation is made more complicated (but more realistic) by the fact that the sliding scales of coherence and adequacy tend to work against each other. The detective may be able to develop a tight case against the suspect if allowed to omit several bits of evidence from consideration. Coherence here finds the criterion of adequacy a bother. But premature coherences need to be resisted when justice is at stake. Still, the police department cannot be ordered simply to go out and collect all and everything, helter-skelter. What is worth going for—the relevance of evidence—is itself largely theory-driven. The insatiable demands of adequacy need limitation, discipline, and definition by coherence.

The polar tensions between the internal and external requirements of theorizing are encountered everywhere, at high levels and at low. If I am trying to decide what kind of person you are, I am, whether I realize it or not, engaging in theory-construction. I have a limited amount of data (on the adequacy pole) of which to "make sense" (on the coherence pole). The evidence is mixed; it does not all fit into neat concepts like "pleasant" or "flighty" or "malicious." These concepts themselves strain against each other. I am tempted to say inconsistent things, but that would not help me understand you; that would only lead me to self-confusion. I would like to wait and let you reveal more of yourself (enlarge the adequacy dimension); but perhaps circumstances do not give me the luxury of delaying before making some decision that will depend on my theory of you. Then I need to select the "more important" evidence from the "less important." How do I do this? For better or worse, I must use partially formed theory-fragments, together with intuition and hunch, to select what I find most significant among the mixed signals you send me. Then I may use this still admittedly imperfect theory in my decision, but, if I am wise, not without full acknowledgment to myself that my conclusion is as shaky as my closure—though *practically* necessary—was *logically* premature. What I must never do, however, is suppose that my new theory of you, once reached, is beyond improvement by more data, when available, and/or by more thinking. Equally, I must not despair and suppose that evidence and reflection are useless simply because I realize that my theory is far from perfect. Jumping thoughtlessly into decisions without considering evidence—however mixed and confusing—is no reasonable response to the elusiveness of theoretical perfection.

HOW METAPHYSICAL THEORIES ARE STRANGE

So far I have stressed the common features of theorizing. But metaphysical thinking is different in one enormous respect from all the rest: it aims at complete comprehensiveness. This makes for trouble.

One troublesome consequence of the unlimited comprehensiveness of metaphysical thinking becomes quickly apparent when we try to make use of the consistency principle. There is so much to be covered. Everything in the universe is to be put under this rule. Have we any right to step into this vast domain with any confidence that our consistency criterion will apply everywhere? What if the universe, taken as a whole, just happens to contain mutually inconsistent features? Who is to say—right from the start—that this is impossible? Is the criterion of consistency, once set to work as a cosmic rule, simply a grand question-begging device?

No, the rule of consistency cannot in principle tell us what we are going to find among the data. Least of all can it rule out the (very probable) outcome that reality, as we get to know it better, may be more bizarre than our wildest fantasies. One of my favorite professors once ended a graduate class in metaphysics with a disclaimer of personal insight into the intimate secrets of ultimate reality; but to this modest conclusion he added a dramatic caution as he folded away his notes: "Whatever reality turns out to be," he rumbled, "it will certainly be *strange*." Apparently inconsistent properties of things appear with regularity in advanced physics; why should this suddenly cease as we cross the line to metaphysics?

My answer is that consistency does not rule out strangeness; it does not in any way legislate for reality. It is a rule *of our thinking*, the precondition *for effective theory*. It is thinkable of course that fundamental reality may be unthinkable. In the long run, all our theorizing about the ultimate may be defeated. That meta-metaphysical possibility is what is finally at stake in the (highly meaningful) question of whether or not reality in its entirety is ultimately hospitable to the rule of consistency. There are no guarantees. But until we are ready to abandon the whole enterprise, our drive to understand, while respecting every apparent inconsistency, will treat each as a challenge to deeper pondering, aiming eventually to resolve paradoxes and show reconciling intelligibilities. This we note is also the pattern in the sciences: even when alternative models remain paradoxical, as in the incompatible properties of "waves" and "particles," their tensions are resolved in underlying mathematical theory.

We may then have a choice whether to theorize, but if we choose to theorize we have no choice but to try to think consistently. This attempt need not be shallow and must not be dogmatic. Unless we open our minds to conflicts, oppositions, and antagonisms—both in the evidence and in what we want to say about it—we shall be left merely with the "foolish consistency" that is the hobgoblin of mediocre theories. And yet inconsistency unresolved ruins thought. This is true in limited domains like physics and is no less true when our thought aims to encompass the whole of things; but as the subject matter enlarges, so do the opportunities for inconsistencies and therewith the difficulties of making sense. Each difficulty, nonetheless, is a challenge for the construction of better theories. Far from posing a question-*begging* substantive doctrine, then, the rule of consistency supplies a firm methodological discipline for question-*answering* and—where the answers clash—for focused new-answer-*seeking*.

If special difficulties are posed for the rule of consistency by the unlimited comprehensiveness of metaphysical thinking, so much the more should we expect troubles to surround the criterion of coherence. Consistency is "merely" a minimal threshold requirement to allow thinking to proceed without self-cancellation. But coherence, as we noted, is far more demanding. Coherence mandates that ideas used for understanding any subject matter fit together, make sense. How can this ideal possibly be approached when the subject matter is (literally) everything?

There are times when we philosophers are morally no less than epistemologically obliged to acknowledge the arrogance—the sheer presumption—of trying to pour the ocean of reality into the thimbles of our minds. This is one of those times. If there is a justifiable ground for rejecting the whole enterprise of metaphysical theorizing, here it is. Many have done just that. I for one cannot bring myself to blame them. In the past I have been in their company. I still recoil from the whiff of dogmatism. If ever a "know-it-all" attitude is radically inappropriate, it is when one is indeed trying to know the *All*.

That acknowledged, what is left? For some of us, at least, there is a powerful counter-intuition that thinking carefully about the small context while failing to do our best at thinking about the largest context is itself irresponsible. Every belief—every action—carries implications for its contexts, all the way up. If I spread my picnic blanket in a pasture, I imply that there is no raging bull behind the bushes. If I first check behind the bushes, I imply that bulls are dependably visible things that can be seen and avoided. By so implying, I take for granted the context of natural regularity and causal predictability. And so it goes toward wider and more inclusive contexts. If any of the larger contexts is not as I assume, everything is changed, all the way down. Meanings shift. Practical precautions are defeated. If the chief of police turns out to have been the head of the crime syndicate, then all the detective's plans and actions, laid in a false context, undergo a sea change in significance, both theoretical and practical. If only our sleuth had thought with more care about that possibility before he stepped into his own trap! Larger contexts count.

The largest context counts, too, despite the difficulties (and the presumption) in thinking carefully about it. Admittedly, it is not a topic that holds charm for everyone. Fortunately, not everyone is required to do it. Yes, it attracts more than its share of cranks and quacks, dogmatists and fanatics. But what can be done "badly" can be done "less badly"—perhaps even "well," considering the given limitations. That is, if standards can be identified that rationally justify assessing a job as *poorly* done, then by the same standards we have some guidance on what would be required if it is to be done *better*.

Coherence as we saw before is a question of better or worse. It is a standard that is hard to measure, and one that is present or absent by degrees, in comparison with alternatives. More coherence, all other things considered, helps; less coherence, hurts. But where do we begin when the job is to bring as high a degree of coherence as possible to the entire realm of reality?

The task of understanding a subject matter is to move from the known to the unknown, or, more accurately, from the relatively better known to the relatively less known. This requires casting around for features in the (relatively) known that make sense to us, particularly for patterns in things that hang together, that can lead our minds with some security from one part of the pattern to another. These features or patterns in relatively well-known things become "models" when we apply them to new, relatively unknown domains. Then they function as analogies. If we are trying to understand sound by imagining it as an ocean wave, there should be something to the subject matter of sound like the height of water waves from crest to trough—call it amplitude. Again, if sound is like a wave, there should be something in the subject matter like the closeness of the waves as they traverse the water—call this frequency. Third, if sound is like a wave, then what kinds of media can perform the "waving"? If we identify air or water or the resonant earth itself, we find (in coherent harmony with our model) that where there is no medium to transmit wave-like motions, there is no possibility of sound. The more we understand how water waves behave—are interfered with, reflected, and the like—the better we understand the phenomena of sound.

Models are aids to coherent thinking, but they are never identical to the subject matter they are brought in to illuminate. There are always differences, or the model would not be simply a model any longer. Sometimes the differences can be surprising, as physicists found when extending the model of waves to light and other electromagnetic phenomena. At first they assumed, naturally, that if light is like waves, there must be some medium in which the "waving" occurs, as in water waves and sound waves. To make the theory coherent, therefore, a medium of very thin "ether" was postulated, spreading throughout space. But this is one of the surprising differences between light waves and water or sound waves. In 1887, Albert A. Michaelson and Edward W. Morley showed, by precise measurements with their newly invented interferometer, that no such medium could be detected. "Ether" was a physical postulate with a systematic function but without any empirical referent.

Metaphysical postulates are also often made for systematic purposes, suggested by great, constitutive analogies that help provide a conceptual pattern for the domain of reality as a whole. To think coherently about such a huge domain requires all the help from models and analogies that philosophers can derive. Is reality like a great machine, a watch perhaps? This would suggest many moving parts finely adjusted to each other, dependably interacting without taking thought. Is reality, rather, like a great living organism? Is it ultimately personality and its products? Or is it more like a dream, all play of illusion on the surface but connected by deep reference to an underlying subconscious? These models and many more have been proposed and developed in human attempts to think about the outermost context of our lives. Unfortunately for the control of such thinking, it is not always clear what would count legitimately as empirical constraints on the fertile coherences cultivated on the suggestion of metaphysical models. What could challenge metaphysical thinking as the Michaelson-Morley interferometer experiment challenged physical theory, showing the referential emptiness of a systematically required concept?

Should metaphysical thought, even in principle, be tied down in any way to the empirical standard of applicability? My contention is that it should and must be so linked. But the "outermost context" character of metaphysical thinking makes one pause. In lesser contexts, when "all" that is wanted is theoretical understanding of some limited domain of actual or possible experience (as in physics), it is obvious that theory needs to be applicable to data in that experiential domain. But at the all-comprehending level of metaphysical theorizing, is not the authority of experience itself one of the open questions?

Should our experiences be granted the honorific title of the *data* (Latin for the givens) to which thinking is fundamentally responsible?

This is not an obvious matter. We must not ignore the old tradition that experience as a whole is misleading or illusory, not the "Way of Truth," as Parmenides put it before the birth of Socrates. Will we not beg the question against Parmenides (and against much profound Asian conviction) if we insist that applicability to data of experience, Parmenides' mere "Way of Seeming," is a necessary condition for good metaphysical thinking?

Perhaps there is no alternative. Our experience is simply there. It provides the given starting point for all thinkers, including those who would think systematically about what is real in general. In what medieval philosophers called the "order of knowing," it comes first. This does not mean that we must take whatever we are given at face value. That the moon *appears* to be about the size of a coin does not mean that it *is* about the size of a coin. The givens of experience are often in much need of mutual correction.

Metaphysical theories such as Parmenides', that hold experience as a whole to be fundamentally flawed, usually make some bold differentiation, as between Truth and Seeming. The data of experience give only Seeming, they say. Truth lies somewhere else. So far, although obscurely expressed, these theories may be right. Our whole experiential apparatus may be in need of critique. But such a position does not (so far) deny the need for the applicability of theory to experience. On the contrary, the door remains open for detailed application of this doctrine, for example, an explanation of why familiar experiences should, on further examination, be considered flawed, and in what ways. What is inadmissible is the self-contradictory implication that a metaphysical theory can be both comprehensive in its "Truth" and also fail to apply to or illuminate the whole domain of experience. Experience may indeed give us mere Seeming, but nevertheless seeming occurs—and needs to be accounted for in terms of what is held as Truth. It is the function of all-inclusive theories to include and explain, not to dismiss and avoid. To the extent that Parmenides' position was merely dismissive of Seeming, the position, however stimulating, was flawed metaphysics. And it may be well to add in this context that the flaw is not simply in complete lack of applicability but also in radical incoherence between the realms of Truth and Seeming. There is no conceptual passage from one to the other. Here is testimony to the power that bold, simplifying abstractions can wield over the judgments of intelligent persons: viz., that Parmenides and his spiritual heirs, to the present day, continue to command prestige despite failing marks both in coherence and in applicability.

Applicability, as we saw, is only a minimal standard compared to adequacy. The former only requires *some* bearing on relevant data; the latter calls for consideration, ideally, of *all*. Even in limited domains of inquiry this is a difficult standard to approach. What then are the prospects of adequacy in the unlimited realms of metaphysical thinking?

There is no point in fooling ourselves. This is an impossible standard to meet, particularly in metaphysics. Like the criterion of coherence, it shows us a direction and holds up an ideal. It provides a scale of ever keener attention to ever richer data, with the high end disappearing beyond our powers to achieve, but a scale on which in the middle ranges we are able to measure comparative approximations.

One obvious handicap in achieving metaphysical adequacy is the human data receptor. Our senses are dull at best. Even perfect vision, for example, is adequate only to the tiny segment of the electromagnetic band in which the visible spectrum falls. Above violet, our unaided eyes are blind to shorter wavelengths and higher frequencies like X-rays or cosmic rays. Similarly, below red, the visible data disappear. But reality as a whole, though invisible to us when infrared or ultraviolet, is still bombarding us with would-be data. That bombardment would be relevant—all data are relevant in principle to metaphysics—if only we could detect the incoming flow. Luckily, instruments have been invented to help expand the range of sensory data collection. In consequence, it is not immodest, only realistic, to acknowledge that our theories today can be graded higher on the adequacy scale—though doubtless not in all respects—than Plato's or Aristotle's, because of the vast increase of available data made possible by the instrumental technologies of modern science. Just as Johannes Kepler's theories were made more adequate because of the patient observations of Tycho Brahe, and just as Galileo's arguments were provided resources of adequacy eventually to trump his scholastic opponents thanks to the concrete data from his telescope, so metaphysical thinking today is blessed (and cursed!) by the immense ranges of data provided by the instruments of the special sciences. The blessings of additional data are obvious: What might Aristotle have done if allowed access to merely as much information as every high school graduate takes for granted today? But the curse shows itself on the other side of the same coin: there are too many data for bold coherences to fit easily; and new data pour in all the time, constantly challenging the models through which those aiming at adequacy try to think comprehensively and coherently as well.

Oddly, in view of the already limited powers of human data receptors, some metaphysical theorists have been inclined to impose further limits on what shall be recognized as relevant data. They have argued that only the intuitions coming from the sense organs (of sight, hearing, smell, taste, and touch) should be attended to. And of those, only a small portion should count: only that portion amenable to quantitative treatment thus excluding all qualitative aspects, not only such aspects as the so-called secondary qualities of heard tones, felt textures, or seen hues, but also such elements as the dim awareness of power and significance or even the vivid sense of beauty. The intuitions expressed through poetry or painting, religion or ethics, must be ruled out in advance as nondata.

This proposal was widely accepted through the modern period. It had the virtue of making the achievement and defense of abstract coherences much easier, since it lops off exactly those would-be data which are hardest to fit into mathematical models of mechanical systems. But this was an achievement cheapened by diminishing the meaning of adequacy. It would seem that real respect for adequacy—at least when placed in its final, comprehensive context—puts the burden of proof on those who propose exclusionary policies. Such exclusions may well be justified when a more limited subject domain is at issue: for example, the domain of physical things only. They become much less easily justified when the domain includes organisms or persons. When the domain expands to cover all reality, however, these policies seem supported only by dogmatism in the service of some treasured metaphysical theory.

How Metaphysical Theories Are Valued

Treasured? Yes, metaphysical theory, however abstract and dry it may seem, is enmeshed with the deepest values. Therefore I need to conclude this opening chapter with a survey of the main ways in which metaphysics and values intertwine.

I have already introduced the distinction between a model, used to advance metaphysical thinking, and the theory it suggests and interprets through its relatively familiar features. The theory itself may be highly abstract. It provides the logical bones and joints that articulate the model in an as literal-minded way as possible, given the metaphorical origins of language as a whole. Inevitably, the suggestive model, drawn from familiar domains of experience, all of which are value-laden positively or negatively, carries with it some implicit value context. When the interpreted theory has articulated a full-fledged metaphysical scheme and has become influential, moving people in the ways they understand themselves, look at others, organize their institutions, and anticipate their destiny, we have what I shall call a worldview.

Worldviews, as I use the term, are not quite the same as metaphysical theories, strictly speaking. Someone may have a worldview without being adept at metaphysical theorizing. Indeed, a worldview may be so pervasive that it is invisible to those who have been reared to see through it, just as a pair of clean eyeglasses is to a reader or, better, as the medium of clear air is to a landscape painter. The painter sees the distant hills as blue, although it is the medium of air refracting light that causes this perception. There is nothing "wrong" with this. We all see the hills in the same way. Similarly, there is nothing necessarily vicious in the systematic influences exerted by worldviews on our beliefs and attitudes about ourselves, our society, and our universe. Still, there is nothing especially admirable in being unaware of influences that may be causing us avoidable problems.

Comprehensive visions of reality, worldviews, need not necessarily derive from prior metaphysical theorizing. They may instead emerge from the "final context" poetry we call myth. Mythic imagery in turn may play a large role in supplying vivid and evocative models to suggest and interpret explicit metaphysical theories. In this way, metaphysical theorizing and mythic traditions may work powerfully in tandem.

Sometimes, however, worldviews in popular culture are the residue of technical and explicit metaphysical theory-construction. This is clearly the case with the mechanical worldview—derived from the careful genius of Descartes, Galileo, Hobbes, Gassendi, Newton, and others—that has claimed and still claims the allegiance of great numbers of intellectuals and ordinary people in the modern period. There are good value-reasons to admire this worldview and the metaphysical theory that underlies it. Besides powerfully validating and further encouraging the mathematical sciences, with which it has always been allied, the mechanical worldview had from its origin the astringent virtue of countering its predecessor magical worldview, in which unchecked superstition, witchcraft, religious wars, and persecutions could and did flourish.

The categories of mechanical metaphysics ruled out in principle, however, the notion of "casting spells" across distances with no intermediate causal means. Witchcraft, given the mechanical model and its articulation in metaphysical theories of contiguous efficient causation, was simply impossible, literally unthinkable. Mind, on the same theory, could in principle have no grip on matter. Fear of hexes or the evil eye could once and for all be set aside. There was no place on the logical map for such concepts. Thus, the mechanical worldview could be treasured for its antiseptic powers in ridding the modern world of goblins and ghosts and the terrible social costs in turmoil and torture that the magical worldview exacted from those trapped inside its transparent, mind-bending medium.

Unfortunately, antiseptics, though immensely valuable for some needs, make a poor permanent diet. The mechanical worldview inherited the grave metaphysical difficulty of accounting for its own value and for values in general. The positive realm of beauty, love, courage, loyalty, creativity, fairness, friendship, and hope seems in principle as vulnerable to dissolution by the antiseptics of the mechanical worldview as the fearsome kingdom of magic and witchcraft. Neither is grounded by, or has any secure counterpart in, the "real" world of matter in motion. As beauty is reduced to something figuratively in the "eye [really the mind] of the beholder," so all values are literally figments of mentality, in this worldview. There is no more place in the logical geography of such a worldview for "values in nature" as there is for "hexes" or "wizards."

But neither is there a secure place for "mind" itself. Mind is as ineffective as it is intangible. It is a mysterious, somewhat embarrassing, addition to the mechanical vision of things, arbitrarily imposing tastes and preferences that have no warrant in purely objective things themselves.

What, then, of the importance of the cleansing power of the mechanical worldview itself? The claim to importance is itself a value judgment. Similarly, shall we conclude that our preference for the austere virtues of the mechanical worldview, if we do prefer them, reflects only an arbitrary taste? Is the magical worldview not really (somehow) worse? Are superstition, intolerance, and persecution only bad "in the eye of the beholder"?

It may be answered that the great theorizers of the seventeenth and eighteenth centuries gave us truer theories; but what is the importance of such an achievement if "importance" itself is only a figment of mentality? Suppose, for argument's sake, we freely grant that effective theorizing "just is" important *to people with minds*, whatever the ultimate grounding—or lack of it—such intuitions may involve. Then it follows that metaphysical theorizing, even assuming the most austere vision of reality, is involved with values from the start. The first value implicit is that such thinking is important enough to be done, and if done, done well. That much granted, other values crowd in as instrumentally essential for the job to succeed. They are such values as honesty before the data, submission to the rules of consistency, coherence, applicability, adequacy, and readiness to respect the criticisms of others who may see more clearly than we where we have gone astray from our commitment to honor such values.

Instrumental values of this sort can be noble and demanding, as we see. To be instrumental need not be trivial; we should never allow ourselves to say "merely" instrumental values, as though they were of little worth or importance. More, instrumental values have the significant trait of being nonarbitrary. Given the goal, they represent the means to reach it. If the goal is valued, some set of them must be valued too.

At the same time, it should be recognized that instrumental values are never valuable in a vacuum. It is only because there are some values that are not instrumental but "final," end-of-the-line, or "intrinsic," that "intermediate," on-the-way, or instrumental values gain what importance they can claim. Some values may be both. Health is a value of intrinsic importance to the organism that enjoys it. But at the same time, being healthy is an important means to many additional ends, both intrinsic and instrumental, that could not be reached without it. My good health is not only enjoyable in itself, for the glow of well-being I treasure without reference to anything more, but also my health allows me to work and earn money. The work in my case is, like health, a dual value: it is intrinsically satisfying and it pays a salary. The money, in contrast, is only instrumentally valuable to me. Earning it allows me to exchange it for other things I value, again either for themselves, intrinsically (e.g., musical recordings), or for both instrumental and intrinsic values (e.g., warm, good-looking clothes), or for further instrumental goals alone (e.g., a shovel for the garden).

What needs to be remembered by metaphysical theorizers is that experience is not neutral. It is not the sensory mirror of a value-free world of mere objects. Experience is instead shot through with intuitions of value, both intrinsic and instrumental. We find the data of experience inseparable from interests and aversions, hopes and fears, joys and pains, sorrows, satisfactions, and obligations. Normal experience is full of vague intuitions of importance, drawing our attention toward some features rather than others. Such intuitions change with added experience; not unlike sensory intuitions, they are corrigible and educable. But only because they are "given," along with all the rest of the contents of experience, can they provide the foundation for the intrinsic valuations which, in turn, give shape and meaning to the instrumental.

One of the most profound questions of metaphysical theory is the status in reality of these intrinsic valuations. One obvious instance is posed by religion. Human beings, since the beginning of recorded history, have reported intuitions of transcendent value. In prehistoric times, archaeologists tell us, there are numerous traces of what can best be interpreted as rituals of worship. What is the "final context" status of these intuitions and practices? For example, are the intuitions purely events in the psyches of individual organisms, simply the firings of neurons or the chemical effects of endocrine secretions? Are the practices simply social manifestations of suggestible groups, frightened by the unknown or coming to terms with the dawning realization of mortality? These are metaphysical hypotheses. They cohere with larger metaphysical theories about the nature of things in general. These theories, in turn, suggest worldviews in which modern churchgoing is seen as high-toned persistence of savage superstition.

Other metaphysical hypotheses and theories are available. It can be maintained that the intuitions of transcendent value experienced by many over long periods of time are points of contact, not purely intra-individual events. Contact with what? Many different theories could offer different answers. But to cohere with the relatively lower-level hypothesis that transcendent value intuitions are referential, not simply psychological, these higher-level theories must allow conceptual place at a minimum for something that is valuable beyond the valuer. For monotheistic religions, an appropriate theory would need to maintain that something in reality is the *most* valuable, uniquely worthy of worship.

Religion affords only one domain in which the question of the metaphysical status of intuitions of intrinsic value strongly arises. Our ethical experience provides another. We often experience some situations as intrinsically bad—the malicious torture of a helpless animal, for example—and others as intrinsically good. Some decisions or actions we regard as right and virtuous, others as wrong and despicable. Are these experiences grounded in something about these situations, decisions, and actions that makes them so? Or is our experience of ethical value purely subjective? Powerful metaphysical theories would preclude any referential status for ethical intuitions, ruling out the hypothesis that there is anything *really* better or worse in the world, assuring us instead that only thinking makes it so. Other theories would allow, in one way or another, the grounding of ethical intuitions in the nature of things. These differing theories give rise to clashing worldviews, in which the weight of moral obligation and the lure of the good are differently perceived, and in which the institutions of human society function in strikingly different ways.

Probably the most difficult domain for modern people considering the reality-grounding of value intuitions is that of beauty. We live surrounded by stimuli that give us experiences of aesthetic aversion and attraction, but our worldview leads us to doubt that there is anything "out there" that is ugly or beautiful. Our dominant metaphysical theories assure us that the hues of the rose in full bloom, the sunset's splendor, or the rainbow's subtle spectrum are not to be reckoned in the world but only in human responses to the world. If this theory can be challenged on grounds of incoherence and inadequacy, and if another can be offered with stronger credentials, the referential character of value intuitions would be strengthened even in its "worst case" context. That should make it correspondingly easier to defend reality-reference for intrinsic value intuitions in other domains, such as ethics and religion. It is a challenge worth pursuing. This book will increasingly focus on it as we progress toward prospects for a postmodern metaphysical theory and a postmodern worldview worthy of humanity's future.

One more thought before we turn to the work ahead, in which this thought will be developed in historical detail. Theories may and do rule on the status of values, as I have illustrated in the foregoing, but that is not the whole story. It is also the case that our values precede our theories in real life and lead us in their construction (or approval). Even in the sciences we have become aware of the degree to which expectations, including such factors as hopes and career commitments, influence what we notice within the total range of the presented data. Attention is selective, and we can hardly expect that when the entire field of reality is before us our powers of attention will grow to match. We should expect, therefore, that our values will have a role in suggesting possible fruitful lines of thought. In addition, these leading values will definitely play a decisive role in influencing us on how long to hang on to a theory, model, or worldview threatened by problems. A treasured worldview is hard to give up. A theory that gives this worldview its cognitive credentials, by the same token, is protected from quick dismissal, even in the face of serious acknowledged flaws. It gathers what I later call "theoretical commitments."

Even in the natural sciences, the limits of rationality, in hanging on to a struggling research program in hopes of its eventual vindication, are flexible. So much the more, then, should we expect latitude in debates between metaphysical theories on which profound values are staked. What seems to some as "ideational loyalty" or "creative hope against hope" will appear to others as sheer obstinacy. This cannot be helped. The domain of metaphysical thinking is not one in which cognitive coercion is a likely outcome.

Even more must this be so since the very standards of cognitive success are themselves involved in the valuational complex that constitutes metaphysical thinking. I call these standards "epistemic norms." They will be more fully treated in volume two, *Knowing and Value,* of the present trilogy. Still, such norms are present from the start of theorizing and are inescapable if we are to think theoretically at all. Choosing (whether boldly and consciously or just absent-mindedly) to think in this theoretical way, however, is already a value-laden act. Its norms cannot be coerced. By citing facts and descriptions, no one can force another to adopt a norm or affirm a prescription. In this chapter, I have therefore proceeded without embarrassment to declare and advocate my suggested epistemic norms—consistency, coherence, applicability, and adequacy—for "effective" (normative word) or "successful" (normative word) metaphysical thinking. If I have not in the process won my readers' free consent, I cannot expect to capture it by bullying or bluster. On matters so fundamental, I can and must hope. So long as these hopes are disappointed, I can only continue to do my best at thinking explicitly within my openly announced norms, so that others can see clearly what is going on, while at the same time I remain willing to listen to proposals of other norms of good thinking. However, what "thinking" could be, without incorporating those four basic epistemic norms, baffles me. I am confident that any dialogue to convince me of additional or revised norms would need to manifest at least the minima I have proposed. They seem too basic to ignore or evade.

Still, even this had better not be said dogmatically. The story of metaphysics is full of surprises. Norms have changed over the history of thought as we shall see in the chapters ahead. Whatever we do, we shall continually need to return to examine our thought in light of the basics—and to reexamine what we take to be "basics"—to see whether there are matters still more basic that demand reexamination. The invitation to join in this process is the best answer to "What is Metaphysics?"

Part One

PREMODERN METAPHYSICS

2

THE GREAT PIONEERS

This is a book about values and reality and how they intertwine. Or is this already the wrong way of putting the issue? Does it not suggest that there are two independent "things," "reality" and "values," and that their relationship, if any, needs to be explored? This seems absurd: how could anything stand wholly *outside* reality and still have relations to it? Worse, such phrasing seems to suggest that reality "by itself" is devoid of values—that they need to be injected into or wrapped around an otherwise valueless mass of some kind.

If, as argued in Chapter 1, metaphysical thinking is aimed at constructing a comprehensive, adequate, and coherent theory of reality, should we not say instead this is a book about the (proper) understanding of value in a (good) theory of reality? Note the value terms. Is this bad? Is it a sign of circular reasoning? If our first formulation seems to beg the question against the intrinsic value-ladenness of reality, does the second beg the question in the opposite way, toward the inescapable inclusion of value in any satisfactory theory of reality?

I believe that the second circularity may in fact be occurring. But at deep enough places, as we shall see, finding great circles in theories that hope to be comprehensive and coherent may be exactly what we should welcome and even seek out. Consider our data. We have no experience of reality in the absence of all value-considerations. As I write these words, I am engaging in an enterprise I must value highly or else I would certainly spend my time in some of the thousands of other ways that beckon to me every day. Each sentence I compose, whether better or worse, is subjected to value assessment. Some sentences fail and are scrapped. All are revised with the aim of improve-

19

ment. Am I saying *well* what I mean to express? Are these the *best* things to be trying to say at this point?

You, too, reader, are not exempt. By picking up this book, you made a value-laden choice. If you continue to read, you will be affirming a certain set of values; if you slam it shut, never to return, you will be affirming another set. There is no escape from valuing. To be a functioning human person is to live in an ocean of values. As in the transparent ocean of air we breathe—and normally look straight through to other objects that more immediately concern us—the eddies and tides of value considerations, positive and negative, may not be particularly noticeable to us most of the time. We are too busy acting on their basis to attend to them explicitly. We could not be the agents we are without them.

Perhaps, for such reasons, the earliest Greek philosophers were not shy about incorporating value categories in the construction of their theories of reality. What could be more obvious? As a start in the long journey toward a metaphysics fit for the postmodern era, we need to survey their naive but seminal attempts to comprehend what they were the first to term *kosmos*.

Cosmos and Decent Order

We are all familiar with a popular current use of "cosmic" (in slang and elsewhere) to express admiration. "Vast," "grandiose," "overwhelming," and "marvelous," are some of the overtones we glean from this use. And in so doing, we still hear some of the authentic echoes of the original Greek sense of kosmos as expressing order or harmony in things.

I wish to give full weight to this first Greek meaning of kosmos in the following discussion. Kosmos is above all, in its origins, a value-laden term. It meant "well-ordered" before it meant "world" or "universe." Its primary application was in such contexts as military formations, which could be well-ordered or not. According to Liddell & Scott's *Greek-English Lexicon*, the verb, *kosmeo*, means first "to order, arrange: esp. to set an army in array, marshal it." This first meaning also includes other ordering activities, as "to arrange a repast." The second meaning of kosmeo is "to order, rule, govern." And the third meaning is "to deck, adorn, trick out, embellish." The residue of this important sense of kosmos remains today in our word "cosmetic," which highlights the domain of aesthetics while perhaps at the same time downgrading (at least among graybeard philosophers) its sense of importance. "*Merely* cosmetic" trips easily from the scholarly tongue. "Cosmetics," therefore, tends not to strike us as of "cosmic" significance. And yet it is exactly that.

"Cosmos" is not simply a synonym for "all that is." That, as mere totality, could in principle be disordered. The fact that it is not so disordered (yet), or is only partially ordered, counts as an empirical discovery. One may speculate without obvious absurdity, for example, that the Second Law of Thermo-dynamics condemns all things to a final state of total randomness in a so-called "heat death." But kosmos, unlike "all things," is a word with an antonym. Its antonym is *chaos*. It would be a literal contradiction in terms, an oxymoron, to speak of a "chaotic" cosmos.

Therefore, when we deal with theories of the cosmos we are dealing with theories of order. And since the "cosmic" has from ancient days acquired the additional sense of all-encompassing, we are in effect dealing with what is taken as finally well-ordered. Not proximate but ultimate orderings are at issue. Theories of kosmos are made up of possible conceptions about what is ultimately comprehensive together with value judgments about what it ultimately means to be ordered "well" or "decently."

THE MILESIANS

The first of the Greek philosophers, Thales, lived around 600 B.C. in the port city of Miletus on the Ionian coast (in what is now Turkey) of the Asian land-mass. That coast was the crossroads of Babylonian, Greek, and Egyptian cul-ture. Thales presents (like many of the pre-Socratics) a somewhat enigmatic picture. His famous dictum, that "everything is made from water," doubtless reflects the same Babylonian water mythology that found its way also into Hebrew creation stories, in which the "Spirit of God moved upon the face of the waters" (Genesis 1952: ch. 1, v. 2), and in which "God said, Let there be a firmament in the midst of the waters, and let it divide the waters from the waters" (Genesis 1952: ch. 1, v. 6).

Thales stepped beyond mythology in his apparent determination to depict a kosmos in which the ordering principles are wholeness and rational intelligibility. Everything, in principle, is accounted for, since everything has the same source. The harmony of things is thus to be complete, all-inclusive. No "holes" are allowed in the theory of reality, no loose ends. Moreover, water as the fundamental harmonizing element is an ideal choice. It is an obvious essential component in life—perhaps it is itself alive (life is widespread, even lodestones, capable of self-movement, can be considered animated)—and water is, also, a substance that obviously can take on many forms and states, from solid to liquid to gas. All this, in addition to the honored status of water in the great myths of his contemporary culture, commended to Thales the "decency" of this ordering of the universe.

The great advance made by Thales was in asking his bold question: "What is everything made from?" It was historic because it demanded for any answer the value-laden standards of unity and intelligibility as applicable to all that is. It is *better* to understand the universe than not. Such understanding should be *complete*. And the universe is assumed to be such a kosmos, well or decently ordered, that these two standards can be achieved by our thinking.

The next of the Ionian philosophers, Anaximander, also of Miletus, was most probably a younger friend and colleague of Thales. At any rate, he took up Thales' question—and therefore adopted his value-laden project—with an insightfulness befitting the first recorded philosophical refutation.

Anaximander posed a simple but devastating challenge to Thales' claim that the sole primal stuff is water by asking: If so, where do all the non-watery aspects of things come from? Water is essentially wet and cool. Whence then the dry and hot? Water is too *definite* a substance to be the source of everything. Rain puts out fires; thus, given an indefinite period of time, there should be no fires left—but this is false by observation. More fundamental, there is no intelligible explanation of where fires came from in the first place if everything originated in water and if water is essentially opposed to fire. The same would be true, by like reasoning, if *any* definite element were chosen to serve as the sole primal stuff accounting for the unity and intelligibility of the universe. Each would clash with, and prevent the appearance of, the traits that are essentially opposed to its basic character. Fire can no more account for water than water for fire.

Rather than abandon Thales' project, Anaximander made a bold proposal of his own: That the fundamental stuff from which all is generated must be itself *indefinite*. The traits of not-hot, not-cold, not-dry, not-wet, etc., must be hypothesized of this primal Indefinite (or Boundless) from which all the definite things of our familiar universe have arisen.

What a leap of abstraction! Anaximander, by this reasoning, presents us with the first theoretical entity, a substance defined in terms of what theory demands in the absence of direct sensory description. Faced with rational difficulty, the powerful attraction of Thales' standards for the kosmos led not to an abandonment of metaphysics but to a great leap of theory.

Anaximander's theoretical creativity was not exhausted by the invention of the Indefinite as theoretical entity. This ancient genius also pondered the question of how the kosmos remains a scene of struggle amongst the opposed elements, but without leading to victory of any single one over the others. The seasons come and go. Heat and drought are replaced by cold and flooding, but again the hot and dry return in orderly sequence. Beneath all this the earth remains stable in its place at the center of things. What can account for that?

The answer Anaximander gave anticipates our modern notion of "equilibrium" as a natural principle, but the theoretical abstraction we take for granted from modern physics was not available to him. The concept had not been invented yet. Thus, Anaximander reached for a parallel concept drawn from familiar social life—"justice."

Nothing is more understandable, unfortunately, than the tendency of people to encroach on one another. Children grab toys and need to be disciplined; neighboring herders let sheep graze beyond proper boundaries and must be pushed back; thieves snatch possessions and require punishment, preferably including restitution of what was wrongly taken. In each case, pressing beyond proper limit is an instance of injustice met by restorative counter-pressure under the guidance of an ideal of fairness. And, alas, in each case, as we well know, the tendency of former victims is to go too far, thus victimizing the former victimizer and requiring further restitution. And so it goes.

This model was available for Anaximander's use in his cosmological theorizing. Winter encroaches on ideal weather with cold and storms; its encroachment needs, in fairness, to be pushed back by summer's warmth and sunshine; but this process tends to go too far and in retribution cold and storms return. All this happens, says Anaximander, "according to necessity; for they pay penalty and retribution to each other for their injustice according to the assessment of Time" (Kirk 1962: 117). The image is of Time sitting in judgment over the conflict of the elements like a parent meting out fairness to squabbling children. Perfect harmony can hardly be achieved in this fractious kosmos, yet the judgments of patient Time in the interests of justice can at least keep inevitable conflicts from getting out of hand.

The same general line of reasoning aids Anaximander in explaining why the earth remains stably in its place. He was the first to argue that it requires nothing physical to hold it where it is. It need not float on water, as Thales had claimed. What holds the water up? Any regress of this sort is subject to the same question, as illustrated by the ancient Hindu account of the world's resting on a great elephant and the elephant standing on the back of a great tortoise. What does the tortoise stand on? (The humorous dodge, "It's tortoises 'all the way down'" hardly satisfies!) No, the best answer would be one that never allows this regress of "holdings" to begin. As Anaximander says, "The earth is on high, held up by nothing, but remaining on account of its similar distance from all things" (Kirk 1962: 134). In this way, Anaximander challenges, in effect, "Where else but in its proper place would one expect the world to be?" Any inclination to move out of that place would amount to an imbalance; justice alone, therefore, maintains the world's position.

Today, we quickly translate "justice" as "equilibrium." This is an advanced abstraction. Anaximander made a great leap toward coherent understanding by extending the notion of "justice," a value-laden concept drawn from the concrete world of crimes and punishments. Perhaps we could say, in our modern terms, that justice itself could be described as a special form of equilibrium in which each element of society functions, without overreaching and without resorting to destabilizing aggression, within its proper place. Plato, in the *Republic*, did come quite close to saying something like this, though still without relying on the impersonal mechanical model of "equilibrium."

What is important for us to notice is that if "justice" is a somewhat abstract way of understanding harmony in the cosmos, "equilibrium" is still more abstract, dispensing with the concrete ideas of what it is that drives the "encroachments" which initially imbalance the system, and dispensing also with the concrete idea of a fair-minded judge, like a parent or tribal elder, who can recognize inappropriate behavior and take measures to correct it. Anaximander's vision of things included agencies at work. Even Time, as we saw, was considered an agent assuring retribution and fairness over the long run.

These are anthropomorphic conceptions, of course. Such conceptions communicate at once to persons attempting to make sense of their world. What would be wrong would be to read back into Anaximander the abstract impersonality of concepts like agentless equilibrium or value-free harmony. It is an anachronism, for example, to write (as a leading scholar has) of Anaximander: "The world, *like a pendulum*, maintains *equilibrium* through the alternation of its extremes" (Allen 1985: 3, emphasis added). Such a simile comes naturally to us, who live after Galileo's epoch-making mathematical studies of the pendulum's motion and are habituated to explanations that ignore nearly everything from actual daily experience; but we should not take for granted that such a simile expresses the mind of Anaximander. Nor should we take for granted that the impersonal mechanical model of explanation is necessarily better in all ways than the dramatic, value-laden, more concrete models used by some of the pioneer Greek cosmologists, like Anaximander.

The third great member of the Milesian trio, probably somewhat younger than his acquaintance, Anaximander, was Anaximenes, thought to have flourished in mid-sixth century B.C., that is, roughly fifty years after Thales. The questions of Thales and Anaximander were also Anaximenes' questions. What makes the universe a kosmos: unified, intelligible, harmonious? But to these questions Anaximenes offered a new answer with powerful implications that resonate to this day.

The *qualitative* differences between things in the observable world were the basis for Anaximander's refutation of Thales. Hot and cold qualities oppose one another, do their best to destroy one another, displace one another periodically, and need to be kept in order by an external magistrate in charge of keeping harmony. Therefore (concluded Anaximander, as we saw) the one stuff that underlies and unites the ordered kosmos cannot have any one of these qualities—cannot be thought to have *any* definite quality at all—lest the other, conflicting qualities be unaccounted for in the first place and, in the long run, be made impossible to survive. But Anaximenes suggests that we approach the whole matter differently by taking a radically dissimilar look at qualities. What are qualities? Are they irreducible "somethings" that can conflict, like children in a sandbox? Or are they, Anaximenes suggests, nothing in themselves but merely the manifestation of particular *quantitative* states in the stuff that comprises the observable world with its many *qualitative* appearances?

If we take Anaximenes' hypothesis, then some natural process resulting in quantitatively different states of affairs could offer a harmonious understanding of the kosmos in all its qualitative variety. The process proposed by Anaximenes is the simple one of condensation-and-rarefaction. Condensation results in more of a given stuff in the same amount of space; rarefaction results in less. For the first time, a quantitative measure was given as the correlate of, and thus the explanation for, qualitative differences in things. Thales had merely observed that water turns into ice and steam. He did not suggest that ice, with its qualities of hardness and cold, was simply *more* water condensed into a given volume, or that steam, with its contrasting gaseous and hot qualities, was simply *less*.

Anaximenes realized that given such a mechanism to account for qualitative differences, he had found a way around Anaximander's argument for the Indefinite. Any state of the primal stuff will have some quantitative measure, therefore, some definite qualities. The underlying common substance of the kosmos, therefore, can be—must be—something commonly experienced, pervasive, and imaginable. Anaximenes proposed that the most plausible candidate for this stuff was air. Air is compressible. Water falls out of it. It is released by earth in evaporation after rain. It, no less than water, can be considered the secret of life; perhaps it is alive, the breath of the world.

If ancient sources can be trusted, Anaximenes even offered experimental evidence that the qualities of warmth and cold can be correlated with rarefaction or condensation of air. Plutarch reports:

> ... let us leave neither the cold nor the hot as belonging to substance, but as common dispositions of matter that supervene on changes; for [Anaximenes] says that matter which is compressed and condensed is cold, while that which is fine and "relaxed" (using this very word) is hot. Therefore, he said, the dictum is not an unreasonable one, that man releases both warmth and cold from his mouth: for the breath is chilled by being compressed and condensed with the lips, but when the mouth is loosened the breath escapes and becomes warm through its rarity (Kirk 1962: 148).

Try it. "Hard" air, blown through pursed lips, will feel colder than "soft," rarefied air exhaled through the open mouth. On such breezes theories of kosmos sometimes rise or fall.

The important thing about Anaximenes from our point of view is not the identification of air as the ultimate stuff of the universe but, rather, the reconception of qualities as nothing but the byproducts of quantities. The qualitative side of life is the side of most values. We must be careful not to overstate. There are quantitative dimensions of value as well. Concepts of "more" and "less" function in value-judgments. But the sensual domain—the realm of the visual arts, the musical arts, the delights of perfume, dining, sexuality, texture, and more—is the kingdom of qualities and intensities. With his suggestion that all the qualitative aspects of the universe are but functions of condensation and rarefaction, nothing in themselves but primal matter in various quantitative states, Anaximenes pioneered a new tradition with more consequences than he could have guessed. No anthropomorphic "judge," like Anaximander's Time, would be needed to maintain the harmony in this kosmos. There are still important values expressed in Anaximenes' thought: the values of unity and intelligibility and order. But the dramatic mode of understanding the "decency" of the kosmos has found a rival. It is what we could call the protomechanical mode, appearing already at the dawning of metaphysics, with values and an agenda of its own.

THE PYTHAGOREANS

Meanwhile, far to the west of Miletus, a somewhat mysterious society was being organized in southern Italy, in the culturally Greek city of Croton. This was being done by a refugee from the Ionian coast where, on the island of Samos (off the coast of present-day Turkey), he had been born sometime during the lifetime of Anaximenes. Pythagoras was the name of this refugee from a tyranny then afflicting Samos. He was a historical figure but one whose actual thought was obscured by hagiography and legends spun by his followers.

In the case of Pythagoreanism, my aim—here to draw attention to the value-implications surrounding theories of reality from their very beginning, is endangered by surfeit rather than a shortage of material. What we know about Pythagoras himself is filtered through the religious cult that he founded and inspired. Value-considerations are pervasive. We need to set aside the cultic rituals, the behavioral restrictions (e.g., refrain, among other things, from stirring a fire with iron, from wearing rings, and from eating beans!), and mythological pronouncements about reincarnation, etc., in order to keep our eyes on the properly theoretical contributions made by Pythagoras to the great human effort to understand reality. We shall find those theoretical contributions not to be value-free (none are) but in their theoretical form they are more universally applicable and arguable. Those are the contributions that have been influential through the ages, to our present time.

Everyone knows the name of Pythagoras from the Pythagorean Theorem we learn in school. It may be that this theorem was his personal discovery; he was said to have sacrificed an ox in gratitude. It may, like many other things, have simply been attributed to him by his admirers. Either way, it is a fitting memorial for at least two reasons. First, the Pythagorean Theorem deals with the numerable character of space. Pythagoras believed that number is fundamental to all things. Indeed, everything, he thought, is derived from number and gains its particular character from the character of its numerical formula. (To these thoughts we shall shortly return.) Second, since the hypotenuse of a right triangle supports a square constructed on it equal in area to the areas of the two squares that can be constructed on the other two legs, the hypotenuse, if it is to achieve this, can never bear a simple arithmetic ratio to the other legs. It is mathematically "irrational." This was the first proof that such irrationals exist in space and must be incorporated into any adequate conception of kosmos. The "decent" harmonies of the universe need to be more complex and perhaps offer more dissonance than first thought.

Pythagoras took the concept of harmony with great seriousness. It is thought that his first important discovery was of the simple mathematical ratios holding between the principal harmonies played on stringed instruments. The octave is a simple but important harmony: the "same" note, qualitatively, but in a different pitch, higher or lower. Pythagoras noticed that the length of the string required to play one octave higher is always just half the length of the total string. This is a formula of 1:2. Whatever the actual notes happen to be, this formula governing the octave harmony remains the same. For modern guitarists this will be quickly recognized as founding the tonic harmony. But similar simple ratios also are behind the subdominant and dominant chords on which most of our music depends. The ratio between the lengths of the strings that provide the sound of fifths is 3:2. The ratio that sounds fourths is 4:3. The same formulas hold for resonating pipes. The material that makes the sounds seems less important than the numbers.

Harmonious sounds are naturally satisfying. Here qualitative and perceptible aspects of the world are once more linked with the quantitative, but in a way strikingly different from Anaximenes'. The linkage is not mechanical, through condensations or rarefactions of material, but formal, through manifestations of a few universal, intelligible ratios behind and within the plethora of particular circumstances.

Where there is beauty of harmony, there is numerical ratio. Conversely, it seemed obvious to Pythagoras that where there is numerable ratio, there is also harmony of beauty. The kosmos is orderly, harmonious, numerical to its core; therefore it is musical with a music of incomparable sublimity. From the Pythagorean perspective, the "music of the spheres" is no casual figure of speech. Behind these convictions is fundamental theory.

Pythagoras was a mathematician, as we know; and in addition to his famous theorem he is credited with many fascinating discoveries about the nature of numbers. One basic Pythagorean observation is that all Even numbers are divisible by 2 and therefore unstable, subject to crumbling, while all Odd numbers are indivisible, thus reliable, stable, and firm. There is something reassuring about the Odd. This Pythagoras illustrated with his invention of the *gnomon* (literally a carpenter's square) as a method of numerical representation:

```
   X      X      X      X

   X      X      X  |   X
 _____|
   X      X  |   X  |   X
 _____|      |
   X  |   X  |   X  |   X
      |      |      |
      3      5      7
```

In this manner of representation it becomes obvious that the ratio between the sides of the gnomon surrounding all Odd numbers is 1:1: perfect rest, tranquility, and assurance. But the situation is far different for the Even:

```
   X      X      X      X      X
 _____
   X      X      X      X  |   X
 _____|
   X      X      X  |   X  |   X
 _____|      |
   X      X  |   X  |   X  |   X
            |      |      |
            4      6      8
```

In this case, and for all Even numbers, the ratio between the sides of the gnomon delimiting them changes (2:3, 3:4, 4:5, etc.) with every step outward. There is no stability, no peace of mind, no rest.

Thus, Pythagoras related numbers to values. The Odd was associated with Rest, Good, and Limited, while the Even was related to Motion, Bad, and Unlimited. To this value-dualism the Pythagoreans (or Pythagoras himself?) added other cultural values to the Odd and Even list: Right-handed was grouped with the Odd, Limited, and Good, along with One and Male and Straight and Light. Left-handed was relegated, with Many and Female and Curved and Dark, to the Even, Unlimited, and Bad.

Even the origin of the universe itself was portrayed as a drama between the forces of One versus Many, Odd versus Even, the Finite versus the Infinite.

In the beginning were the Limited and the Unlimited. There is nothing more fundamental than they. This willing embrace of dualism is something new after the determined monisms of the Milesians. But despite the irreducible duality of things, the One, the original Unit, is still more fundamental to the origin of the universe, since it was through the One's "breathing in" of the surrounding Void (itself the product of the Unlimited) that it began to grow and gave birth to the number 2, the dyad. In so doing, it created the first line, that is, two-dimensionality. In continuing this process it gave birth to the number 3, the triad, that is, three-dimensionality in the form of the triangle. And from this the primal Unit gave birth to the number 4 and through it to the simplest solid figure, the tetrahedron or pyramid, constructed with four triangular faces (Kirk 1962: 254). Once the number 4 had been created, all the numbers were in their essence available for world-making, since the "perfect" number 10, the decad, which contains all numbers potentially, can be created by cumulatively adding 1 to 2 to 3 and then to 4. This wonderful number, displayed by Pythagoras through the *tetractys*, looks like a triangle and contains both points and lines:

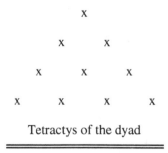

Tetractys of the dyad

Equilateral; symmetrical no matter which way approached; stable; containing, yet limiting, the dangerous principle of Even—the tetractys of the dyad was a figure of sacred significance to the Pythagoreans, on which solemn oaths could be sworn.

Hard though it may be for us to imagine what "inhaling" Void might be like, or how what is essentially One can "become" or "give birth to" Duality, problems with details should not obscure the shape of the whole, which is immensely impressive. Mathematics and empirical reality, quantity and quality, change and stability, order and chaos, were here brought into a single perspective in which Limit and Rest were given pride of place while at the same time their opposites were not wholly rejected. The cultic aspects of Pythagoreanism need to be washed away from the worldview, as much as possible, if we are to be fair to this achievement. In particular, we need to stand back from the sexist values that pain our contemporary sensibilities. There is no logical necessity within this metaphysics for Female to have been linked with Left, Even, and Bad. These were historically contingent linkages.

Yes, we may say, but are not *all* such value-linkages logically independent of the theories that carry them? Were not Pythagoras' preference for Stability and Limit, as well as Right-handedness and Maleness, contingent on his or his culture's historically conditioned preference for form, symmetry, and the predictable? In asking this question, perhaps we are making progress toward a deeper understanding of the relations between values and theories of the ultimate. Values are inescapable; but the particular items valued positively or negatively are likely to be highly contingent. It helps, in awakening to our own underlying assumptions, to appreciate the variety of alternatives defended by others.

CHANGE OR PERMANENCE?

Certainly the preference of ancient Greek culture for Limit, Form, Symmetry, and the like, did not determine in any detail the value-laden answers of early philosophers as to whether the well-formed kosmos should be considered fundamentally dynamic or perfectly static. Pythagoras had shown his preference for Rest, but had not excluded Motion from his dualistic universe. Can they be reconciled?

Two immensely important early thinkers took opposite positions on this key question. The first, a slightly younger contemporary of Pythagoras, was Heraclitus. He, like the three earliest Milesian philosophers, lived on the western edge of the Asian landmass in the city of Ephesus. The second, Parmenides, a still younger contemporary, was born about 515 B.C. in Elea, a culturally Greek city in Italy, not far from the center of Pythagorean activity.

Heraclitus was famous in his time for a sour, misanthropic disposition and an obscure, riddling style. If we can summon enough charity to set these traits aside, we shall find much to admire in this pioneering Ephesian's contributions at the beginning of inclusive metaphysical synthesis. Above all, he wished to draw attention to the balanced stability of the changing universe, the *intelligibility* of things even within their ceaseless *flux*.

Often, Heraclitus is remembered simply as the one responsible for the famous observation that "you cannot step twice into the same river" (Kirk 1962: 197) because the river is always becoming a "different" river with new waters, altered banks, and the like; but this statement, no matter how important for Heraclitus, might, unless treated carefully, overemphasize the idea of change alone. The river, after all, is an identifiable feature of the landscape. It has banks; it has a bottom; it contains a huge amount of water that flows in orderly ways between its banks and over its bottom, even though riverbanks and riverbottom are constantly subject to erosion and resedimentation. Later

Heracliteans, like Cratylus, exaggerated Heraclitus' own stress on the changing character of things. Cratylus went so far as to claim that one cannot step into the same river even once.

True, everything changes; but Heraclitus himself stressed that the intelligibility and form within the universal change is at least equally worthy of note. Nor did he claim that everything from rocks to rafters was changing exactly as rivers change. Heraclitus portrayed the world as in flux but not as mere fluid. Behind all things lies what he called *Logos*, the literal word for "word," but his usage more appropriately translated to "measure" or "meaning" or "proportion." This cosmic Logos, reminiscent of Anaximander's Time, maintains balance within all change, Heraclitus says; thus Logos assures fair equilibrium between opposed qualities. Unlike Anaximander's Time, however, which, as we saw, allows excesses to occur that later require correction, often leading to equal and opposite excesses, Heraclitus' equilibrium is constant, a steady "strife." Rather than picturing the swinging pendulum as a modern image for this worldview, we might better imagine massive continental plates maintaining dynamic balance by grinding against one another, basing stability on enormous, often invisible, counter-pressures.

Unlike our horizontal tectonic forces, Heraclitus' own "strife" was imagined as vertical. The "way up" balances the "way down." In this way, the various changes, some rapid, some slow, are kept in fair proportion thanks to the Logos of the universe. Here we find the answer to Heraclitus' apparent riddle: "Right is strife" (Kirk 1962: 195). And we see also the meaning behind another obscure saying: "War is the father of all and king of all" (Kirk 1962: 195). The "decency" of Heraclitus' kosmos is expressed in terms of meaningful balance between opposites, all assured by Logos.

The proportion-assuring Logos, for Heraclitus, is neither immaterial nor abstract. In the spirit of the Milesians before him, Heraclitus chose a familiar physical substance as his primary principle. Appropriately, his choice was fire. Flame is in constant change, but is far from amorphous. One might even define fire as extremely rapid flux maintaining form. Both flux and form are essential and positively valued in Heraclitus' thought.

Such an embrace of *both* flux and form was not accepted by Heraclitus' younger contemporary, Parmenides. Like Pythagoras, an older neighbor and probably an early mentor, Parmenides intensely (but more single-mindedly) valued Rest and Unity over Motion and Multiplicity. Moreover, and no less important, Parmenides trusted the outcome of theoretical trains of inference over the direct deliverances of experience. In this, he may have been the first "pure" rationalist. He was certainly not to be the last.

Behind Parmenides' various arguments, which were to be of enormous influence in the course of Hellenic and post-Hellenic philosophy, was a profound value-intuition that reality—whatever it is—must be *perfect*. It must admit to no flaw, no chink through which corruption could in principle creep.

Only in one rather curious respect was Parmenides dualistic. His great poem, through which he expresses his views, contains two parts, the "Way of Truth" and the "Way of Seeming." The first part purports to deduce what must be the truth about reality: that it is absolutely one, full, eternal, and unchanging. The second part (of which most is missing today) reinstates change, even to the point of proposing a cosmogony to rival those of his predecessors. Parmenides' motive in appending the second part is obscure, since there is no logical connection between it and what he holds in the first part to be necessarily true. The fact that the poem's two parts are incoherent is a good symbol for the radical break Parmenides makes between what seems to everyone to be the case and what he holds must actually be so. His faith in the power of his deductive logic allowed him to ignore the inability of his account of Truth to explain in any way the possibility of Seeming.

What is this account of Truth? It begins from the simplest of premises about ultimate Reality: "It is" (Kirk 1962: 269, 273). So much can truthfully be said for reality, whatever it may be. All must agree to that much. Indeed, Parmenides presses on, *only* this much is thinkable. We cannot—logically cannot—think about nothing at all. Thinking about nothing is strictly equivalent to not thinking at all.

If nothing is an unthinkable topic, then any putative concept that includes the unthinkable is itself a pseudo-thought. Not only does logic rule out "It is not," by itself, but also ruled out is any compound containing the expression, such as "It is and it is not." This latter expression, on which some might wish to rest the possibility of change within being, for example, "It [the unripe apple] is [green] and it [later, the ripe apple] is not [green, any longer]," is according to Parmenides pure contradiction on its face and is further undermined (if this should be necessary) by containing a meaningless second clause. It is by confused compromises like this, Parmenides chides, that "ignorant mortals wander knowing nothing, two-headed . . . [also rendered two-faced], who are persuaded that to be and to be-not are the same, yet not the same. . . ." (Kirk 1962: 271).

The implications of this sweeping logical rejection of negative statements are huge and startling. Being must be completely perfect. To claim the opposite would be meaningless, involving the pseudo-idea that being could be not-this or not-that. Thus being must be a *plenum*, completely full (without any "holes" or "bubbles" in it, which would be unthinkable nothingness invading being); and by the same token it must be completely *spherical*. This perfect shape follows from two premises: (1) being must be granted the Pythagorean perfection of Limit, but (2) there must be no imbalance in it, no place "lacking" relative to any other place. As Parmenides puts it: "But since there is a furthest limit, it is bounded on every side, like the bulk of a well-rounded sphere, from the centre equally balanced in every direction; for it needs must not be somewhat more here or somewhat less there" (Kirk 1962: 276).

Furthermore, "It is" implies that there is no second being; it must be *one* not only in the sense of being *indivisible* but also in the sense of being *unique*. To suppose that there were a second being would require one to suppose that the first being "is not" the second and that the second "is not" the first. But that is impossible. No more could it have come into existence or go out of existence, because these suggestions must imply either coming from what "is not" or going to what "is not"—equally unthinkable consequences. Thus, being must be *eternal*. Not only is being eternal as a whole, but also being cannot contain within it the slightest change. Change implies that something comes into being from what "is not" or goes from being into what "is not." Neither of these is a possible thought. Therefore, time, if it implies "becoming," or any differences between past, present, or future, is an inappropriate concept for Truth.

Above all, it is obvious that for Parmenides there can be no place in Truth for a concept of the Void (as in Pythagorean cosmogony) "inhaled" by the primal One to generate Two, and then a world. The Void is just nothing, and "nothing" is excluded in principle from rational consideration in the Parmenidean universe. If Parmenides is right, there is no reality to change, to multiplicity, to the basic experiences of human life. Since men and women value their world of sense perceptions, moral deliberation, and change, we should not be surprised by the stir that Parmenides caused with his radical challenge to the conceptual possibility of that world. His arguments, however, were grounded in deductions from the most basic premises of thought itself. Must his successors choose between the daily world of qualities and change, on one side, and the values of honest thought, on the other?

PLURALISTS AND ATOMISTS

Parmenides chose to challenge the reality of the everyday world of human affairs. His sense of the proper "decency" of the kosmos led him to affirm only the traits listed on the Odd, Limited, and Good side of the Pythagorean list of dualities. We saw that the Even or Unlimited side contained such entries as Void, Female, Motion, and Bad. All of these were utterly rejected by Parmenides along with the concept of duality itself. In this he was expressing his deepest judgments of value, even while exercising deductive logic in their establishment and defense. This blending of valuing with theorizing illustrates again an important thesis of this book. The two activities—judging and thinking—are not only not incompatible but pervasively intertwined. At the widest levels of theoretical comprehensiveness and the highest levels of value-intensity, we find that metaphysics blends into religion and vice versa. Parmenides' poem qualifies for both genres even in its explicit form, in which it is introduced as revelation from a goddess to the author as a "youth" (Kirk 1962: 268). In many ways, a foreshadowing of Anselm's *Proslogion*, written 1500 years later, Parmenides' epoch-making poem can be seen as an instance of "faith seeking understanding."

Faith, no matter how profound, is often unshared, especially by those with sharply differing value-commitments. Like the Pythagoreans, Parmenides found Motion, Plurality, and Void *unworthy*, as well as *unthinkable*, of Being. Similarly, in the clash between his logical conclusions and his daily experiences, he chose to *disdain* experience as "ignorant" rather than taking its deliverances as providing a *reductio ad absurdum* for his arguments. But such basic judgments cannot be expected to legislate for others.

Earlier, we noted that the Pythagoreans' negative valuation of Female in their list of dualities is, in contemporary culture, obviously open to challenge as arbitrary and misguided. In like manner but in his own time and culture, important contemporaries of Parmenides found nothing Bad or "unthinkable" about Multiplicity and Change or even Void. The Pluralists and Atomists of the mid-fifth century B.C. simply reversed the value judgments of Parmenides and his followers (notably the brilliant Zeno of Elea, he of the "paradoxes"—which were essentially preemptive *reductio ad absurdum* strikes against common sense), and affirmed, despite Parmenides and Zeno, the reality of multiplicity, change, and empty space as eminently "fitting" for a "decent" kosmos.

There is no need, for our purposes, to go into any detail about the metaphysical proposals of the Pluralists. In general, they tend to accede to Parmenides the traits he claims for genuine being (indivisibility, unchangingness, impenetrability, inability to be created or destroyed, etc.) but to argue that there are several or many kinds of beings and a great many mixtures made out of these kinds. For Empedocles, there are four different basic kinds, the sensible opposites of hot and cold, wet and dry. Additionally, there are two dynamic principles of change, Love and Strife. The universe as a whole is, he holds, a Parmenidean sphere, but within it the attractions of Love and the repulsions of Strife mix the elements into the sort of world we find in experience. For Anaxagoras, the first of the famous Athenian philosophers (who contributed importantly to Athens' Golden Age until his exile on grounds of impiety), there are indefinitely many different kinds of indestructible beings, one for every substance and quality we encounter. Moreover, he adds, all empirical things are mixtures of all of these kinds, their perceived character depending on what element in the mixture happens to be dominant. Their change is governed by a single principle (rather than Empedocles' two): namely, Mind, which is not a mixture but is purely itself. If it were a mixture, on a par with everything else, Mind could not properly "rule" the mixed things over which it has in fact complete control. Still, Anaxagoras, though he attributes all "knowledge" to Mind, as well as all power to govern, should not be thought to be attributing moral purposes to the Mind of the kosmos (Kirk 1962: 372–3). Socrates, as we shall see, strongly complains about this omission. But we must remember that not all values are moral ones. Anaxagoras shows more interest in the values of cosmic order and reliability, in intelligence itself, and in the interpretation of common experience, than in matters of right or wrong.

The Atomists of the fifth century, like the Pluralists, were also prepared to embrace radically non-Pythagorean, non-Parmenidean judgments as the basis for an alternative world picture. While Void and the Unlimited, as we have seen, had been strongly disvalued by both Pythagoreans and Eleatics, these formerly repellant notions were to become essential pillars of a new theory of kosmos, created in this early era and destined to inspire the dominant worldview of our own modern mechanical civilization.

This new theory was originally worked out early in the second half of the fifth century by the philosopher Leucippus, about whom very little is known, and his younger associate, Democritus. The intellectual and valuational key to their respective books describing the "World System" (Kirk 1962: 402–3) was the bold espousal of Void. As Aristotle later expressed their view: "Being is full and solid, not-being is void and rare. Since the void exists no less than body, it follows that not-being exists no less than being" (Kirk 1962: 407). Initially, this conclusion sounds like a contradiction, and indeed the Atomists deliberately seem to make their point through a provocative paradox; but the key to its solution is suggested in Aristotle's quotation, wherein he contrasts void not with "being" alone, but with "body." Perhaps not all reality is *bodily* reality. Perhaps there is some other kind of genuine reality—empty space—within which bodily reality can exist and move.

We find here a major turn in thinking, worth pondering. None of the previous philosophers seems to have considered the logical possibility of disembodied kinds of reality. Even Heraclitus' cosmic Logos, though made of very fine material, was no exception; it was fire. No exception, either, was Anaxagoras' Mind, which was portrayed as very fine and pure, but still embodied. It is not often remarked that the Atomists, by overcoming nearly universal repugnance against Unlimited Void, paved the way for wider theories of reality including Plato's proposal of real immaterial Forms, by challenging hitherto unquestioned associations of "being" with "body."

Bodily being, then, for Leucippus and Democritus, could be described just as Parmenides would wish: perfectly dense, completely impenetrable, ungenerated, indestructible, and unchanging in itself. The Void would simply be the empty space, perfectly "rare" and wholly without resistance, that could contain bodily being. It would be unlimited in its extent, and thus it could allow infinite numbers of tiny, indestructible bodily beings. Once the antipathy to bodiless space is overcome, the Eleatic block against multiplicity is removed.

At the same time, once room is provided for many beings, the possibility of their motion relative to one another (no matter how unchanging they are in themselves) is opened again.

Change, Democritus argued, is not in the bits of being themselves, not in the "atoms" (from *a-tomos*, "uncuttable" entities) from which everything else is made, but in the rearrangements of these extremely small and numerous Parmenidean universes within the perfect hospitality of infinite Void.

The happy consequence is that change and the empirical world is once again made theoretically intelligible. We no longer seem forced to choose between the values of our common life and responsible thinking. But there are other consequences as well. What seems solid is really not so; only the atoms are truly solid, but they are not visible to our eyes or sensible to our touch. The colors of things, the textures, the odors, tastes, sounds—all the qualities of experience must on this theory be somehow the byproduct of interactions of certain atoms (specifically, those in perceiving organisms) with other atoms making up the world around us. Atoms themselves, since they are nothing but "being" (of the bodily sort) can have none but geometrical qualities. Democritus departed from Parmenides in allowing "being" to take on an infinite number of geometrical shapes, not merely the spherical, but no other qualities would be fitting. "Soul atoms" of spherical shape and extremely fine, are distributed throughout living bodies and are contacted by other atoms by touch, giving rise to all the apparent qualities by "convention." As Democritus holds: "By convention are sweet and bitter, hot and cold, by convention is colour; in truth are atoms and the void. . . . In reality we apprehend nothing exactly, but only as it changes according to the condition of our body and of the things that impinge on or offer resistance to it" (Kirk 1962: 422).

Atomism has brought revolutions on several fronts. First, the age-old revulsion against the Unlimited, the Void, is rejected and reversed. "Naught" is just as real—and thinkable—as "aught." Second, a disembodied form of being is accepted as not merely intelligible but even essential to understanding change and plurality. And third, the world of time, qualities, and common sense, though rescued from Eleatic unthinkability, is rendered a realm of appearance and "convention" rather than truth. These are revolutions with large implications for values. The first to exploit these implications were the Sophists.

THE SOPHISTS

The Sophists, who flourished about the time of Socrates in the second half of the fifth century B.C. were a loose grouping of itinerant teachers who were "wise" to the ways of the world—the social world of lawsuits and political advancement, in which cleverness in argument (or its lack) could make or break a reputation, a career, or a life. They were less interested in metaphysical theories about the nature of nature than in teaching—for a fee—the rhetorical devices required to persuade an electorate or a jury.

It seems plausible to suppose that at least part of their move to shift attention from the world of nature itself, *phusis*, to the world of human convention and laws, *nomos*, was due to discouragement with the conflicting multiplicity of theories about the former, linked with their lively sense of the equally conflicting multiplicity of human customs and laws. Dwelling on all these disagreements certainly may lead to urbane skepticism about the powers of human reason to establish reliable truth in either domain. Moreover, if the thesis of this book is correct, the root of both sorts of disagreements is the same: conflict, open or hidden, in fundamental judgments of value, on which theoretical as well as practical priorities always rest.

Be this as it may, Protagoras (from Abdera in Thrace), who was the eldest and most distinguished of the Sophists, proclaimed a moratorium on the disputes we have been following in this chapter. Instead, he offered a new dispute-avoiding standard: "Man is the measure of all things, of things that are that [or 'how'] they are and of things that are not that [or 'how'] they are not" (Plato *Theaetetus* 152 A-B in Kerferd 1967: 505). What seems right or true is right or true to that person or group; what seems otherwise to others is right or true to the others who judge of the matter.

In the first instance, these seemings are applied to sensory qualities, like hot and cold. A person can hardly be wrong about what seems directly a quality of sense perception. If a wind seems cold to me, it *is* cold to me, whether it is cold or warm to you or anyone else. Likewise, if the same wind seems warm to you, I must grant that it *is* warm for you, even though it is not warm for me. My mistake would be in trying to force the issue to universal truth or falsity as though there could be some "objectively" warm or cold wind, in itself, apart from a perceiver. That way lies nonsense.

Beyond this application to the world of sensory qualities, Protagoras added the relativity of judgments of right and wrong, good and evil, which always depend upon the community doing the judging. "Whatever seems just to a city is just for that city so long as it seems so" (Kerferd 1967: 506). These are matters of convention. Conventions, which depend only on customary agreements, differ from place to place and from age to age; customary agreements seem to hold sway in everything from table manners to definitions of crimes and virtues. We should not look for any *phusis* beneath such customs; they are purely matters of *nomos*.

These laws and conventions are open to change by human decision. They are constantly in the state of being reaffirmed or amended, depending upon the eloquence commanded by defenders or challengers of the status quo. This fact makes it immensely important to influence how matters "seem" to other per-

sons. Thus is justified the profession of Sophists to instruct citizens in fundamental tools for advancement and survival.

The practical values of the Sophists and their wealthy patrons become
clear from all this. What is not always so clear is the realization that buried in
Protagorean relativism, as practiced by the various Sophists, is also an implicit
metaphysics. It may be a metaphysics of "opposites" indwelling in all substances (a reminder of Empedocles, perhaps, with "seeds" of everything in
everything), in which different people perceive differently what is really there
to be perceived. Or it may be, instead, a metaphysics of radical idealism in
which phenomena are created by perceivers in the act of perceiving and judging. It may be the avowal of an inconsistent universe, not to be bound by the
law of noncontradiction. In any event, it is not a value-standpoint that can be
metaphysics-free, no more than can any metaphysical standpoint be finally
value-free.

3

THE GREAT HELLENES

The contrasting judgments made by the pre-Socratic thinkers set the agenda for metaphysical controversy for thousands of years to come. Is reason more to be trusted than experience? Can being really change? Must everything be made from one underlying stuff? Can anything really be infinite? Is plurality possible?

Today, the controversies continue over theories of reality: are particles "fundamental" or are fields? Is the space-time universe closed or open? Is time really a feature of the universe, or is it simply a mind-dependent appearance? Does the universe have a unique present, or does it exist all at once in a multi-dimensional complex of time lines that simply "are," durationless?

The pre-Socratics opened the conversation. Soon, the three great Hellenic philosophers, Socrates, Plato, and Aristotle, reacted to the babble of voices with responses that moved the story of metaphysical thinking to a new level of system and profundity.

SOCRATES

Socrates is the odd one out in this regard. He was neither a systematizer, nor even, so far as we can tell, much interested in metaphysics. He never published anything. But he was such a fulcrum figure in the history of philosophy that his passionate intervention in the discussion marked the passing of an era from "pre-" to "post-" as surely as "B.C." is set off from "A.D."; and, like the figure whose celebrated birth in a manger still defines the calendar for much of the modern world, Socrates cared enough to die for his values.

The quest for the historical Socrates is full of uncertainty. Our best guide is no doubt Plato, his student and admirer, but since Plato himself was such a powerful thinker, it is difficult to discern where the line between his own thought and that of his master might be found. For the purposes of this book, this question may be set aside in favor of the consensus among scholars—that Plato's earlier dialogues, depicting Socrates at work among famous Athenians and embroiled in the final, highly public arguments of his life, are trustworthy.

The Socrates who emerges from these dialogues is a man with a mission—a divine mission to seek wisdom—who took his mission with greater seriousness than he took himself. Socrates is shown as someone full of irony, playfulness, modesty about his own knowledge, but also as someone with an iron determination to probe beyond his own ignorance and that of those around him.

The sort of ignorance that bothered Socrates so intensely was not ignorance about the kosmos, whether it is made up of One or Many substances, or how Being and Becoming can be related. In Plato's *Phaedo,* Socrates recounts his youthful enthusiasm for such traditional pre-Socratic issues, but he was disillusioned early about these questions. He saw such speculations as *valueless for life.* Even when they seem to promise much, as in Anaxagoras' evocation of Mind as the controlling causal power in the universe, they leave out the main point as long as they omit explicit notice of why whatever is ordered is ordered for the *best.* In explanations of the latter sort Socrates could rest content. Short of that, mechanical or material causal accounts seemed to him arbitrary. Worse, they seemed profoundly incomplete. As he said (addressing his disciples who were visiting him in jail, where—he had decided after reasoned examination—it was better to die rather than break the law by escaping):

> It seemed to me that [Anaxagoras'] position was like that of a man who said that all the actions of Socrates are due to his mind, and then attempted to give the causes of my several actions by saying that the reason why I am now sitting here is that my body is composed of bones and sinews, and the bones are hard and separated by joints, while the sinews, which can be tightened or relaxed, envelop the bones along with the flesh and skin which hold them together; so that when the bones move about in their sockets, the sinews, by lessening or increasing the tension, make it possible for me at this moment to bend my limbs, and that is the cause of my sitting here in this bent position. Analogous causes might also be given of my conversing with you, sounds, air-currents, streams of hearing and so on and so forth, to the neglect of the true causes, to wit that, inasmuch as the Athenians have thought it better to condemn me, I too in my turn think it better to sit here, and more right and proper to stay where I am and submit to such punishment as they enjoin. For, by Jingo, I fancy

these same sinews and bones would long since have been somewhere in Megara or Beoetia, impelled by their notion of what was best, if I had not thought it right and proper to submit to the penalty appointed by the State rather than to take to my heels and run away (Plato 1985c: 98b–99).

The trouble with that kind of mechanical "explaining" is that it confuses *necessary* causes (if the bones were not so and so, it would not be possible to sit like this) with *sufficient* causes that together really explain why the situation unfolded as it did. Only the valuational "why," showing that a situation is for the best, will be allowed as a proper resting place by Socrates' probing mind. Anything short of this ultimate designation of rightness leaves the matter underdetermined, arbitrary, and unsatisfying to one who takes with all due seriousness the concept of kosmos as an ultimately "well-ordered" domain.

Before these concepts can meaningfully be applied to the kosmos, however, they need to be understood in themselves. What does "best" mean? What is "good"? Here is the locus of the sort of wisdom Socrates sought with the concentrated passion of his sense of divine mission. Considering something even more basic than purportedly descriptive accounts of the universe, Socrates determined to probe with all the rigor of his unflagging reason into the prescriptive issues that had long been implicit in (and driving) the metaphysics of his predecessors.

His methods were revolutionary. He did not lecture, like the Sophists. He did not write books, like most of his predecessors. Instead, he questioned other people about what they thought they knew. In this questioning, speaking back and forth—"dialogue"—Socrates invented a method to analyze and clarify the meaning of fundamental value terms.

All methods, as regular ways of doing something, rest on values affirming the worth of the "something" that is to be done, and embody other values reflected in what sorts of specific actions are allowed or avoided. The revolutionary force of Socratic dialogue, as a method for seeking wisdom of the sort he passionately wanted, becomes clear when we reflect on the sorts of values it embodies.

First, Socratic dialogue is a social act. It requires a hospitable social context. Plato later compared all philosophical thinking to having an internal dialogue with oneself, but this seems not to have been Socrates' own way. Socrates needed other people with whom he could work—people with a supportive set of values of their own—people who were ready to stop and talk, accustomed to the art of conversation, and convinced that large, difficult issues were worth spending time to examine. At the turn of the fourth century B.C., Athens was a place where such people could be found. Socrates recognizes, however, when he rejects the idea of even trying to fulfill his mission elsewhere in the Greek world, that these social value prerequisites were not available elsewhere. Exile or escape into less cultivated lands would be tantamount to abandoning the divine assignment (Plato 1985a).

Socrates' search for wisdom entails valuing real people engaged in the affairs of daily life. The method presupposes a starting place that is never valuationally neutral, never a blank slate, for those involved in it. Socrates takes for granted that questioning starts in the middle of things, with beliefs and prejudices already firmly in place at the outset. We never start philosophizing *de novo*, as though we had not lived, made choices, shaped our character, experienced much—learned something from life to this point.

In this, Socrates broke entirely with the more or less oracular tradition of his predecessors, in which pronouncements were dropped as into a vacuum, or in which writings or lectures were sown like seed on passive soil. Socrates, in contrast, needed—insisted on—an active partner for his mission. The search for wisdom was to be a genuine search, by two or more interactive but relatively independent seekers.

Therefore, a second major value reflected in Socratic dialogue is respect for the intellectual autonomy of the other. Rote learning is not valued. Socrates' interlocutor must see for himself (historically, alas, "herselves" were not recorded) what is wrong with his initial answers. In the end, if the dialogue develops that far, he must be able to see for himself why his achieved answer must be right and necessary.

This does not mean that Socrates does not lead the questioning, make suggestions, offer analogies, prod, and cajole. He does all of this and more, even offering poor suggestions, misleading analogies, sometimes, when his partner runs out of imagination (Plato 1985b). The point is that Socrates' partner can never rely on these suggestions. If he takes them up he may well have them shot down. Socrates is a fellow seeker, not an authority. The authority must be internal, the power of reason possessed by each thinker who uses it to see directly, without external props or authorities on which to lean. This must hold always, even when the suggestions and hints are not misleading. Only by seeing for himself can the interlocutor finally tell the difference.

Third, this places a major value on the power of reason in each thinker and especially on the importance of recognizing logical consistency and inconsistency. The argument develops where consistency leads it. From one statement another statement follows and yet another. Eventually something follows that is inconsistent with something else that has been elicited earlier in the questioning, and a choice must be made: Shall we go back and withdraw what earlier seemed so clear, or shall we abandon the line of assertions that has led to the present contradiction? One or the other must go.

A fourth value follows directly from the valuing of consistency: it is the (counter-intuitive) valuing of finding oneself caught in just such a dilemma, of finding oneself refuted out of one's own mouth. To learn—to see for oneself—that something is wrong with an opinion one had expressed is to learn something important. One is well ahead of where one had been before. Now there is knowledge that something is wrong; before the refutation there was only ignorance. Not ignorance but ignorance of ignorance is the danger.

Of course not everyone shares such a valuation of refutation (especially if one is self-important and if there are witnesses to the process of discovery), and Socrates was not always thanked for his services. One handsome young aristocrat said insulting things about Socrates' physical appearance, comparing him to an ugly, flat-faced electric catfish of the Nile who had "shocked" the aristocrat's usually eloquent tongue into numbness; but the fulcrum of the Socratic method is exactly this shock of recognition—that what one had been accustomed to saying cannot any longer be said without self-contradiction. This shock spurs some to fresh determination: to learn what can and must be said instead, as it did an untutored slave boy who was questioned by Socrates into finally understanding certain geometrical truths he eventually could see for himself. Others, who set a higher valuation on prestige than on wisdom, retreat from the learning process in frustration and anger (Plato 1985b).

Frustration is not such a bad thing, from the viewpoint of Socratic method. A fifth value implicit in the method is the importance of partial achievement in the quest for wisdom. A conversation, no matter how probing and sincere, will hardly solve all problems. Dialogues begin in real life and usually must end in real life before everything is tidy. Final answers are elusive. Systems are not even sought. But if some knowledge has been achieved, even if it is knowledge about blind alleys and false trails not recognized as such before, then something worthwhile has been done. Another day a different path may beckon.

Valuing such partial achievements does not mean that the goal of Socratic dialogue does not remain fully comprehensive solutions, if only those can be found that withstand the stress of testing. Therefore, the sixth implicit value in Socratic method is the quest for all-comprehensive, yet exact, meanings for key valuative terms. The Sophists, we saw, stressed the variability of customs, fashions, and norms of all sorts in the human world of nomos. Socrates was not content with such a swarm of answers to his great questions about good and justice. Is there no underlying meaning by virtue of which all these variations are variations of the same basic idea? Why otherwise use the same word for all these different instances? His method was bent on searching for the universal, however difficult it might be to articulate. Only by insisting on this (what today might be called a research program) will the goal of true wisdom—of the unified, comprehensive sort needed for a true science of ethics—be gradually approached.

For all the murkiness of the textual data, one outstanding characteristic of the historical Socrates, besides his method of questioning and his sense of divine mission, is his insistence that there *is* a truth to be had about fundamental value terms. Opinions on the subject are not equally trustworthy. Some, at least, are clearly worse: full of muddle and outright contradiction. But in some fields of interest we plainly see there can be special competency in what is better and worse. Horse trainers, for example, are expert in knowing what kinds of treatment are better and worse for the animals in their care.

This difference between expert knowledge and unqualified opinion is one of the touchstones of Socratic thinking. For this reason, he turned frequently to "experts" in various excellences—"courage," "piety," and the like—for his public questioning. He was disappointed in particular cases, but never gave up the distinction. To abandon the ideal of an exact science of ethics would be to open the door to sophistical relativism. This was something against which Socrates fought to the end of his life. There must be some things that are really good, just, and pious, not just in appearance or "for me," but in truth and for anyone who thinks clearly about the principles that apply in all cases.

Even being correct in one's opinion about fundamental values is not enough. Correctness is possible without knowledge. Having a right opinion on something can be a matter of good luck. The trouble with mere right opinion is that it has no stability, no universal application. A jury may convict someone of a crime because his eyes are too close-set for their liking, and they may happen to be correct in their guilty verdict. He may actually have done the deed. But the correctness of the verdict in this case does not rest on any principle that can assure correctness in every case. There is no reliable connection between close-set eyes and criminality. Knowledge requires more than right opinion: it requires also that our opinions, even when correct, be further supported by some principled "account" that shows why what is believed is and must be so. The person with this sort of knowledge will be regularly, not randomly, right.

Can this sort of knowledge be obtained for ethics? Leaning in one direction, Socrates stresses the degree to which the various virtues rest essentially on reason. True courage depends on understanding when and under what circumstances it is appropriate to advance, when it is appropriate to make an orderly retreat to fight another day. Courage is not just insensibility to fear; it is more principled than that. It depends, essentially, on a thoughtful component that can discriminate in a principled way between craven cowardice at one extreme and foolish rashness at the other. Temperance, likewise, is possible only when a reasoning mind can discriminate between too much and too little and give an account of itself that is convincing and appropriate. Piety and justice are both deeply dependent on understanding circumstances and weighing obligations. It seems that ethics must necessarily be a science, since all the virtues depend on knowledge.

Leaning in the other direction, however, Socrates is fully aware of the facts emphasized by the Sophists. There are many conflicting opinions; no one seems to possess the explicit, principled "accounts" that would turn ethical opinions into the items of firm knowledge they should be. If ethics were really a science, and if teaching such knowledge could actually make people virtuous, it would be the top priority of every virtuous parent to pass it on. No virtuous parent wants vicious children. And yet, unfortunately, this is not the way we find the world. Many parents are disappointed. Since good parents would if they could and do not, this finding implies that they cannot—they simply do not have the "accounts" that would turn their right opinion into established knowledge. It seems, then, that ethics cannot be an exact science but, even among the most virtuous, must be merely matters of opinion—or, equally random, be divine "gifts"—unable to support themselves in principle, beyond the level of "lucky shots."

Socrates accepts both findings as true. Since all the virtues do essentially require a knowledge component, ethics should in principle be able to be made a science; but actual virtue, as we find it, seems far removed from a science of universal ethics that can straightforwardly be taught. Our value-judgments are made sloppily, without bothering to clarify key meanings and without even attempting to give the principled "accounts" that would make them more than opinion.

Patient questioning, examining opinion for its logical consequences and seeking consistency in fundamental definitions of meaning, might improve the actual situation. The ideal beckons. For Socrates it beckoned urgently, as a divine command. It seems not impossible in principle; it seems simply a matter of putting in the effort and sincerity and humility required for self-examination. But somehow the recognized "experts" are always "too busy" doing what they are doing to reflect deeply on whether what they are doing is right. In one of Plato's most charming early dialogues, *Euthyphro*, Socrates is shown patiently exposing the ill-considered views of a pompous young theologian on what "piety" means and what sorts of duties the gods may require of us. The "electric catfish" aspect of Socrates is once again effective in stunning the tongue of his interlocutor, who is made to realize that he has no clear idea of what service to the gods entails. At this crucial point Socrates invites Euthyphro to begin again, but the young man refuses: he is "too busy." But what is he so busy with? He is busying himself with a most questionable indictment of his father for a borderline capital crime that might well lead to the death of his father. He asserts that it is his pious duty to do this dreadful thing—but he is "too busy" to work out a consistent meaning for "piety." He has just discovered that he literally does not know the moral meaning of what he is doing; but rather than try to understand the character of his intended actions, he throws himself back into those actions without further examination. Here, the unexamined life becomes a danger to others as well as to itself.

This is a fitting parable of tragic irony. When he recounted it, Plato must have been sick at heart, remembering his admired master's recent execution on grounds of "impiety," among others. What did the Athenian multitudes know about this matter? In their ignorance, they had rejected and condemned the very one who was struggling hardest to overcome their ignorance. A new era had arrived with the new century; how should philosophy after Socrates proceed?

PLATO

If my thesis about the interpenetration of theorizing and valuing is correct, it would be misleadingly abstract to discuss metaphysics without paying attention to historical context. Metaphysicians do their thinking always in the midst of things, always in some particular place and time. However much they may try to insulate themselves from turmoil, they must eat and sleep and have some social position or other; their thinking does not rise from a *tabula rasa*. No less than every participant in a marketplace dialogue, they always start from within a framework of values and beliefs.

Respect for concreteness does not entail that philosophical thinking is a mere by-product of historical circumstances, for example, economics or geography. Such an extreme of historicism underestimates the degree of universality attained by concepts deployed in free discursive thought; and universality, by its nature, shakes loose from the particularities of circumstance. It abstracts from these grubby details, deliberately leaves them out of account, forgets them. But the details remain present and influential—though conceptually invisible at high levels of abstraction—in swaying decisions on which concepts will be early deployed, what consequences will be welcome, and what conclusions will be distasteful enough to force the thinker to reconsider.

Plato lived in troubled times. Born in 428 B.C. into a highly aristocratic family, his youthful years coincided with the moral and political erosions of the long Peloponnesian War. The glories of Periclean Athens were ground down in military conflict with Sparta, the Athenian democracy became increasingly corrupt, and in 404 B.C., when Plato was twenty-four, members of his own aristocratic class launched a successful revolution against the democracy after defeats in war. The resulting dictatorship of the "gentlemen" dismayed Plato. He saw his aged and honorable teacher Socrates placed in grave jeopardy by being commanded by The Thirty, against his conscience, to participate in an illegal arrest. Socrates refused, preferring the mortal danger of defiance to the certainty of moral corruption. On that occasion he was saved from the oligarchs by another revolution, which reinstated democracy; but before long Plato observed the new democratic régime presiding over the outrageous trial and execution of his admired master on trumped up charges of impiety.

My concern in what follows is of course not to deal in any comprehensive way with Plato's philosophy. Rather, it is to reflect briefly but I hope illuminatingly on the way his values influenced his metaphysics and, in turn, on the way his metaphysics established value in ultimate reality. All of Plato's dialogues dealt in one way or another with these issues, but I shall concentrate most of my attention on three key writings: the *Republic*, *Symposium*, and *Timaeus*.

The great *Republic*, long Plato's most famous dialogue among the educated public at large, can be seen at one level as an attempt to work out a viable basis for Socrates' burning quest after a science of values. It is the depiction of a city-state in which there is no longer division between nomos, law (norm, custom, ethics), on the one hand, and phusis, nature (given character, established reality), on the other. The laws and customs of this state would be grounded in the nature of the universe itself. Policy, domestic and foreign, would be made by those who were qualified to know what is really so and really best for all concerned.

This means that the ignorant multitudes could not be trusted with the helm of state, as in the turbulent democracies that Plato himself had experienced from childhood. Plato's aristocratic mistrust of the mob comes through plainly in this prescription. But it also means that mere lineage and family distinction could not be allowed to rule, either. Plato's disillusionment with aristocratic terror and oligarchic corruption blocks easy solutions in that direction. The need is for leaders who know what is good and can see the truth beyond temptations of venality and family interest.

It is striking that in Plato's state the most radical barriers ever imagined are placed between rulers and family favoritism. No child should even know who his or her parents are, much less the family tree. Everyone should rise on aptitude alone, not on favors or inheritance. Only those who rise unhindered to the top through the rigorous educational system Plato describes should be allowed to rule. The rest should follow their aptitudes for other activities, economic or military. In this design for a state, power is insulated from both the unqualified many and the potentially venal few. Neither democracy nor aristocracy can be trusted, if instead there is a way of placing power in the hands of policy makers with genuine knowledge, not mere opinion, about the good and real.

The all-important question then becomes whether Socrates' quest can have a happy outcome. For those who assume that the answer must be negative—that the "really good" is either a forever elusive mystery or a logical category mistake—Plato's state is the terrible archetype of all totalitarian "closed societies" (Popper 1963). If a genuine science of value is an illusion, then the so-called "experts" whose hands are on the levers of control turn out to be no more than overachieving test takers who promote their own interests arbitrarily, perpetuating their control by lying propaganda and rigid distinctions of social function that insure monopoly of power. However, for those who are open to the possibility of genuine ethical knowledge, not mere opinion, Plato's state is not "closed" at all, because it is open "at the top," as it were, to inspiring visions of the truth, by which policy makers who are entrusted with this personally thankless role faithfully guide the fortunes of all concerned toward the best (Thorson 1963).

Plato clearly favored the latter alternative. He was no lover of democracy, but he would doubtless have been astonished (and wounded) at allegations that someone with his principles might have been sympathetic to Hitler or Stalin. The Greece of his day knew tyrants galore; the rule of sheer power, imposition of policy by force of will rather than by the "account" of intellect, was explicitly rejected in Plato's *Republic* (Plato 1985d). Instead, the radical idea of a society led by assured truth in matters of better and worse was offered to replace tyranny either by the many or the few. What would the kosmos need to be like if such an idea is to have any plausibility at all?

In his *Republic*, Plato builds his metaphysics on the distinction we saw to be of such great importance for Socrates: the distinction between mere opinion and genuine knowledge. Mere opinion is uncertain, changes over time, and is relative to particular persons in particular circumstances; knowledge, in contrast, must be necessary, eternal, and universal. If reality is to be knowable, it must be like that. What served as a guiding principle in Socrates' search for knowledge becomes for Plato the foundation of a theory of reality.

Socrates acknowledged the split between the *world as it is actually experienced*, in which virtue is not understood and thus cannot be taught, even by virtuous parents, and the *world as it must ideally be*, in which the knowledge that infuses every virtue shines with its own universal and necessary light, allowing firm understanding to replace the lucky hits of divine inspiration. In an earlier dialogue, Plato depicts Socrates as summarizing the situation:

> Whoever has [virtue] gets it by divine inspiration without taking thought, unless he be the kind of statesman who can create another like himself. Should there be such a man, he would be among the living practically what Homer said Tiresias was among the dead, when he described him as the only one in the underworld who kept his wits—"the others are mere flitting shades." Where virtue is concerned such a man would be just like that, a solid reality among shadows (Plato 1985b: 100).

In the *Republic*, this hint is expanded into the famous parable of the Cave. Ordinary, unexamined perception in our daily world of opinion and change is compared to flickering shadows cast on a wall by a fire. The shadows are not even shadows of real things, but cutouts, simulacra of natural objects passed with some degree of regularity in front of the fire. In this "underworld" of "flitting shades," perceivers trapped there, forced to look only at the wall, dutifully spend their time closely observing the shadows and studying their regularities, guessing which will come next, developing a quasi-science of opinion. But one prisoner is released and forced up from his world of copies and their shadows, seeing for himself what is going on in the cave and eventually encountering— half blinded by the blazing light—real objects, illuminated by the effulgent sun. Having seen reality itself he returns to the cave to spread the news, but is scoffed at by the others. His eyes, dimmed in the cave because of the bright light outside, are no longer fit for distinguishing the regularities of the shadows. He has to suffer the taunts and hostility of the other prisoners who reject the idea of going outside (and perhaps, we may add, reject the very notion of an "outside" itself).

The parable presents in an image what Plato offers as the outline of his metaphysical solution to the paradox of *Meno*: that virtue *must* be a matter of knowledge (can be taught) but obviously *is not* a matter of knowledge (cannot be taught). If we are concerned with the domain of reality—the realm of the unchanging, the intelligible, the absolute—virtue can in principle be taught by those who can attain knowledge of it. But if we are concerned with the domain of ordinary appearances, alas, we are dealing with inconstant shadows, mere opinion, and must rely on luck or the inspiration of the gods.

Plato's dualism between the realm of reality and the realm of daily experience may remind us of another similar-sounding dualism in the thought of Parmenides, who, as we saw earlier, distinguished sharply between the Way of Being and the Way of Seeming. True, Plato accepted many of Parmenides' basic values: reality, to be worthy of the name, must be eternal and absolute, perfect, lacking in nothing, ungenerated, ultimately unified. But the differences between the two are vast, outweighing the similarities in importance. First, and most telling, the Being of Parmenides was through and through material. It was not until the Atomists, who declared independence ("Naught is just as real as Aught") of the assumption that material existence is the only possible kind, that philosophers were freed to think of nonmaterial reality. The Atomists themselves restricted their nonmaterial alternative to the Void, empty space with no properties except the capacity to hold material atoms and allow them to move within itself. The path had been broken. Plato's alternative to *material* being is *intelligible* being: perfect and eternal like Parmenides' Being; free from material particularity, like Democritus' Void; but richly qualitative, consisting solely in character.

The exact range of fundamentally real characters, thus the exact number of Intelligible Realities, Forms, or Archetypes, was a finally unresolved question for Plato. At different times in his life he seems to have held different views on the question. But however few or many might be granted ultimate and noncomposite status, the realm of Form was always considered a system. In the *Republic*, the "lesser" Forms are those that unify and make sense of flitting sensory qualities, allowing us to build beliefs about relatively stable things from swarms of sense-images that, in themselves, though universal (like hues and tones), fade off into chaotic illusion.

"Higher" than these are the Pythagorean-like mathematical Forms, not themselves open to sensory imagination, that provide us with intelligible laws for such unified things. Here emerges knowledge, the possibility of giving "accounts" that provide self-evident necessity and universality to belief.

Finally, "highest" of all, Plato propounds a realm of interrelated qualitative Forms, unified by a Form of Forms which makes all the others intelligible. This he names the Form of the Good, something beyond description in language, because while language always divides subjects and predicates, the Good is wholly unitary. It is the one self-justifying, all-encompassing ground for intelligibility and explanation. As such, it combines in itself exactly those finally satisfying qualities Socrates looked for, but could not find, in Anaxagoras' invocation of Mind. If something is of the Good, it is for the best; the restless mind can slake its thirst in fulfilled contentment: moral, intellectual, and aesthetic. The Good, the True, and the Beautiful are ultimately real and are at one—are the One on which all lesser realities depend and through which alone they can be understood.

With this theory of reality, based on the distinction between opinion and knowledge, appearance and reality, becoming and being, Plato seems in danger of falling into the same sort of incoherence—the same lack of connectedness between fundamental elements in his system—that we noticed in Parmenides. What does the realm of being have to do with the familiar daily realm of becoming? How can there be any positive relation between the eternal and the temporal?

At some points Plato seems tempted to raise his key distinctions to a pitch of absolute dualism and thus to fall into this waiting trap. In the dialogue *Phaedo*, for example, he depicts the ideal "philosopher," the "lover of wisdom," as properly obliged to fight the material world of fleshly yearnings to such an extreme extent that he should have nothing at all to do with it, in principle, so far as possible. His mind should so dwell with and for the perfect Forms that when it comes time for his body to die, the passage will be easy. No, it will be a positive relief. His soul, already at home with the eternal, will not be shackled to the temporal; accustomed to the universal, it will not be dragged down by particulars. Interpreted in this mood, Plato's metaphysics reminds us of the ascetic dualism of Pythagorean cults. The soul must struggle against the body, reason must reject experience, the sacred must separate itself from the profane. Here is dualism both of values and in theory. Both are defined in terms of oppositions. In this direction lies ineradicable incoherence.

Fortunately, this is not Plato's only mood. The dualist, ascetic mood suitable for a vigil before an unjust execution is not appropriate for a wine party. In the *Symposium*, Plato provides a different account of the relationship between experience and truth, in which eternal reality shines through its particular temporal embodiments, drawing the lover of wisdom up to ever more nearly perfect levels on the "ladder of love."

The wise woman, Diotima, instructs Plato's Socrates in the secrets of this ladder toward perfection. The crucial lesson is to *use*, not to reject, the world of sense, change, and particularity in the pilgrimage toward the intelligible, eternal, and universal. At the outset, she reminds Socrates that we should be suspicious of premature disjunctions. Either/or is an easy assumption to make. But it leads to fallacy. If something is not beautiful, must it be ugly? Socrates is shown jumping to this conclusion, but this is not so. Likewise, opinion is not knowledge; but for that it need not be sheer ignorance. Intermediate between them lies right opinion, embodying substantive truth but lacking the "account" that would make it proper understanding.

The lover of the Good, True, and Beautiful is, consciously or not, seeking the eternal. But the eternal does not appear as such in the world of change. Instead, there are approximations. Even sexual love, of which ascetics have such horror, is in the service of an approximation of the eternal. Diotima points out:

> It is in this manner that all mortal nature is preserved: not by being ever completely the same, like the divine, but by leaving behind a new thing of the same sort in place of the old as it departs. That is the means, Socrates, she said, by which mortal partakes of immortality, both body and all the rest; but the immortal is otherwise. Do not then be surprised if every animal by nature cherishes its own offspring: it is for the sake of immortality that this zeal and love obtain (Plato 1985e: 208b).

The urgent mating of animals in the wild is already on the ladder of love leading to the eternal. So, likewise, is human sexuality. Biological fertility is a kind of quest for immortality, of the sort appropriate to the world of becoming. Even more clearly a product of the urge for everlasting glory, despite its moral ambiguity, is the "terrible intensity of the desire for fame" (Plato 1985e: 208d). Writing poetry, designing cities, and the like, are analogous acts of lovemaking by those fertile in mind.

Diotima leads Socrates to see the full sequence. First we are attracted to particular beautiful bodies. Sexual attraction at this level is in the service of the divine because it draws us insistently to notice the beautiful and to want it. But then, on the next rung of the ladder, we notice that beauty is present in many bodies. It is a universal quality with many instances. Among these instances, the lover discovers, is beauty in character or soul, and this is to be even more treasured and sought after, as more long lasting and satisfying than beauty of body. Still higher on the ladder comes love of the beauty in laws and practices. Knowledge, the lover finds, has its own type of beauty and corresponding satisfactions; but above all attractive is the study of beauty itself, not as instanced here or there in one body or another, in one law or theorem or argument or another, but for what it is in itself: pure, absolute, and eternal. This is the goal of philosophy, to know "finally and perfectly, that very thing, what it is to be beautiful" (Plato 1985e: 211d).

In all this sequence Plato has not suggested that we reject or scorn the lower rungs of the ladder. At each stage the Form of Beauty is present, the eternal draws the temporal toward itself, and the world of becoming is recognized as suffused with the Forms of Being. In this way, the seeker of wisdom, the one who faithfully maintains his quest for the science of value, will be rewarded, as Socrates had hoped. "He will give birth, not to an image of virtue, since he does not touch an image, but to true virtue, since he touches the truth. And in giving birth to true virtue, and nurturing it, becomes dear to god; and he, if any man, is immortal" (Plato 1985e: 212a).

What sort of kosmos would be required to allow such thorough penetration by Beauty—the eternal, intelligible, and perfect realm of Forms that constitutes ultimate reality—and still to present itself as daily life actually finds it in changing, far from perfect, often ugly, experience? Plato's *Timaeus*, a late work of great intellectual maturity and poetic power, describes how all the mixed and muddled data of this observed universe can be coherently conceived from within the valuational framework to which he and Socrates before him were committed.

For this, Plato tells a story of origins: a myth of genesis. In so doing he takes advantage of the wonderful simplification provided by this story form, in which one can highlight the essential few elements that constitute the necessary ingredients for "putting together" a universe. Myths of origins, telling what it was like "in the beginning," clarify by stepping back from the turmoil and complexity of the present age, in which everything is confused. They (like myths of endings) set in bold relief what is primary and what is derivative. They need not be taken literally as temporal sequences; rather, as imaginative recipes for world making, they draw attention to the ingredients in their pure state, before everything got "cooked."

What were the motives of the great chef who combined the ingredients into our world? Motive is not one more of the ingredients, but it is an essential part of the story, answering not only why the world is *as* it is but also why it *is* at all. Plato's answer: "He was good" (Plato 1985f: 29). That is, perfect goodness entails perfect generosity. The world is only because altruistic benevolence lies at the heart of reality. In the end this will be the resting place of intellectual as well as moral satisfaction that Socrates looked for (in vain) from Anaxagoras' world system. The kosmos is, as Socrates insisted that it must be, "for the best," since it comes from an imagined divine agency characterized by perfect goodness; thus,

> . . . being without jealousy, he desired that all things should come as near as possible to being like himself. . . . Desiring, then, that all things should be good and, so far as might be, nothing imperfect, the god took over all that is visible—not at rest, but in discordant and unordered motion—and brought it from disorder into order, since he judged that order was in every way the better (Plato 1985f: 30).

Order is better than disorder. Another major value premise that runs through Greek metaphysical thought from the beginning is again clearly articulated. Discord in itself is ugly. The universe is for the sake of being, "so far as might be," beautiful.

Clearly this last is an important proviso. The world is not, as we observe, perfectly beautiful. It is not perfect in any respect. There must be some impediment to the perfection of our world which is logically necessary, an insuperable handicap even for perfect benevolence.

Before we return to examine the world ingredient that both allows our world to be and, simultaneously, blocks its perfection, we should canvass further for other values that govern Plato's world making. "Goodness" unifies all values, but a number of these can be identified in their own right, as we have seen in the case of order, which is "in every way better" than disorder. Others include uniqueness, which is better than multiplicity. To be one of many resembling others is to share qualities with them and thus to require subsumption with them under something higher. The highest and best will not therefore permit a second like itself. Since beauty is a major value, proportion will be better than disproportion; and concord or amity (i.e., harmony) will be preferable to discord, strife, and dissonance. Likewise, wholeness or completeness is to be valued over composition, which allows "aging" and "sickness." This should remind us of Parmenides' emphasis on absolute unity, as also of his selection of spherical shape as the only "fitting" one for Being. Plato here agrees and adds that only the sphere is "equidistant every way from centre to extremity— a figure the most perfect and uniform of all; for he judged uniformity to be immeasurably better than its opposite." Not only this, but Plato adds an ecological value that sounds oddly contemporary when he insists that self-sufficiency is a key value for any "good" universe:

> There was no surrounding air to require breathing, nor yet was it in need of any organ by which to receive food into itself or to discharge it again when drained of its juices. For nothing went out or came into it from anywhere, since there was nothing: it was designed to feed itself on its own waste and to act and be acted upon entirely by itself and within itself; because its framer thought that it would be better self-sufficient, rather than dependent upon anything else (Plato 1985f: 33).

Clearly the universe as living ecosystem is better than a dead or merely mechanical system, for Plato. This implies that it has soul, senior to and of more value than its body.

These are some of the important values indicated in the *Timaeus* as subsumed by the Good. Likewise, eternity is valued over temporality. At this point, when we return to contemplate why the universe, whose story of generation is being told, cannot possibly be perfect in every respect, we see that some perfections are logically impossible, even for perfect benevolence. A generated world cannot possibly be eternal, simply by virtue of having been generated. But without being generated, it could not have any of the good qualities that it does have. Benevolence would have been stymied at the outset. The condition of the existence of a temporal world like this is thus also an absolute obstacle to its perfection. The closest way a temporal thing, even a universe, can approximate the eternal is to be everlasting. This approximation is reflected in the constant regular rotation of the spherical universe about its center. With this rotation, the "moving image of eternity," Time itself, is also generated. It is the "everlasting likeness [of eternity] moving according to number" (Plato 1985f: 37).

This shows us how a necessary condition of the world's being can also be a block to its absolute perfection, but the world as we experience it has many more blemishes than merely failing to be eternal. How does Plato square this with the perfection of the Forms and the altruism behind the temporal world's existence?

The answer lies in Space. Hitherto we have considered only two of the three ingredients which go into the making of our world: the eternal, immaterial Forms and the generated world itself, twirling everlastingly in Time. Now Plato introduces the necessary third ingredient: a Receptacle into which the Forms can be copied. Without such a Receptacle, no Copy of the Forms, no actual, separate instantiation of those archetypal qualities that give intelligibility and order to the chaos of mere movement, would be logically possible. The matrix of temporal Space has no definite characters of its own, since character is exclusive of the realm of Form, but it is the logical precondition for character becoming instantiated into a concrete world. In this, the Receptacle is "like" nothing at all, since everything that can be "like" or "unlike" is so by virtue of some definite character. And, as a consequence, it is impossible to have a normal concept of the Receptacle. It strains the mind, Plato admits. It is something "difficult and obscure" (Plato 1985f: 49) as, figuratively, the "nurse—of all Becoming." This third world ingredient "is Space, which is everlasting, not admitting destruction; providing a situation for all things that come into being, but itself apprehended without the senses by a sort of bastard reasoning, and hardly an object of belief" (Plato 1985f: 52).

Illegitimate though our quasi-concept of this third ingredient may be, it helps to account for what we have seen needs to be held together: both that eternal Qualities are everywhere pervasive in our temporal world, to be recognized by intellects alerted to their presence and drawn to their universal Beauty, and that the world is a changing, messy place in which there is much actual disagreement over matters of fact and value. Just as what is in time must fall short of perfection, so what is in space is by virtue of that very fact less than the perfect Archetype of which it is a copy. Space-Time distorts "like an instrument for shaking" (Plato 1985f: 53) even as it serves as necessary ground for any world at all.

This is a world in which Socrates' dream of a rigorous science of ethics, as well as of other lesser matters, could be accommodated. Ordinary people tend not to notice the Forms as such, though they are always present. By active training of the mind and discipline of life, clarity is possible and needful. A mathematics of morals is not a contradiction; it is certainly not contradicted by the empirical fact of much confusion and relativism in opinion; perhaps the way is paved, metaphysically, for temporal human society ruled by wisdom grounded in the eternal.

ARISTOTLE

Aristotle, the last of the great philosophers of the Hellenic age, was not a mathematician. The son of a prominent court physician, he had a lifelong penchant for the biological. Living organisms develop and change according to some internal principle. These changes are not random; they are intelligible and largely predictable. But they are far from exact or perfect. Illness occurs; birth defects happen; death and decay are as universal as generation and development.

This nonmathematical perspective did not keep Aristotle from making great contributions to the formal disciplines: he founded what came to be known as formal logic. His general cast of mind, however, despite twenty years studying and in residence with Plato at the Academy in Athens, was never that of a purely formal thinker. After Plato's death in 347 B.C., the leadership of the

Academy was inherited by the mathematically oriented Speusippus, a nephew of Plato, and Aristotle promptly departed from Athens to plunge himself into pioneering zoological studies on the island of Lesbos.

Because Aristotle had been born in Stagira, a Macedonian city in Ionia where where he had lived until being sent to Athens at about age seventeen, it was natural for the King of Macedonia, Phillip II, to invite him to become the tutor of his son Alexander. In 342 B.C., Alexander was a tender thirteen years old. Aristotle accepted the royal invitation and left Lesbos to spend the next three years imparting what wisdom he could to the young man who was to conquer the known world and, thereby, with the opening of the Hellenistic era, end the Hellenic.

Royal duties done, Aristotle returned to Stagira for a few years before founding his own school, the Lyceum, in Athens in 335 B.C. The Lyceum quickly became a center of learning that rivalled the Academy of Speusippus and other mathematically oriented Platonists. It remained flavored by its Macedonian origins, however; and after Alexander the Great died in 323 B.C., what had been an advantage (being Macedonian) turned to a danger in Athens. Aristotle at age sixty-one was forced to depart, leaving the Lyceum to others. He died the next year.

This active, engaged man of the world resembled his mentor Plato in many respects: they both founded and led schools, were at home in ruling circles, and were fascinated by politics, actual and ideal. But Aristotle differed in a deep way. While Plato wrote the *Republic*, Aristotle collected actual constitutions of his day and published them in his *Politics* (Aristotle 1967). Plato first polished the ideal and moved down only later in his works to compromises with the actual (Plato 1937a); Aristotle begins his study of politics with the premise that "man is a political animal" (Aristotle 1967: Book I), from which it follows that civic orders rise and develop by nature, empirically from "below" and "within," as it were, in the manner of organic unfoldings.

As noted earlier, this profound shift of emphasis from the formal to the empirical in Aristotle's approach does not imply scorn for the exact and necessary, where it is appropriate. First philosophy, what we have come to call metaphysics, arises also by nature in us, since "all men naturally desire knowledge," as Aristotle announces at the very start of his *Metaphysics*. It begins in "wonder," a kind of ignorance with a built-in urge to understanding; but at its best it ends with a sense of the necessity of what had earlier been problematic.

> All begin, as we have said, by wondering that things should be as they are, *e.g.* with regard to marionettes, or the solstices, or the incommensurability of the diagonal of a square; because it seems wonderful to everyone who has not yet perceived the cause that a thing should not be measurable by the smallest unit. But we must end with the contrary and

(according to the proverb) the better view, as men do even in these cases when they understand them; for a geometrician would wonder at nothing so much as if the diagonal were to become measurable (Aristotle 1935a: Book I, 983A).

This "better view"—of the necessity of what had once been perplexing—rests squarely on the Law of Noncontradiction, the utterly unprovable but no less utterly fundamental principle that "it is impossible for anyone to suppose that the same thing is and is not"; or, more fully stated, that "it is impossible for the same attribute at once to belong and not to belong to the same thing and in the same relation" (Aristotle 1935a: Book IV, 1005B). Its unprovability hangs on the fact that every proof depends upon at least tacitly assuming it. To claim anything at all would be impossible if a claim did not exclude its own contradiction. Therefore, says Aristotle, "it shows lack of education not to know of what we should require proof, and of what we should not. For it is quite impossible that everything should have a proof; the process would go on to infinity, so that even so there would be no proof" (Aristotle 1935a: Book IV, 1006A). Though unprovable, nothing could be more certain, since to say anything at all is to invoke it.

Still, between the state of sheer wonder and the state of complete understanding grounded in the necessities of Noncontradiction, there are many worthwhile things to investigate and learn about in less rigorous ways than those of mathematics. An exact science of ethics, for example, is an illusion. It shows poor judgment to look for the same level of precision in every field of human endeavor. Mathematical rigor is an inappropriate ideal for inquiries that lack mathematically exact starting places. Aristotle feels no need to be loyal to Socrates' dream of a perfectly certain ethics. It will be enough, he writes, "if it achieves that amount of precision which belongs to its subject matter" (Aristotle 1946: Book I, 1094B). Once again he invokes the broad intuitive standard of good judgment and "education" to defend his more relaxed, empirical, and practical standard:

We must . . . be content if, in dealing with subjects and starting from premises thus uncertain, we succeed in presenting a broad outline of the truth: when our subjects and our premises are merely generalities, it is enough if we arrive at generally valid conclusions. Accordingly we may ask the student also to accept the various views we put forward in the same spirit; for it is the mark of an educated mind to expect that amount of exactness in each kind which the nature of the particular subject admits. It is equally unreasonable to accept merely probable conclusions from a mathematician and to demand strict demonstration from an orator (Aristotle 1946: Book I, 1094B).

For Aristotle the point is appropriateness. Mathematical rigor has its place—in mathematics, of course; and also as an ideal for full understanding. Whether the latter is attainable or not is an open question. But between ignorance and intellectual bliss lies the main work of human thinking.

For the purposes of this book, the kind of human thinking of special interest is addressed toward understanding the kosmos in its most inclusive sense, the "well- or decently-ordered" universe in which we find ourselves. For Aristotle, the biologically minded student of Plato, such thinking will inevitably show similarities to and differences from his great mentor.

The most important similarity is their agreement on the need for ideal universals as ingredients in the world. Qualities are not limited to any particular space or time. The very same hue of red can be present in a space over here and also over there, a different space. It can be present in an indefinite number of instances in a limitless number of places. Qualities somehow transcend the particularizing localism provided by space. Likewise, this identical shade of red that existed yesterday or a thousand years ago can exist today or tomorrow or at any time that offers subjects suitable for having color. Qualities can be manifested, received, instanced in space and time—just *how* must be debated—but the qualities themselves, in their purely qualitative characters, are not subject to space and time. They are quite literally eternal, out of time, when considered merely as qualitative rather than as somewhere/somewhen instanced.

It is these universals, not only including sensory universals like colors or tones or textures but also including purely intelligible universals as found in mathematics or science, ethics or religion, that provide the possibility of structure and understanding in our world. They provide the basis for common meanings in languages shared by many thinkers. They are the necessary condition for order, repetition, recognition of "the same again"—literally the *same* quality in new circumstances—that permits familiarity, regularity, and eventually law.

Following Plato, Aristotle called these universal entities Forms and accepted their necessity for any satisfactory theory of the kosmos. But "how" and "where" the Forms should be held to exist was a matter of deep controversy. On one question, of course, they could easily agree: the Forms exist at least in our minds. And Aristotle, student of biology that he was, would have added, for sensory qualities, also in our sense organs. On another point, too, there was agreement: the Forms exist when and where they are instanced in things, the objects with definite qualities and characteristics that make up our world. Our sense organs, Aristotle says, are so constituted by nature that they can (and normally do) conform themselves, within the proper range of qualities of the things in their presence, to the same Forms that are in those things. Thus, sense organs are intermediaries offering possibilities of further abstraction and contemplation.

The question remains whether the Forms exist in any way apart from or in addition to minds, sense organs, and things. Plato, as we saw, insisted that they do. "Before" the world came to be, through the benevolence of the Maker, the Forms timelessly "are" and therefore are apart from the world, in addition to it, independent of it. This answer postulates a special Realm of Forms which the liberated human mind, properly drawn by Eros, can rise to contemplate. Mathematical entities are "there." Ethical qualities are "there." The experienced world, at its best, is only an imperfect Copy.

For one with Aristotle's empirical preferences, this answer was unnecessary or worse. True, the world of nature could not be conceived without the qualitative, universal aspect that gives it character and structure, but there is no need for a doubling of this aspect in some separate Realm. The Forms are present in things (the substances around us) and in us (our sense organs and our minds); and that is sufficient for an ordered, intelligible kosmos.

The natural world is not only ordered and intelligible (these rational qualities, as we have seen, represent fundamental values for all the pioneer Greek theorists). It is also in itself, especially for Aristotle, inescapably normative in additional ways. For the purpose of our narrative on the place of values in reality, it will suffice to conclude this chapter with a reflection on the concept of "nature," both respecting the nature of individual substances and respecting the nature of nature as a whole.

Individual substances have natures. This applies to inanimate things, such as air or water, and to artifacts, such as knives or bedsteads. But, for Aristotle, who had devoted much attention to their empirical study, the obvious paradigm of "substances with natures" is located in living organisms. One thing Aristotle never doubted: that things are many and changing. Eleatic doubts about plurality and becoming are properly to be refuted, not seriously entertained. But how do things change? And how can change be understood?

The natures of things are provided by those characteristics inherent in them that are "not separable from the things themselves, save conceptually" (Aristotle 1935b: Book II, 193B). That is, the natures of things are the essential properties without which they would no longer be what they are. If a fire loses hotness, it is simply no longer a fire. It has "gone out," as we say: it has disappeared *as fire*. If water loses wetness, it has ceased to be water. These fundamental properties are what determine from within how individual substances will change, move, or remain still. A stone's nature will determine from within how firmly it remains at rest and how much force will be required to stir it. More clearly, an acorn's nature will determine from within how it will germinate in the moist earth and grow according to inbuilt principles of development into a great oak tree productive of more acorns. The "oakness" of the oak is constant throughout many changes in inessentials such as size or appearance. Leaves (and even limbs) can fall or be plucked away, but the oak remains oak, from acorn to old age. It determines its changes, to the extent its environmental good fortune allows, from within its own nature.

Several observations flow from this principle. First, the development of finite substances is not always—perhaps not even usually—permitted to follow its "natural" course. A strong prevailing wind may distort the tree from its natural handsome shape. A squirrel may eat the acorn, according to the squirrel's own nature, and prevent the germination of a tree that might have been. There are different natures in nature, interacting and interfering with one another. Some substances have the good luck to develop according to their essential characters; some suffer other ends. Second, we see that Aristotle's vision of the kosmos is deeply teleological. Each finite substance, having its own nature, has its own ideal state. This is especially clear (and poignant) in living things. Biological substances have ideal states toward which they develop—if they can. They have individual goods to pursue. The acorn is self-directed toward its fulfilled state in becoming a productive oak tree, under fortunate circumstances. This is what is meant by having a distinct nature, an essential character bringing about internal self-development. Similarly, the squirrel is self-directed toward nourishment and reproduction—survival as an individual and as a species—for which the acorn may need to perish as a potential oak tree to become food for a finite living substance with a different goal and a conflicting good.

What allows orderly change (or stability) in things with natures is the presence in particular substances of universal characters, what Aristotle and Plato called Forms. But universal characters are not effective unless they are somewhere and somewhen. The characters must be embedded in a substrate that is spatial and temporal and, thus localized, particular. The substrate is capable of taking on general characteristics, thereby becoming something definite and, at the same time, giving universal characteristics a definite place in the world. The principle of individuation Aristotle called matter. It is the function of matter to provide both *particularization* for whatever universal forms it takes on and *continuity* as some of these universal properties are replaced by others.

The replacement of properties by other properties can be rapid or slow and regular, as in the gradual ripening of an apple, when traits such as "green" and "sour" are insensibly replaced by "red" and "sweet." Change does not infect the eternal Forms themselves: "green" itself does not somehow turn into "red" itself. That would indeed destroy the intelligibility of the universe and, since "red" is essentially "not-green," would violate the inviolable Law of Noncontradiction. Yet change occurs. Therefore, it is the whole *substance*, made up of both its formal, qualitative aspect and its material, particularized aspect, that changes.

To understand such change, Aristotle insisted that four distinct dimensions be considered. His famous four "causes" require accounts of what *prop-*

erties are involved (the Formal aspect), what *ends* are involved (the Final aspect), what *agency* is involved (the Efficient aspect), and what *stuff* is involved (the Material aspect). All this is so well known that it would barely warrant repeating except for the immensely important role for values that is entailed by this way of looking at change in the kosmos. Forms are ideals, perfect exemplars of their kind. And each of the first three "causes" are aspects of these ideals.

Consider our earlier example of natural changes in finite living substances, oaks and squirrels. The Formal Cause of the oak would encompass all the qualities necessary to the ideal of fully exemplified oakness; this is exactly the same as the Final Cause, since the end of the acorn (as of the sapling) is to attain just this set of characteristics, if possible; and the Efficient Cause for living things, at least, is again the same, since it is the mature oak that is the agency which gives the process its push, developing its acorns and spreading them abroad to flourish, if that be their fortune. (There is no chicken-or-egg problem for Aristotle: since actuality takes priority over potentiality, it is the adult form of any species that "comes first" in every case.) This leaves us with two Causes, the Ideal and its localized "Stuff." But every actual "stuff" we ever encounter is already characterized by universal properties. Therefore, we never experience directly, and cannot—except through what Plato called "bastard reasoning"—even theorize to ourselves about Prime Matter by itself. It is a necessary theoretical principle of individuality and continuity, but for Aristotle Prime Matter could no more exist alone than could the Forms. Every finite entity requires both aspects. Together they are sufficient.

What of nature as a whole? Does it have a nature, too? Or is the kosmos only a collection of finite substances giving spatio-temporal location to ideals often in conflict, as entities with different goods seek their diverse ends?

The natural world as a whole, as defined by Aristotle, could be considered to have a nature only if it has a goal or end as a whole. Everything that has a nature has one, as we noted, only insofar as it has an internal principle of change or stability with a Final cause as well as Formal, Efficient, and Material causes. Does nature have such a purpose? Aristotle's answer is positive, but we must be cautious not to over-interpret the answer in modern terms influenced by Christianity.

The world, full of finite natures seeking goods after their kinds, is thereby full of purposes. These purposes are aided, especially in living substances, by natures of great complexity and refinement, nicely attuned to their ends. For example, "the front teeth come up with an edge, suited to dividing the food, and the back ones flat and good for grinding it" (Aristotle 1935b: Book II, 198B). It may of course be argued that this attunement is mere coincidence, Aristotle acknowledges, as he considers a version of the natural selection hypothesis attributed to Empedocles (Aristotle 1935b: Book II, 198B). But the attunement is regular, not sporadic as chance and coincidence must be; therefore, if the choice is between coincidence and purpose, it must be admitted that behind nature's many attunements is purpose.

> Now, when a thing is produced by Nature, the earlier stages in every case lead up to the final development in the same way as in the operation of art, and *vice versa*, provided that no impediment balks the process. The operation [of art] is directed by a purpose; we may, therefore, infer that the natural process was guided by a purpose to the end that is realized (Aristotle 1935b: Book II, 199A).

All this remains purpose *in* nature, not addressing the end *of* nature. Nature is both agent and patient at once, giving itself purposes and following them. Purpose is not introduced from outside nature, as suggested by the image of the Maker in Plato's *Timaeus*. Aristotle's early medical surroundings, mentioned earlier, may have suggested to him a different metaphor: "If purpose, then, is inherent in art, so is it in Nature also. The best illustration is the case of a man being his own physician, for Nature is like that—agent and patient at once" (Aristotle 1935b: Book II, 199B).

What then of nature's "end as a whole"? Beyond nature as a whole lies nature's Final Cause, says Aristotle; but this is not some Designer laying plans for the world. It is the Unmoved Mover, pure Actuality with no trace of potentiality: perfection of self-existence and self-enjoyment. As Thought thinking Itself, God is unaware of the world, necessarily, since to know this world of change would introduce potentiality into the supreme Mind, destroying its perfection. Nature is moved by such perfection, but not through efficient causality. The allure of perfection draws the world as a whole, while nature gives itself, agent and patient, its own lesser goals. Nature ultimately has a nature, then, since it has a single end that transcends its many purposes; with this conclusion we leave the subject of value in nature for realms of theology.

To summarize: the worldview shaped by Aristotle admits value into the heart of reality. No, values are required, not merely admitted. Even to speak of "birth defects," for example, is to assume a norm relative to which natural processes somehow have gone wrong. Purposes in nature are toward something good for the purposing agent. Final causes are not defined in terms merely of what actually happens to happen. It would be an unintended joke, Aristotle says, for a poet to say, in eulogizing a man's death, that "He has reached his end, for the sake of which he was born" (Aristotle 1935b: Book II, 194A). It is not just termination that counts as one's "end" in life. One's "end" is one's ideal best.

That this is not always or even often achieved is a different matter. There are as many ends as there are natures and as many exemplifications of natures as there are actual finite substances striving toward their ideal goals. These will inevitably conflict, sometimes, and cooperate at other times. Just as it is not the "end" of a human to be eaten by a grizzly, it is not the "end" of an acorn to be nourishment for a squirrel. But these things happen—the latter, fortunately, more often than the former. And in the case of the acorn, it is clearly no tragedy that the world is so structured that finite entities can serve many goods besides their own self-fulfillment. The world would not be enhanced by being so full of oak trees that nothing else could grow. It would be diminished, to some extent, by having no squirrels (no matter how they may frustrate us in stealing from our bird feeders).

Aristotle leaves us with a mixed world of many purposes and many limited goods. Like Plato's world, it has its inevitable defects. Unlike Plato's, it dispenses with a separate realm of perfect intelligible ideals that would have satisfied Socrates' thirst for perfect value-knowledge. Quality, mind, purpose, and value are woven into the fabric of the kosmos in such a tight pattern that this general worldview would remain an essential background tapestry for human thought, in agreement or not, for many centuries to come.

4

THE GREAT TRANSITION

The narrative of this chapter has a long way to go. Between the breakup of the Hellenic world (which followed quickly upon Alexander's youthful death) and the birth of modern European thought, lie roughly eighteen centuries and many huge upheavals. We shall need to cross the rise and fall of the Roman Empire, the emergence of Christianity, the waxing and waning of feudalism, the appearance and spread of Islam, the establishment of two great churches—one at Constantinople and one at Rome—both called Catholic, a Protestant Reform, and the founding of European nation states. On the way, we shall find techno-logical innovations such as the introduction of the stirrup and invention of the moldboard plough, eyeglasses, the mechanical clock, printing, the compass needle, and gunpowder.

My aim is not general history nor even a general history of thought. Instead, I am more specifically interested in reflecting on the intertwinement of values with reality; both for considering the influence of values on key exam-ples of thought about reality, and for examining the status in reality allowed values and qualities by important metaphysical theories. With this more limited goal, we can afford to simplify the long transition from the great Hellenes to early modern thinkers by considering the period under four aspects. In the immediately ensuing Hellenistic age, metaphysical thought is full of echoes, sometimes significantly distorted but clearly identifiable, from the heroic pre-Socratic pioneers. Under this echo metaphor we may more clearly hear the value-laden metaphysical reverberations emanating from the Epicureans, the Stoics, and the Skeptics, who fill the transition from Athens to Rome. Second, a lens metaphor also applies. Plato's powerful theory of reality works as a lens for many significant thinkers, focusing the vision of thinkers from Philo of Alexandria to Anselm of Cluny. A still different lens, provided by Plato's great alternative, Aristotle, shapes the thinking of a third selection of important thinkers, Muslim and Jewish as well as Christian. Finally, a fourth set of late premodern critics demand to be seen in terms of the surprisingly protomodern values they express in their evident impatience with either of the great Hellenic foci available to them in their time.

VALUE-ECHOES OF SOME PRE-SOCRATICS

An echo begins as a strong, distinct sound that bounces off structures in the environment until the sound that eventually strikes the ear is returned changed, to some extent: perhaps changed only in amplitude (loudness), but usually in other ways as well. By noting the changes, as in sonar, one may learn something about the structures of the environment.

In this section we shall find that metaphysical theories reaching our ears from the major philosophical schools of the Hellenistic age bear strong resemblances to originals enunciated in the pioneering pre-Socratic age, but incorporate important changes. These changes were introduced by bouncing off value-structures in the cultural environment. Therefore, we can observe how interventions of value can alter theories of reality. This happens all the time, but not always so clearly.

Epicureanism is named for its founder Epicurus, a person of Athenian heritage, born in 341 B.C. on the island of Samos. As a youth, travelling the coast of Asia Minor, where Greek philosophy had originated, Epicurus encountered followers of Democritus, the Atomist; he began his own teaching, at about the age of thirty, on the island of Lesbos and later on the Hellespont. He moved to Athens around 306 B.C., when he purchased the walled garden that was to become the center of his teaching and of the Epicurean movement.

In many ways Epicurus was a faithful echo of Democritus. He argued for the reality of Void, or empty space, for example, in which an infinite number of atoms could move. Each atom must be indivisible and indestructible, a bit of Being that would satisfy the rigorous logical criteria of Parmenides, just as Democritus had said. Only the direct impacts of mechanical interaction could influence such atoms. Even our dreams are caused by the direct collision of images (made from very fine atoms capable of passing directly through our bodies) upon the especially rarefied soul-atoms inside. Ordinary sense experiences are the result of grosser but still very thin images, which are constantly being thrown off material objects around us, impacting our sense organs. The atoms themselves have no colors or other qualities, but their combination, especially in combination with our soul-atoms, give rise to these images along with the other macroscopic phenomena of our experienced universe.

This strong echo of Democritean Atomism is changed in ways important for Epicurus, though apparently not for Democritus in his more serene era. The Hellenistic age was a time of great anxiety. There was much to fear as kingdoms swayed and customs seemed ready to totter for lack of stability. Epicurus identified the three great sources of fear in his time as (1) fear of fate, that implacable but unknown future before which we are powerless, (2) fear of the gods, those arbitrary interveners whose irrationalities require constant placating, and (3) fear of death. For the consolation of the pains caused by these fears, and as prophylaxis against the generation of the fears themselves, Epicurus put his metaphysical theory to the service of peace of mind.

First, *ataraxia*, peace of mind, may be secured against the fear of fate as long as the universe is not perceived as "locked up" and unresponsive in every way to human efforts for voluntary change. To meet this need Epicurus modified Democritus in a crucial way: in addition to the purely regular motions of the atoms in the void, falling forever together and impacting one another exactly in accordance with necessity, Epicurus declared that here and there within the crowd an individual occasionally "swerves" from the predictable course of nature.

The introduction of the "swerve" serves a double theoretical function for the Epicurean theory. On the purely physical side, it explains how the jostlings come about, in the first place, among the free-falling atoms. Such jostlings are necessary, on the atomic theory, for clumps of atoms to form and for a world to take shape. Two hundred years later, Epicurus' famous follower, Lucretius, in his philosophical poem, *On the Nature of Things*, puts it in a way that anticipates Galileo's great discovery that heavier things fall no more rapidly than light things (disregarding air resistance):

> But contrariwise the empty void cannot
> On any side, at any time, to aught
> Oppose resistance, but will ever yield,
> True to its bent of nature. Wherefore all,
> With equal speed, though equal not in weight,
> Must rush, borne downward through the still inane.
> Thus ne'er at all have heavier from above
> Been swift to strike the lighter, gendering strokes
> Which cause those divers motions, by whose means
> Nature transacts her work. And so I say,
> The atoms must a little swerve at times—
> But only the least, lest we should seem to feign

> Motions oblique, and the fact refute us there
> (Lucretius 1957: 54–55).

We never observe such "oblique" motions, he admits, but they need not be large enough for the senses to detect. After all, the unaided senses are crude, shifting the burden of proof to the other side; thus,

> ... [W]ho
> Is there can mark by sense that naught can swerve
> *At all* aside from off its road's straight line? (Lucretius 1957: 55).

On the valuational side, similarly (but exciting more than double the lines of poetry from Lucretius), the empirically unobservable "swerve" is a necessary theoretical assumption if we are to avoid the fear of fate.

> Again, if ev'r all motions are co-linked,
> And from the old ever arise the new
> In fixèd order, and primordial seeds
> Produce not by their swerving some new start
> Of motion to sunder the covenants of fate,
> That cause succeed not cause from everlasting,
> Whence this free will for creatures o'er the lands,
> Whence is it wrested from the fates,—this will
> Whereby we step right forward where desire
> Leads each man on, whereby the same we swerve
> In motions, not as at some fixèd time,
> Nor at some fixèd line of space, but where
> The mind itself has urged? (Lucretius 1957: 55).

The argument goes from valuational premises to metaphysical conclusions. After a number of examples Lucretius draws the needed moral:

> So seest thou not, how, though external force
> Drive men before, and often make them move,
> Onward against desire, and headlong snatched,
> Yet there is something in these breasts of ours
> Strong to combat, strong to withstand the same?—
> Wherefore no less within the primal seeds
> Thou must admit, besides all blows and weight,
> Some other cause of motion, whence derives
> This power in us inborn, of some free act.—

> Since naught from nothing can become, we see
> (Lucretius 1957: 56).

Mere mechanical necessity, such as Democritus originally seemed to place in the saddle, gives rise to fears that everything is compelled, as by external force.

> But that man's mind itself in all it does
> Hath not a fixed necessity within,
> Nor *is* not, like a conquered thing, compelled
> To bear and suffer,—*this* state comes to man
> From that slight swervement of the elements
> In no fixed line of space, in no fixed time
> (Lucretius 1957: 56, emphases original).

The second fear. of the arbitrary whims of the gods, is also an enemy of peace of mind. Epicureans did not deny the existence of these gods, since, as we have noted, they were realists even about the objects of dreams and imagination. If Zeus or Aphrodite appeared in dreams—and no doubt they frequently did in those days, at least as often as Krishna or the Virgin Mary do in ours, then these dream images must have been flung off from some real entity. The bare existence of the gods being granted, there is still no need to fear them. Epicurus comforted his followers that the gods are not interested in the human realm and, even if they should be interested, they are too ethereal in nature to engage in causal influence over the grosser atoms of ordinary life. Ataraxia may be maintained, against this second fear, by hanging firmly to the assurances derivable from this metaphysics: that god-stuff is and must be wholly uninfluential upon daily world-stuff.

Death, the third great fear, is also no match for atomism, properly interpreted. Democritus, so far as we know, had not deployed his theory of reality against the fear of death; but Epicurus gained fame for his preachment that death, for those with the proper metaphysics, is nothing to fear. This follows from a thoroughgoing application to ourselves of the basic metaphysical premise that besides atoms and the void there is nothing at all. A fortiori, we living, conscious beings are complexes of atoms moving in empty space, and nothing more. Our organs of consciousness too, our souls, must be made of fine atoms, even finer than the air we breathe. While we are alive, we act, we think, we feel—and *death* is not present to *us*; when we die, our soul-atoms disperse, scattered like dust motes in the wind—and *we* are not present to *death*. Therefore, neither while living nor after life's end, is death anything to trouble the wise, who understand the hidden nature of things.

The metaphysics of atomism is used, then, as an instrument in the service of an ethics of moderation, of pursuit of the "natural," of this worldly satisfaction through cultivated friendships and simple physical pleasures, of the avoidance of pain—in general, in the service of a spirituality of ataraxia, or peace of mind. Where the original atomism of Democritus can be used without modification, it is put to use directly; where its apparent determinism might make for spiritual distress, as in fostering a fear of fate, it is amended as needful, within the generous limits of empirical plausibility, so as to contain a subtle, undetectable "swerve" that allows free will. In this way, Epicureanism offered a value-rich application of pre-Socratic atomism in an appealing echo that resonated throughout the Greco-Roman world well into the new millennium marked by the rise of Christianity.

Returning to the end of the fourth century B.C. and to Athens, we discover the first sounds of another major Hellenistic tradition that was to be locked for centuries in unrelenting combat with the Epicurean. These were the early lectures of Zeno of Citium, a Phoenician from Crete, who began his new school in the year 300 B.C., lecturing from the Painted Porch (or *Stoa Poikile*) of the main marketplace in Athens. The Zenonians soon took on the name "Stoic" from the site of their lectures and enjoyed a long history distinguished by adherents of all social classes, from slave to emperor.

Cultural values, at the time of Zeno's first lectures and for the entire span of Stoic history, were in profound flux. The problem for the Stoics was to find constancy within all the change, lawfulness ruling the ceaseless transformation.

One of the main changes was begun by Alexander the Great, whose world empire made the city-state form of government obsolete. Even after his death, the age of empires had begun. First, Alexander's principal generals maintained control over the armies they had in place at the time of his death, transforming their military domains into smaller empires and themselves into hereditary emperors. Over the years, Rome rose to dominate the previously Greek world and its Middle Eastern and Egyptian dependencies, gradually evolving from an Italian republic into the hub of a huge world state, maintained by might and commerce through its magnificent stone highways and aqueducts.

World citizenship was a new ideal. Universal laws, governing the clash of many against many, unifying the far reaches of empire despite local variations in language, custom, and religion—these were the norms of the new age into which the Stoics directed their voices from the Painted Porch.

For these ideals, supporting cosmic lawfulness and rationality against apparent strife, interpreting stability beneath constant flux, the metaphysics of Heraclitus was highly serviceable to the Stoics. Their echo was not exact reproduction of the original pre-Socratic message, since it was offered with political and ethical modifications unknown to Heraclitus himself. But the worldview of the Stoics was at least as strong an echo of Heraclitus as that of the Epicureans was of Democritus.

The clash was nearly total. The Epicureans were empirical and moderate in their approach, careful not to trip over observable facts like the absence of pronounced "oblique" motions in falling bodies. The Stoics were rational and uncompromising, taking an argument and following it to its utmost conclusion. The Epicureans welcomed a chance "swerve" at the heart of reality; the Stoics praised lawful order to the point of worship. For example, Cleanthes, first successor to Zeno at the Stoa in the marketplace, expressed his adoration of lawfulness in his *Hymn to Zeus*, "Zeus" now taken as one of the innumerable names for the cosmic Logos that rules the fiery universe of constant change:

> Hail, O Zeus, most glorious of the immortals, named by many names, forever all-powerful, leader of nature, you who govern the universe with laws . . . (Cleanthes 1988: 281).

Universal law, for a world evolving toward universal government, was an obvious treasure to be mined from Heraclitus' doctrine of the Logos (meaning, intelligibility) behind and in all things. In addition, the presence of bits of the Logos in human beings, providing for each a seed of rationality, supplies the ontological basis for a human community reaching far beyond the obsolete walls of city-states, transcending even the particularities of language, race, or religion. Heraclitean metaphysics could meld with and support the ideal of universal dignity for humanity *qua* humanity. Reason, our defining property, is our personal share of the general Logos of the universe; it is this which constitutes all humankind as one large family.

Living by this inner reason then is living according to the nature of Nature itself. It is accepting the will of Zeus as one's own will. Thereby, it transcends all local customs, which may be disregarded without loss. The only thing that matters is virtue defined by universal Reason, accessible from within but linking all virtuous persons to the heart of the universe. At different times in its long history, the Stoics were in varying degrees crude in their righteous separation from the ignorant and unvirtuous. At the outset, Zeno had been impressed by Crates of Thebes, the Cynic, who like his master, Diogenes, spared no pains to show contempt for the moral laxities of normal society. Three centuries later, the former slave Epictetus was also influenced by fiercely independent Cynic spirits he came to admire in first century, A.D., Rome. But the tone of Stoicism was not necessarily quite so extreme at all times or with all its leaders. The gentle Emperor Marcus Aurelius, in his *Meditations*, found unity with reason to be less off-putting and more a basis for bonding with one another and the world.

In either mood, however, Stoic insistence on echoing the worldview of Heraclitus required them to affirm that since Reason rules the flux, all is well. Apparent evil gives way to good when seen as the product of Logos. As Cleanthes put it, in his mid-third century, B.C., *Hymn*:

> Nothing is done in the world without you, god, neither in the holy air of the sky, nor in the sea, except for what the evil do in their folly. But you know how to make extraordinary things normal, and to make order out of chaos; you love even unlovely things. In this way you have joined everything into one, the evil and the good, so that the eternal Word becomes one, which those who are evil among mortals avoid and abandon (Cleanthes 1988: 284).

The problem of evil thus turns into a problem of "folly." But whence, then, folly? How, if Logos rules all, can there be evil mortals who do foolish things, think foolish thoughts, and "avoid" or "abandon" the eternal Word? The problem of evil, if given Cleanthes' response, drives consistent thinkers to the problem of free will. If the Logos rules *all*, then how can mortals engage in folly?

These intellectual problems of accounting for free will and apparent evil in a perfectly rational universe plagued Stoicism throughout its history, and no perfect answers were found. But the spiritual state of calm confidence in the order of things—control of the mere emotions, rational insight so strong as to induce *apatheia*, or feelinglessness—this state was so strongly valued by the adherents of Stoicism, that such unsolved theoretical problems were not enough to force abandonment of a metaphysics which, though not designed for these spiritual purposes, could support them in difficult times.

Unsolved theoretical problems can roil the mind and destroy ataraxia in those who yearn to find satisfying theoretical answers to such large questions. The third philosophical movement of the Hellenistic period bent all its efforts to wipe away such disturbances, caused, they argued, by the dangerous tendency to want dogmatic answers to metaphysical questions. This was the movement of the Skeptics.

The founder of the long and distinguished Skeptical tradition was Pyrrho, who was born in the Peloponnesian city of Elis in 360 B.C., only a quarter of a century after Aristotle's birth in Ionia. His youth coincided with the ascendancy of the Macedonian Empire. At twenty-four years of age, he joined Alexander's entourage as court philosopher and travelled with the Emperor's armies throughout the world. In India, tradition has it, he was impressed with the ascetic holy men and fakirs. At the same time he was deeply influenced by his own teacher (also a court philosopher in Alexander's train) Anaxarchus, who, following Democritus, stressed the unreliability of the senses for giving accurate knowledge of the real world of atoms. Anaxarchus, however, stressed the still greater importance of happiness and peace of mind. These themes combined in Pyrrho's teaching: the supreme importance of cultivating peace of mind—the same ataraxia sought by the Epicureans—within a context of carelessness about the body and the alleged regularities of nature. In Pyrrho, we hear echoes from several sources: from the Atomists, from whom he drew the fundamental lesson that we know nothing directly about things in themselves, but are constantly living merely in appearance; from the Sophists, in all likelihood, who argued for the doubtfulness of cultural and moral fixities; and from ascetic world-deniers he met in his travels.

These voices were echoed in Pyrrho's distinctive teachings and even more in his life of relative poverty, simplicity, and peace of mind. After Alexander's death, he returned to his home on the Peloponnesus. His townspeople of Elis listened to his lectures and observed his life with such favor that in due course he was made high priest of the city and exempted (with all fellow philosophers) from taxes.

The principal teachings were simple: We know nothing with the kind of assurance that warrants drawing conclusions. That way lies dogmatism. Where claims can always be met by equally plausible counterclaims (the Skeptic symbol was an evenly balanced scale), one has no need—no right—to a conclusion. The proper attitude to cultivate is *epoche*, suspension of judgment. This alone allows peace of mind to replace the never-ending process of argument and rebuttal, with its consequent anxieties. If this is the proper stance toward the issues that torment the dogmatists, the proper response of the wise is *aphasia*, or silence. Combining epoche with aphasia, we find ataraxia. The soul is cured.

The distinctive new element in the echoes we hear from the Atomists, the Sophists, and various ascetics (roughly speaking, we could group these with the Cynics), is the subordination of argument to the service of a spiritual goal, peace of mind. In each case, the original doctrines were enunciated for other ends; but Pyrrho blended and reflected them for what was quite literally a priestly service to anxious times.

Later Skeptics were often less beloved than Pyrrho. Plato's Academy itself became a hotbed of Skepticism in the second century B.C., as the implications of Plato's views on the illusory character of the world of becoming were emphasized over his hope that the eternal Forms could be known by mortal minds. Carneades, for example, born in North Africa toward the end of the third century and living through most of the second, was best known for his invincible dialectical skills in "proving" either side of any question. On one occasion, on a diplomatic mission to Rome in the midst of the second century, he delivered two orations on justice, showing with equal clarity that justice had to be—but could not be—grounded in the nature of things. For this he earned enduring hostility from the upright Cato, but he gained the admiration of many others, who sought to emulate his brilliant advocacy of the Skeptical epoche. The main efforts of the Skeptics of this period, however, were in opposition to the "dogmatism" of the Epicureans and Stoics. The Stoics especially fell under the lash of the Skeptics, who were only too happy to point out the flaws and inconsistencies, for instance, in their defense of free will in conjunction with an allegedly total determination of all events by the Logos of the universe, or their attempts to justify the "perfect" ways of Zeus to the suffering, sick, and dying.

The Skeptic tradition survived, often in contentious, sometimes priestly modes, through centuries of turbulence and dispute. Toward the end of the era in the third century A.D., shortly before Greek-inspired pagan philosophy was banned by the growing power of Christianity in the Roman Empire, it made one more value-laden appearance in the medical thinking of Sextus Empiricus. Sextus was the historian of Skepticism as well as its proponent in a new context of practical healing. Several leading Skeptics, both before and after Sextus, were medical practitioners. For Sextus and for them, the key to wisdom lies in retaining peace of mind from performing epoche concerning in all things "hidden" or cosmic in scope, while refusing to let doubt undermine trust in the observable phenomena of daily life. In this way, on a case by case basis, genuinely "empirical" medicine could protect itself from the ignorant dogmatism of a priori theorists while gradually building a reliable repertoire of modest cures. To the end of defending against theory, Sextus developed elaborate dialectical methods, offering ten tropes as standard weapons against all dogmatists. But this end itself was still a means to a further, more fundamental, end: the end of contentment, spiritual equilibrium, peace of mind, health, and happiness.

We have seen all three of the primary traditions of philosophy, through this era between the breakup of Alexander's empire and the flowering of Rome's, as echoes of earlier voices. All these echoes were transformed by being bounced off the same great structures of the times: the need for spiritual equipoise. All served this profoundly valuational, indeed, religious, function, shaping theory to the needs of the spirit.

There is little wonder that when Christianity, offering a rival spiritual ideal to the Hellenistic quest for ataraxia, rose from persecution to power after the conversion of Constantine to Christian faith in 324, that conflict between Christian authorities and pagan philosophers gradually heated to the boiling point. Now that the tables were turned, the persecution was directed at the pagans by the Christians. Finally, in 529, only two years after the accession of Byzantine Emperor Justinian the Great, the Schools of Athens were officially closed, and pagan philosophy of all traditions was proscribed on pain of death. In 533, Justinian negotiated a treaty with the rulers of Persia, who were eager to be rid of the philosophers who had fled across their borders for safety, and the demoralized refugees were allowed to return to their homes to live in peace, but not to teach again. The end of institutional Greek philosophy had come.

THE PLATONIC VALUE-LENS

Centuries before the coerced ending of the philosophical schools of Athens, the intellectual predominance of that city had been challenged by other great centers of learning in the world inherited from the breakup of Alexander's empire. Of these, Alexandria, on Egypt's Mediterranean coast, was the most distinguished. Founded by Alexander himself in 332 B.C., the city had become the leading center of Hellenistic culture by the third century B.C., after the founding of its great museum and unrivalled library near the turn of that century by Ptolemy I, one of Alexander's Macedonian generals, who made himself king after Alexander's death.

In Alexandria, roughly two decades before the birth of Christ, another Jewish family celebrated the birth of a son who was to become the most important Jewish philosopher of the Greco-Roman period. Philo of Alexandria, also known as Philo Judaeus, lived until about the middle of the first century A.D. and left behind a major legacy influencing two religions.

Philo was well-educated in the Jewish scriptures and in Platonic philosophy. Hitherto they had flowed in mainly isolated streams of development; it was Philo's task to unite these streams for the first time. He saw them both as true. Therefore, given adjustments to both, he was convinced that both could be understood as saying essentially the same thing.

This agenda, the aim to harmonize a philosophical system with a religious tradition, is today so familiar that it is easy to pass it over without recognizing the striking values implicit in it. One key value is commitment to the fundamental importance of *coherence*; that is, to the insistence that truth is ultimately unified. This is a theoretical value so deep that we sometimes forget how plausible its alternative can be in an age of great multiplicity of claims and theories. It was a basic commitment, as we saw, of the great pioneers of theory in the pre-Socratic age, but in Hellenistic times it must have been hard to maintain in the face of cafeteria-style offerings in religious beliefs, customary practices, and theories about the universe flowing in from all quadrants of the known world. In this climate, an easygoing relativism can become a defense against worrying overmuch about consistency between such beliefs. After all, it may be asked, what does one have to do with the other? They use different languages. (Sometimes this can be taken quite literally: Judaism turned to Hebrew scriptures, the Platonists argued in Greek; thus there were at least different—often hardly overlapping—vocabularies.) They are set in different institutional contexts. They turn to different authorities. It is much easier to let such different types of claims, which seem not even to be *about* each other, much less in significant conflict with one another, lie peacefully next to one another rather than to stir trouble by trying to decide between them or, even more difficult, to resolve their differences into a unified view of reality.

Philo, however, had embraced two viewpoints, Hebrew scripture (fortunately translated, by the Septuagint version, into Greek) and Platonic philosophy, which both insist on ultimate oneness. Judaism had long, and in the end successfully, fought the tendencies, in itself as well as in its neighbors, toward polycentric "tolerance" of many ultimates. "The Lord is One" is one of the central statements of any faithful Jew. Plato's philosophical enterprise, as well, fairly shines with the rays of the Form of the Good, which, like its allegorical counterpart, the Sun, is held to be the radiant One that renders all multiplicity finally intelligible in its light. Not only is the world of Becoming given intellectual coherence by the presence in it of the eternal Forms, but also the Forms themselves, in so far as they also constitute a multiplicity of intelligibles, are brought to ultimate unity in Plato's ideal for philosophical knowledge.

Commitment to the value of coherence and the unity of truth is an important value, then; but even more fundamental is the readiness of Philo to value the enterprise of *theorizing* itself in connection with his religion. By no means all religions embrace the contemplative, logically restrained, truth-seeking aspect of human life among their primary values. Some value frenzy, for example, to the denigration of theoretical moods and standards. Some are entirely focused on rituals, with no interest in theoretical speculations beyond. Some place their highest value on mystical states incompatible with reasoning. Some deliberately mortify logical thought, just as in many religions the flesh is sacrificed and punished.

Philo, however, accepted a form of Judaism that was learning to live without its ritual center, the Temple at Jerusalem. During Philo's life the Temple still existed as a site of animal sacrifice and other ritual expressions derived from time immemorial; but for Jews like Philo, Rabbinic Judaism and the growing importance of synagogues as local centers for religious discussion and argument in distant lands made the values of theorizing a natural part of religious observance. Twenty years after Philo's death, when the Roman authorities in Palestine utterly destroyed the Temple itself, sprinkling salt on the ruins, this trait favoring the theorizing—and consequent universalizing—of Judaism provided this religion a unique flexibility and independence from particular circumstances that allowed it to survive, while untold numbers of similar faiths disappeared, victims of historical specificity.

Philo's great achievement was to learn how to see his Judaic heritage, in particular the scriptures, through the lens of Platonic philosophy. The method is allegory. Plato provides the plain text; the biblical texts say the same thing in allegorical figures. The need, then, is simply to explain these figures in accordance with the Platonic doctrine—adjusting the doctrine, too, when it becomes necessary to harmonize it with authoritative scripture.

In this harmonization, Philo took Plato's *Timaeus* as the primary source for understanding biblical stories of the creation of the world. God is eternal. At some point, according to God's inscrutable will, the world was created. At first the Ideas were only in the mind of God, subject like everything else to God's will, but prior to the creation of the world God created another Mind, or thinking Soul, which can be interpreted as the Realm of the Forms, or the "intelligible world" (Wolfson 1967: 152). This ensouled Realm of the Forms Philo called the "Logos," perhaps in honor of current Stoic vocabulary (Dodd 1953). It was through the intermediary of the Logos that the one eternal, all-powerful God created the world. Although the *Timaeus* seems to hold that the preexistent "stuff" of the world was eternal, Philo harmonizes this with what he accepts as the Scriptural account of "creation out of nothing" by postulating an earlier creation by God "out of nothing" of the Matrix, which later allows the informing and particularization of the Ideas through the ministrations of the Logos.

In the debates between the current Stoic and Epicurean schools in early first century Alexandria, Philo selectively took sides. On the one hand, he agreed with the Stoics that God's actions are completely lawful. No random "swerves" allowed! On the other hand, the God of Moses is too great to be captive to any so-called "inexorable" laws. Nothing can be thought to reign above God's will. Rather, God can and does suspend normal regularities *for God's own reasons*, to perform what we view as miracles. And just as God's will can override normal causal regularities, so likewise our finite human wills can also freely initiate new causal chains. In this, Philo accepted the Epicurean answer to the question of free will, against the Stoics, while rejecting the Epicurean embrace of mere chance. However, against the Epicureans, Philo insisted, with Plato, on the immortality of the human soul—at least its rational part—but against Plato he recognizes this immortality as purely conditional on the will of God who alone is eternal and immortal necessarily.

Philo is guarded in his claims about God, beyond this, since, he argued, God cannot be known in essence. True to the Jewish unwillingness to pronounce the secret name of God, and true also to the image of Moses, who, even on Sinai, was not allowed to look on the face of the divine lawgiver, Philo invents an important distinction: we know the *existence* of God, but not God's *essence*. The existence of the Creator is easily shown by the fact of the existence of the creation. The cosmological argument from the necessary dependency of the effect (universe) on the cause (God) seems obvious to Philo. Certain other general truths from the convergence of scripture and philosophical insight, such as the eternity and uniqueness of God, can be asserted—without, however, violating the sacred prohibition against human knowledge of God as properly only

God should be entitled to know. In this way, from a mixture of grounds, religious (proper respect for the holy) and epistemological (the genus of all genuses cannot be defined since there is no wider genus by which to define), Philo introduces the basis for two thousand years of "negative theology."

In these and still more ways, Philo did not simply teach himself to see biblical religion through the lens of Plato's great system. He taught others, as well. His influence, therefore, can hardly be overstated, both within his own Jewish tradition and, even more strikingly, within the new Christian phenomenon that was unfolding even as he wrote.

In the turbulence following the crucifixion of Jesus in Jerusalem—first, the spontaneous formation of small groups of followers, then the gathering of churches, soon the transformation of Saul of Tarsus into the indefatigable Paul the Apostle, and, throughout, the valiant efforts to remember and write down events and vital sayings for the nurture of the infant Christian religion—one author is of special importance to this narrative. Writing in the latter part of the first century, probably in Ephesus (the city of Heraclitus, with strong cultural ties to Alexandria), or perhaps in Alexandria itself, this anonymous author wrote the small book of Christian theological discourses and symbolic stories about Jesus that was later placed into the canon as the Fourth Gospel, the *Gospel According to John.*

John, unlike the other three Gospels (the Synoptics, so-called because they can be "seen together" as three tellings, with minor variations, of the same story in the same sequence) is a book principally of ideas. It is introduced with a prologue placing Christian beliefs about Christ into the philosophical context provided by Stoic-Platonic concepts, especially into the synthesis achieved by Philo. In *John,* events are rearranged for the sake of intellectual development. New stories are introduced for their symbolic value in reinforcing conceptual structure (Dodd 1953; Howard 1952: 442).

The key to the thinking behind the Fourth Gospel is the Logos doctrine circulating within Hellenistic culture in the latter part of the first century. *John*'s opening words, "In the beginning was 'the Logos'," would have communicated well, especially to those (e.g., cultivated Jews) familiar with Philo's various works, where the word λόγος appears thirteen hundred times (Howard 1952: 453). "The Logos," *John* is saying, was not subject to the temporal constraints of our historical existence; it was "in the beginning." But also, *John* continues: "'the Logos' was with God and 'the Logos' was divine." (Many familiar translations of the latter phrase read "'the Logos' was God," but the absence of a definite article in the Greek makes it clear that θεὸς is here used adjectivally.) All this would be familiar in the first century context, as would be the next sentence: "He was in the beginning with God; all things were made through him, and without him was not made anything that was made." The Hellenistic reader would recognize the indirect allusion to the *Timaeus* and the making of the world by copying the intelligible Forms. The personal pronoun, too, would not be disturbing in light of Plato's own mythic language and even more in view of the eclectic imagery of the later Stoics and, more recently, Philo's rich allegorizing.

Where *John*'s Prologue would startle the philosophically acute Hellenist, however, would be at the point where the general language suddenly becomes concrete and personal:

> There was a man sent from God, whose name was John. He came for testimony, to bear witness to the light, that all might believe through him. He was not the light, but came to bear witness to the light.
>
> The true light that enlightens every man was coming into the world; he was in the world, and the world was made through him, yet the world knew him not; he came to his own home, and his own people received him not (John 1952: ch. 1, vs. 6–11).

What was this jarring historical reference to John the Baptist doing in a philosophical reflection on the nontemporality of the Realm of Forms? The answer was soon to come:

> And "the Logos" became flesh and dwelt among us, full of grace and truth; we have beheld his glory, glory as of the only Son from the Father. . . . For the law was given through Moses; grace and truth came through Jesus Christ. No one has ever seen God; the only Son, who is in the bosom of the Father, he has made him known (John 1952: ch. 1, vs. 14–18).

The writer of the Fourth Gospel begins by announcing a novel, not to say peculiar, thesis: that Jesus, the flesh-and-blood protagonist of the stories he would be telling, *was* the cosmic Logos, the eternal Realm of Forms acting in time, the universal made particular. Plato, the Stoics, and Philo would doubtless have been appalled at this "confusion" of categories, but for the writer of the Fourth Gospel, as for those in the Christian churches who treasured this document for its many symbolically rich stories and beautifully enunciated theological discourses, this paradoxical thesis was of the essence: the key to understanding who Jesus really was and how God works, first to create, then to reveal and reconcile. The other Gospels offer no hint of this Platonic lens through which to see Christian truth. But with the incorporation of the *Gospel According to John* into the official Christian canon of the New Testament, when this was gradually accomplished by church leaders over the next four centuries, a strong strain of Platonism was made a permanent part of scripture itself.

Thus supported, it is not surprising that Christian Platonism was a strong movement in early theology. Titus Flavius Clemens, one of the major figures in this movement, was born a pagan, about the middle of the second century, perhaps in Athens. After many travels, he found a mentor in Pantaenus, then the head of a Christian school in Alexandria. Later, as a Christian lay-scholar (and now known as Clement of Alexandria) he became head of the school and used his position to defend the values of theorizing against the anti-intellectualism of such "simple believers" who might prefer to rely on literalism and ecclesiastical authority rather than on consistency, coherence, and the resources of high Hellenistic culture. Clement argued for an allegorical, Platonized interpretation of scripture and maintained that Christianity could, as sheer philosophy, far outstrip its pagan alternatives. Attempting to fashion a genuinely Christian gnosticism, one that could rival and defeat on their own ground the various gnostic cults of his day, he believed that the great philosophers of old had plagiarized from the Old Testament, to the extent that they shared the same truths that Christian philosophy offers; and through his life and teaching he supported a mellow, inclusive ethic against fanaticisms of all sorts.

His immediate successor, Origen, resembled him in some ways, but differed radically in others. Origen was a brilliant youth who studied both with Clement, at his broad-minded Christian school, and with the Platonizing philosopher, Ammonius Saccas, who converted to Hellenic religion from a Christian upbringing and is best known for his Platonic arguments against the Stoic doctrine of the materiality of the soul and for two of his pupils. He taught both Origen, who became the leading thinker of the Church prior to Augustine, and Plotinus, who was to reform the Platonic Academy itself.

Origen was born about 185. His was a dramatic life. When he was seventeen he barely avoided going to death with his father, who was killed in the great persecution of Christians in 202 by the militant Emperor Septimius Severus. The next year he was appointed to succeed Clement (who had been forced to flee at the time of the persecution) as head of the Christian school in Alexandria. From 203 until 231, Origen taught, wrote, and led by example. Unlike his mentor Clement, he was not easygoing. He read in *The Gospel According to Matthew* a passage wherein Jesus is cited as saying:

> "For there are eunuchs who have been so from birth, and there are eunuchs who have been made eunuchs by men, and there are eunuchs who have made themselves eunuchs for the sake of the kingdom of heaven. He who is able to receive this, let him receive it" (Matthew 1952: ch. 19, v. 12).

Taking this challenge as personally obligatory, he dutifully castrated himself. He was not ordained in the clergy, but he was much admired and of great influence in the Church. This did not please Bishop Demetrius of Alexandria. On one of his trips to Palestine, when Origen dared to preach (at the invitation of the local bishops), Bishop Demetrius was outraged and ordered him home. The period after his return produced some of his most important work. At age forty-five, in 230, Origen finally decided to accept ordination at the hands of the friendly bishops in Palestine. Outraged again, Bishop Demetrius excommunicated Origen and ordered him into exile. Sensibly, Origen took his exile in the safety of Palestine at Caesarea where he founded a theological school in 231, which he headed with distinction for twenty more years. Caught in a spasm of persecution from Rome in 250, a period of terrible political instability, Origen was nearly tortured to death and died, four years later.

The intellectual ideals accepted by Origen throughout his stormy life were those we have identified with Plato and to some degree with Stoic thought. He was committed to universality and to unity of truth. He spent much of his energy on thoughtful examination of scripture, both the Old Testament and the New. His *Hexapla* attempted to establish a critical text for the Old Testament, and his studies of the Gospels were in many ways the beginning of serious biblical scholarship in the Christian Church. But the focus of his contribution was on *understanding*, in a more coherent way than hitherto, how the concepts of God the Father, God the Son, and God the Holy Ghost could relate to one another and to the created kosmos. In this effort, Origen saw the issues through the lens provided by Plato's thought. All are eternal. The Father is transcendent, though not so remote, as Philo had argued, that none of our categories can attach to Him. We can meaningfully and truthfully assert the goodness, the power, and the justice of the Father, even though these terms, with their human limitations, fail to convey the full truth. The Son (following Clement, and before him the author of the Fourth Gospel) is the Mind or Wisdom of the Father, the Logos through which, by copying the eternal Ideas, the Father creates the world. The Holy Spirit is God as immanent, working intimately with human souls, preparing them to receive truth and salvation. All are God, who is one οὐσία (essence or nature) existing eternally in three *hypostases* (characters or "masks"—as in a theatre production—or "personae"). Unfortunately, it did not help Origen's aim at coherence that *both* these Greek words, *ousia* and *hypostasis*, can be translated into Latin as "substance," making them ambiguous when brought to the Western church, thus stimulating endless controversies (Wolfson 1970: Vol. 1).

One place Origen's Christian values forced a change in his Platonist heritage was in the sharp distinction between the world and the divine maker. For the Platonists, the kosmos we live in is obviously less perfect than the Model from which it was copied. But for Christians, like Origen and Clement before him, the world is valuationally so far below being able to claim the status of a less perfect, but still ontologically continuous copy, that it must be a wholly different, lower, order of being. It alone is simply *made*. The Son, however, as eternal Logos is *begotten* by the Father; the Holy Spirit *proceeds* from Father and Son. Neither of these *personae* is merely *made*. The world is not an emanation, however remote, from God. That would be to praise it too much. Still, Origen could not conceive of God not creative; therefore, he considered the made world co-eternal. Its ontological difference from God is not merely temporal but in kind.

The Platonists tended to take the soul as preexistent and eternal, the "principle of life itself" in things that are living, as Plato put it in the *Phaedo*, where he argued for its everlasting preexistence as well as its never-ending reincarnation. Origen accepted preexistence but probably not reincarnation. After death, however, even without reincarnation, the human soul is not through with its adventures. There will still be opportunity for testing, learning, growth, and for making a free decision whether or not to accept salvation. God does not slam the door on our spiritual opportunities just because of the incident of our body's death, which often comes too early for fair judgment to occur.

Freedom of the soul to choose is high among the values defended by Origen. Even the sin that surrounds our mortal state cannot destroy that precious freedom, without which we would not count as morally responsible agents. Indeed, Origen concludes, even God's foreknowledge cannot extend so far as to our free choices in the future, since they *are* not yet to be a subject for anyone's knowledge.

Origen's views were not gratefully accepted by the Church. In 553, the Fifth Ecumenical Council at Constantinople condemned "Origenism," but this is not a consideration that matters for our purposes. We see in Origen's thought a Christian scholar dedicated to viewing his faith as a whole, and doing so in terms of the best theoretical resources at his command. His blending of Christian concerns with Greek philosophy remains one of the paradigmatic achievements of its kind.

The other great student of Ammonius Saccas in Alexandria, Plotinus, was nineteen years younger than Origen. Hardly a "classmate" (in the year Plotinus was born, Origen was already in his second year heading the Christian school), he nevertheless shared the inspiration of Ammonius' reportedly brilliant teaching, which he absorbed for eleven years. At age thirty-nine, he left Alexandria with a military expedition headed for Persia and India. There he hoped to learn more about the philosophy of the East; but the murder of the commander put his life in jeopardy, forcing him to flee back to Antioch and thence to Rome. Reaching Rome in the same year, 244, Plotinus set up a school and began to lecture. He did not write until persuaded to do so by his students, around the age of fifty. His *Enneads*, six great discourses with nine sections each ('*ennea*',

Greek for 'nine'), were written in Greek between 253 and 270. After the first ten years, Plotinus acquired a student, Porphyry, who organized all his works, finally editing and publishing them posthumously, with a biography.

Plotinus was no Christian. He never mentions Christianity in his works, and during the same era in which Origen underwent his tortures, Plotinus enjoyed special patronage from the Roman Emperor, Gallienus, and his Empress, Salonina. Plotinus' thoroughly pagan philosophy, however, reflects and even intensifies the same fundamental values, focused through the Platonic lens, that we have seen in the Jewish thinking of Philo and in the Christian theologies of Clement and Origen.

Above all Plotinus valued unity. Plato held all the Forms to be unified in the Form of Forms, the Good; and, beyond this, he had in the *Parmenides* speculated about "the One" which, since utterly simple, would be beyond speech or knowledge. These Platonic themes were seized by Plotinus with all the power of a mighty intellect. "The One" for him, becomes the indefinable ultimate: completely satisfying the Eleatic criteria—simplicity, eternity, indestructibility, self-sufficiency, uniqueness—that Plato himself had embraced as finally worthy of ultimate reality. Such an ultimate, indescribably full of all reality, would inevitably (not consciously or deliberately but necessarily) overflow. In place of the image of the "benevolence" of the Maker in Plato's *Timaeus*, we now have a process of outflow or "emanation" which brings about a second eternal order of Intelligence or Reason that contains all the eternal Ideas. As in Philo's Logos, this Realm of Forms is not free-standing but is instead embedded in eternal intellect generated from the transcendent One. Plurality is generated at this level because of the inevitable plurality of Ideas. For Plotinus, this second level is less excellent than the first, but still wonderful. From the second level, a third level, the order of Soul, is emanated. Here Plotinus finds many different types and qualities of souls. Some are admirable and live only for the realm of Intelligence, which, having given rise to them, is their proper home; some are low, so low that a least worthy fourth level, matter, is generated out of this lowest level of Soul—indeterminate matter in which weak souls become entangled and lose touch with Intelligence, in which alone they can find proper fulfillment.

Once we are aware of this "downward way," from One to Intelligence, from Intelligence to Soul and, finally, from Soul to the material world of our bodily existence, there is a chance, Plotinus taught, that our souls may successfully struggle upward again, given right instruction. This "upward way" involves strict self-discipline of the material body, of course, but also sustained embrace of beauty and every sort of excellence, climbing what, in connection with Plato's *Symposium,* we called "the ladder of love." By virtue of such efforts it may be possible to commune again with Intelligence and the Forms; but one more step is needed for perfect fulfillment: unity with the One. There is no way the One can be known in normal discursive ways, obviously, since discourse rests on plurality of concepts, distinctions between knower and known, and the like. Therefore, only by a mystic union—"flying alone to the Alone," becoming simple with the Simple, one with the One—does one finally reascend the fountain of being to its source. Plotinus claimed four such experiences of ecstasy in his own life.

Plotinus' comprehensive Neoplatonic vision, combined with his personal magnetism and the hunger of his time for an alternative to the materialistic decadence of Roman society, won enormous influence. The leaders of Plato's Academy in the late third century were impressed. Their alliance with the Skeptics had been based on the Platonic doctrine that in order to know, one must be able to contemplate the Forms directly. They had argued by *modus tollens* from this premise: since one cannot see the Forms directly, therefore there is no genuine knowledge. But Plotinus and his followers argued from the same premise by *modus ponens*: since there is knowledge, it must be that the Forms are directly accessible. The tired skepticism of the late Academy gave way to a surge of Neoplatonic affirmation, and from then until its forced closing in 529 the Academy was increasingly hospitable to mysticism and emanationist theories inspired by Plotinus.

Meanwhile, another giant figure in the history of thought was inspired by Plotinus to envision Christianity, and thus the character of all reality, through Plato's lens. Thanks in part to a translation of Plotinus' Greek *Enneads* into Latin by Victorinus during the second half of the fourth century, young Augustine, a rhetorician from North Africa then living in Milan, was able to encounter a philosophical framework compatible with his mother's Christian values. Augustine, born in 354 in Thagaste (now in Algeria), had admired his mother's simple faith, but had been unable to think honestly in any way consistent with the religion in which he was raised. He intensely valued theorizing. During his education in Carthage he had encountered and accepted the value of pursuit of truth and could not be content with less than intellectual excellence. A previous attempt to theorize via the highly dualistic Manichaeism imported from Persia left him intellectually disappointed and disillusioned. But after wandering from job to job in Carthage, Rome, and finally Milan, he discovered, in reading Plotinus and other Neoplatonists, that with their help he might well be able to think of Christianity coherently, without sacrificing his deepest values. In 386, at age thirty-two, Augustine converted dramatically back to the faith of his childhood, but now he was armed with a powerful conceptual scheme through which to interpret all reality.

It would be out of place, for our purposes, even to survey the magisterial viewpoint developed by Augustine through the remainder of his highly productive life. He enjoyed the freedoms of a lay religious philosopher for only a few years, from 386 (when immediately after his conversion he returned from Italy with a few friends to a quiet monastic life in Thagaste) until 391 (when clerical orders were pressed upon him by popular demand while he was on a visit to Hippo). In four more years he was made bishop of Hippo, and much of his writing was from that point on directed to pastoral issues, especially to warning his flock against falling into various religious and intellectual traps like Donatism and Pelagianism, rife at the time. Despite the controversies and the administrative distractions, Augustine remained true to his early commitment to the values of theoretical activity and the pursuit of truth for its own sake.

For Augustine, however, truth is not simply a philosophical abstraction. Truth *is* God; God *is* Truth. In a quick but revealing demonstration of the necessity of the existence of God, Augustine argues that since we know there is truth, and since Truth and God are identical, we know already that God is (Augustine 1964). If God cannot be truly known apart from God's own self-revelation through Christ and if God *is* Truth, then full truth cannot successfully be found by philosophers, however hard and honestly they search, apart from Christian belief. This unification of truth and God lies behind Augustine's famous formulae, "I believe in order to understand," and "Unless you believe, you will not understand."

God alone is Truth; God alone is fully Being. Everything else is a falling away from the fullness of Being. Since (as Parmenides insisted and Plato agreed) there can only be one true Being, if there is anything else besides the One, then all the other existences can only be by virtue of nonbeing, or finitude, entering into their characters. Augustine accepts this principle, even for the angels, and emphatically also for the human condition and for the rest of the created world. When he discusses the origin of the disobedience of Adam and Eve, he argues that nothing caused this cosmic Fall: Adam and Eve could not have been at all without being finite (as Plato argues also in the *Timaeus*), since this was a condition of their being something besides God; but the finitude in their composition was a lacuna that did not force but allowed for the inevitability of human disobedience to God's command (Augustine 1950). Therefore, it follows, says Augustine, that the first sin was caused by nothing. This can be read two ways, both correct. Nothing caused it; at the same time it was made possible by the presence of that inevitable nothing that dilutes the being of all finite existences.

The Platonic and Neoplatonic conception of degrees of being, with finite things declining from the full reality of the Eternal One by increasing admixtures of nothingness, gives Augustine the answer he offers to the problem of evil. As we have seen, the Stoics were constantly plagued with the problem of accounting for apparent evils and imperfections in what is supposed by them to be a perfectly rational universe ordered by a perfectly good Logos. Augustine, however, answered the problem by arguing that only the One True Being, God, can be perfectly good. The Good and the True are identical in Being, but since there are degrees of being, so there can be degrees of goodness. All beings are good, insofar as they have being (and being, as such, is good), but some are higher, some lower, in the degree of being/goodness they possess. That there are lower goods is no indictment of the perfection of Being, since it is better that all degrees of being be actual than not; and the alternative to finite being/goodness would be the sheer absence of such being/goodness from the universe. The problem comes from misplacements in the hierarchy of finite goods. If something with a lesser degree of being/goodness usurps the place of something else with a greater degree of being/goodness, then it is not the Creator of all these varieties of being/goodness that is to be blamed, but the usurper. If the brightest angel, Lucifer, is not content with his brightness and great goodness but envies and schemes to usurp the only one higher, God, then the next-best becomes the worst. Evil ontologically is nothing but the privation of good. Evil morally consists in preferring the lesser over the greater good. What we love (as Plato taught in the *Symposium*) is the key to our virtue. As long as we keep our love centered on the highest Good, our preferences and decisions will fall into the proper priorities. "Love God," Augustine summarized, "and do what you will."

But of course we are not able to love God without knowing Christ, and we only come to Christ by God's Grace, unmerited by anything we do. Therefore, Augustine insists, Pelagians are wrong in insisting too much upon their freedom to do virtuous things and thereby earning their way to God's favor. They court spiritual pride, accepting an impossible (and fundamentally rebellious) dream of salvation by their own moral achievements. Freedom at one fundamental level is real. Adam freely sinned, with nothing causing the act of misplaced preference. Since Adam's Fall and the consequent disordering of the universe, we are all entangled in the resultant world of jumbled goods, misordered preferences, and self-centeredness.

Augustine's reflections on human freedom, its genuineness (enough to warrant blame), but its limitations (not enough to earn our own salvation), are inevitably tied to his views on time and eternity and God's perfect knowledge. What is time? In the *Confessions* Augustine expresses his frustration with this topic. Time is easy to recognize as we live through it, but it is hard to theorize. He is adamant that the temporal order, our world, cannot properly be thought (as Origen and Plotinus did) as co-eternal with the One Eternal Being. This grates against all of Augustine's deepest values. There is and can be nothing necessary about our world; we are not that important; nothing forced or automatic happens when God freely decides to create. God must have created time itself, therefore, along with the world (as Plato suggests in the *Timaeus*). But what of the "period" in God's eternal life "before" time? Does this not presuppose a time line at some point on which the world and time were brought into being? What was God "doing" before getting busy with the Creation? Augustine approaches humor mixed with exasperation when he declares:

> I answer not as one is said to have done merrily (eluding the pressure of the question), "He was preparing hell (saith he) for pryers into mysteries." It is one thing to answer enquiries, another to make sport of enquirers. So I answer not; for rather had I answer, "I know not," what I know not, than so as to raise a laugh at him who asketh deep things and gain praise for one who answereth false things. But I say that Thou, our God, art the Creator of every creature: and if by the name "heaven and earth," every creature be understood; I boldly say, "that before God made heaven and earth, He did not make any thing." For if He made, what did He make but a creature? And would I knew whatsoever I desire to know to my profit, as I know, that no creature was made, before there was made any creature (Augustine 1960: 223).

Still, whatever baffling reality time should be, it is only a creature and can be no limitation on God's knowledge. God has foreknowledge of all events. For God, the whole of created time is laid out like a landscape seen from a high perspective. For those of us on ground level, the future and past are not directly seen, only the present. But even for us the present is not simply the abstract knife-edge that causes so many conceptual puzzles. Our minds can and do hold together immediate past and immediate future in one field of awareness. The former rhetorician Augustine reminds us that while we speak a sentence, only the syllable being voiced qualifies on the "knife-edge" theory as "present," but in fact we recognize that the whole sentence is somehow present and active in our speaking or listening. The past of the sentence is still influential, even while the words to come are actively pulling us toward their enunciation. Our minds are capable of transcending the given instant to hold together a larger swath of time. God, by huge analogy, must be thought capable of holding together the entire expanse of time, from its creation until its disappearance at the End of the World.

This means that God must see all our actions, from birth to death, as accomplished fact, even before, from our perspective, they have happened. Does this allow them to be free, in the morally relevant sense, so that we can be held responsible for them? Augustine's answer is that God's cognition is not causal coercion; God knows all that we freely decide to do. They still remain our actions, not those of God. Therefore God can justly foreordain salvation or damnation. In this, Augustine breaks decisively with Origen, who, as we saw, rejected the consistency of the idea that God can know in advance what we have not yet freely decided to do, since a free decision *is* not yet to be known, before it is made, even by one who knows all that truly is. These differences rest not only on different conceptions of omniscience but also on wholly different ontologies of time. These premodern issues remain important. We shall return to them as they continue to resonate.

Although no longer temporally qualified to be called a Father of the Church, a monk named Anselm, living seven centuries later than Augustine, shows how persistent the Platonic lens continued to be in focusing thought during the great transition between the end of the Hellenic period and the beginning of the modern.

Anselm was born in Italy in 1033. In 1056 he travelled to France to study, and in 1059 he joined the theologian Lanfranc at the monastery school in Bec (Normandy), where he became a monk. After William of Normandy conquered England in 1066, Lanfranc was appointed Archbishop of Canterbury by William I, then King of England. After Lanfranc's death and the accession of William II to the throne, Anselm, too, reluctantly agreed to be consecrated Archbishop of Canterbury in 1093, soon beginning a stormy era of struggle for supremacy between the representatives of Catholic popes and English kings.

Anselm is best remembered by philosophers for his great *Proslogion*, a book written in the mood of prayer and addressed to God, in which the Ontological Argument appears in its classical formulation. At the outset of his book, Anselm confesses to God his profound valuation of theoretical reason. He believes in God with all his heart. His head, however, lacks the same level of assurance. He pleads with God to provide him something adequate and fitting for his mind, something he could share with others in the more universal and public discourse of reason.

For Anselm, the prayer is answered by the realization of what it means, within the Catholic tradition, to be God. What "we" mean by God, he muses, is absolute perfection. Others may have different understandings of God, but the Augustinian-Christian tradition holds unwaveringly to the vision of God as the unique union of Truth, Beauty, Goodness, and Being. Anselm accepts this tradition, deeply focused through the lens of Platonic excellences, as revelation. He believes, but he still wants to understand. Like Augustine, he believes in order to understand; and as he contemplates the meaning of God thus conveyed in the Christian tradition, he realizes that an understanding worthy of his heart's passionate faith is being granted him. If God is taken as perfect, as "that than which nothing greater can be conceived," then anything allowing any deficiency or lack whatsoever will not be God, as "we" define God. But this means that the God so believed by Christians cannot be understood not to be. It would be contradictory—literally unthinkable—for something to be identified as perfect but still lacking in some excellence. To say that something is lacking in God would be like saying that "that than which nothing greater can be conceived" is not "that than which nothing greater can be conceived," since the subject of our thought would be greater if conceived instead with that lack filled. If we compare a concept of God as having existence both as a thought in our mind and as mighty Creator independent of our mind, with another concept of God as having existence as merely a thought in our mind but lacking existence outside our mind, it is clear, Anselm argues, that the former is greater than the latter. In a second version of the same argument, Anselm compares the concept of a being having *necessary* existence to that of one lacking it, again concluding that the former is greater than the latter. If so, then the latter (in either version) is not a thought about *God*, since the very meaning of God excludes that a "greater" is conceivable. Thus such a God's nonexistence is logically unthinkable. God, according to the Catholic tradition, cannot be understood in any way except as existing, and existing necessarily. Therefore, we can logically doubt other gods, as indeed we should. They are, after all, false gods. But we cannot meaningfully doubt the necessary existence of the God we worship. Faith has led to understanding, with a theoretical power and a clarity worthy of ultimate commitment itself. Now that I have been given such understanding, as Anselm concludes, I could not not believe, even without prior belief.

At least three Platonic values are taken for granted in this ever-fascinating proof. The first is the positive valuation placed on Being itself. Without making this valuational judgment, God would not be lacking any good thing in lacking existence, and the argument would not work. Since the *Timaeus*, however, and the image of the benevolent Maker, sharing good by generously multiplying existence as widely as possible, it is taken for granted that it is good to be rather than not to be, and that "having existence" is a positive quality. This value, like any value, can be challenged. Not all cultures, not all major religions of the world, place a positive value on existence. Some, e.g., Buddhism, which seeks release from the wheel of existence, make quite the opposite judgment. But it is clear that for Anselm this was not an issue. The Platonic lens through which he contemplated the ultimate did not waver on this point.

The second value judgment deals with what sorts of qualities can count as "perfections" in this context. Objections are often made to Anselm's argument that it can prove too much, too many things. A contemporary monk, Gaunilo, was among the first. He argued that Anselm's logic could prove the existence of a "perfect island" by simply claiming that it has no faults (including nonexistence, if that is granted as a "fault"). This would lead to endless absurdities. However, all these founder on failure to keep clear on what the Platonic lens allows real perfection to mean. Perfection, taken in the strong sense intended by Anselm, can apply only to one referent: that which is lacking in nothing at all. Plato's Form of the Good, Plotinus' One, Augustine's God— these would qualify for perfection as such. But islands, by definition, are from the wrong category of referents. Islands are bounded by water. They are not infinite, by definition. From the Platonic viewpoint, Gaunilo made a terrible choice of example. Nothing finite could be a good example. Throughout the Platonic tradition, Infinite Being must be unique, Alone. How could there be two? "They" would limit one another; or, to put the point differently, insofar as they were conceived to have different properties, one would lack what the other possessed, and vice versa, thereby neither would qualify as infinite.

Finally, Anselm shared with the Platonic tradition the confidence that intellectual contemplation can put minds in touch with reality. Valuing pure thought over the derivatives of sense experience is another old tradition. We saw it in an early clear form in the distinction made by Parmenides between the *Way of Truth* and the *Way of Seeming*. We saw it in Plato's low estimate of beliefs based merely on the shadowy Appearances we are provided in the World of Becoming, relative to the eternal truths grounded in the Eternal Realm of Forms. We have encountered it even in the antiempiricism of the Atomists, who maintain that the world of common life is derivative from and wholly unlike the really Real things, which can never be experienced in themselves.

All of these values and in particular the last of these—the trust in contemplative reason and a priori thought—were not unchallenged in the transition to the modern. The most powerful alternative to the lens of Plato was the thought of his student and successor, Aristotle.

THE ARISTOTELIAN VALUE-LENS

The story of the transmission of Aristotle's thought from its original Hellenic context to Medieval Europe is complex and interesting in its own right, but not of the essence for our purposes. Suffice it to say that Syrian Christians were instrumental in beginning the process of translation into Syriac and Persian during the first five centuries A.D. Early in the sixth century, even before the time of Mohammed in the latter half of that century, these works were retranslated into Arabic, making them available to scholars in the world of Islam following the powerful spread of Muslim belief and culture through the Middle East and North Africa, and later, in the tenth century, into Spain.

In Baghdad, the early tenth century scholar al-Farabi did much to introduce Aristotle's thought to the world of Islam. He offered Aristotle's logical works as a propaedeutic both to philosophy and to theology, which logic ought also to serve. He also made clear distinctions between philosophy and theology, adding arguments for the existence of God based on our experience of a kosmos in which there is motion and change. Such experienced motion requires a First Mover to account for what is evident to our senses. We also experience death and decay all around us; therefore, there must be something that itself is not contingent and perishing—a necessary being that, precisely by its necessity, accounts for its own existence while also accounting for all the other contingent existences we see around ourselves in ordinary life.

Blending a share of Neoplatonic thinking into his Aristotelianism, al-Farabi, like Plotinus, postulated emanations, to link the Necessary One, through lesser entities like Intelligence and the World-Soul, to our changing and contingent world.

Another Persian, living in the second half of the tenth century and into the eleventh, was Avicenna. His works, all in Arabic rather than his native tongue, greatly advanced interest in Aristotle in the Islamic world. Avicenna had a strong sense of the necessity of things. Not only must there be a necessary being to account for all contingency, as al-Farabi had argued, but all these "contingent" things need to be seen as themselves "necessary" in another sense: that is, they do not possess their own necessity as part of their essence, as God does; but they are as they are thanks to the external necessity of God's creative activity. More, God *creates* necessarily. Like Origen (whose work Avicenna could hardly have known), Avicenna cannot conceive of an uncreative God. Therefore, God must always be creating—and the world thereby becomes necessary, too. God—the One—would be defiled, however, by too close contact with the created world. Avicenna, following the lead of al-Farabi, insists on intermediaries. The One, creative though it be, can hardly be conceived to emanate anything less than another perfect being, as much like itself as logically possible. Thus, the first intermediate is Intelligence, resembling the One in all respects except for its created status. This single difference, however, entails the fact that its principle of existence (having been created) lies outside its essence. So duality enters the universe. From then on, Avicenna postulates intermediary after intermediary until, finally, the tenth intermediary Intelligence creates the world we inhabit. In consequence, the One, though ultimately responsible for all, is entirely unaware of the world. Such awareness would be a defilement. In this, if not in his Neoplatonic (even gnostic) multiplication of intermediaries, Avicenna was close to Aristotle's own conception of a God too perfect to be sullied with thoughts of a changing world.

The Aristotelian lens becomes more focused in the philosophy of Averroës, who lived at the far western edge of the Islamic world, in twelfth-century Spain. Born in Córdoba in 1126, Averroës was trained in law and medicine as well as theology and philosophy, and served his Caliph, both as judge and physician. He found in Aristotle's works the correct guide to truth. Therefore, he poured his immense energies into writing commentaries, often multiple commentaries at various depths for various readers, on all the writings of Aristotle available to him, including the *Posterior Analytics*, the *Physics*, the *De Caelo*, the *De Anima*, and the *Metaphysics*. His commentaries were so full and compelling that Thomas Aquinas later called Averroës simply, "The Commentator."

Averroës opened Europe to Aristotle with his Commentaries, but he was more than simply a commentator. He developed a powerful system for understanding the nature of things in an Aristotelian way. Inheriting Avicenna's ten Intelligences but rejecting the Neoplatonic notion of emanation, he reduces these Intelligences simply to lesser Movers of the etherial Spheres. In this, he retreats from the constant tendency toward pantheism that emanationism brings. In contrast to all varieties of Platonism, Averroës celebrates matter for its limitless potentialities, rather than condemning it for its "lower" status and its tendency to drag the mind away from the universal.

In particular, the matter of our human bodies is not just the prison of the soul but shows, rather, what the union of immanent Form and prepared organic matter can achieve. The soul, as Aristotle held, is the form of the living body. What happens when the body dies? This sensitive question has enormous value-implications both in Christianity and in Islam. Orthodoxy in both religions requires the answer of personal immortality; but Averroës resists this position. Aristotle himself held out the possibility that the purely rational part of the soul might, because of its association with the universal and eternal character of intelligible truths, be able to survive the death of the thinker. That is as far as Averroës will go. This aspect of our rational souls is not private or personal; it is shared, like truth itself, with all who are rational. There may be life for this universal aspect of the soul after the death of our material bodies, then, but this will not count as personal immortality.

Another point at which Averroës parts company with orthodox Islam deals with the eternity and necessity of the world. It is inconceivable that time could "begin," since beginning already assumes a temporal context. Thus, time and the changing universe must be co-everlasting with God. Certainly Prime Matter is no fit subject for direct creation. Uncreated, it stands ready forever, at any time, to realize its myriad potentialities.

These clashes with religious orthodoxy could be dangerous. Therefore, Averroës developed a theory for overcoming the pain of conflict between philosophy and religion. Philosophy utters literal statements, providing truth of this blunt sort to those who can rise to the rigors of logical thought. Religion, however, speaks in allegory and symbol, also providing truth to those who need the imagery of parable and myth to guide them. Let the two truths flourish side-by-side. But since Averroës left it entirely to the philosophical side to decide when religion was speaking in allegory and what the correct interpretation of these allegories might be, it is not surprising that orthodox theologians of Islam did not care for this subordination. A turbulent decade after the death of his longtime sponsoring Caliph, Yusuf, the new Almohad Caliph, al-Mansūr, was persuaded by these theologians to order Averroës into banishment. The study of Greek philosophy was banned in Muslim Spain, and Averroës' books were burned. His principal legacy was to be bequeathed not to Islam but to Judaism and Christianity.

The leading Jewish thinker of the Middle Ages was Moses, son of Maimon (in the name's more familiar Latinized form, "Maimonides"), who was born just nine years after Averroës in Córdoba, Spain. The Almohad Muslim rulers of Córdoba were not tolerant of Jews, however, and when young Moses was only thirteen the family was forced to flee, first in 1148 to North Africa and finally in 1165 to Egypt. Maimonides became a court physician and a leader of the Jewish community in Cairo. He, like Averroës, was an ardent Aristotelian.

His philosophical approach led him to break with the Platonic conception of soul as an immortal substance encased in a body and to prefer the Aristotelian conception of hylomorphic unity between body and soul. If this means that only the impersonal part of our soul, the active intellect, can possibly survive the death of our particular body, so be it. Likewise Maimonides employs highly Aristotelian arguments in his proofs for God's existence. He argues for God as First Mover, as First Cause, and as Necessary Being—all arguments, as we have seen, that depend upon at least general experiential premises, that is, the experience of motion, the experience of causality, and the experience of decay and contingency.

His greatest philosophical work, *The Guide for the Perplexed*, was originally written in Arabic for Arabic-speaking Jews who were "perplexed" ("torn," "confused") about the conflicts between the authoritative statements and observances of Jewish religion and the compelling findings of Greek philosophy. It is a deliberately daunting, esoteric work, meant to fend off readers who might lack the intellectual capacity or motivation to persevere. Maimonides was concerned about undermining the authority of religious tradition for those unable to cope with the bare truths of philosophy. But for those who can follow, literal truth as seen through the Aristotelian lens is normally offered as the proper interpretation of scriptural language understood as allegorical. Maimonides reserves his right to differ with Aristotle, however, when the scriptural tradition is clear and the theoretical case is inconclusive. Aristotle argues, for example, that the world and time must be everlasting, co-eternal with the Unmoved Mover, distinguished not with regard to their everlastingness but, rather, with regard to their different levels of actualization. The Unmoved Mover is completely actual, Pure Act, while lesser things are not completely actual but are full of potentiality, striving everlastingly and not always successfully, as we saw, to actualize their natures. Maimonides is repelled by the idea that the Absolute God would not, on this theory of the kosmos, be free to create or refrain from creating, according to what (religiously) must be a completely unhindered will. Aristotle's argument from the unthinkability of a "time before time" is declared not entirely convincing; and, in the case of such theoretical balance, the clear teaching of religious tradition can be affirmed.

Maimonides takes the absoluteness of God so intensely that he propounds the strongest case since Plotinus for the utter ineffability of God. Nothing positive can be said about God, he insists. The only thing possible for us, without sullying God with our mundane concepts, is to utter negations: what God is not. He adds that this *via negativa* does not leave us speechless or even empty-headed. There is such a thing as "full silence" in contrast to the empty silence of the ignorant or muddle-headed. If we conduct our negations long and sensitively enough, as in a sacred game of twenty questions, a direction appears, pointing the way toward God without disgracing Deity with the dross of human comparisons.

This is true, of course, only in a prior context. In a game of twenty questions we have at least a positive category: animal, vegetable, or mineral. Maimonides does not concede this point explicitly, but he makes the positive context clear for the sake of his "full silence" by allowing two exceptions to his rule of negations-only. One is from the general understanding of philosophy (what later came to be called "natural theology"), supplied by the conceptual lens of Aristotle, as to what God in the most general sense *is* and *does*. God is simple; God is actual; God is Mover; God is Cause; God is necessary. The second is from the particular authoritative traditions of Maimonides' own religious community (what later came to be called "revealed theology"), supplied by the core authorized practices and statements of prayer. These, too, must not be taken out of context, but they may legitimately be uttered *in prayer*, and these authorized words give affirmative clues, along with the findings of philosophical reason, that make negations about God not merely negative. No one has insisted on the via negativa more fiercely than Maimonides. If his position requires such a two-pronged, prior *via affirmativa* to save it from sheer nescience, this finding may be significant (Ferré 1992).

Thomas Aquinas, the leading Christian Aristotelian of the Middle Ages, was most appreciative of Maimonides' strictures against illegitimate use of anthropomorphic language about God, but despite this appreciation he pulled back from the extremes of via negativa in favor of an important doctrine of analogy. Thomas was born near Naples, Italy, some thirty years after the death of Maimonides in Cairo. His father was the Count of Aquino and his uncle a prominent Benedictine Abbot at the Monte Cassino monastery. At age five, Thomas was placed in this monastery by his family, but armed strife in the region required him to withdraw at age fourteen and enroll at the University of Naples. There, he dismayed his family by joining the Dominican order, rather than the Benedictine. At age twenty, while travelling under the protection of the Dominicans to Paris for further study, he was kidnapped by his own brothers and held prisoner by his family in a failed attempt to force him back to the Benedictines. After a year he escaped and made his way to the University of

Paris, where he studied for three years with the greatest intellect of the day, Albert (called "the Great" even during his lifetime), a wide-ranging thinker interested in a vast array of topics, from theology to empirical science, but especially in the newly discovered philosophy of Aristotle.

When Albert was sent to Cologne to found a new school, Thomas accompanied his master and remained part of his busy intellectual and administrative life. At twenty-eight, Thomas returned to Paris to study for his own teaching credentials. These acquired, he taught at Paris or in Italy for the rest of his short life. After a three-year phase at Paris, he taught for nine years in various Italian cities in the courts of various popes, then returned for a four-year phase at Paris before being sent to Naples in 1272 (now age forty-eight) to head the Dominican school. Early in 1274, on a trip to attend a Church Council, Thomas fell ill and died, not quite fifty.

The philosophy of Aristotle was considered dangerous by the theological conservatives of the time. For one thing, it was tainted by association. Not only had Aristotle himself been a pagan, but, worse, the path of his rediscovery had led through generations of non-Christian thinkers, Muslim and Jewish. More important for our account, it was associated with ideas that were discordant with central Christian values.

First, Aristotelianism seemed to clash with the high value put on immortality of the soul. This was no problem for Christian Platonism, which could carry over into theology Plato's apparent conception of the soul as an independent, immaterial, eternal substance. There might be a clash with Plato's doctrine of the preexistence of the soul—Christians leaned toward thinking of God as specially creating each soul (the alternative would be to consider souls as coeternal with God, which would be to exalt our finite selves too much)—but at least there were no conceptual problems, while looking through the Platonic lens, in seeing souls capable of existing apart from bodies in an afterlife, having direct moral significance for the personal souls which once, for better or for worse, had inhabited flesh. Aristotle's lens, however, showed soul and body intimately—perhaps inseparably—entwined: soul, for him, is the "form" of the animated body. If, as Aristotle taught, forms have no separate existence, then, when the body's animation ceases, how can soul be thought to continue? Aristotle allowed a possible exception for the active human intellect, dealing with rational, eternal truths and, therefore, needing to be in some way like these truths, perhaps itself immortal. But this is just that part of the soul which is completely devoid of the particular quirks that give us personal identities. Therefore, this sort of survival, even if hazily visible through the Aristotelian lens, would be irrelevant to the morally portentous concerns of Christians toward a future life.

Thomas inherited this serious value-problem with his Aristotelianism. He was not prepared to abandon Christian hope for a meaningful, personal afterlife;

but, at the same time, he was not ready to give up the widely illuminating hylo-morphism provided by his Aristotelian lens. His solution was to insist on both, but now in a new synthesis reviving the doctrine of the resurrection of the body to replace the doctrine of the survival of the soul. The idea of resurrection was not really new. Imagery of the dead rising had been part of the biblical tradition, at least since *Ezekiel*, with its vision of the valley of the dry bones. Jewish thought-forms (before Philo of Alexandria, at least) were less comfortable with Platonic dualism than with the more intimate soul-body interdependence of Aris-totelian hylomorphism. New with Thomas was the carefully developed theo-retical substructure in which personal identity and individuation were to be sup-plied by God's miraculous reanimation of one's former flesh, as a necessary condition of a personally identifiable and morally meaningful afterlife. There were problems occasioned by this solution, of course: What would happen if cannibals ate one's flesh, turning it into theirs? What if they later converted to Christianity and themselves deserved resurrection? Whose bodies would then be reanimated with whose soul-principle? But these are distinctly theoretical problems, generated within shared value-commitments and with a clear con-ceptual framework for solution; thus, granted adequate access to divine miracle and to the category (from St. Paul) of "spiritual body," they pose no insuperable problems to future generations of Christian theorists.

A second Aristotelian clash with Christian values was over the problem of God's knowledge of the created world. For "The Philosopher" it would seem that the Pure Act could only think Itself in order to remain perfect and pure. Thought contemplating anything less would need to admit potentiality, change, and unworthiness. On the other side, the God of the Bible was treasured pre-cisely for knowing every detail, with boundless compassion for every creature. Again Thomas could not, without abandoning basic values, release either side of this tension: on the one hand, God must know the world, on pain of ceasing to be the Heavenly Father, the Good Shepherd; on the other hand, God must not know the world, at least directly, on pain of corrupting Pure Act with fini-tude and potentiality. For Thomas, the solution was again to insist on—and find a way to have—both. God certainly knows God's own nature with perfect knowledge. But God is Creator of this world. Therefore, in God's knowing everything about the Creator, God knows perfectly (though indirectly, and non-corruptingly) what the Creator has created: our world in all its detail. The val-ues of Christian piety can in this way be combined with the values of philo-sophical purity.

Philosophical purity, through an Aristotelian lens, however, does not permit a reciprocal human knowledge of God's divine essence. Aristotle, unlike Plato, had stressed the need for the bodily senses in coming to knowl-edge of any of the eternal forms. If a form is not first in the appropriate sense organ, there to be abstracted by the mind, then it cannot later be in the intellect.

There are many things we can know in this way; but God's own essence is never to be one of them. The Ontological Argument offered by Anselm was not dependent upon our knowing the true divine essence. Anselm disclaimed such pretensions quite explicitly. But this argument is more suited to the Platonic lens. It moves entirely in the domain of concepts, drawing conclusions about reality from necessities of thought. It contemplates meanings "than which nothing greater can be conceived," far removed from the empirical order. Admittedly, this is not a positive conception of God's essence, since it is negative and comparative, but it purports to prove to us that God's essence must include existence. Thomas, a Christian fully committed to the existence of God and also to the identity of God's existence and essence, is torn between strongly valuing what the proof concludes and disagreeing with the whole a priori framework of meaning in which Anselm's thought operated. Again, Thomas insists on both. For any intellect that can know the essence of God, he admits, the Anselmian proof would be completely sound and convincing. Even for us it is valid; God's essence does entail God's existence. But the argument cannot be convincing (to us) since we cannot know the meaning toward which Anselm's formula points in its negative, comparative way. Only by contemplating positively what it is that "nothing greater can be conceived" could we know the meaning of that definition. Since we cannot, it remains only a formula, a form of words vainly searching for a conceptual referent. Though valid, and though its conclusion "God (necessarily) exists" is true, the argument fails to gain purchase on human minds. Only God knows God's essence. For God (alone), the Ontological Argument would succeed. God sees that existence is included in the divine essence; thus, for God the argument would not only be formally valid but also meaningful and true. But God is the one intellect for which the Ontological Argument is not needed.

Such a solution to the Anselmian heritage leaves the problem of how God can be known. This cannot be by pure intellection, not if the Aristotelian lens is to be retained. But, Thomas argues, the world itself, as experienced, can point our minds to knowledge of God's existence. We experience change, and this must be accounted for by something unchanging while still capable of explaining change. Everyone allows this First Cause can be called "God." Likewise, we experience motion, and this needs grounding in something unmoved. Everyone grants this Unmoved Mover the name of "God." Again, we experience generation and destruction, contingency in the finite world, and this demands for explanation something other than just more of the same contingent order—it demands a basis in what accounts for itself, as necessary, as well as for all that is not necessary. Everyone permits this Necessary Being the name of "God." We experience qualities of different degrees, better and worse, but this means there must be a maximum, a best. Everyone acknowledges this Highest Good to be called "God." Finally, we experience order beyond the inherent capacity of the orderly things themselves to explain, and this requires a purposive, intelligent orderer. Everyone allows the Designer to be called "God." To discover all this is still not to know the essence of God, as in syllogistic reasoning, wherein the "essence" of something serves as the fulcrum "middle term" of argument. But it is to know something about what God *does*, even if it falls short of full understanding of what God *is*. In this way, the values of Aristotelian empiricism, the principle that whatever we think about we have abstracted from our senses, may be retained without abandoning the values at stake in claiming knowledge of God's existence.

In these and many other comparable ways, Thomas of Aquino wove, by his teaching and writings, the greatest of all the medieval tapestries of Christian intellectual vision, its warp from Aristotelian theory, with its own characteristic value implications, shot through with the woof of Christian traditions and symbols, laden with commitment to the final values of worship.

It should be clear from the exemplars chosen for this section that values and theory wind inseparably around one another. Sometimes in the lead are the values of a great philosophical vision, which pull even deeply religious persons to rethink and reportray their doctrines and images in terms of the large values provided by the vision itself. Sometimes in the lead, instead, are the values of a religious perspective, which urge reformulation and modification of philosophical views. Often in the same persons, as in Averroës or Maimonides or Thomas, there are pulls in both directions at once, to modify a religious tradition here, to marginalize a philosophical argument there.

My metaphor of the lens, which has organized the last two sections of this chapter, should not be allowed to mislead. Although it might be argued that Jewish, pagan, Christian, and Muslim thinkers tend to see the world more alike when looking through the same basic lenses, whether of Platonism or Aristotelianism, the differences between them are also deep and instructive. It must be realized that all these "lenses" are compound: the primary lens of Plato is never entirely without the additional lenses of Stoicism and neo-Pythagoreanism. The primary lens of Aristotle is usually attached to Neoplatonic and sometimes even Gnostic secondary lenses.

When parallel primary lenses from Islam, Christianity, or Judaism are added, the resulting visions of reality will inevitably diverge in many respects. This granted, it remains impressive how long, through the many centuries of transition between the death of the Hellenic world and the birth of the Modern, the metaphysical landscape, as viewed by the major thinkers of this period, remains in general respects recognizable, whatever particular lenses are used. Just as the Great Hellenes shared more than they disputed, so the Great Transition, suffused by the vision of Plato and/or Aristotle, rested on values too deep to question—at least within the focal power of the lenses at hand.

PREMODERN TO PROTOMODERN

The Thomistic synthesis had many vigorous opponents, of course. After Thomas' untimely death, charges were brought in Paris against his thinking. Against these, his surviving teacher, Albert, came stoutly to the rescue. Despite controversies, the great Thomistic blending of faith and reason had the strength to survive early attacks at Paris and Oxford, and soon it became the standard of correct teaching among the Dominicans. Much later it became official teaching for the Church as a whole (Copelston 1962: Vol. 2, Part 2, 153–5).

In the first turbulent decades after Thomas' death, his synthesis stimulated different sorts of dissatisfaction. One sort we may consider essentially premodern in character; the other, which will interest us even more, is what I shall call "protomodern."

Of the medieval opponents, two figures illustrate opposite poles of reaction. Meister Eckhart, who was twenty-six when Thomas died, was deeply offended by Thomas' heavy stress on Aristotelian reason. Although himself a fellow Dominican, Eckhart passionately defended faith as the way to God, returning to a Neoplatonic form of mysticism in which God, the ineffable, emanates all things through the Word and the Holy Spirit, and the soul returns to the source of its Being in mystic ecstasy. Eckhart received his teaching credentials from Paris at the turn of the fourteenth century and taught at Cologne (ironically, the site of Albert's platform for Aristotelianism a generation before) until his death in 1329. At the time of his death, condemnation activities were brewing because of perceived dangers of pantheism in Eckhart's unity-mysticism.

Duns Scotus, at the other pole, was born in the year of Thomas' death, eventually joining the Franciscan order and teaching (though only in his twenties) at Oxford. His grievance with the Thomistic synthesis was not its excessive stress on reason, but what he thought was its inadequate logic. The arguments for God, for example, are logically irrelevant to *God*, since they fail to deal with God's own nature but only with certain effects "everyone agrees" should be attributed to God. All a posteriori arguments of this sort are only probable and thus inadequate to the subject matter: the perfect One. Scotus demanded that God not be tangled in the limitations of an Aristotelian "nature" that would determine God's actions. Even though the divine nature was understood as good, benevolent, just, and so on, to every superlative degree, God's unlimitable will must transcend and choose even those qualities. Indeed, for Scotus, all the qualities, all ideas, all Forms must be the free creations of God. They are not co-eternal. God created both the matter and the Forms of the universe by sheer fiat. Afterward, we may say this creation was "good," but "goodness" is a creature of the divine will. God's will is not bound by goodness; rather, it defines goodness by what it decides. Since Forms come into being along with matter, individuated from the start, it is not matter that is the principle of individuation, as Aristotle and Thomas taught, but Forms themselves, "contracting" to provide a particular "thisness," as well as the general "whatness," of an entity. Matter, no longer simply a principle of individuation, is a spatio-temporal receptacle which, if God so willed, could in principle be stripped of all Form and still remain real as Void, with no characteristics at all. This brilliant, complex metaphysical system was taught briefly at Oxford, then for four years at Paris, when Scotus left Oxford in 1304. In 1308, Scotus moved on to Cologne, but in that year, only thirty-four, he died.

Both these objections to the Thomistic synthesis were distinctly premodern. Eckhart looked through the familiar lens of Neoplatonism and mystical spirituality; Scotus looked (critically) through the equally familiar lens of Form and matter provided by Aristotelianism. His thinking, though original, called for more of the same, albeit sharply modified by the logic of God's absolute will.

Two other exemplar figures warrant the term "protomodern." With them we complete the transition from the last days of the Hellenic to the first days of the distinctly Modern modes of thought. There were many others involved, as there have been at every stage of our story. But to illustrate deep shifts in values across the fourteenth and fifteenth centuries, we shall limit ourselves to a brief look at William of Ockham and Nicholas of Cusa.

William was born in England in the village of Ockham in Surry, not far from London, around 1285. When he went to Oxford in 1310, he had missed his chance to study with Duns Scotus in person, since Scotus had left for Paris in 1304, when William was only nineteen. But Ockham became, like Scotus, a Franciscan; and he undoubtedly encountered the highly critical, obscurely complex logical thought of Scotus during his Oxford studies.

He most certainly did not become a Scotist. On the contrary, the metaphysics of the Forms became for him the subject of slashing attack. What he did pick up from Scotus, perhaps, was the supreme value of the will of God over all else: emphatically over any alleged universal characteristics of the divine "nature." At Oxford, he lectured on the Bible, then on Peter Lombard's *Sentences*, before entering a period of writing and disputation. He had qualified to teach by 1324, but never actually began, since he was then commanded by Pope John XXII to come to the papal court at Avignon to answer charges of heresy. Four years went by without a verdict, but Ockham's case became entangled in the ongoing struggle between pope and emperor through the case of another important Franciscan who had in the meantime been haled on charges to Avignon. In 1328, Ockham, with three others under suspicion, fled from Avignon to avail themselves of the protection of Emperor Ludwig IV of Bavaria, who supported them in Munich. Ockham was excommunicated, but retaliated with polemics against the popes in the battle for supremacy between Church and State. When Ludwig died in 1347, Ockham negotiated a reconciliation with the papacy, but he himself, independent to the end, was taken by the plague in Munich in 1349.

In a life of resistance against the heavy hand of authority, Ockham's most radical revolt, as history shows, was not directly political but was against the reality of Forms. As we noted, both Platonic and Aristotelian lenses show the world as characterized by universals. There was a difference between Plato and Aristotle as to whether the Forms could exist somehow entirely by themselves or whether they needed a mind or matter to support them. But their existence, their necessary place in an intelligible kosmos, was unquestioned. Ockham, however, in the first half of the fourteenth century, exemplifies the coming Modern spirit by his radical denial of the reality of anything besides particular individuals. Only particulars exist. If an apple is red, its red consists in its particular pigmentation. If we think about the similarity between this apple's color and a red sunset, our concept itself is a particular event in our mind. Universality is simply our disposition to use particular words to draw together a range of similarities among individual things. Besides particulars, which give us all we need for knowledge, there is no need to posit another "realm" of universals (with Plato) or another ontological "type" formally ingredient in substances (with Aristotle). To do so is to "multiply entities beyond necessity." With this methodological principle of simplicity in explanation (which is implicitly also the expression of metaphysical preference), Ockham armed his followers with a logical "Razor" for the counterattack on premodern thinking as a whole.

Ockham's Razor makes nonsense of the concept of God as somehow either the repository of the Forms or creator of the Forms. There are no Forms. God, the unique One beyond all Universals and unbound by any "nature," cannot be thought by human reason or proved by any natural theology. With this slash of his Razor, Ockham shreds the Thomistic synthesis of faith and reason. Theology is no science, as Thomas held. Matters having to do with God must be taken entirely on faith; matters of philosophical interest have no authority over religion. Secular and sacred are utterly different domains, each with its own legitimacy. (The indirect political implications for the independence of imperial from papal authority show themselves at this point.)

More, if God is not bound by Universal Good, since there is no such Form of the Good, so much the more is human society not under obligations to any so-called "absolute" moral qualities of right or justice or benevolence. The duty of the creature is simply to obey the Will of God. If God had willed otherwise, our duties would have been different but our obedience no less required. Therefore, ethics cannot logically seek independent, objective truths. There is no "science" of ethics, no more ·han there is a "science" of theology.

With these conclusions, Ockham rejects a crucial value, which we have traced from the days of the pre-Socratic pioneers—the final unity of truth under a single coherence-making principle or perspective. For Ockham, sensory intuition, on which alone individual existences can be known, and logical understanding, in which he made powerful contributions, stand on one side, the secular knowable; theological and ethical pronouncement stand on an entirely different side, the sacred revealed-but-unknowable. In future years, forwarded by such thinkers as Jean Buridan (1300–1358) and Nicholas of Autrecourt (1300-c.1355), thinking based on these new values would be called the *via moderna*, in contrast to the *via antiqua* of the medieval synthesis. Buridan advanced a newly empirical physics, developing a theory of impetus for projectiles totally at variance with Aristotle's theory of motion as requiring an ever-present mover. Nicholas, though harassed in his time for his unorthodoxies, is best remembered as the one who, accepting Ockham's rejection of inherent universal qualities in things, pushed on to deny the existence of real substances and real causal connections between things, as well. In this he became the fourteenth-century precursor of eighteenth-century David Hume.

An entirely different thinker, a Neoplatonist, a believer in Forms, a mystic, provides our final link to modernity. He is Nicholas of Cusa, born in Kues, Germany, in 1401. His life and thought during the first part of the fifteenth century are in complete contrast to that of Ockham in the fourteenth century. Ockham was a rebel against the church; Nicholas was a churchman, a papal delegate, a cardinal. Ockham derided the Forms; Nicholas embraced them, rejoiced in them, played with them in new logical and mathematical ways.

Nicholas was in many ways a paradigmatic man of the early Renaissance. He urged a return to classical culture, in particular to the Neoplatonism of Augustine, Anselm, and Meister Eckhart. He searched for and found classical manuscripts, including a dozen lost Latin plays by the comedian Plautus. He was a reformer with broad vision and boundless hopes for reorganizing the church; and he worked for his vision through councils and delegations. With one of his delegations he even succeeded, temporarily, in overcoming the rift between Rome and Constantinople, bringing together the two Catholic churches through the Council of Florence in 1439.

His protomodernity, however, is evident in two respects: his profound valuation of mathematics and his positive assessment of the infinite. Nicholas was alarmed by the rigid use made by the ascendent Aristotelians and their Ockhamite opponents of the Law of Non-Contradiction. Logic-chopping, distinction-making, had become an industry. Even God was widely held, by the Thomists, the Scotists, and most of the Ockhamites, to be subject to this Law. On its basis, God was absolved from doing nonsense things, for example, God making a stone so heavy God could not move it, and was defended, too, from doing frightening things, for example, God driving God insanely evil. But these, Nicholas protested, are to trivialize infinity. God is absolute infinity, the absolute maximum containing all perfections. As such, God is completely incommensurable with finites. If so, God's infinity admits of no degrees of "greater" or "lesser." That being the case, it is as true to say that God is the "minimum" as it is to say that God is the "maximum." "Maximum" and "minimum" coincide in infinity. There is in God a "coincidence of opposites" that stubborn allegiance to the Law of Non-Contradiction blinds us to, just as it undermines all efforts to fulfill our intellects by resting them in God's own infinity.

Not only is *God* infinite, so must be any *world* created by such a God. This is not to say that the universe is absolutely infinite, challenging God's infinity, but it is to insist that the universe is infinite in all respects except that it does not contain God, who remains unencompassed by anything whatsoever. How then should we think about the world?

Mathematical thinking is helpful to restore the mind's flexibility and wonder. Syllogistic proofs are too stiff. Nicholas calls on us instead to think about the circumference of a large circle. The circumference is clearly curved. Now think about doubling the diameter of the circle: the curvature of the circumference has become more gradual, to cover the larger area. Now extend the diameter to infinity: the infinite circle's circumference is no longer curved at all. The circumference of an infinite circle turns out to be a straight line. The circumference, by the coincidence of opposites, has become indistinguishable from the diameter. Further, for an infinite circle, every point is at its center. Total relativity holds. Even though my place is different from your place, it is both true that my location will be at the center of an infinite universe and that your location will also be at the center.

By celebrating, rather than shrinking from, conceptions of infinity, Nicholas of Cusa clearly exemplifies one of the greatest changes in values that has occurred between the time of Pythagoras or Parmenides and the early Renaissance. The change from early Hellenic unease and dread was fostered by consistently positive evaluation of God's status as the Unlimited, which Judaism, Christianity, and Islam all share. Worship of the Infinite, joy in the Infinite, had become fully established in thought and emotion over the intervening centuries. Now, with the vision of an infinite cosmos, with a principle of spatio-temporal relativity, with mathematical modes of expression that represent a newly resurgent Pythagorean spirit—but with a value-inversion embracing the infinite as wonderful and good—the stage is set at last for the emergence, from Ockham's analytical nominalism and Nicholas' Renaissance optimism, of the distinctly Modern.

Part 2

MODERN METAPHYSICS

5

THE FOUNDERS

There are no absolute discontinuities in history. This is certainly the case when we move from premodern to modern metaphysics. Since everything is related to everything else, it is possible to trace micro-continuities until the large differences we thought we had seen blur and fade away.

Still, there are important watersheds in history. By the end of this chapter, thoughts about being and value will flow in a different dominant direction from those we have become accustomed to seeing in premodern metaphysics. This is not to say that there are no precursors. Indeed there are. Much of what counts as the modern revolution in worldview flows from the rediscovery and reevaluation of ancient views, now put to new uses. Nor is it to say that all who live after a certain date are automatically "modern" in outlook, even on fundamentals. Opponents of the dominant view are important in part because they show, by contrast, how widespread and taken-for-granted the dominant position comes to be.

It is true that modernity, as a historical phenomenon, arose at a certain time. This means that dates are relevant. In this book, however, the word "modern" will not be used primarily in terms of dates. More important is the character, or content, of what arises, especially as it becomes enmeshed with and gives shape to the civilization we also call "modern." This means that beliefs about value and basic reality had a bearing on the institutions of modern life as they were invented and grew in power (and geographical spread) during the seventeenth through the twentieth centuries. Economics, politics, education, religion, art, the family, and so on, are bound together in a network of beliefs and values that can be characterized without essential reference to dates. Therefore, it makes sense to say that recognizably "modern" ideas appeared sporadically before the rise of modern civilization, and that "modern" ideas and institutions can and do coexist with "premodern" and "postmodern" ones.

RENAISSANCE EARLY MODERNS

One celebrated instance of a person with remarkably modern ideas well before the "official" rise of modernity is Leonardo da Vinci. Leonardo was born during the Renaissance—he is often taken as the very paradigm of the "Renaissance man" (in the sense that before our age of specialization he was free to do everything supremely well)—but the date of his birth in 1452, as the illegitimate son of a Florentine lawyer, is more misleading than illuminating about his mind. There was of course plenty of "Renaissance" in Leonardo: his involvement with the great families of Italy and their hunger for commemoration in monumental works of art, his relish for the sensual appreciation of nature, his organization and direction of lavish pageants and spectacles loved by that era. But Leonardo was in his genius a person not contained by his temporal context. His intellect would have been far more at home centuries later, amid modern scientists probing into the hidden secrets of things, and among modern engineers designing weapons of death or amenities of life. He loved to think about gadgets, great and small. He planned cities with elevated highways and sanitary systems; he designed flame-throwers and pontoon bridges and new weapons for siege warfare for his military sponsors; he considered problems of civil engineering, canals with locks, dredges for digging canals and draining swamps (including the principle of the siphon in his plans); he invented the turbine; he played with ideas about the steam engine; he designed spinning machines; he planned cranes for lifting heavy weights; he worked out machines for sawing marble and wood; he played with ideas for a heavier-than-air flying machine and a submarine. With all this, he engaged in close anatomical studies not only for his art but also for pure understanding of the nervous system and the functioning of the eye. He studied the mathematical principles of perspective. He theorized about geology, suggesting an emergent theory of land from the oceans on the basis of fossil findings on hilltops. He studied Archimedes' mechanics and advanced beyond these with a sweeping theory of universal mechanism and a consequent theory of universal determinism, which he welcomed with spiritual joy in the impersonal wonder of nature, to which he believed we must acquiesce. He also theorized about the heavens and rejected the standard Ptolemaic system on mechanical grounds: all those supposed "crystalline spheres" holding the planets and fixed stars could never coexist because of the huge frictional forces they would exert on each other.

Methodologically, Leonardo combined fierce empiricism (he mocked those who engaged in endless "verbal disputes" over questions taken from books when experience should rule discovery) with strong support for mathematics as the arbiter of conflicting, revisable theories. "He who is not a mathematician according to my principles must not read me," he wrote. And, again, "Oh, students, study mathematics, and do not build without a foundation" (Burtt 1954: 42–43). Here he drew from a major Renaissance event, the Florentine revival of Plato through Marsilio Ficino's translations and commentaries (particularly from the *Timaeus*), a theme—the centrality of mathematics for the understanding of reality—that was utterly to transform modern science and metaphysics in centuries to come.

These centuries were not Leonardo's. He was a largely solitary figure in his time, manifesting in his spirit, interests, values, and methods, what might be called the "modern syndrome" before the arrival of modernity.

Another Renaissance figure who combined in himself powerful premodern commitments—strikingly more so than Leonardo, though Leonardo was twenty-one years his senior—with important elements of the "modern syndrome" was Mikolaj Kopernik, a Polish clergyman and physician with an interest in astronomy. Copernicus, as we Latinize his name, was born in 1473 and educated in Poland and Italy, returning to Poland to practice medicine and to engage in ecclesiastical administrative duties after the turn of the sixteenth century. Though recognized as early as 1514 by Pope Leo X for his astronomical competence, Copernicus was shy about publishing his theories during his lifetime. Better known locally for his medical and financial skills than for his astronomical speculations, his theories were first described to the public in 1540 by his follower and biographer, Georg Joachim Rheticus. It was Rheticus, too, who finally persuaded Copernicus on his deathbed to allow publication of *De Revolutionibus Orbium Coelestium*, which appeared in 1543, the year of his death.

Copernicus was no revolutionary in spirit. On the contrary, there were behind his agenda for astronomical reform many deep premodern values. What seems to have disturbed him most was the failure of the Ptolemaic approach to be sufficiently systematic in defense of what we have seen to be the oldest and most precious assumptions about the heavens: that astronomical motions must be "worthy" of a kosmos, that is, must be perfectly regular and uniform. The Ptolemaic approach (too ad hoc properly to be called a "system," Copernicus complained) mocked Plato's and Aristotle's requirement that such intrinsically intelligible motions be used to make sense of things. In his privately circulated *Commentariolus*, written perhaps as early as 1512, as he began to search for better ways to honor the commitments of "our ancestors," Copernicus writes that

> . . . they considered it absolutely absurd that a heavenly body, which is a perfect sphere, should not always move in a uniform manner. . . . Yet

the planetary theories of Ptolemy and most other astronomers, although consistent with the numerical data . . . present no small difficulty. For these theories were not adequate unless one also thought up certain equants: it then seemed that the planets moved with uniform velocity neither on their deferent circles nor around the centres of their epicycles. Such a system appears neither sufficiently absolute nor sufficiently attractive to the mind (Toulmin 1961: 170–71).

"Equants"—theoretical centers of planetary motion located in empty space— were the most outrageous affront against intelligibility. Copernicus called them "monstrous" (Kuhn 1957: 139) because they were not only completely without physical interpretation but also completely without coherence (like "hands, feet, head and other members . . . each part excellently drawn, but not related to a single body") with other elements of the theory. They were simply the *computational* center from which the motions of the planetary epicycles *would* be uniform. But these equants had nothing to do with (and were not in the same place as) the *observational* center for astronomers, nor were either of these points the same as the recomputed *geometrical* center of the universe from which distances of the planets were to be measured. This was intellectually scandalous, not at all in keeping with the high ideals appropriate to the subject. For this reason Copernicus reported in his early *Commentariolus* that:

Being aware of these defects, I spent much time considering whether one might perhaps find a more reasonable arrangement of circles, from which every apparent inequality could be calculated, and in which every element would move uniformly about its own centre, as the rule of absolute motion requires (Toulmin 1961: 171).

Copernicus' second great premodern value assumption—that the geometry of heavenly realities and motions must be no less than perfect circles— goes intimately together with commitment to perfect uniformity of motion, as these quotations have already indicated. As long ago as Parmenides, the sphere was postulated as the only shape adequate for a perfect kosmos, lacking in nothing, allowing no pits or holes or declivities, and yet comfortingly finite and intelligible. This stood to reason for Plato and Aristotle and to all their followers; it stood to reason for Copernicus as well. Book One, Part One of *De Revolutionibus* is entitled "That the Universe is Spherical," and begins:

In the first place we must observe that the Universe is spherical. This is either because that figure is the most perfect, as not being articulated but whole and complete in itself; or because it is the most capacious and therefore best suited for that which is to contain and preserve all things . . . (Kuhn 1957: 145).

And in Book One, Part Four he continues, concerning the motions appropriate to the heavens:

> We now note that the motion of heavenly bodies is circular. Rotation is natural to a sphere and by that very act is its shape expressed. For here we deal with the simplest kind of body, wherein neither beginning nor end may be discerned nor, if it rotate ever in the same place, may the one be distinguished from the other (Kuhn 1957: 147).

From our vantage there seem many irregularities in the motions of the planets, even apparent retrograde motion, but these must be accounted for by none but perfect circular, uniform motions.

> Now therein it must be that divers motions are conjoined, since a simple celestial body cannot move irregularly in a single circle. For such irregularity must come of unevenness either in the moving force (whether inherent or acquired) or in the form of the revolving body. Both these alike the mind abhors regarding the most perfectly disposed bodies (Kuhn 1957: 147).

Copernicus launched his effort at reform out of shared commitment with the "ancestors" concerning the values a worthy theory must reflect. In this he was not alone. Certain other medieval thinkers had been aware of the intellectually shabby methods employed in Ptolemaic calculation. Nicholas of Cusa, for example, had been among them. Nor was Copernicus alone in his reverence for the Sun. Plato, we saw, had taken the Sun as symbol in the Myth of the Cave for the Form of Forms, the Good itself, from which being and value and intelligibility all endlessly flow. Copernicus shared this tradition of deep respect (if not—as a good Christian—of literal worship) for the Sun, and reasoned that it, not Earth, is far more worthy of centrality in a properly ordered kosmos. Marsilio Ficino, whose importance for Leonardo we noted, had written in his influential treatise, *On the Sun:*

> Nothing reveals the nature of the Good [which is God] more fully than the light [of the sun]. First, light is the most brilliant and clearest of sensible objects. Second, there is nothing which spreads out so easily, broadly, or rapidly as light. Third, like a caress, it penetrates all things harmlessly and most gently. Fourth, the heat which accompanies it fosters and nourishes all things and is the universal generator and mover. . . .

Similarly the Good is itself spread everywhere, and it soothes and entices all things. It does not work by compulsion, but through the love which accompanies it, like heat [which accompanies light]. This love allures all objects so that they freely embrace the Good. . . . Perhaps light is itself the celestial spirit's sense of sight, or its act of seeing, operating from a distance, linking all things to heaven, yet never leaving heaven nor mixing with external things. . . . Just look at the skies, I pray you, citizens of heavenly fatherland. . . . The sun can signify God himself to you, and who shall dare to say the sun is false (Kuhn 1957: 130).

The tenor of Ficino is echoed in Copernicus' Chapter 10, Book One, of his *De Revolutionibus* when, waxing eloquent about his heliocentric "hypothesis," he writes:

In the middle of all sits Sun enthroned. In this most beautiful temple could we place this luminary in any better position from which he can illuminate the whole at once? He is rightly called the Lamp, the Mind, the Ruler of the Universe; Hermes Trismegistus names him the Visible God, Sophocles' Electra calls him the All-seeing. So the Sun sits as upon a royal throne ruling his children the planets which circle round him. The Earth has the Moon at her service. As Aristotle says, in his *On [the Generation of] Animals*, the Moon has the closest relationship with the Earth. Meanwhile the Earth conceives by the Sun, and becomes pregnant with an annual rebirth (Kuhn 1957: 179–80).

Despite this obvious matrix of central premodern values, the marks of distinctly modern values are visible not only in the later consequences of the Copernican reform, when modernity itself arises in the next century, but also in other attitudes of Copernicus himself. A powerful motivation in his labors was the search for conceptual simplicity. William of Ockham himself could hardly have been more outraged at the "multiplication of entities" represented by the "monstrous" astronomical theories of Copernicus' Ptolemaic adversaries. The simplicity sought was of course not psychological ease. For common sense the Copernican system made everything more complicated, since it made the world whirl and spin in most unnerving ways. John Donne expressed this common sense vertigo when he wrote:

> [The] new Philosophy calls all in doubt,
> The Element of fire is quite put out;
> The Sun is lost, and th'earth, and no man's wit
> Can well direct him where to look for it
> (Donne 1990: lines 205–8).

But for Copernicus the simplicity was in the system. One interlocking arrangement, using only perfect circles and uniform motions, dispensing with those loathsome equants, could now account for the observations. True, there was still need for a few remaining epicycles to be postulated to accommodate the observations; but their number was down from eighty-three to seventeen; and motions and distances could at last be plotted from the same point.

A second distinctly modern value for Copernicus was reflected in his willingness to accept the humbling fact that this central point is no longer the same as the location of the human observer. The distinct anthropocentric bias of much premodern valuing is gone. This is the first step in a long journey away from the centrality of the human position. The vector is set. We shall make more stops along it.

Third, more characteristic of modern than premodern attitudes, Copernicus was quite willing to challenge the literal reading of Scripture. This was tolerated in his own time, but it did not sit well with conservatives, Catholic or Protestant. We shall encounter the Catholic Inquisition later, but Protestant opposition was nearly immediate. Martin Luther, hearing rumors in 1539, even before the appearance of *De Revolutionibus*, that some astronomer (he says "astrologer") was working on a heliocentric theory, pronounced his disfavor:

> People give ear to an upstart astrologer who strove to show that the earth revolves, not the heavens or the firmament, the sun and the moon. . . . This fool wishes to reverse the entire science of astronomy; but sacred Scripture tells us [Joshua 10:13] that Joshua commanded the sun to stand still, and not the earth (Kuhn 1957: 191).

Shortly after Copernicus' death, John Calvin similarly condemns the theory: "Who will venture to place the authority of Copernicus above that of the Holy Spirit?" For evidence he quotes Psalm 93, "The earth also is established, that it cannot be moved." And Philipp Melanchthon, friend of Luther and leader of the Reformation, thundered:

> The eyes are witnesses that the heavens revolve in the space of twenty-four hours. But certain men, either from the love of novelty, or to make a display of ingenuity, have concluded that the earth moves; and they maintain that neither the eighth sphere nor the sun revolves. . . . Now, it is a want of honesty and decency to assert such notions publicly, and the example is pernicious. It is the part of a good mind to accept the truth as revealed by God and to acquiesce in it (Kuhn 1957: 191).

Beyond his readiness to challenge Scripture, we finally see in Copernicus a modern readiness (also highly objectionable to the Protestants just quoted) to prefer the results of abstruse mathematics to the deliverances of common sense and prima facie experience. This too has the makings of a major story in the formation of the modern worldview. To it we shall soon return.

NONMATHEMATICAL EARLY MODERNS

Meanwhile, it will be worthwhile casting an eye on three early founders of modernity who are noteworthy precisely because mathematics did *not* stand high in their scheme of values. All three were conscious of a historical threshold being passed from the "old" to something "new." All wanted nothing more than to contribute to the unformed but promising age they felt ready to be born.

The oldest of the three was William Gilbert, born just a year after the publication of *De Revolutionibus*, in Colchester, England, in 1544. Gilbert, a court physician, distinguished himself by research in electricity and magnetism. He accepted part of Copernicus' theory: the part involving the daily rotation of the earth. But on the more radical motion of the earth annually around the sun he was noncommittal.

Gilbert's special fascination was with the magnet, and most particularly with the globular lodestone, which he saw as a micro-earth. To understand the lodestone would be to advance understanding of the great ball on which we live, he argued.

Why does the lodestone draw iron to itself? Gilbert's classic contribution to magnetic theory, *De Magnete magneticisque corporibus et de magno magnete Tellure physiologia nova* (New Physics of the Magnet and of Magnetic Bodies, and of the Big Magnet, the Earth), appeared in 1600 and drew much admiring attention. Galileo, who tended to read few works by others, read it as early as 1602 and discussed it extensively in his *Dialogues*. Johannes Kepler too made favorable references to *De Magnete* in his own writings. As we shall see, Gilbert's methods were entirely different from theirs. He observed carefully, but he did not convert his observations into measurements that could in turn be converted into mathematical formulae.

Galileo and Kepler are representative of the age to come; Gilbert is not fully part of that age. He is, instead, a nonmathematical, sheerly qualitative empiricist. Yet neither is he fully part of the age coming to its end. Unlike the scholastic thinkers of the "old" era that Gilbert is consciously leaving behind, he rejects all arguments from authority. He urges us to let nature speak for itself, and to let it speak directly to our eyes and ears. Gilbert wants to give credit to the wise of olden times when credit is due, but he is not shy about making claims for the new age. "Our time has discovered and revealed a good deal which [the Ancients] would gladly welcome if they were still living" (Dijksterhuis 1961: 392).

The qualitative observations made by Gilbert reinforced his belief that the earth is a huge magnet, whose poles attract, and repel, respectively, the opposite poles of such smaller magnets as compass needles. This observed attraction and repulsion across large distances led him to argue further that the magnetic influence of the earth must extend out indefinitely far into the solar system. He also credited the magnetic powers of earth with holding the whole globe together in one piece as it spins and with maintaining the axis of rotation stable, pointing always at the same fixed stars.

But what exactly accounts for the attraction and repulsion phenomena? Gilbert found it necessary to give an account of what lies behind the observed facts. This commitment to "deep" explanation, sometimes shared and sometimes rejected by later moderns, is familiar from premodern times. Gilbert chose a theory familiar from the earliest of premodern philosophy for his own explanation: animate agency. Thales, the first of the great metaphysical pioneers (Chapter 2), had theorized, among other things, that all things—and magnets in particular—are full of *psyche*, or soul, the principle of self-movement. The presence of soul in self-moving things was taken as fundamental by Plato and Aristotle (Chapter 3) and by their successors (Chapter 4) for many hundreds of years. Combining a modern insistence on empirical observation with a long premodern tradition, Gilbert concluded that the *coito*, or coming together, of magnets is a matter of soul reaching out to soul. The very principle of the unity of the earth itself is at work drawing—not violently or coercively but quasi-voluntarily—magnetized things to one another. The souls of magnets are not rational, they do not even work through sense-organs; but in this they have a certain advantage over human souls, since magnets work directly and infallibly, while human souls, requiring so many intermediaries between themselves and the world, allow mistakes unheard of in simpler magnetic realms.

The earth itself, being a huge magnet, also has a soul. It would be an indignity, indeed, to deny a soul to the earth when souls are readily granted to such lowly animate things as ants, Gilbert says. All the astronomical bodies are ensouled as well, relating to one another across space with mutual attraction in the cosmic solidarity of systematic unity. In this way, Gilbert offers a world picture uniting the rocks of the earth with the planets and the stars. It is not a mathematical or mechanical picture, but in its own way it provides a semi-Copernican vision of the kosmos that goes beyond positional astronomy to a kind of astrophysics, giving an account not attempted by Copernicus of how our universe is held together. As a theory of reality it is a transition between old and new, valuing the need for coherence and insisting on experimental adequacy based on firsthand observation, but not requiring quantification or microanalysis. The former values allow the theory its holistic charm; the latter values allow it to rest with vague qualitative conceptions that future moderns would find it necessary to replace.

In contrast to Gilbert, Giordano Bruno was in many respects not modern at all. He was in his own time more a magus, or magician, figure and certainly was no scientist. Born in 1548 near Naples, Italy, he early joined the Dominican order; while still in his twenties, he fled his monastery when charged with heresy, and never returned to Christianity, either Catholic or Protestant. He spent most of his life wandering Europe, giving lessons in memory magic, lecturing on his views of the universe at centers of learning, and dodging warrants for his arrest. He was picked up in 1591 in Venice, while on a trip to teach a nobleman the secrets of memory, was tried twice by the Inquisition, once in Venice and once in Rome, and, refusing to recant his views, was publicly burnt alive in 1600 in the Campo di' Fiori in Rome.

He fits into this narrative, whether he is officially classed as a "modern" or not, for at least two reasons. First, his rejection of Christianity was deliberate and bold. He could have had a secure position at the University of Paris, but refused it rather than attend Mass. He was an independent thinker who made no pretense of joining in the consensus of Christendom. Even when he explicated his views on the universe, which reflected an interesting amalgam of Nicholas of Cusa's embrace of the infinite and Copernicus' demotion of the earth from central place, he made no effort to relate his ideas to Christian doctrine, even when it would have been easy and obvious to have done so (as both these Nicholases, solid churchmen, had in fact done before him). In Bruno's story we see embodied a significant modern value: the importance of independent, secular theorizing, outside the Church, unbeholden to any of the constraints of orthodoxy.

Second, Bruno was an unqualified supporter of heliocentrism, but he expanded Copernicanism beyond its limit to populate Cusa's infinite space with infinite numbers of solar systems and infinite worlds—indefinitely many of which must be populated, he held, by intelligent species like ours. Of Copernicus himself, Bruno was more than a little contemptuous, calling him "only a mathematician," who had missed the larger significance of his own revolution. In Bruno's positive evaluation of the infinite, particularly of infinite space and an infinite creation, we see a foretaste of modern Newtonian cosmology.

It is a proto-Newtonianism, however, without its mechanism and without its mathematics. Bruno did not merely ignore the values of mathematics, as Gilbert did; he lashed out against mathematics, especially the mathematicians of Oxford, where he spent some years, as fostering "pedantry." To replace mathematics, he offered his own magical numerology, full of qualitative meanings; and to replace theology, a metaphysics strikingly anticipatory of Spinoza (Chapter 6) and Leibniz (Chapter 7). God, he argued, is the first *monad*, the creator of all the infinitely many others, and the sustaining indweller as both matter and mind in all. Creating, God is *natura naturans*; created, God is *natura naturata*. The creative emanation from God is experienced as matter, but all matter is alive; when matter gains consciousness in the human person and thinks of God, it is God returning again to God, the One who ties all the infinite universe together, vibrant in its energy of life.

This of course is not modern at all. Or is it? If Spinoza and Leibniz belong uncontroversially to the modern, why not Bruno? The difference lies largely in attitudes toward mathematics and magic. Spinoza was deeply imbued in geometrical method; and Leibniz was a mathematical genius, in a class with Newton, with whom he disputed priority for the invention of calculus. Bruno despised mathematics and reveled in the occult arts. Some of his values make him an early founder of modernity; others make him an antithesis to the modern spirit. It sharpens our concept of modernity itself to reflect on which values are which.

Unlike Bruno, Sir Francis Bacon, Baron Verulam, Viscount St. Albans, is nearly always credited with a role—sometimes a central role—in the founding of modernity. But it is quite reasonable to wonder why. He made no scientific discoveries on his own. His proposed scientific method was never used and is unworkable. He dismissed Copernicus. He ignored mathematics. He offered a complex (and obscure) theory of "forms" less clear than the Aristotelianism he denounced. And yet he was possessed by the sense of standing on the brink of a new age, in which government-sponsored scientific institutions would revolutionize human thought and—no less important—the comforts and securities of human life.

Bacon was born in 1561 when both Gilbert and Bruno were in their teens. His father was Sir Nicholas Bacon, a high ranking official of Queen Elizabeth's court. As the youngest son, he inherited nothing on his father's death and needed, from the age of eighteen, to live by his wits and on his "connections"—which he proceeded to do without scruple. His greatest benefactor was Queen Elizabeth's favorite, the Earl of Essex, who wangled him as many preferments as possible, guided his career on its rapid upward rise, and eventually provided generously for him out of his own estates. Later, when Bacon had risen in the Queen's favor and Essex had fallen, it was Bacon who, to please the Queen, brought the prosecutions against his greatest benefactor and saw to his execution. When James I succeeded the childless Elizabeth to the throne in 1603, Bacon continued to please and to rise. He argued for an absolute monarch and acted accordingly, fawning over his monarch's every wish, thus being steadily rewarded with lands, ennoblement, and the highest post in the country, Lord Chancellor. At age sixty, three years after reaching this pinnacle, he was discovered taking petty bribes in a court case and was utterly disgraced, stripped of all his offices and "connections." His remaining five years were spent quietly in seclusion at Gorhambury, writing and dreaming about the advancement of science. He died in 1626, after catching cold while standing in bad weather, stuffing a chicken's body with snow to see how long it would last when thus refrigerated.

This sort of empiricism, collection of facts such as the preservation of chicken meat under snow-cooled conditions, is a good symbol for Bacon's idea of scientific method. Like William Gilbert, he valued looking for himself at the world and letting the world speak directly, not from books. Like Gilbert, too, he valued carefully contrived experiments. But Bacon added an extra tone— that of a high judicial prosecutor—to the engines of experiment that would force nature to reveal the truth. Accustomed to authorizing torture to gain confessions (which he had agreeably consented to at the king's whim in at least one famous instance), Bacon writes of his project for a scientific "natural history":

> I mean it to be a history not only of nature free and at large (when she is left to her own course and does her work her own way)—such as that of the heavenly bodies, meteors, earth and sea, minerals, plants, animals— but much more of nature under constraint and vexed; that is to say, when by art and the hand of man she is forced out of her natural state, and squeezed and moulded (Bacon 1960: 25).

In Bacon's gender-specific language, we may even have the hint of a sadistic sexual gratification at the thought of nature bound, twisted, and squeezed. This use of coercion is not an incidental element in his recommended method for scientists. "Nay (to say the plain truth), I do in fact (low and vulgar as men may think it) count more upon this part both for helps and safeguards than upon the other, seeing that the nature of things betrays itself more readily under the vexations of art than in its natural freedom."

The delightful process of forcing nature to tell us her secrets establishes modern science, as Bacon envisions it, both in a phase of dominance—where nature is "squeezed and moulded"—and in a phase of submission, as well, where she must be obeyed.

> For man is but the servant and interpreter of nature: what he does and what he knows is only what he has observed of nature's order in fact or in thought; beyond this he knows nothing and can do nothing. For the chain of causes cannot by any force be loosed or broken, nor can nature be commanded except by being obeyed (Bacon 1960: 29).

Until his disgrace, Bacon was a man of power. For him the point of science was not mere theory but action. He mocks the ancient Greeks for not having reached intellectual puberty. They were just boys. "Assuredly they have that which is characteristic of boys: they are prompt to prattle, but cannot generate: for their wisdom abounds in words, but is barren of works" (Bacon 1960: 70). For Bacon, the priorities are reversed.

> For the end which this science of mine proposes is the invention not of arguments but of arts; not of things in accordance with principles, but of principles themselves; not of probable reasons, but of designations and directions for works. And as the intention is different, so, accordingly, is the effect; the effect of the one being to overcome an opponent in argument, of the other to command nature in action (Bacon 1960: 19).

For this we need to get beyond the "old" sciences, which in Bacon's sexual metaphor are simply impotent in the loins—or worse.

> So that the state of learning as it now is appears to be represented to the life in the old fable of Scylla, who had the head and face of a virgin, but her womb was hung round with barking monsters, from which she could not be delivered. For in like manner the sciences to which we are accustomed have certain general positions which are specious and flattering; but as soon as they come to particulars, which are as the parts of generation, when they should produce fruit and works, then arise contentions and barking disputations, which are the end of the matter and all the issue they can yield (Bacon 1960: 8).

To end this frustrating situation, Bacon foresees a world with large government-supported scientific institutions engaging in experiment after experiment to fill up his suggested Tables (of Affirmation, of Negation, and of Comparison) that will eventually reveal "not empty notions but well defined, and such as nature would really recognize as her first principle, and such as lie at the heart and marrow of things" (Bacon 1960: 20).

In all this, Bacon has no interest in mathematical reasoning or indeed in abstruse theorizing. "First principles" are useless. Since what really matters is applications for the betterment of human life, science should shun both abstraction and what he calls "dissection," (what we think of as analysis) and remain firmly committed to the middle level of daily experience. In this atomic age, it is ironic to hear Bacon on this point:

> Nor again is it a lesser evil that in [premodern] philosophies and contemplations their labor is spent in investigating and handling the first principles of things and the highest generalities of nature; whereas utility and the means of working result entirely from things intermediate. Hence it is that men cease not from abstracting nature till they come to potential and uninformed matter, nor on the other hand from dissecting nature till

they reach the atom; things which, even if true, can do but little for the welfare of mankind (Bacon 1960: 65).

A founder of modernity? In important ways, Bacon was a trumpet player, a herald, and a visionary of some values of modernity, for better or for worse. Though enormously influential as rhetorical defender of scientific manipulation and domination of nature, he was certainly not, as Voltaire and Diderot later termed him, "the father of modern science." But he was the cheerleader (and brilliantly eloquent voice) for experimentalism, institutional scientific exploration, and knowledge-generated, systematic technological exploitation of nature. His vision was powerful and admired by important future scientists including Isaac Newton. To them, we now return.

KEPLER AND GALILEO

One of the most notable of these is Johannes Kepler, born in 1571 in Württemberg, Germany, in the town of Weil, where his grandfather was mayor. At the age of three, already weakened by premature birth, Kepler survived smallpox with hands and eyesight permanently impaired; at eight, he suffered the desertion of his family by his father, who fled to escape both debts and an extremely shrewish wife. In her later years she would be tried (and acquitted, thanks to her scholar son's heroic efforts) for witchcraft. Family bankruptcy, requiring him to engage in farmwork, interrupted his first schooling. But by the age of thirteen, Kepler's intelligence shone through his physical handicaps and he was given a chance for theological education at the Lutheran seminaries of Adelberg and Maulbronn. At seventeen, his examinations were so brilliant that he was admitted on a scholarship to the University of Tübingen, where he both absorbed classical lore and, in private, was introduced to Copernican theory by his lifelong mentor Michael Maestlin, an astronomer. Although personally convinced that Copernicus was right, Maestlin was reluctant to open his public lectures to controversy. Thanks to him and Kepler's other professors, at twenty-three he was chosen to fill the vacant chair of astronomy at the University of Gratz, which the Lutheran state of Styria in southern Austria had placed at the disposal of the Tübingen faculty.

At Gratz and throughout his career, Kepler supplemented his income by casting astrological predictions, as was expected of all astronomers. He defended the making of such horoscopes. His vision of the solar system allowed for "influences"; at any rate, it was a way of supplementing official salaries that seemed always in arrears. "Nature," he later wrote, "which has conferred upon every animal the means of subsistence, has given astrology as an adjunct and ally to astronomy" (Clerke 1882: 46).

Kepler's principal work was in bringing together the values of mathematical beauty with the values of rigorous observational precision. As early as his Tübingen days, he was convinced—in a Pythagorean spirit—that reality must be mathematically meaningful. Abstract formal reasons are the fundamental causes in the kosmos. This must be shown, not in some vague hand-waving way, but with full detail and in exact conformity to the best evidence available.

Only a year after his arrival in Gratz, Kepler experienced the ecstasy of success in realizing these values. On July 9, 1595, while not yet twenty-four, he rejoiced in his notes on "discovering" that the distances of the six (then known) planets from one another can be understood by fitting their greatest and least distances, as measured from the central Sun, into the five regular solids. The orbit of Mercury would fit inside an octahedron that just defines the outer orbit of Venus; between the orbit of Venus and Earth just fits an icosahedron; between Earth and Mars there is just room for a dodecahedron; between Mars and Jupiter fits a tetrahedron; and the space between Jupiter and Saturn is exactly right for a cube. Plato's disciple had proven that these and *only* these five could be the regular solids. And now, using each only once but using them *all*, Kepler could interpret the observable universe in the light of geometrical principle. He published his results in *Mysterium Cosmographicum* in 1596 through Tübingen and was rewarded with immediate fame and praise, including favorable correspondence from Galileo, then professor of mathematics at Padua, and from the Danish astronomer, Tycho Brahe, professor of astronomy at Prague.

Unfortunately for Kepler, the new ruler of Styria, Archduke Ferdinand, adopted a policy of intolerance against Protestant clergy and professors, issuing a decree of banishment in 1598. Kepler fled toward Hungary, but thanks to the benevolent intervention of the Jesuits, was allowed to return to his post. His classrooms soon emptied, however, and he was acutely uncomfortable in the prevailing atmosphere. He considered returning to Tübingen, but by then the theologians there had imposed a rigid code of belief for all faculty that Kepler could not bring himself to accept. It was with relief that he received an invitation from Tycho Brahe to become his assistant in Prague. About the same time that Bruno was being burned in Rome, Kepler moved north from Gratz to work with Brahe.

Brahe was the most distinguished astronomer of his time. He had not accepted the full Copernican theory, particularly the centrality of the Sun with its implication of an Earth in motion. He had worked out a compromise theory in which the five planets, excluding Earth, could be described as heliocentric, with the whole system swinging around the stationary Earth. It was a "middle of the road," common-sense position, squaring the greater mathematical simplicities of Copernicanism with the perceived stability of the ground beneath our feet. Kepler, a convinced Copernican, was not persuaded. But in addition and with greater long-run import, Brahe was a superb observer and had amassed the most accurate readings of the sky possible before the invention of the telescope. When Brahe unexpectedly died in 1601, this treasure of observations fell to Kepler, who was immediately appointed Brahe's successor. The empirical anchor for Kepler's rigorously disciplined mathematical speculations over the coming years had been provided by Brahe's patient labors.

From the beginning of his residency in Prague, Kepler devoted himself to an especially close analysis of the orbit of Mars, whose eccentricities had long been especially difficult to rationalize. Finally, with the aid of Brahe's observational data and his own dogged insistence on mathematical intelligibility, Kepler announced a stunning result. In 1609, the same year Galileo first placed a homemade telescope to his eye, Kepler published *Astronomia nova*, in which he abandoned the long commitment of astronomers, including Copernicus, to perfect circles and uniform motions, of the ideal sort that Plato and Aristotle had imagined worthy of any "decent" kosmos. Kepler proposed instead, as his First Law of Planetary motion, that the actual mathematical form of all the planets' orbits is an ellipse with the Sun at one focus. To achieve this took years of trial and error, false starts, failed hypotheses, and frustration. But the reward was in the formal simplicity of the result: no need for epicycles, equants, deferents, or ad hoc mathematical fix-up procedures. The planets in their elliptical orbits could not be thought to be moving at the same speed all the time: as they get farther from the Sun, they slow down, as they get closer, they speed up. Yet, Kepler announced, a wonderful hidden mathematical uniformity could be expressed by a Second Law: the *area* within the ellipse swept out by a line between the Sun and a planet in its orbit is always equal for equal times.

Kepler also suggested that the motions of the planets are caused by the central Sun, reaching out somehow to push its dependent associates around and around. Invoking the principle of the lever, which is stronger when the distance between fulcrum and weight is shorter, he argued that the force of the Sun on the planets is diminished by distance in a similar way. He appealed also to the principle of magnetism, citing William Gilbert (though himself a non-Copernican) as an inspiration. Beneath it all, however, is the calm assurance that mathematical reasons are themselves causes for things, sufficient for satisfaction of the understanding.

More radically, and vitally for our narrative, Kepler thereby narrowed the conception of "intelligible Forms" from the broadly inclusive Platonic and Aristotelian tradition that welcomed as "Forms" *all* universal characteristics (including time-and-space-transcending general properties such as colors and tones and odors) to a rigorously exclusive *mathematical*—quantitative and geometrical—definition of what counts as "formal." The other (sensible) Forms might well exist. Kepler did not go so far as to deny them metaphysical standing in the universe. But from his perspective they were useless for theory or explanation. For the question of the status of values in nature—especially values other than those open to measurement and mathematics—this was to be a portentous preference.

Kepler continued to work for such formally precise understanding during the decade following publication of *Astronomia nova* and turned to the mathematics of musical harmony to explain, more fully than his earlier theory of the five regular solids could, the distances of the planets from one another. He became dissatisfied with the imprecision of his youthful theory of the solids, recognizing approximations and deficiencies that led him to conclude (without abandoning the theory) that "the true proportions of the distances between the planets and the Sun have not been taken from the regular solids alone. For the Creator, who is the very source of geometry and (as Plato puts it) 'is forever doing geometry', does not depart from his own specifications . . ." (Toulmin 1961: 205–206). Kepler's Third Law of Motion published in *Harmonices mundi* in 1619, rests on a highly abstract mathematical relation between the orbital period of a planet and its distance from the Sun. It is that the square of the planetary year (the time required for one complete revolution in orbit) varies with the cube of the distance from the Sun.

The human mind, Kepler held, is especially created for such mathematical understanding. "Just as the eye was made to see colours, and the ear to hear sound, so the human mind was made to understand, not whatever you please, but quantity" (Burtt 1954: 68). When such quantity is presented in coherent form, as in mathematical ratios or other formulae, the mind's yen for understanding is ipso facto satisfied. Only mathematics gives full understanding, then; merely qualitative experience, insofar as it is not subject to quantification and mathematical formulation, evades our grasp.

It is a short (but metaphysically portentous) step from declaring a quality *unknowable*—outside the scope of cognitive capture, but nonetheless real—to dismissing it as *purely subjective*, the ephemeral by-product of the actual mathematical world and an observing mind. This step was to be taken by Galileo.

Galileo Galilei, Kepler's slightly older contemporary and friendly correspondent, was born in Pisa to a relatively impoverished (but historically distinguished) family in February 1564. Vincenzo Galilei, his father, was a mathematician and a musician who hoped his son would make a better fortune by becoming a physician. Young Galileo was a child prodigy, showing the sort of universal aptitude that an earlier Tuscan, Leonardo da Vinci—born in the neighborhood of Florence—had manifested in similar measure. Galileo's earliest education began with monks at the monastery of Vallombrosa, near Florence, where he excelled in all but Aristotelian logic, which he loathed. Before the young man could become too involved in the religious life, Vincenzo Galilei removed him from the monastery and enrolled him in November 1581 in medical studies at the University of Pisa. While carrying on his program, Galileo showed astonishing skills in music, painting, and literature. The turning point of his early life came when he happened to overhear a lecture on geometry given by Ostilio Ricci. The subject (from which his father had apparently protected him) set him afire; and, with Ricci's help, he mastered the field in short order. Before completing his degree, Galileo was forced by family finances to withdraw from the university; but he returned to Florence prepared to lecture, tinker, and publish on his own. His first publication on his invention of a hydrostatic balance was a resounding success, leading to patronage by a nobleman, Marchese Guidubaldo del Monte, who was much interested in science. After commissioning Galileo to solve scientific problems for him, the Marchese arranged his appointment in 1589 as mathematical lecturer at the University of Pisa, from which he had been obliged earlier to withdraw, still uncredentialed.

After two youthful years at Pisa, where he delighted in embarrassing the Aristotelians with their errors in the dynamics of motion (he may really have dropped heavy and light objects from the Tower of Pisa to show that velocity is proportional not to weight but to time), he realized, after being publicly hissed in class, that he had made too many enemies. Resigning his post, he returned unemployed to Florence just before his father died and the family fortunes came to rest on his shoulders. Luckily, the benevolent Marchese Guidubaldo had influence with the Venetian Senate, which controlled professorships at Padua, and Galileo was appointed to the chair of mathematics in 1592. He remained at the University of Padua from 1592 until 1610, a period of great productivity and general popularity. For once in his life, Galileo avoided controversy, lecturing publicly from Ptolemaic principles while privately accepting Copernicanism, as he revealed to Kepler in his enthusiastic letter of August 4, 1597, praising *Mysterium Cosmographicum* in lavish terms.

In April 1609, word reached Venice from Holland about a new device capable of increasing the apparent size of distant objects, invented in the previous year by the Dutch optician Hans Lippershey. Galileo's genius immediately asserted itself, and in short order he produced his own telescope, improving on his own models until he had at least a 20-power instrument, which he manufactured in quantity, sending them around Europe where they were in great demand. In Prague, Kepler happily received his in 1610.

Once Galileo turned this many-powered instrument toward the heavens he held his peace no more. Copernicus was right. What had been an attractive theoretical possibility was now open to plain sight. The universe could be seen to be much larger, just as Copernicus had predicted, than the Ptolemaic theory allowed. Through the telescope, many more stars appeared than were visible to the naked eye. Further, the apparent size of fixed stars did not increase but remained point sources, thus indicating (also as Copernicus had concluded) that they were all much farther away than previously thought. The planets all grew in apparent size. Jupiter in particular could be seen to have satellites of its own, in a wonderful visible analogy to the Copernican solar system and in suggestive similarity to our Earth and Moon. The Moon, too, showed mountains and craters revealed by changing shadows on its surface. Later, Galileo even observed the phases of Venus predicted by Copernicus as a consequence of that inner planet's location between Sun and Earth. The Sun could be seen to have spots on its surface, which rotated regularly, in a grand analogy to the Copernican diurnal rotation of the Earth.

Galileo's discoveries with the telescope so impressed the Venetian Senate that he was given a professorship for life, with no attached teaching duties, but with a splendid salary. Therefore, in September 1610, he returned to Florence to press his astronomical research and his campaign for Copernicanism. He took his case to Rome in 1611, impressing the dignitaries who heard him lecture and demonstrate his telescope. For five years, the argument was in the balance, and Galileo was full of hope; but in February 1616, the decision of the Holy Office was negative. He was warned not to hold or teach the Copernican doctrine. In the next month, the Congregation of the Index placed *De Revolutionibus* off limits to everyone, except as an *ex hypothesi* theory. For seven years, Galileo remained silent and in seclusion in Florence. He broke this silence in 1623 with his book on comets, *Saggiatore*, which was warmly received despite its thinly veiled Copernican sympathies. Thus encouraged and with a personal friend now elected to the papacy as Pope Urban VIII, who gave him permission to write a "neutral" discussion on the Ptolemaic and Copernican systems, he went to work on the book that was to undo him, *Dialogues Concerning the Two Great Systems of the World*. Galileo was simply not ready to be impartial. Despite pro forma disclaimers at the beginning and end, the overwhelming force of his argument was pro-Copernican, a brilliant destruction of the premodern world scheme.

Arrested, threatened, and thoroughly intimidated by the authorities, Galileo did what was needed to survive. In 1633, he publicly renounced his Copernicanism. This submission to raw power turned out not particularly important for the course of modern thought. The damage to the premodern world picture had been done. His *Dialogues*, widely translated, were devoured throughout Europe, even as his telescopes were telling their own first-hand tale. Kepler's theories, especially as embodied in his unprecedentedly accurate *Rudolphine Tables* of planetary appearances (1627), were gradually winning the day on theoretical elegance and practical applicability. Galileo's remaining nine years, spent comfortably under house arrest near Florence, were devoted to consolidating the Paduan studies on motion and on the strength of materials. These mature reflections, sent from Italy for publication in Leiden as *Discourses and*

Mathematical Demonstrations Concerning Two New Sciences, appeared in 1638. Despite blindness, he continued to correspond with colleagues and to work on the development of pendulum clock mechanisms. Galileo died near his seventy-eighth birthday, in the year of Isaac Newton's birth.

We must not be misled by the drama of Galileo's life, especially by the famous controversies with the Church over Copernicanism, in discerning the main significances his thought carries for modern values in our dominant picture of reality. As I suggested, the Copernican revolution was on its way to winning acceptance quite apart from Galileo's contributions to the battle. He contributed very little to enhancing the state of theory itself. In fact, he took a large step backward, so far as theory is concerned, by ignoring his friend Kepler's brilliant Laws of Planetary Motion. Many have puzzled about why this should have been. Some have put it down to a kind of egoism, that discoveries like the Law of Elliptical Motion could not count for Galileo if they were not made by himself. But it seems more likely that he tactfully ignored his friend's work at this point because he did not agree that this was a true discovery. Galileo never abandoned the commitment to the ancient value of perfect circular motion. Insofar as he tried his hand at matters of planetary motion, he continued to play at "saving the appearances" with circular epicycles on circular orbits.

This may seem strange, since Galileo's greatest contribution to astronomy was to destroy the isolation of that science from terrestrial sciences. It was his telescope, enhancing the power of the human eye, not the content of pure theory itself, that was his main contribution to astronomy. And what power the eye—multiplied by hundreds of other confirming eyes—had thus been given to erode ancient attitudes! From earliest times, as we have seen, the notion of kosmos has carried the value of "well ordered," "decent," and even "perfect." The heavens had been the realm of the unsullied, the divine. True, the implication of heavenly "immutability" had been seriously challenged by the appearance of new stars, especially by the nova of 1572, carefully observed by Tycho Brahe, and by another nova of 1604, observed and argued over by Kepler, Galileo, and many others. (Apparently earlier novae, now known to have existed, were simply not "seen" by eyes convinced of their impossibility.) But now Galileo's telescope was making the ancient division between "sacred" heavens and "profane" earth impossible to feel. The Sun could be seen to have spots and blemishes that rolled around its surface; the Moon was clearly made of something like rocks and dirt, mere mountains and valleys similar to terrestrial ones; and our queenly Moon was discovered not to be unique, but merely one of a class of satellites similar to Jovian ones. The sacred heavens were rudely secularized. Or to take the inverse, Earth was offered the honor of becoming a heavenly body. Either way, the valuational segregation of heaven from earth was suddenly gone. Astronomy and terrestrial physics could be presumed continuous. If Earth is a heavenly body, then learning the principles of motions on earth would be to learn something about the dynamics of the (other) planets. And vice versa; if certain motions are natural in the heavens, they can be presumed natural on earth as well.

It turns out not so strange, after all, that Galileo retained the value of circular motion as "natural" despite Kepler's First Law, since he had a use for it in the terrestrial context, not merely in astronomy. Galileo was one of many who rejected the Aristotelian notion that for every motion there had to be a continuous mover at work. It had been obvious for some time that arrows were not really "pushed" from behind as they flew between the bow and the target. Strings attached to the arrowhead did not stream out in front as they should have if air were pushing the arrow from behind. Lances tapered at both ends flew just as fast as lances blunt at the rear. Galileo therefore postulated the important principle of inertia, that motion is a natural state—just as natural as rest—and that unless something stops an object in motion, it will simply keep moving forever. Motion does get stopped, of course. Friction from the earth keeps sledges from sliding unless continuous effort is applied. Friction with air slows projectiles and items dropped from towers. Friction with water keeps boats, once kicked off from the dock, from floating off forever. But in principle, Galileo argued, if there were no resisting medium, such as that provided by the water in this case, the boat once started in motion would glide all the way around the world and return to its starting place, still going at the same rate.

It did not occur to Galileo to wonder why his boat would not leave the surface of the water and fly off at a tangent to the earth's round surface in a rectilinear straight line. Since circular motion was natural and right both in the heavens and on earth, this was not a problem for him. The benefits of continuing his commitment to the cosmic—now also terrestrial—appropriateness of uniform circular motion were larger than the costs.

A second great value change brought by Galileo, besides the abandonment of special status for the heavens, was commitment to the thorough mathematicization of the newly unified world picture. From boyhood days, when he counted in pulse beats the period of the great swinging chandelier at Pisa's Cathedral, Galileo's passion was to *count*. A mathematician to the core, he loved to find ratios, constants, hidden relationships between units he could measure and enumerate. When these relationships emerged he had a sense of clarity, of understanding. For this to happen he had to measure with extreme exactness and devise mechanisms for getting the units precisely right. At Pisa and later at Padua, he invented a water clock (we would call it a stopwatch today) to determine the exact time taken for one of his balls to roll between two points on his carefully smoothed inclined plane. When the ball began rolling, a thin stream of water would be released into a cup, then shut off when the exact distance had been reached. This allowed Galileo to weigh the contents of the cup on an extremely accurate balance, thus pinning down the times in units of weight. Then these accurate time-units could be put into meaningful mathematical ratios with accurate distance-units, providing constant formal outcomes, over many trials, for different distances, different speeds (different angles of the inclined plane), and different times. Acceleration was constant. The distances measured always varied as the square of the times measured. A natural regularity, a law of uniform acceleration, had been drawn forth from the welter of qualitative data.

Where the world of ordinary experience was vague and qualitative only, Galileo did his utmost to find ways of turning it into measurable units. Besides his water stopwatch, he worked untiringly on the principle of the pendulum and in particular on the mechanics of a pendulum clock, devising ways of turning the qualitative flow of time into quantifiable units. The verge escapement used in clocks of the time was not sufficiently accurate for Galileo; as we saw, even in his blind old age he was working on the pendulum clock, assisting Christiaan Huygens in its development. Other merely qualitative aspects of experience, like feeling warm or cool or very hot or very cold were also to be turned by Galileo into quantitative measures allowing of mathematical treatment. It was he who invented the first thermometer, in which different qualitative intensities of heat could be transformed into points along a line that could be measured accurately and put into mathematical relationships. In this way *felt qualities* could be translated into *spatial quantities*. Galileo's first thermometer was contrived out of a glass bulb filled with air, out of which a tube protruded downward, dipping at the bottom into a vessel containing colored fluid (at first water, later alcohol); expansion of warm air pushing the liquid lower in the tube gave a linear correlation between cooler and warmer. This was a huge breakthrough in making the quality of heat subject to mathematical treatment, though unfortunately it was imperfect for measuring heat alone since it made no compensation for differing levels of atmospheric pressure, which (unbeknownst to Galileo) also affected the height of the water in the tube. True to his master's ideals, Evangelista Torricelli, Galileo's secretary and disciple, allowed the reduction of even this invisible air pressure to quantitative measure by proposing an experiment (inverting a tube of liquid into an open dish containing the same liquid) that led both to establishing the reality of air pressure and (simultaneously) to the invention of the barometer. The spatial length of the liquid in the tube, water at first, then mercury, provides a foothold for mathematics; marks inscribed on the tube allow counting and correlating.

With all this counting and measuring of the world, Galileo was firmly committed to appreciating only the results of mathematical thinking. In one famous passage he declares:

> Philosophy is written in that great book which ever lies before our eyes— I mean the universe—but we cannot understand it if we do not first learn

the language and grasp the symbols, in which it is written. This book is written in the mathematical language, and the symbols are triangles, circles, and other geometrical figures, without whose help it is impossible to comprehend a single word of it; without which one wanders in vain through a dark labyrinth (Burtt 1954: 75).

In this insistence on the knowability only of the mathematical aspects of things we are reminded of Kepler, who said similar things about the essentially mathematical character of knowledge. But Galileo went an important step further. Unlike Kepler, who seems to have assumed the presence of influences and qualities in the universe that may not be strictly knowable but are still there, Galileo, polemicist and ardent mathematician that he was, demanded that the picture of the world as it really is be cleansed of what finally evades reduction to quantitative methods. What is not measurable, in the end, is not.

For Galileo, this means that what is real about heat is not the quality of warmth we feel, but the tiny corpuscles of heat that are in warm things and that can be measured by our thermometers. It is the measurable aspects of things that are genuine, not the notoriously unreliable, vague feelings of coolness or warmth that human beings report. Those feeling are in us, not in the real world. In the same way, we certainly do not attribute the tickle that we feel in our armpit or foot or nostril to the feather that does the tickling. The tickle exists only in the interaction of the objectively real world with our subjective feelings. Take away the feeling subject and there will be no tickle left. As Galileo put it, "Now this tickling is all in us, and not in the feather, and if the animate and sensitive body be removed, it is nothing more than a mere name." Generalizing, he presses on: "Of precisely a similar and not greater existence do I believe these various qualities to be possessed, which are attributed to natural bodies, such as tastes, odours, colours, and others" (Burtt 1954: 86). The *primary* qualities of things are those that are subject to mathematical treatment, like number, figure, magnitude, position, and motion; all the other traits that things seem to have, like unquantifiable smells, tones, textures, hues, warmths, sourness, sweetness, and the like, can be classified as *secondary* and dismissed from the real world. Not only is beauty in the eye (or ear or nose) of the beholder; more fundamentally so are the harmonies of hues (or tones or perfumes) that make it up.

Besides dismissing the qualitative dimensions of experience, Galileo's commitment to the values of exact mathematical method lead him to reject any imprecision in the behavior of the real world. Just as the mathematical formulae of physical science are exact and categorical, so nature must be seen as inexorable and precisely regular in its behavior. Nature is the domain of complete determinism. Galileo invokes this trait of the real world, indeed, in defense of the proper freedom of physical science from the authority of Scripture. Both the world as it is and the Bible came from the same divine source, who should be the only ultimate authority:

> Methinks that in the discussion of natural problems, we ought not to begin at the authority or place of scripture, but at sensible experiments and necessary demonstrations. For, from the Divine Word, the sacred scripture and nature did both alike proceed. . . . Nature, being inexorable and immutable, and never passing the bounds of the laws assigned her, . . . I conceive that, concerning natural effects, that which either sensible experience sets before our eyes, or necessary demonstrations do prove unto us, ought not, upon any account, to be called into question . . . (Burtt 1954: 83).

Therefore, freedom, indeterminacy of any sort, is not to be found in nature. The unified mathematical realm of reality runs by perfectly consistent laws.

Qualities and freedom in nature turn into *dis*values in Galileo's vision of the kosmos. Likewise, emphatically, so does the very idea of purpose. Notoriously, Galileo used his gift for sarcasm and mockery against the Aristotelian conviction (Chapter 3), that to understand an event fully requires an account of the end or goal of the phenomenon in question. Aristotle, as we remember, took his paradigms largely from organic nature, wherein the development of individuals could be represented as in search of the goal of maturity or fulfillment in an ideal species' form, or from instances of human artisanship, wherein the actions of a painter or a house builder could be understood in terms of the purpose or plan guiding individual steps of craftsmanship. In both cases, a *telos* or future outcome was represented as active, a "final cause" drawing potentialities into actuality. Over the years, Aristotelian scientists had done their best to supply final causes for all happenings, including such phenomena as the acceleration of falling bodies with which Galileo did so much work. These premoderns had portrayed falling bodies as of earth and as returning with a "natural" motion to Mother Earth. Things made of earth-stuff would naturally be drawn to find fulfillment "at home" and would accelerate to actualize their potential telos as they drew nearer and nearer. From Galileo's vantage, this anthropomorphic account not only betrayed a ludicrous imagination—attributing mounting "enthusiasm" to the "breasts" of stones and other inanimate objects—but also explained absolutely nothing. How *much* faster would these little earthlings be found to be travelling at various points along their route "home" to Mother? Premodern qualitative vagueness on such questions showed the emptiness of the invocation of final causation.

It is still meaningful to ask what things are made of: their "material causes" in the archaic Aristotelian terminology. It is even meaningful (in an extended sense) to ask for their "formal causes," if all this calls for is the formal mathematical principle describing their motion. Of course, mathematical descriptions are not in fact *causes* at all (here Galileo departed from Kepler who seems to have accepted the opposite view). The only actual causes, strictly speaking, are the pushes and pulls of real material things shoving against one another and bouncing off one another. These qualities of things can be rendered numerically. But it is by no means needful—not even intelligible—to ask in Galileo's kosmos what end or goal or telos is being pursued. The future is made by material particles being moved by prior efficient causes, themselves moving according to exact, immutable mathematical laws. The future has no power to influence or "draw" the present. Corpuscles made of purely mathematical properties can have no final causes; no intelligible meaning can attach to "purpose" in nature. Serious science will laugh it out of the modern world picture.

In sum, Galileo ties together such a large cluster of the distinctive values that characterize the modern way of feeling, seeing, and thinking the world, that he represents in many ways the fulcrum figure of modernity. He is an ardent enthusiast for mathematics, so much so that he relegates to nonreality whatever is not amenable to mathematical treatment; but at the same time he is a vigorous empiricist who insists on highly precise observations on earth and revels in the new powers of instrumented seeing into the heavens. Paradoxically, he demands that we abandon common sense in favor of what powerful theories, Copernicanism and atomism, tell us must be so; but he defends the initially implausible by more precise and carefully chosen experiments, correcting common sense by better sense. Fiercely, he extrudes from nature those traits which are most pervasive in human experience: the sensory qualities in which everything comes clothed, our intuitions of the freedom to choose alternative futures, and the purposes that guide such choices. All these traits he attributes to mind alone, though mind is not among his subjects for study. Brilliant, confident in his gifts, sarcastic, immensely successful in invention and research, profoundly suspect by the opponents he humiliates and outmaneuvers, admired and feared by the popes and other pillars of the old order he is undermining—Galileo rests an authentic martyr-hero, an "in your face" controversialist, physically "prudent" (compared, at least, to Bruno), and, finally, the paradigmatic modern genius. Little wonder, then, that his values, methods, and commitments won an enormous following in decades and centuries to come.

HOBBES AND DESCARTES

Among the admirers who visited Galileo and drank deeply of his spirit was Thomas Hobbes, then an English tutor employed by the great Cavendish family. At the time of Hobbes' visit, on his third trip to the Continent (1634–1637), Galileo was already under condemnation and house arrest. Hobbes himself was to know the pangs of exile for his royalist sentiments during the English Civil

War; in 1646, he became tutor to the also-exiled Prince of Wales, the future Charles II, from whom in later years he was to win honors and pensions.

Hobbes was born in 1588, the year of the great Spanish Armada. In the year that Bruno was burned and Kepler removed to Prague, young Thomas was preparing himself, as the son of an Anglican clergyman, for education at Oxford. After graduation in 1608, Hobbes accepted employment as tutor for the Cavendish family, and travelled to the Continent with his charges during 1608–1610, while Galileo was first probing the skies with his telescope. Back in England, Hobbes became acquainted with the still-powerful Sir Francis Bacon, some of whose essays he translated into Latin, and with William Harvey, a physician ten years his elder, whose research leading to the publication of *On the Motions of the Heart and Blood* (1628) was then under way. Significantly, Harvey was the first to apply quantitative methods in the life sciences, showing that the heart functions essentially as a mechanical pump and that the blood must circulate, since more is pumped each hour than is contained in the entire body. Hobbes took note of these important currents, but at this point he was still not engrossed in philosophy.

In his early thirties, during his second trip to the Continent, 1629–1631, Hobbes was transfixed by reading Euclid's *Elements* for the first time. He was thrilled to the core in a reaction reminiscent of Galileo's in Pisa. Although Hobbes never came close to the mathematical genius of Galileo, the Euclidian system remained for him a model of method.

Hobbes made a third trip to the Continent, 1634–1637, during which time he paid his visit to Galileo and in Paris was introduced to the inner intellectual circles by the priest-philosopher-theologian-mathematician Marin Mersenne (1588–1648), who knew everyone. At this time, Hobbes met Pierre Gassendi (1592–1655), whose Atomist enthusiasms were to influence his own thinking, and was invited by Mersenne to write a set of formal *Objections* to René Descartes' thought, soon to be published as the great *Meditations* (1641). Hobbes' career as a philosopher, though now in his middle years, was well and truly launched. With a Euclidean care for organization, he outlined his system, beginning most generally with bodies, of which all things are composed, then moving to human beings, individually, and finally to human political community.

Politics in England prompted Hobbes to flee for his life in 1640; safely in Paris, he began to compose the third (political) part of his system, which he published as *De Cive* in 1642. During this period of exile, he wrote also his most famous work, *Leviathan* (1651), and tutored, as previously mentioned, the future Charles II, whose father, Charles I, was beheaded in 1649. Hobbes' political values, as we shall see, favored absolutism; but any absolutism, the King's or Cromwell's, would do. In 1652, he reconciled himself to the Commonwealth and returned to England, where his services were rendered to the scions of the earl of Devonshire. During this time, he published the delayed first and second parts of his system: *De Corpore* (1655) and *De Hominem* (1658). After the Restoration in 1660, he lived in the good graces of his former pupil Charles II, and happily engaged himself in controversies over his doctrine of determinism and over his mathematical views, until his peaceful death at age ninety-one in 1679.

The attitudes and values of Thomas Hobbes and his views on the status of values in reality make for a fascinating reflection. He deeply shared Bacon's preference for a philosophy that was practical. Ideas should work. Like Bacon, he was an empiricist. It is only through the body's senses that information of any kind comes to the mind. At the same time, he was a follower of Euclid in seeing knowledge as ratiocination, the deductive working through and logical arrangement of ideas which, in their raw state of mere reception, are not yet knowledge.

Substantively, the influence of Pierre Gassendi, William Harvey, and Galileo form the framework for Hobbes' view of the world. Gassendi, enthralled by the rediscovery of Democritus and Epicurus, was a committed Christian priest who labored to show (analogous to the work of Thomas Aquinas with Aristotle) that atomism, as a theory of reality, could be compatible with an orthodox Christian faith. Galileo had accepted corpuscularism too as an available alternative to Aristotelianism, without exploring its full implications; Gassendi wanted to take it as a metaphysics and baptize it for the dawning modern age. For him, the compatibility with Christianity was to be achieved by adding a doctrine of creation to the ancients' view of an unbegun universe of atoms and void. God had *created* the atoms—a finite though unimaginably large number of them—in an infinite space to allow for their motion, and had given each atom its quantity of impetus. These atoms are controlled in their collisions by the direct intervention of divine lawfulness, ever constant; once created, they can be destroyed only by God at the Last Judgment. There is nothing real but atoms, void, and, of course, God.

Hobbes, valuing Euclidean minimalization of initial principles, accepts the great simplification of all things to material atoms moving according to immutable law, then simplifies still further by dropping as unintelligible any notion of God as an "incorporeal reality." Whatever is real is body, Hobbes postulates. Therefore, a "nonbodily existence" is as meaningless as a "round square." The phrase contains a contradiction, destroys itself, and can have no reference. If someone still were to persist in mouthing these phrases, Hobbes says, "I should not say he were in an error, but that his words were without meaning, that is to say, absurd" (Hobbes 1969: 43). And if the only things that truly *are* consist in tiny material bodies or larger aggregates and compounds of these bodies, then it follows that the only kind of causation, as the great Galileo recognized, is efficient causation communicated by motion and the impact of moving body upon moving body.

Empirically, human beings are parts of this world; therefore, deductively, they are no more than compounds of atoms and are moved by nothing more than material impacts, whether external or internal. This implies there can be no such things as universals, of course, since all atoms are particular and only atoms exist. Ideas are particular names we give to a number of other particulars or groupings of particulars. The secondary qualities, experienced colors, tastes, and tones, are nonexistent in the world of atoms. They simply are the by-products of motions entering the body and combining with the body's own responsive motions. Hobbes calls them "phantasms." The mind, of course, is material, to the extent that it is real. It projects its self-generated phantasms outward, where they seem falsely to be part of the observed world, by a sort of reactive pressing back against the incoming influences that carry primary qualities alone. Mental motions synthesize experienced qualities that are entirely absent from the world itself. Similarly, decisions are the end result of a train of motions that begin (for the subject) with an external stimulus, resonate in subtle, often unnoticed internal motions, and finally resolve in some action by the whole complex of atoms that equals a person. Since all motions are lawful and perfectly regular, the outcome must—given the character of the stimulus and the character of the complex entity stimulated—be entirely ordained by the laws of motion. This is logically entailed by the immutability and universality of the laws of nature, together with the beautiful simplicity of one sort of existence, material atoms, and one sort of cause, motion. Nothing less perfect would be acceptable in a decent kosmos.

It follows that each human bundle of atoms must follow its own inclinations. This is not a moral judgment but a necessary deduction from what it is to be an entity in action; it has moral consequences. Every individual is inevitably selfish, and when there are other selfish entities competing for scarce goods (including such inevitably scarce goods as self-esteem, reputation, feelings of superiority, and concern for future security), there will be savage conflict. Just as primal atoms naturally collide with one another, so the "natural" state of those compounds of atoms that constitute human beings is to abrade and aggress against one another endlessly without check or mercy, to the perpetual misery of all concerned. If we object that this is a nightmare universe, Hobbes readily agrees. His values are attuned with ours. Nothing worse could be imagined. This is why it is to the selfish interest of each to escape from this awful state of nature, this "war of all against all," into civil society. This can only be done by each giving up individual natural sovereignty over personal behavior, transferring it to a common sovereign who will protect all against each other. This new all-powerful figure will be part of the common universe and subject to all its categories, of course, and will demand absolute obedience to his selfish interests; but the alternative, the collapse of civil restraints, would be far worse.

In this sketch of Hobbes' outlook, his personal fears, priorities, prejudices, and temperament, as well as his theoretical commitments, are clear. Though the latter are as familiar as Galileo and are characteristically modern, the former are doubtless idiosyncratic. It is probably not just coincidence, but not wholly required, either, that the first attempt at creating a comprehensive metaphysics based on a radical acceptance of the theoretical values of *simplicity* (stripping entities to their bare mathematical properties, eliminating all causes except efficient ones, allowing only mechanical interactions between material corpuscles, taking motion as the only cause), together with those of *uniformity*, *exactness*, and *necessity*—this early example of the empirico-deductive method—should have had precisely the moral and political consequences that Hobbes actually gave it. These are contingent matters. Gassendi, the committed Christian, handled them very differently. Still, for some reason, Hobbes' association of the quality-bare atoms with amoral human predators has resonated powerfully through the modern civilization constructed with values attuned to the severely shorn premises required by Hobbes and Galileo.

Much is at stake in deciding the status allowed for qualities and, hence, all value in the scheme of things. For Galileo, the physical world was empty of characteristics other than those his mathematics could comprehend. The other characteristics of daily life, what he called the secondary qualities, were left within mind, with its purposes, preferences, commitments, hopes, and fears. Concerning mind he had next to nothing to say. It was not his department; it was a loose end. For Hobbes, in contrast, mind was to be fully incorporated into nature. With geometric assurance he insisted that, after all, there is nowhere else where mind can intelligibly be imagined to function. Experience teaches us that there is thought, deliberation, sensory appreciation, feeling. Deductive ratiocination requires that only material bodies in motion can be real. If so, the products of mind must be the effects of material causes; and since the only causes are matter moving, mind is matter moving. Free choice must be an illusion, just as the entire sensory appearance of the world of experience must be "phantasm." What "phantasms" are, how they come to be, where they could possibly "be" in a world admitting nothing but matter in motion, is not explained.

Yet another approach, not ignoring mind, with Galileo, but not reducing mind to matter, with Hobbes, seems called for. This is the way of René Descartes, long honored by many as the "Father of Modern Philosophy."

Descartes was not always a "father." For much of his life he was insecure, self-doubting, a wanderer and a recluse. He was born in March 1596 in a small town in central France in the Touraine district defined by the Loire River. Since his mother died when he was an infant, his upbringing was left to one of his grandmothers until he was ten. Then, he was entrusted to the Jesuits at their school at La Flèche (near Le Mans of current racing car fame), where he remained for eight years, an eager student, and appreciative of his mentors at the time, though reporting later the sense that he had learned nothing solid. From eighteen to twenty years of age he studied law at the University of Poitiers, but never practiced. Instead, he travelled to Holland in 1617, and volunteered for officer's service in the army of Maurice of Nassau. There was no question of combat. Nor did Descartes need or accept pay. For the most part, he was bored with barracks life, but his encounter with the mathematician Isaac Beeckman among the other officers was stimulating intellectually. From Holland, Descartes drifted to Germany, where he signed up, briefly, with the army of the Duke of Bavaria; he left military service for good in 1619, at the age of twenty-three. While in Germany, Descartes had continued to work at the mathematical interests roused by Beeckman and experienced some remarkable success. In the fall of 1619, intellectually exhausted, he suffered a spell of deep self-doubt climaxed by three vivid dreams on the night of November 10, 1619. These dreams he took to be signs of a special mission to continue work and to create a new system of thought, a worldview unified by mathematics, that was emerging in his mind.

In and out of Paris, frequently on the road for the next eight years, Descartes worked episodically both on his mathematical ideas and with a telescope that had recently come into his hands, solving various issues in optics. At intervals, however, he lived the unfocused life of a dandy. Finally, in 1627, he had an important conversation with Pierre Cardinal de Bérulle, a leading scientific figure in the Church. Bérulle urged him to discipline himself to the great work he had within. Descartes took his advice and left France, with its whirl of social distractions, moving instead to the peace and intellectual freedom of Holland, where he remained almost until the end of his life. In his new ambiance, he settled down with a Dutch woman, with whom he had one child (who died as a young girl, to Descartes' intense grief), and wrote the great works of his life. The first of these, *Le Monde*, his cosmography, was ready for publication in 1633—just as Galileo was being condemned in Rome. Since Descartes' views were nearly identical, he suppressed publication of the book. He was always extremely anxious to be in good standing with the Roman Catholic Church, even hinting that his views could become the approved view of the Church itself. This was not to be. After his death, his works were put on the Index of Forbidden Books, but that did not prevent Descartes from holding out hope during his productive years.

The major works then came steadily from his pen. In 1637, he published, as a long preface to three scientific essays (on geometry, optics, and meteorology), his *Discours de la méthode* (the *Discourse on Method*). This was written, against the fashion, in the "vulgar" language of French rather than Latin, in hopes that common literate people could read it without depending on the turgid medium of traditional scholarship, which, after all, he explicitly wanted to supplant. In 1641, Descartes returned to Latin, publishing his most important metaphysical work, *Meditationes de prima philosophia* (the *Meditations Concerning First Philosophy*). In 1644, came *Principia philosophiae* (the *Principles of Philosophy*), also in Latin, presenting his scientific views in a form he hoped would be adopted as a text. Finally, in 1649, publishing again in French, he offered what was to be his last book, *Les passions de l'âme* (usually translated *Treatise on the Passions*). Another book, begun in 1628 but uncompleted, was published much later in 1701 as *Regulae ad directionem ingenii* (*Rules for the Direction of the Mind*).

Descartes' productive period in the Netherlands ended with an honor—an invitation from Queen Christina of Sweden in 1649 requesting help for the establishment of a scientific institute and for personal tutoring in philosophy. Descartes responded, moving promptly to Stockholm, where, at royal request, he gave lessons to Her Majesty at extremely early hours, long before dawn. The endless, wintry Scandinavian mornings took their toll on a constitution unaccustomed to these rigors, and Descartes died of pneumonia in February 1650, just short of his fifty-fourth birthday.

Descartes' childhood insecurity and youthful aimlessness can provide an apt metaphor for the intellectual life of his time. The old views, the traditional methods, offered no conviction to those most aware of the tides of thought sweeping Europe. But there was yet no clear alternative to provide hope and direction. All that was evident in advanced intellectual circles was that a new, some might simply say a "postmedieval" age, was beginning. Some of its lines were starting to emerge, dimly, from the contributions of Copernicus, Kepler, and (controversially) Galileo; Bacon's trumpet blasts were stirring, though hardly focussed. The famous poem of John Donne, cited earlier in this chapter, published in 1611 while Descartes was still a student at La Flèche, well expresses the rootlessness—the deep intellectual frustration—of the time by continuing:

> And freely men confess that this world's spent,
> When in the Planets, and the Firmament
> They seek so many new; then see that this
> Is crumbled out again to his Atomies.
> 'Tis all in pieces, all coherence gone;
> All just supply, and all Relation . . .
> (Donne 1990: lines 209–14).

Descartes' great inspiration, in the context of all this "postmedieval" failure of nerve, was to conceive a theory of the world, inclusive of all reality, constructed with the methods of mathematics. For him, even while attached to his military regiments, mathematics had been a constant preoccupation, exhausting but rewarding. Its method must above all be unremittingly analytical, breaking down all questions to their ultimately simple parts, whose necessity would shine in their own light. Then, by slow and deductively sure steps—each self-evidently correct, checked and double-checked—larger answers could be offered with the assurance that, since they were nothing more than the combined function of these simple parts and certain steps, they could be trusted with equal certainty.

The genius of Descartes was to use the intellectual malaise of his time against itself. Skeptics abounded. Michel de Montaigne (1533–1592), Pierre Charron (1541–1603), and even a group of ethical libertines and freethinkers had operated in the penumbra of "postmedieval" society. But Descartes, inspired by the mathematical method of analysis, was determined to drive skepticism to its grave by pushing it to lengths where it would have to surrender to certainty. This he set out systematically to do, setting aside ethical doubts for practical reasons, but attacking every theoretical belief to see whether it could withstand assault. The first and easiest to go were all beliefs about the sensory qualities. Skepticism of their truth was by now well-trodden territory. They are too inconstant and relative to our perceiving bodies to be reliably real. But what about the world of primary qualities and our bodies themselves? Descartes found these beliefs dubitable, in principle, since—who knows—we might be dreaming. We often dream "worlds" and "events" that are not real. And mathematical operations themselves? If we assume for the sake of argument, far-fetched though it may be, that there is a great, malevolent demon who makes us commit mistakes of calculation (e.g., forgetting where we began to count the sides of a square and coming up with five sides or three), then we cannot trust even mathematics without prior assurance that such a demon does not exist. Skepticism—of our senses, of our world, of other people, even of mathematical calculations—has reached its fever pitch.

But here the fever breaks. Because even if we assume that a malignant demon is constantly deceiving us, we cannot think the logical possibility that we (as minds, at least) do not exist, at least while we are being deceived. To be deceived is undeniably to think; and to be *thinking*, even erroneously, is to *be*. Certainty at last! More, the certainty itself can be analyzed into what makes it certain: this discovered certainty is entirely distinct, not mixed up with others (it is one of the ultimate simples mathematical method seeks), and it is entirely clear, not hazed with mere probability but transparently true. By finding this example of a necessary truth, Descartes has, by analyzing it, found the criteria—clarity and distinctness (of this perfect degree)—by which other truths may also painstakingly be added. Two of these, no less clear and distinct, are that nothing comes from nothing, something of which thinkers have been rightly assured since the pre-Socratics, and that qualities presuppose a substance, that is, a quality must be a quality *of* something—a "free-floating quality" is an obvious absurdity.

Given such basic, indubitable truths, Descartes employs his method of cautious steps to build back the world, temporarily lost to the skeptical onslaught. His mind, he now knows, exists as long as he is thinking; but his mind hardly accounts for itself. If nothing comes from nothing, his mind's existence must be accounted for either by its own necessity or by something else adequate to account for it. Search his mental qualities as he may, he cannot find within himself any necessary basis for his own existence, therefore, it must be accounted for by some other. That other must either account for itself or must be accounted for by another. But the latter route is endless until ended by something that accounts for itself. What accounts for itself and everything else is what is meant by God. Moreover, he realizes he has an idea of God within the inventory of his ideas. This idea is of a perfect being. Descartes, by being a doubting, potentially confused and imperfect thinker, is by no means capable of producing such an enormously positive idea. It cannot have come from nothing; therefore, it must have come from the only being that could in principle be capable of producing it, Perfect Being itself: that is, God. (Descartes even takes a leaf from Anselm's book, though he gives it a mathematical tone foreign to the prayerful monk.) God's nature, being perfect, contains actual existence as certainly as a triangle contains 180 degrees. A triangle is unthinkable—one is not truly thinking about triangularity—unless one admits its interior angles equal 180 degrees (even if one might not be aware of this prior to going through the steps of Euclid's proof); God is not thinkable without all perfections, including existence.

But since God exists and is perfect, then in such a divinely governed universe we can be sure that the malevolent demon of our skeptical fantasies cannot exist. A perfect God would not allow it. We can trust our mathematical calculations, if we are careful. We can trust that there is a world. God, being perfect, would not deceive us about this very large matter, either. And we can trust that we can know this world as long as we limit our claims to what is genuinely clear and distinct about it, that is, as long as we consider it only in its mathematical aspects.

With this, Descartes comes full circle back to science and mathematics, but now with renewed confidence, having defeated on its own ground the skepticism of his age and his own insecurity. The world of nature is defined by its geometry. It is *res extensa*, extended reality, and in its quantifiable properties lies not only everything knowable but also everything real about it. Human reason, if it remains obedient to the injunction to restrain its claims to what can be dealt with mathematically, can confidently make new discoveries into what Bacon called the "marrow of things." At its simplest, the material order is just extension; therefore, the idea of a literal vacuum, "empty space" void of all reality, is a self-contradiction to Descartes. By being extended it has been *admitted* to be res extensa. Thus, material nature is a plenum, is full, though with different quantitative degrees of impenetrability, different shapes and sizes and speeds and positions. All causal influence in this plenum is by pushing, direct contact between efficient causes and their effects. For this reason, Descartes developed an elaborate theory of "vortices" between apparently distant things, so that the occult concept of action at a distance—a dangerous exception to pure mechanical causality—could be eliminated from postmedieval thought. The attempt to cleanse the world of such invisible, noncontiguous causes was a many-faceted one. Among other more theoretically motivated reasons for insisting on a purely mechanical universe of contiguous pushes and pulls was the need to fight lingering (and dangerous) superstitions crediting magic and witchcraft in a world where credulous people still delighted in tormenting, typically, unpopular old women for allegedly casting spells across the town or mysteriously blighting a neighbor's cow or corn. "Occult" in its original derivation simply means "hidden from view." But there is a far more sinister sense of the term that can be unleashed—a cruel reality in the sixteenth and seventeenth centuries—when "actions at a distance" are not extirpated, root and branch, as unthinkable absurdities.

Since res extensa has none but mathematical properties and operates on none but mechanical principles, there must be another sort of reality in which can be located the secondary qualities, the values, the hopes, the fears, the purposes, and the thoughts that constitute our constant experience as human beings. This is *res cogitans*, or thinking reality, the very reality that comes first in order of certainty, after the method of doubt has burned away all the dross of confused belief. Descartes' method would not—could not—remain vague about mind, with Galileo, much less allow a reduction of mind to matter, with Hobbes. Mental qualities are real; that cannot be doubted. Therefore, since there can be no "free floating" qualities, mental substance is real. It is primary reality, as fundamental as the mechanical world of geometrical extension, but even more intimately known. The only substance that could be considered more fundamental than mind-substance and matter-substance, which cannot account for their own existence and have no power to perpetuate themselves by themselves, is God, who can and does both. In this ultimate sense of having the capacity to exist "alone," that is, needing no further underpinning, only God is Substance; but granting God's constant sustenance across the abyss of nonbeing represented by every next moment, mind and matter are equally substances. One supports mental qualities; the other supports geometrical qualities. The former, not being extended, are indivisible; the latter, consisting essentially in extension, are infinitely divisible. The former, not being in space, are influenced only by persuasion or argument or similar mental motives; the latter, being utterly unthinking, are influenced only by pressures of immediate contact, motion communicated from surface to extended surface.

The fruits of Descartes' commitment to certainty, analysis, and mathematics are God plus two entirely different kinds of substance. The concern for God, doubtless sincere in Descartes himself, will fade as the modern world establishes itself on these foundations. This leaves the other two substances, matter and mind. It is notorious that as they are defined by Descartes, they can have no intelligible interaction. Minds are influenced only by mental qualities, but matter, defined as unthinking, has none of these. Material bodies are influenced only by pushes and pulls in extended space, but mind, defined as nonextended substance, has no place to stand and no way to push. *Treatise on the Passions* attempts to deal with this yawning gap, since it seems obvious on its face that our thoughts influence our bodily behaviors and that our bodies (through our senses, at least, but also probably in many other ways) influence our minds.

As we know, Descartes' life was cut short soon after publication of that book. He probably knew that his answers, suggesting a tiny place in the brain where immateriality could touch materiality and materiality could persuade immateriality, were inadequate. As early as 1643 he wrote privately:

> It does not seem to me that the human mind is capable of conceiving distinctly and simultaneously the distinction and the union between body and soul, because to do so it is necessary to think of them as a single thing and at the same time to think of them as two distinct things; and this is absurd (Clarke 1982: 26).

If he had been given another decade, would he have modified his definitions of res extensa and res cogitans to allow a solution? We shall never know. We do know that his values were profoundly engaged in the quest for certainty and for adequacy, to the full range of the data given human beings. The quest for certainly led him to highly abstract formulations, highly simplified inventories of possible substances, highly restricted ranges of causes. But Descartes' commitment to adequacy required that he admit purpose, freedom, value, thought, sensory enjoyment, and all the rest, as somehow genuinely real. It also required him to admit the obvious: that our minds influence our bodies and vice versa. All these he held but could not hold logically together. In the end he was forced to choose between abstract clarity, quantification, simplicity, and analysis, and the pesky empirical adequacy that he was unwilling to deny. He might not have admitted to his associates that he was sacrificing coherence by these preferences. He was characteristically aloof and haughty toward his critics. His mind was too keen, however, not to have seen the crucial trouble undermining his entire vision of the whole. It has been, in many ways, the crucial trouble undermining the worldview he bequeathed. In more recent days (as we shall discuss in Volume Three of this trilogy) it has eaten at the institutions of the civilization constructed implicitly on his preferences. At any rate, the "postmedieval" worldview, after Descartes and the other founders who preceded him, has earned a name and an agenda. The name is "modern," and the agenda is our own.

6

THE PREVALENCE OF MATTER

Now comes a change in narrative approach. Until this point, we have moved relatively steadily across time with a minimum of what, in the old astronomy, would have been called "retrograde motion." But now, with the posing of the modern agenda for dealing with mind, purpose, quality, freedom, and value in the nature of things, the exposition will change. The next two chapters root in the period just after Descartes, but diverge as they follow different main branches to the twentieth century. The third and final chapter of the narrative will start one hundred years from the early twentieth century to follow new shoots appearing in the nineteenth.

The present chapter will explore the main branch constituted by those thinkers whose values reflect what turns out to be the dominant view in the modern world: the principal importance of the material and the measurable. Chapter 7 will move across the same temporal territory, but will follow the implications for metaphysics of valuing mind over matter. Chapter 8, concluding the historical parts of the book, will take the path least travelled, but now of special relevance, in which primary stress is placed on neither mind nor matter as mutually exclusive alternatives, but on history, change, evolution, or process.

As we proceed, it is vital to avoid oversimple pigeonholing of complex thinkers. It should not be supposed, for instance, that Baruch Spinoza or Isaac Newton, main figures in this chapter, had little interest in the phenomena of mind. That would be downright false. Spinoza, as we shall see, explicitly understands mind to be co-equal with matter among the infinite attributes of reality. Newton devotes himself privately to theology. Nonetheless, the theories of both thinkers contribute to the steady press toward an exhaustively material account of all things: to the mechanization and materialization and—after Einstein—the eternalization of a "block universe" that squeezes freedom, purpose, creativity, and quality out of the character of the really real.

MALEBRANCHE AND SPINOZA

Before we trace the path leading to the material/mechanical depiction of the universe, let us pause to consider—and illustrate with two nonmaterialists— the profound but sometimes underestimated phenomenon we might call "theoretical commitment." By this I mean the readiness to prefer accepting awkward, even (apparently) absurd consequences to sacrificing a favored theory. Major theoretical abstractions often have the power to win such commitment. Sometimes the circumstances are obviously psychopathic. My grandfather, a physician in general practice, told a story (he swore it had happened to him) of a man who came to him convinced he was dead. Grandfather argued with him but to no avail. Eventually, to prove the man wrong, he drew a little blood from the man's finger. "There," said my grandfather, "that proves you can't be dead, since corpses do not bleed." "No," replied his patient, "it just shows that corpses do, after all, sometimes bleed."

Theoretical commitment need not be pathological; but preference for a refined theory over raw experience can persuade people to accept conclusions that may strike others, uncommitted to the theory, as odd indeed. Immediately following Descartes' triumphant establishment of the duality of material and mental substances, with the unresolved issue of mind-body interaction, two dualist philosophers illustrate this phenomenon. One was Arnold Geulincx (1624–1669), a Flemish Cartesian philosopher, a midlife convert to Calvinism, and a professor of philosophy at Louvain and later at Leiden. Geulincx was completely committed to the Cartesian theoretical framework, except for the late unconvincing attempt of Descartes to account for body and mind affecting one another. This is theoretically impossible. Mind can only affect mind, never body. Only the omnipotence of God, who had created matter in the first place, could alter physical states at will. Therefore, Geulincx concludes, God is the only real cause of our bodily movements, not our own intentions or efforts. Harmonizing well with his Calvinist sense of God's total control over events, Geulincx's conclusion is that our moral duty is to humble our will to accept our metaphysical dependence on God for every action. Our intentions are only the occasions for God's gracious interventions into the material order.

The other Cartesian occasionalist was the slightly younger Nicholas Malebranche (1638–1715), who remained Roman Catholic, entered the priesthood, and spent his energy as a member of the Society of the Oratory, harmonizing Augustinian theology with Descartes' dualistic philosophy. Malebranche carried his commitment to Cartesian theory a step beyond Geulincx. Geulincx had not seriously questioned where our information about the physical world comes from. But Malebranche followed the logic of Cartesian mind-matter duality to its complete conclusion: the senses are physical, organic, therefore, in principle, precluded from influencing the conscious mind. A physical sensation, for example, a pin pricking a finger to draw blood, may flow directly through the nerves to the brain; at the brain it is blocked by its material, extended character from influencing the mind, which is nonspatial. At that point, Malebranche argues, the extended brain-event becomes the occasion for God to bring about the appropriate mental event, the conscious feeling of pain, together with other mental events of seeing images of the pin, the finger, the blood, and the like. If, at that moment, the mental intention is formed to pull the finger back from the invading pin, this cannot go directly to the muscles through the nerves; it must again be forwarded, first through God's omniscience and then back, by God's omnipotent cooperation with this second occasion for intervention, into the physical creation and thence through the brain and nerves to the muscles. More, Malebranche contends, without God's creative action, nothing at all could even *be* in the next moment. Finite entities, whether mental or physical, have no power of self-existence from one time to a later time. Therefore, even purely physical trains of causation are not independent of God. God must create and recreate the world according to faithful regularities. These events are constantly conjoined because of God's rationality and order; but there is no causal power there. Thus, the world is not at all what it seems. What it "seems" is in reality only God's production of mental events in us, since there is no possibility of the material world's communicating itself to our minds directly. And what it "does" is—nothing at all. The material universe is simply the field of God's constant recreative activity in space, indirectly providing the occasions for God's parallel constant recreative activity in finite consciousness. What we "do," likewise, is only to signal God our intentions. Our will is our responsibility; to God goes credit for all the rest.

The value placed on Descartes' brilliant theoretical achievements, together with a predisposition to value theologies of predestination and total divine sovereignty (exemplified here in the thought of Calvin and Augustine), outweighed the apparent "givens" of moment-by-moment interactive experience. To reiterate, these philosophers were far from the materialists with whom this chapter will end. They are noted here mainly to illustrate how far it is possible to go for the sake of preserving a valued theory when "matter" and "mind" are initially defined in such incompatible ways—and to underscore how utterly "lifeless" matter, so defined, seemed to the early successors of Descartes.

A quite different theoretical answer to the modern agenda of relating mind with body, thought with extension, would soon be given by Benedict

Spinoza, although the presence of theoretical commitment to many of the same principles would remain a strong element in his system.

Born toward the end of 1632 in Amsterdam to a family of Portuguese Jews seeking refuge from persecution, he was initially given the Jewish name Baruch. After his education in Hebrew, Talmud, Kabbalah, Maimonides, Renaissance Neoplatonism, Stoicism, and Descartes' philosophy, however, Spinoza, at twenty-four, was officially excluded from his Jewish community, even from his family, for expressions of unorthodox views. Thus, expelled from Judaism, Spinoza renamed himself Benedict, the Latinized version of his old name, and entered into a remarkable life of solitary thought, tied loosely to the larger society by correspondence and by occasional visits from others, including Gottfried Wilhelm von Leibniz, fourteen years his junior. After various moves, attempting to find complete peace and freedom for thought—all the while supporting himself in marked simplicity by his craft of lens grinding—Spinoza ended in The Hague, from which he refused an offer of a professorship at the University of Heidelberg, despite promises of academic freedom. The life of a university professor, he thought, would take away too much time from his writing. At the age of forty-five he died of tuberculosis, probably aggravated by the glass dust from his lenses.

The writing he left as his sole bequest was profound and fascinating. Two items had been published during his lifetime. The first (published in 1663 at age thirty-one) was a reduction of Descartes' *Principles of Philosophy* to geometric form, an attempt to express Descartes' views through Descartes' favored method. The second was an anonymously published *Tractatus theologico-politicus* (published in 1670, at age thirty-eight), in which he made, among other things, a strong case for complete intellectual noninterference from Church or State. His principal legacy was the book, *Ethica ordine geometrico demonstrata* (*Ethics Demonstrated in Geometrical Order*), on which he had been working unassumingly in the privacy of his lens grinding shop. A draft had been completed in 1665 and was subsequently revised, over the next dozen years, in the quiet hours after work.

Spinoza's intense valuing of the infinity of ultimate reality—a profound turn away from the ancient Greek dread of the infinite—is no longer a surprise, after the interventions of such thinkers as Philo of Alexandria, Maimonides, Nicholas of Cusa, and Bruno. Quite apart from Spinoza's knowledge of Descartes' philosophy, which he knew intimately from the geometrical version he had done of it in his first published work, young Spinoza was predisposed by his studies of the Kabbalah and the Neoplatonists to venerate Self-existent Being. But a Cartesian definition of "substance," taken with full seriousness (as Descartes did not) in this previous context, can mean nothing less. As Spinoza states in Definition III at the start of his *Ethics*: "By *substance*, I mean that which is in itself, and is conceived through itself: in other words, that of which a conception can be formed independently of any other conception." To understand what is implied in being "in itself" and in being able to be conceived entirely "through itself," is to realize that whatever is truly substance, so defined, cannot be caused by another. If it were, then it would have to be understood "through another" and it would not properly be "in itself." Therefore, if it is to be the cause of itself and conceivable entirely through itself, a true substance cannot in principle be limited by anything else, lest that something else enter into the understanding of it and make it no longer a true substance. But what is in no way limited is absolutely infinite. Since it is absolutely infinite, there is no room in reality for beginnings or endings or for any second substance, which would inevitably (simply by being something genuinely "other") put limits on the first—now one-and-only—substance.

Whatever is, then, has existence only in reference to the one unique, absolutely infinite substance. This one Reality might as well be called "God." As Spinoza expresses it in Definition VI: "By *God*, I mean a being absolutely infinite—that is, a substance consisting in infinite attributes, of which each expresses eternal and infinite essentiality." God and only God is exactly what the one Substance must be, as Descartes half-saw, but finally spoiled with his loose talk of res extensa and res cogitans as "also" substances created by but somehow impossibly existing alongside of God.

Instead, Descartes should have recognized that Substance, essentially characterized in principle by an infinite array of attributes, is the true reality of whatever is spatial and whatever is mental. Mentality and materiality are totally incompatible in essence, Spinoza agrees, but they are only different attributes of a common Substance, which has both of these and infinitely many more. We are not equipped to be aware of any but these two, but we should *think* of everything, as it ultimately is, as having an infinite expression of attributes. This means a fortiori that everything has at least the two attributes of materiality and mentality. My body, for example, is Substance understood as a modal appearance of its matter attribute; my mind is Substance understood as a modal appearance of its mental attribute. For every change in a mental attribute, there is, whether we detect it or not, a corresponding change in a physical attribute, and vice versa. There need not be "interaction" between the two attributes; such interaction would be absurd. But individual modal appearances of these incommensurable attributes are finally unified—coherence is regained—by reference to the whole of which they are common manifestations.

This whole is unlimited by any reference to anything but itself, as we have seen. Therefore it is, in Spinoza's Definition VII, perfectly free: "That thing is called free, which exists solely by the necessity of its own nature, and of which the action is determined by itself alone." God, Substance, the Universe, and Nature, in this sense, is entirely free. The freedom of God, on the one hand, we have seen valued intensely by Jews, Muslims, and Christians for centuries. Spinoza agrees. Taking the phrases we saw earlier to have been coined by Giordano Bruno, Spinoza says that this way of seeing nature as active, self-creative, untrammelled, is as natura naturans. At the same time, Spinoza, with Kepler, Galileo, and Descartes, values intensely the perfect mathematical order of nature. On this second hand, every change is necessitated by "inexorable" laws, as Galileo called them. Spinoza again agrees and offers a way of seeing nature also as passive, constrained, necessitated, as natura naturata. Depending upon the viewpoint, nature (active) is God, defining itself with absolute freedom from external constraint; or Substance is nature (passive), totally ordered and necessitated.

Is reality Substance, Nature, God? Is reality free or determined? All depends upon the viewpoint taken. A similar relativity of viewpoint can permit us to look at reality either as a realm of infinitely extended matter, or under the no less infinite attribute of mind. The important thing for our narrative at the moment is that for Spinoza, everything, without exception, can be understood as material, extended, quantifiable, and determined. Matter is everywhere prevalent. Complete explanations can be found, in principle, for all things, using only mechanical categories.

In fairness to Spinoza it must be acknowledged that he would have had to say the same things, with equal emphasis and with equal comprehensiveness, on behalf of complete explanations based on categories of mind alone. This follows from his position. But the momentum at the time was with the mechanists. The heady young sciences of mathematical physics and astronomy were moving from triumph to triumph, applying the tools appropriate to the "infinite attribute of matter," ignoring the "infinite attribute of mind." Spinoza's modest influence at the time was, if anything, to encourage the research programs of those committed to the exclusive use of material explanations. In later years, he encouraged Albert Einstein in additional ways, as we shall see at the end of this chapter.

BOYLE AND NEWTON

Back from the predominantly a priori reasonings of the occasionalists and Spinoza on the European continent, we find Great Britain abuzz with efforts to combine the abstract, minimalist values of atomistic materialism with rigorous experimental discipline—and to maintain the resulting physical world picture alongside the values of mind and religious faith. This is the main story of the second half of the seventeenth century in England, as illustrated by the great works of Robert Boyle (with Robert Hooke) in chemistry, pneumatics, and theory of matter, and of the incomparable Isaac Newton. As we review their accomplishments in establishing the "mechanical world picture," which eventually left no significant place for purpose, quality, or religion, we should note especially the degree to which both of these two great progenitors retained the humanistic range of values they personally found immensely dear.

Robert Boyle, the seventh son of the first Earl of Cork, was born in Ireland in 1627 (the year in which Kepler published his *Rudolphine Tables*, and Descartes, resolving to follow Cardinal Bérulle's advice, left Paris for peaceful Holland). Unhappy with his schooling at Eton, young Robert at age eleven was fortunate enough to be able to continue his studies privately in Geneva and Padua. Galileo was still alive, both in his guarded villa near Florence and in the minds of venturesome youth in the university where he had taught. Boyle's excitement was kindled by reading Galileo's discoveries; and when he inherited part of the family estates at the time of his father's death in 1644, he resolved to spend his life in the same scientific pursuits. In 1654, during Cromwell's rule, Boyle moved to Oxford to avoid political disruptions, and set up a small laboratory, which he enlarged in 1657 upon hiring Robert Hooke (later famous in his own right) as his assistant. It was in Oxford that he set up the experiments in pneumatics. He invented the vacuum pump, to determine empirically whether the old tradition that "nature abhors a vacuum" is true; and he performed the experiments that led to his formulation of "Boyle's Law," stating the constant mathematical relationships of pressure and volume in gases. Also, during the Oxford years, he played a leading role among the group of intellectuals who later founded the Royal Society of London, the importance of which we shall repeatedly see.

Ill health prompted a move to London in 1668, where he stayed at the home of his sister, but continued his research. At this time, he became the friend of Isaac Newton, who was fifteen years his junior. Still true to his youthful scientific enthusiasms, even in middle age, Boyle refused offers of a peerage and even a bishopric, on grounds that these responsibilities would interfere with his scientific work. At the end of December 1691, a month before his sixty-fifth birthday, he died, widely honored and admired.

Boyle's no-nonsense attitude toward thinking about the world was to combine abstract thought with carefully controlled observations. He was not at all antitheoretical, but he reported that he did not want to let Gassendi and Descartes overwhelm him too early, "that I might not be prepossessed with any theory or principles, till I had spent some time in trying what things themselves would incline me to think" (Burtt 1954: 168). Now that the "corpuscular philosophy" (as he called the combination of Gassendi's revived Democritean atomism with geometrical Cartesianism) had taken hold so strongly, however, Boyle was happy to advance it further, as long as experimental verification continued to be forthcoming. His own pneumatic experiments leading to his Law he thought best explained by imagining air to consist of tiny coiled springs, thus conforming to the corpuscular model. His mission was to bridge the gap between abstract world theory and concrete experiment. As he wrote:

> Since the mechanical philosophers have brought so few experiments to verify their assertions, . . . I hoped I might at least do no unseasonable piece of service to the corpuscular philosophers, by illustrating some of their notions with sensible experiments, and manifesting that the things by me treated of may be at least plausibly explicated without having recourse to inexplicable forms, real qualities, the four peripatetic elements, or so much as the three chemical principles (Burtt 1954: 170).

While fully adhering to the corpuscular philosophy, even arguing that all things in nature (except living things) could be fully explained simply in terms of the mathematical features of material atoms in motion according to geometrical principles, Boyle insisted also on bridging the looming gap between his science and religion. As a lifelong, convinced Christian, one of the points he found unnecessarily stringent in Descartes and Galileo was their banishment of final causation from approved thought about nature. Boyle saw evidences of God's purposive design everywhere in nature—the wonderful adaptations of things to one another and the sheer glory of the rational order of creation—and argued at length in support of the teleological argument for God. This did not mean that he was open to explanations of particular physical happenings by reference to *their* tendencies or goals. In this Boyle was firmly dualistic. Final causation of the world is found in God's great purposes, but only there. Once created according to God's aims, the physical universe is simply the domain of matter in motion, and all efficient causality is communicated direct contact. Where there is apparent "empty space," this too is full (as Descartes insisted it must be) with extremely thin stuff Boyle called "ether." This means that in the heavens as on the earth, "The world being once constituted by the great Author of things as it now is, I look upon the phenomena of nature to be caused by the local motion of one part of matter hitting against another" (Burtt 1954: 179).

In like manner, insisting on "both/and" rather than "either/or," Boyle would not exclude the so-called "secondary qualities" from the real world. Of course, they do not apply to the material corpuscles of the physical world itself. Here, Boyle accepts the orthodoxy of Galileo, Gassendi, and Descartes. But since human souls really exist, the qualitative dimensions of the universe are just as real as the mathematical. *If* human beings did not exist, there would be no qualities or values in the finite order of things; but this is a false conditional. Boyle simply reminds us that "there are *de facto* in the world certain sensible and rational beings that we call men" (Burtt 1954: 181–2). If it comes to questions of value, Boyle sides with quality against quantity, even though his laboratory science rests exclusively on the latter.

> Matter, how vastly extended, and how curiously shaped soever, is but a brute thing that is only capable of local motion, and its effects and con-

sequents on other bodies, or the brain of man, without being capable of any true, or at least any intellectual perception, or true love or hatred, and when I consider the rational soul as an immaterial and immortal being, that bears the image of its divine maker, being endowed with a capacious intellect, and a will, that no creature can force; I am by these considerations disposed to think the soul of man a nobler and more valuable being, than the whole corporeal world (Burtt 1954: 183).

Still, considered in its physicality, the human body that does this valuable perceiving is still a mechanical thing. Human beings are "engines endowed with wills" (Burtt 1954: 183). How can the soul transform mechanical impulses into the grandeur of the multi-hued, -textured, -odored, -toned universe of living human experience? That is not explicable by finite minds. Boyle is willing to leave the issue to God.

For I demand why, for instance, when I look upon a bell that is ringing, such a motion or impression in the conarion produces in the mind that peculiar sort of perception, seeing and not hearing; and another motion, though coming from the same bell, at the same time, produces that quite different sort of perception, that we call sound, but not vision; what can be answered but that it was the good pleasure of the author of human nature to have it so (Burtt 1954: 184).

Boyle was confident, however, that such questions as may be left will not damage the harmony between Christianity and the corpuscular philosophy. Perhaps in future times, he might have thought, still more answers will be found. In his final testament, he bequeathed funds for a lectureship, in perpetuity to see to the defense of Christianity in face of science. The Boyle Lectures remain today among the most prestigious in the world. In every way, by his advances in mechanical science as in his determination to remain faithful to his religion and his human experiences of quality and purpose, even if unable to explain how they could go together, Boyle's legacy to future generations was generous.

Isaac Newton was born into far less generous circumstances than the fortunate Robert Boyle. By the time of his (premature) birth on Christmas Day 1642 (Old Style), his father, an unlettered small farmer in the tiny hamlet of Woolsthorpe in Lincolnshire, England, had died. At age three, Isaac's mother handed him over for rearing to her mother to free herself for marriage to a wealthier man in a neighboring village. We can only speculate what scars this treatment and the acknowledged hatred Isaac felt toward his stepfather might have left on Newton's later years, marked as they were by emotional breakdowns, furious controversies, and insatiable hungers for recognition.

When he was eleven, Isaac was taken out of school and back to Woolsthorpe by his mother, who was again widowed and looking for help from her
eldest son in managing her now much-enlarged farms. Isaac proved incompe-
tent at farming, and, by 1661, when he was nineteen, his family decided that he
should go away to Cambridge University to fit himself for some other way of
life.

At Cambridge, Newton did not distinguish himself with his teachers.
One of them, Isaac Barrow, Lucasian Professor of Mathematics, came close to
failing him on an examination covering Euclid's *Elements* in 1664. But Newton was engaging in self-study of an even more advanced sort. He was reading
and mastering Descartes' *Géométrie* and the works of Francis Bacon, Pierre
Gassendi, Thomas Hobbes, and at least some of the later works of Johannes
Kepler. In 1665, Newton received his bachelor's degree without distinction.
He would normally have continued immediately for the master's degree, but a
great plague broke out in England in that year and he was obliged to return
home for safety.

Newton's plague years, 1665–1667, while he was quarantined in Woolsthorpe, turned out to be some of his most creative. All three of his major contributions were germinated then. First, in mathematical theory, Newton worked
out a unified method for dealing with numerous problems, such as finding
areas, lengths of curves, tangents, maxima and minima, that had previously
been left to ad hoc mathematical devices. This was what he called his "method
of fluxions," what we now know as calculus. Second, in optics, he turned the
tables on all prior theories of light with his famous prism experiments, to which
we shall shortly return. And third, in celestial mechanics, with or without the
help of the legendary Woolsthorpe apple tree, he began to work on the problem
of the Moon's orbit. He did not, as he later misreported the matter, immediately
think in terms of a universal gravitation pulling on the Moon (as well as
apples). Rather, in those years, he started thinking about the Moon as subject
to a great centrifugal force, as swinging around the Earth, forcing it out and
away. Obviously, something keeps it from flying off into space. That "something" Newton conceived to be a mechanical pressure of some sort, equal and
opposite to the supposed centrifugal force. This meant that the mechanical
"inward push" would need to drop off as the square of the distance; only this
would balance the assumed centrifugal force which, as Newton already knew,
manifests that mathematical form. Taking Galileo's estimate, that the distance
between Earth and Moon is about 60 times the radius of the Earth, the acceleration of the Moon "away" from the Earth should diminish to being 60^2 (3,600)
times less strong than the opposite acceleration of falling objects 60 times
closer to (just one radius from) the center of the Earth. Putting actual estimated
distances, observed speeds of acceleration for falling objects, and the Moon's
observed rate of rotation into his equation, Newton came out with 4,000 rather

than 3,600. Since the result was, as he said, "pretty near," but not near enough (he had been using too-small estimates of the size of the Earth), Newton set the matter aside.

The plague ended in 1667 and Newton returned to Cambridge, where he completed his master's degree and was elected a Senior Fellow at Trinity College. When he shared his "method of fluxions" with Isaac Barrow, the same professor who had nearly flunked him on Euclid, Barrow was so impressed with the achievement that, in 1669, on resigning his chair to pursue theological interests, he arranged for Newton, only twenty-seven, to succeed him as Lucasian Professor of Mathematics.

The years in Cambridge were rewarding. In 1672, Newton consolidated his optical research and presented his first public paper on the topic to the Royal Society, chartered a decade earlier by King Charles II, the former tutee of Thomas Hobbes. The Society was first organized in 1645 as "The Royal Society of London for the Improvement of Natural Knowledge" by a group of intellectuals, prominently including Robert Boyle's former assistant, the energetic and talented experimentalist Robert Hooke, who was named its first Curator of Experiments.

Newton's paper was a thunderclap. From antiquity, everyone had assumed that plain white light is simple and that colors are qualitative additions to or modifications of fundamental white. But when Newton admitted a thin beam of white light through a hole in the shutter of his room at Woolsthorpe and then passed it through a clear prism, producing a spectrum of colors on his wall, it occurred to him that instead of *adding* something to the light as it went through, the prism might be *bending* different primary elements of the light to different degrees, thus *analyzing* it into its basic parts. To check this idea, he placed a second prism into the path of a thin beam of some of the colored light coming from the first prism, to see whether this already refracted light could still further be refracted or analyzed. It could not. Newton's paper went on to argue, in keeping with the atomism in which he had been immersed through his private reading at Cambridge, that the fundamental light elements, those colored rays, must themselves be made up of tiny particles deflected to different degrees in the prism because of different mechanical characteristics. Their straight line path, the sharp edges of the shadows they make, the absence of any sign of periodicity in their behavior, also weighed against their being waves, as Christiaan Huygens and Robert Hooke had been contending.

Hooke, in his position as Curator of Experiments for the Royal Society, strongly objected. In particular, he objected that Newton's experiments alone were insufficient to require the corpuscular conclusion that Newton was drawing from them, as of course they were not. Indeed, Newton himself later modified his theory in view of his own discovery of "Newton's Rings," circular refractions visible in thin films, mathematically proportional to the thickness of the films. In response, he postulated a vibratory motion for his particles to account for the signs of periodicity he himself had uncovered. But that came later. The brilliant simplicity of Newton's experimental achievement, together with the irresistible prestige of the corpuscular philosophy, won the day in the Royal Society, despite curatorial objections. And not only the day—the corpuscular view of light reigned virtually unchallenged in the world of science generally for two centuries to come. It is easy to see why. At last another dimension of purely qualitative experience, like heat and duration, but in this case even the paradigmatic "secondary quality" of color itself, proved reducible to geometrical quantification. The *real* ray of light is now to be defined by the geometrical property of its angle of refraction, not by subjective hue. Analysis and mathematics triumph again. As Newton put it in his *Optics*, these hues are not even qualities of light, much less of things:

> If at any time I speak of light and rays as coloured or endued with colours, I would be understood to speak not philosophically and properly, but grossly, and according to such conceptions as vulgar people in seeing all these experiments would be apt to frame. For the rays to speak properly are not coloured. In them there is nothing else than a certain power and disposition to stir up a sensation of this or that colour. For as sound in a bell or musical string or other sounding body, is nothing but a trembling motion, and in the air nothing but that motion propagated from the object, and in the sensorium 'tis a sense of that motion under the form of sound; so colours in the object are nothing but a disposition to reflect this or that sort of rays more copiously than the rest; in the rays they are nothing but their dispositions to propagate this or that motion into the sensorium, and in the sensorium they are sensations of those motions under the forms of colours (Burtt 1954: 235–36).

The dispute with Robert Hooke was bitter and increasingly personal. Newton waxed hot and haughtier, then withdrew into himself in Cambridge. In 1678, he suffered an emotional breakdown during which he wrote his friends vindictive and bizarre letters that alarmed them deeply. By 1679, he seems to have recovered his stability, just in time to receive a series of letters from his enemy Hooke, politely inquiring about the problem of planetary dynamics. Hooke, whose intuitions and experimental talents always outstripped his mathematical abilities, suggested that instead of a centrifugal tendency balanced by some unknown centripetal mechanism (as he had imagined for the Moon), Newton might consider for the planets a centripetal attraction of some sort, toward the central body (the Sun) but combined with rectilinear inertia diverting the planets into continuous circular orbits. He suggested a sort of local gravitational relationship between Sun and planets, the force of the attraction dropping off as the square of the distance. Newton answered initially but soon broke off the correspondence. During the following years he immersed himself in studies of alchemy and magic, the literature of which was rife with discussions of mysterious attractions and repulsions, actions at a distance, and occult causes. Later historians, thoroughly imbued with the exclusive claims for "decency" of the modern mechanical worldview, have been scandalized by those studies, often averting their attention, but it seems quite possible that Newton was intensely following the lead of Hooke's suggestion of an unknown attracting force. At any rate, nothing came out of these researches that Newton would ever officially acknowledge.

His mind was much on the topic, however, by 1684, when the young astronomer Edmund Halley (1656–1742), a close friend of Hooke's, came from London to ask him to calculate (as Hooke, despite his promises, evidently could not) the geometric form for motion of a body under the influence of a central force diminishing as the inverse square of distance. Newton's answer was immediate: it would be elliptical. He had calculated it some years before, but had mislaid his notes. Halley was thrilled. It was the first physical explanation for Kepler's First Law of Planetary Motion, which until that point had been purely descriptive. As such, it had enjoyed surprisingly little influence among astronomical theorists. Galileo, as we noted, ignored it, preferring perfect circles. Newton and Hooke had apparently not been much impressed by it, since their first calculations were based also on the assumption of circular motion. The commitment to perfect circularity went deep. Even Kepler, who first broke the spell, was not happy about it. The ellipse was awkward and unbeautiful compared to perfect circularity. It was, as he put it, just "one more cart-load of dung"—a brute fact to be endured—though it got rid of a "vaster amount of dung" (Toulmin 1961: 247). But thanks to Newton's calculation, a new sort of intellectual simplicity replaced the old. The algebraically simple numerical relationships of masses multiplied, divided by distances squared, could replace the geometrically simple relationship of centers and circumferences. Even the egg-shaped ellipse with its two funny foci began to look intellectually beautiful under the new circumstances. It was a theoretically necessary consequence of a mathematically elegant formula.

Halley's enthusiasm was infectious. At his imploring, Newton reconstructed his lost notes, added to them and expanded them, until, in 1687, with Halley personally bearing the expense of publication and seeing the manuscript through the press, the world was given Newton's *Philosophiae naturalis principia mathematica*. In this work, the most famous and influential work in the history of science, the synthesis of terrestrial mechanics and astronomy was complete in three Books. At the time, it seemed Newton's system could explain everything worthy of attention.

The world picture presented, in keeping with the mathematical ideals forged by Kepler, Galileo, and Descartes, was highly abstract. In Book I, space and time are defined as absolute, homogeneous, and infinite. Motion, in principle, is defined as geometrically rectilinear, following Descartes' ideal of perfect natural motion rather than Galileo's great circles. Bodies in this infinite universe of perfect geometry can be treated as dimensionless points, centers of gravity. Motion of such bodies would be endless unless disturbed by other bodies. Stationary bodies would remain forever at rest; moving bodies would remain forever in motion along Euclidean straight lines. Disturbances, when impressed upon bodies, would be rectilinear too and exactly proportional to the quantity of the impressed force. Every actual motion, no matter how complex, could in principle be analyzed into component simple, perfectly rectilinear motions. And for every action, an exactly equal and opposite action will occur.

In Book II, Newton meticulously examines the physics of motion of bodies in resistant media and the motions of these media themselves. The climax of the study is the demonstration that Descartes' theory of a plenum, in which the planets are moved by "vortices" of matter tangible enough to impress motion upon anything, is mathematically impossible. The supposed vortices themselves could not sustain their own motion indefinitely; even overlooking that problem, the vortices could not impart motion that conforms to Kepler's observational laws. The main rival theory of planetary motion is thereby demolished.

In Book III, the harvest is gathered. The laws of motion defined in Book I are extended to the whole universe. One elegant formula

$$F = G\frac{Mm}{R^2}$$

could express and predict all the variety of phenomena that Copernicus, Kepler, Galileo, and others had long labored to understand. The tides on earth, the moons of Jupiter, all the planets around the Sun, the Moon, the movement of the comets, the precession of the equinoxes—all were open to understanding by multiplying the masses involved, dividing by the square of the distances concerned, and multiplying by a constant, "G," chosen on the basis of the units used for mass and distance.

There is just one problem. There is no physical explanation—not even an imaginative suggestion—of what this universal force of gravity *is*. Newton has demolished the theory of vortices, which at least provided the notion of a mechanical agency to account for the motions of the planets. Now he gives nothing at all to replace the vortices. Gravity seems the very paradigm of an occult force, reaching invisibly across space, against which no shield is possible, remorselessly working its effects on distant objects. The outcry was immediate and intense. Along with paeans of praise, Newton had to suffer denunciations for flouting a fundamental value of modernity. Is this a wedge for witchcraft and superstition? No, Newton insists, there obviously *must* be some mechanism. In a letter to a friend he wrote:

> It is inconceivable, that inanimate brute matter should, without the mediation of something else, which is not material, operate upon, and affect other matter without mutual contact. . . . That gravity should be innate, inherent, and essential to matter, so that one body may act upon another, at a distance through a vacuum, without the mediation of anything else, by that through which their action and force may be conveyed from one to another, is to me so great an absurdity, that I believe no man who has in philosophical matters a competent faculty of thinking, can ever fall into it. Gravity must be caused by an agent acting constantly according to certain laws; but whether this agent be material or immaterial, I have left to the consideration of my readers (Burtt 1954: 266).

This suggestion of an "immaterial agent," however, was not made in his public writings. There he simply "stonewalled," as we would say today, all demands for explanatory hypotheses. All he had attempted, he repeatedly insists, was the *mathematical* explanation of observed phenomena. The mathematics works. The Laws hold. Beyond this he will not venture. As he states in the *Principia*, "But hitherto I have been unable to discover the cause of those properties of gravity from phenomena, and I frame no hypotheses" (Burtt 1954: 314).

In private, Newton tried out many hypotheses, including an elaborate theory involving the circulation of the ether, an extremely thin material or spirit:

> So may the gravitating attraction of the earth be caused by the continual condensation of some other such like ethereal spirit, not of the main body of phlegmatic ether, but of something very thinly and subtly diffused through it, perhaps of an unctuous, or gummy, tenacious and springy nature; and bearing much the same relation to ether which the vital aerial spirit requisite for the conservation of flame and vital motions does to air. For if such an ethereal spirit may be condensed in fermenting or burning bodies, or otherwise coagulated in the pores of the earth and water into some kind of humid active matter for the continual uses of nature . . . , the vast body of the earth, which may be everywhere to the very centre in perpetual working, may continually condense so much of this spirit as to cause it from above to descend with great celerity for a supply; in which descent it may bear down with it the bodies it pervades with force proportional to the superficies of all their parts its acts upon, nature making a circulation by the slow ascent of as much matter out of the bowels

of the earth in an aerial form, which for a time constitutes the atmosphere, but being continually buoyed up by the new air, exhalations, and vapours rising underneath, at length . . . vanishes again into the etherial spaces, and there perhaps in time relents and is attenuated into its first principle (Burtt 1954: 273).

These hypotheses and more were tested by Newton but not published. As he wrote to his friend Robert Boyle after an elaborate exercise in hypothetical imagination in which "grosser" particles of ether above the earth push bodies toward "finer" ether below, this is not really to his taste.

From this supposed gradual subtilty of the parts of ether some things above might be further illustrated and made more intelligible; but by what has been said, you will easily discern whether in these conjectures there be any degree of probability, which is all I aim at. For my own part, I have so little fancy to things of this nature, that had not your encouragement moved me to it, I should never, I think, have thus far set pen to paper about them (Burtt 1954: 277).

Through all this, Newton stubbornly refused to provide a mechanical account in public for the force of gravity. Thereby, he became not only high priest of modernity but also heretic, at least for a time. Later, the prestige of his achievement came so to dominate the world of thought that the very definition of "mechanism" began to lose the necessary element of pushes and pulls between surfaces in contact; and the ideal of explanation itself changed to match Newton's mathematical method of establishing laws without offering "hypotheses." The classical Positivism of Auguste Comte (1798–1857) a century and a half later (as we shall see) took Newton's refusal to go beyond the mathematical covariation of observable variables as the very essence of modernity.

Behind the scenes, however, Newton was deeply engaged not only in the physical "hypotheses" he rejected in public; he was also a prolific theologian. His manuscripts on theology and biblical studies contain well over a million words. He considered these matters important. It was his fate that his successors remembered and admired the abstract mechanical world picture he, more than anyone else, brought to coherent unity, but forgot (or scorned) the other side of his values.

Newton's theological values were deep but neither ordinary nor orthodox. He accepted the existence of God, whose sensorium comprised all of infinite space and time and gave to them whatever absoluteness of reference they could allow. He accepted not only the necessity for the original creation, but also the continuing influence of God in the universe: the need for occasional subtle corrections in the world machine as it ran down or became erratic. But he had no sympathy for cant or superstition; at the end of his life, he rejected the sacrament and died in 1727 at age eighty-five, unshriven by the church. His bequest to history was not to the realm of the spirit, though he cared about it, but to the realm of matter and mechanics. After Newton's era, ironically in large part because of his immense triumphs of abstraction, the palette of values available to him, Robert Boyle, and other early architects of the modern materialist worldview, begins to lose many of its hues.

PHILOSOPHES AND IDÉOLOGUES

For the most part, this gradual transformation occurred on the continent of Europe, rather than in England, where the penchant for compromise and "muddling through" tended to blur the sharp focus that materialism attained, especially in France. In addition, in England there rose, to the relative eclipse of metaphysics, a strong concentration on epistemology, which will be given proper attention in the next volume of this work. This epistemological turn, itself characteristically modern, made itself also felt in France, particularly through the influence of John Locke, Newton's London associate and, in the estimation of many, Newton's parallel and peer in the field of mental science.

Artificial though it is to separate metaphysics from epistemology, our narrative at this point needs to continue without dwelling in any detail on what, in Volume Two, will be of central interest. Thus, in this section, we will follow the values that entwine with the triumph of metaphysical materialism through the eighteenth century, first through Voltaire, then the philosophes of the *Encyclopédie* and *Idéologue* movements, and last, to the brink of nineteenth-century Positivism. Although epistemological themes will be present, our main focus will be the theories of reality, the commitments underlying them, and the place they assign to qualities, moral responsibility, mind, and purpose.

François-Marie Arouet, as Voltaire was then called, was born to a comfortable family in Paris in 1694, about the time Isaac Newton (his creativity exhausted and again recovering from another nervous breakdown) was preparing to take over intellectually undemanding but financially rewarding duties as Master of the Mint in London. Young François-Marie had received a good education from Jesuit schools and was launched toward a career in law when the literary muse captured him with a vengeance. Taking "de Voltaire" as his pen name, he was one of the authentic geniuses of his century. In and out of exile, in and out of prison, in and out of controversies of every sort, Voltaire breathed a liberating Newtonian-Lockean atmosphere into what was a repressive police state sustained by premodern ideas promulgated by the Church and enforced by the Monarchy. Voltaire's youthful talents were so successfully manifested in satirical plays against the *ancien régime* that first, he was forced to flee Paris, then at age nineteen, to take refuge in Holland, and finally, four years later, to endure the inside of the Bastille for nearly a year. After a second imprisonment, Voltaire, now thirty-two, moved to England. There he learned English, studied English ways, and read deeply in English philosophy and science. It has been said that Voltaire, in 1726, fled to England a poet and, in 1729, returned to France a philosopher.

His admiration for English thought and political practices was expressed in his *Lettres philosophique* (1734), composed after his return to Paris but written as though still enthusiastically absorbing impressions in England, home of the free and enlightened. To these *Lettres*, which contained much on Newton's triumphant unification of heaven and earth, Voltaire added a careful summary of the main lines of the Newtonian theory itself in *Éléments de la philosophie de Newton* (1738). These *Éléments* were later a principal channel for the entrance into French thought of the Newtonian alternative to still-dominant Cartesianism. Its impact will occupy our attention shortly.

Voltaire himself found life in Paris too dangerous for comfort and kept his distance for many years: First, in Cirey, he paid a fifteen-year visit to the intellectual Mme. du Châtelet, until her death; he then, for three years, tried living in the court of Frederick the Great; and, after quarrelling with Frederick, settled in 1755 on an estate in Switzerland. There, in 1759, (at age sixty-five), Voltaire published his masterpiece, *Candide*. He lived long enough to return in 1788 to Paris, where, before his death, he was acclaimed the world's greatest exponent of enlightenment, democracy, and justice.

The materialist world picture inevitably reflected the halo effect of these latter values. The ancien régime was authoritarian, cruel, obscurantist. The clean air of Newtonian empiricism and high mathematical abstraction was a tonic. To stand in favor of the mechanical world picture was to stand against superstition, priestcraft, and repression. Voltaire was no extremist, despite the alarm of the authorities; rather, he was, in his well-modulated views, an authentic Newtonian. He vigorously affirmed—specifically against a form of undiluted atheism that we will shortly encounter—the existence of God, but only the "demythologized" God of Newton's world machine. As Voltaire said, the existence of a watch calls for a watchmaker. Thus, the cosmic watchmaker's reality must be acknowledged, along with appropriate properties of intelligence and power, but there are strong reasons to doubt traditional attributions of divine goodness, and certainly to deny providential concern for the small problems of human actors on Earth's insignificant stage.

In one respect, Voltaire ventured to a topic beyond those considered by Newton's philosophy: the power of matter to think. In his reaction against Descartes' dualism, Voltaire preferred to entertain the possibility of thought being simply one function of matter, rather than the activity of a separate, immaterial, unextended, soul-substance. For this view he could cite John Locke, since Locke admitted he had found no argument strong enough to rule out absolutely that God's omnipotence could create matter capable of thought. Newton, as we saw, had referred to the human "sensorium," as well as to God's, but had not accounted for it within the material order. Voltaire, and after him an important strand of modern thought, was prepared to take that fateful step.

One of the first to be directly influenced by Voltaire's tributes to Newton and the English way of thinking was, paradoxically, a priest: Étienne Bonnot de Condillac. Condillac was born in 1715 in Grenoble, completed his theological education at the Sorbonne, and in 1740, entered the priesthood. His interests, however, were never particularly religious. It was rumored he performed only one mass in his entire life. On the way to holy orders, he encountered Voltaire's freshly published *Lettres philosophic* and the *Élément de la philosophie de Newton*. From then on, he was fascinated by and devoted to science and the Newtonian way of thought.

Condillac did not contribute directly to the natural sciences, though his cousin, Jean le Rond d'Alembert, whose influence we shall soon note, helped him with his mathematics, and Denis Diderot, d'Alembert's friend (and employer at the *Encyclopédie*) gave him much encouragement. Condillac's principal role was as an analyzer of experience. His particular fascination was in tracing all human thought to origins in the organs of sense. Although he retained belief in God (and never explicitly challenged Cartesian dualism between mind and matter), he applied what he viewed as a Newtonian-Lockean method of reduction of thought about the world to bodily stimuli. Indeed, so complete was his empirico-deductive reduction that his friend Diderot raised in print the question of whether he needed a material external world at all, or was in danger of drifting off into a sort of Berkeleian idealism (Chapter 7). Condillac recoiled at this thought and attempted to show, in his major work, *Traité des sensations* (1754), that even the externality of the material world is rooted in a *perception* of externality. Berkeley would probably not have been convinced by the argument, but the energy and ingenuity spent by Condillac in this enterprise underscored how intensely he and his circle of fellow thinkers valued the notion of an external material world.

Condillac's cousin Jean le Rond d'Alembert shared these values with no less intensity; "d'Alembert," by the way, was not his original name; he adopted it, perhaps for its euphony, as a young man. But, for that matter, "Jean le Rond" was acquired in an unusual way, too: his mother, after giving birth out of wedlock, abandoned him on the steps of the church St. Jean-le-Rond in Paris. His father, a man of means and some honor, claimed the infant boy, providing for his upbringing and later his education in a Jansenist school. Alas, the Jansenist-Jesuit controversies were in full cry at the time; young Jean le Rond found the endless polemics excruciating. For the rest of his days, he was emotionally opposed to such metaphysical quibbles.

Aiming first at law, then medicine, d'Alembert later turned enthusiastically to mathematics. Here, in mathematics, he found his remarkable talent and eventual fame, being admitted in 1743, at age twenty-six, to the Académie des Sciences. He knew English. At least two years earlier, he had read Francis Bacon in the original and was thrilled at the empirical wind he felt blowing away the cobwebs of French apriorism. Mathematical truths are fine, he argued, even before his admission to the Académie, but (à la Newton even more than Bacon) mathematical principles, no matter how demonstratively necessary, require empirical verification before being accepted as representing physical truth.

D'Alembert's additional talents as an English translator were recognized by Denis Diderot, four years his senior and already launched toward the career of an encyclopedist. In 1746, Diderot hired d'Alembert to translate Chambers' *Cyclopaedia* from the English; and, in 1751, d'Alembert was given the honor of publishing the *Discourse préliminaire* to Diderot's own *Encyclopédie*. In this *Discourse*, a philosophical work in its own right, d'Alembert praises Newton in particular for choosing not to offer behind-the-scenes "hypotheses" to account for the mathematical law of gravitation. We simply cannot know these ultimate causes at work. They are inaccessible to reason. At the same time, he forcefully rejects, as his cousin Condillac rejects, the Berkeleian subjective idealism that would lose the world of matter. Thus, in the name of antimetaphysical modesty, d'Alembert assumes the metaphysical reality of matter. Materialism is not recognized as a "metaphysical" position—it is just the obvious truth about the way things are. With Newton, it is good to acknowledge that our minds cannot penetrate the ultimate springs of action in things, like the causes of gravitation; but d'Alembert and his circle are sure that whatever these causes are, could we know them, they are material.

For most of his career, d'Alembert balanced a more traditional theism and mind-matter dualism with his other views. He argued, for example, that God must exist since something must account for the existence of intelligence—and intelligence cannot possibly arise from brute matter. But later, after years of association with Diderot, it seems the latter premise began to crumble. *Why*, apart from Cartesian (and Christian) dogma, can matter not give rise to intelligence? Diderot, like Voltaire, was convinced it was quite possible not only to entertain this idea without absurdity but to accept it as true, as he did early on. It is appropriate to look more closely at the circumstances under which the formerly treasured separation of mind from matter is debunked.

For this narrative, we need to step back one or two paces before Diderot, to look at the flow of influence eroding d'Alembert's convictions about the special character of mind. One important influence came from an eminent Dutch professor of botany and medicine, the author of large Latin medical texts, Hermann Boerhaave (1668–1738), who, in his approach to healing and the treatment of the human body, was a methodological mechanist, after the manner of William Harvey's studies of the human heart.

Boerhaave, celebrated and honored for his contributions to medicine, might not have figured in this narrative of modern materialism had it not been for a student of his who seemed to have relished outraging orthodox opinion as deeply and frequently as possible. This student was Julien Offray de La Mettrie, born in Brittany in 1709. La Mettrie studied medicine at the University of Paris, completed his doctoral work at Rheims, and, in 1733, engaged in postdoctoral studies in Leiden with the famous Dr. Boerhaave. After his return to Brittany to practice medicine, and, after a brief stormy marriage, La Mettrie published his first challenge to public sensibilities, *Histoire naturelle de l'âme* (*Natural History of the Soul*), in 1745. In it, he argued that the study of the soul is basically the province of medicine. The central nervous system, in particular the brain, is sufficient for the understanding of all the genuine phenomena of consciousness, memory, judgment, and the like. Matter—here he departs both from Descartes and Newton—is animated with intrinsic formal properties—as the Aristotelian doctors claim (here he may have been tweaking the establishment by the nose)—and needs no further additions from alleged "mind-substances."

The oppressive authorities went into their predictable frenzy, and La Mettrie took leave of France for tolerant Holland. There he penned his next outrage, *L'Homme machine* (*Man as Machine*), published two years later. If anything, this was more cunningly designed to stimulate apoplexy than his first work. Here he drops the quasi-Aristotelian metaphysical trappings of *Histoire naturelle de l'âme* for an explicitly antimetaphysical posture: the equivalent, as we have seen, of an implicit metaphysics of sheer materialism, outdoing even Hobbes for assertiveness. The general outcome is to treat human beings as the "living machines," or automata, as Descartes viewed the nonhuman animal world. There could, in such automata, be no place for free will, of course; the balance of aversions and desires at any given moment determines completely the behavior of any machine. More, since matter alone is capable of producing such elaborate behavior as human (and plant and animal) life manifests, there is no need for a spiritual creator. La Mettrie therefore expounds an explicitly atheistical position, which, though it seemed gratuitously offensive to many at the time, is perfectly in keeping with, though not logically required by, the thoroughgoing materialism of his anthropology.

Even Holland was outraged. La Mettrie fled once again. This time he took refuge in Berlin under the "enlightened despotism" of Frederick the Great. Frederick, amused by this stormy petrel, made him an official of his court. Thus secure, La Mettrie wrote more nose-thumbing works aimed at his stalemated opponents. *L'Homme plante* (*Man a Plant*) appeared in 1748, and *Le Système d'Epicure* (*The System of Epicurus*) followed in 1750, as did *Discours sur le bonheur* (*Discourse on Happiness*). The ethical works followed the predictable argument from the man-machine premise: Happiness is the state of maximum individual pleasure-sensations. The attainment of happiness of this sort is entirely independent of moral deserving. It is a medical question, like health, and is indeed a form of health that all—including criminals and the like—should enjoy.

Of course, La Mettrie was attacked at every level. He was depicted not only as a wrong thinker but as an immoralist, a monster of every sort of vice. These reactions no doubt provided hearty entertainment for La Mettrie and Frederick. The amusement ended abruptly, however, when La Mettrie, always a corpulent figure, died suddenly at age forty-two from what were probably the effects of overindulgence in food and drink.

Denis Diderot was another materialist, though far more subtle in his manner of fencing with the oppressive authorities. Diderot, as we already noted, was a significant influence in the lives of Condillac and d'Alembert. Diderot's talents were wide-ranging, his mind supple and keen. He was born to a bourgeois family in the old Roman town of Langres, Champagne, in 1713, and received his early education, at which he excelled, at Jesuit schools. Obtaining his master's degree from the University of Paris at the astonishing age of nineteen, he then dropped out, against his family's wishes and at the sacrifice of their support, for a prolonged period of private study. Having mastered the English language, he supported himself with translation and, through his work, absorbed the values of freedom, empiricism, and mechanism. His first independent philosophical publication, *Pensées philosophique* (*Philosophical Thoughts*), appeared in 1746, stirring concern from the ever-vigilant authorities. In the same year, he became associated with the great project of the *Encyclopédie* and soon rose to become its editor-in-chief. In that position, he was required to walk a fine line in the police state in which he had to operate. His *Lettre sur les aveugles* (*Letter on the Blind*), which he published in 1749, contained a deathbed conversation with a blind professor who, unable to see the wonders of the world, questioned the providential design of the universe. For this, Diderot spent several months in jail. In 1759, the *Encyclopédie* was officially suspended for a time, and Diderot was required to pull several of his best manuscripts, fearful of their destruction at the hands of the authorities. Some of these were not published until after the French Revolution. With tact and guile, however, Diderot, in 1772, completed the great project.

It is striking how, over and over again, in this tumultuous century, political values become intertwined with metaphysical views. Once free of editing the *Encyclopédie*, Diderot immediately travelled to Russia to the court of yet another "enlightened despot," Catherine the Great. Though repressive enough in her own way, she was glad to receive and support this leading representative of the intellectual underground in the West. To help him financially, she purchased his entire library, then gave him a permanent stipend for the libary's care and upkeep. She also commissioned him to advise her on the revamping of her country's legal system.

Diderot's advice came from a philosophical position that had, by that time, been thoroughly radicalized by his struggles with the forces of premodern repression in France. Earlier in his life, Diderot had been a deist; but the steady drumbeat of opposition to everything the brutal authorities stood for had moved him to atheism. Later, he was known to remark that deism represents just a transition for one who has not yet become an atheist. In his interactions with Condillac, he was sympathetic to the analysis of human thought to sensation, but his sensationalism was a reductive materialism in which sense experience is nothing but the functioning of the sense organs, something the priest in Condillac never accepted. The mind, as La Mettrie had also argued, is nothing but the brain at work. The will, too, is no more than the outcome of the net equilibrium attained at any point by a person's aversions and desires. There can, in principle, be no such thing as free will. All events in the universe, including all the phenomena of mind, are simply the functioning of matter. Matter, therefore, is naturally capable of mind-properties.

Catherine the Great and her counterpart Frederick were not prepared for such radicalism, even in their enlightened courts. The issue of atheism especially was sharpened by controversy over yet another radical materialist who had exploded into public consciousness, Baron d'Holbach. Catherine and Frederick were more comfortable with the moderate enlightenment of Voltaire, who was stimulated to write his defense of deism against Holbach. Since Diderot sympathized with Holbach on this issue, he was, as far as Catherine was concerned, too radical to be trusted to revise Russia's legal code. His work was promptly seized and thoroughly suppressed. Disillusioned, Diderot returned in 1774 to France where he lived quietly among his friends until his death a decade later.

Who was this Baron d'Holbach, who had squeezed a defense of God from even Voltaire and had turned enlightened despots against Diderot, merely for taking his side? Paul-Henri Thiry, Baron d'Holbach, was born in 1723 in the westernmost part of Germany, the Palatinate region bordering France. His mother's brother, wealthy Baron d'Holbach of Paris, invited the young man (then named Paul Heinrich Dietrich) to join his household as a surrogate son after his education in Holland was complete. The invitation was accepted, and Paul Heinrich became Paul-Henri, soon a French subject, who, at thirty years of age, inherited his uncle's title and estates. The new Baron d'Holbach was an eager participant in the excitement of new ideas in mid-century Paris. He spent his great wealth liberally entertaining the circle gathered around the *Encyclopédie* project. Besides Diderot, who was his closest friend, this circle included Voltaire, Condillac, d'Alembert, Jean-Jacques Rousseau, and many more, such as, from time to time, David Hume, Edward Gibbon, Adam Smith, Joseph Priestly, Horace Walpole, Benjamin Franklin, and Thomas Jefferson. His salon was the unofficial headquarters of the philosophes, who held regular dinner meetings at his city home and country estates to exchange and expand upon the most radical ideas of the day. He himself was patient, kind, and generous. He also was a passionate atheist and absolute materialist: author of unbridled polemics against Christianity, monarchy, feudalism, and all the "old" ideas still fiercely protected by the police state in which such views were extremely dangerous to maintain. Many of his manuscripts were published anonymously after being smuggled to Holland for publication. More officially, he wrote hundreds of articles for the *Encyclopédie*, principally on earth sciences such as geology, chemistry, and mineralogy; and, in 1770, he published his *Système de la nature* (*System of Nature*), his comprehensive defense of atheistic materialism sometimes called the "atheist's bible." This work pulled no punches. It depicted humanity as entirely a product of nonintelligent natural forces acting under necessary laws. The "soul" is an illusion. "Mind" is purely organic. Matter is inherently endowed with energy enough to account for all observed events. Nature is self-created and eternal. The book was immediately suppressed, of course, but nonetheless attracted a wide readership. It polarized discussion as nothing hitherto had done. Even within the close circle of Holbach's salon, there were divisions, as between Voltaire and Diderot. In addition, Jean-Jacques Rousseau, who had taken Holbach as his model for the virtuous atheist in *La Nouvelle Héloïse*, was offended. But Holbach's ideas simply carried to a logical and systematic conclusion the metaphysical ideas most diametrically opposed to those of the establishment. They harmonized, without need for explicit argument, with the widespread sensed need for general reform, even revolution. As Holbach himself put it in his second book, *Le Bon-Sens, ou Idées naturelles opposées aux surnaturelles* (*Common Sense, or Natural Ideas Opposed to Supernatural*), published in 1772, since in a materialist universe happiness is the supreme good, the people have the unhindered right to overthrow their rulers—monarchs, "enlightened" despots, whomever—to attain that end. Thus, as the age of revolutions approached, Holbach wove together his metaphysical sources from ancient and modern Epicureanism, Cartesian matter-in-geometrical-motion, Hobbesian atomism, Spinozistic determinism, and contemporary concepts such as Diderot's idea-generating matter and La Mettrie's *L'Homme machine*—all in Voltaire's spirit of "*Écrasez l'infâme!*" In the end, Voltaire sensed Holbach had gone too far, that his polemics had outpaced his judgment; but the values of cleansing radicalism were completely shared. All this makes it more than a little ironic that this most revolutionary of Barons should have been among those first selected by the Revolutionary tribunals of France for the guillotine.

The same end awaited another member of Holbach's circle, Antoine Laurent Lavoisier, but not until five years later during the Terror. Lavoisier, born in 1743, was expected to go into his father's legal profession, but like many others in our narrative, fell in love with mathematics and the sciences instead. A brilliant youth, he won election to the Royal Academy of Sciences in 1768 on the basis of a chemical analysis of gypsum. In the same year, he made the financially wise but politically fateful decision to join the "Farmers-General," who collected taxes for the government at a handy profit for themselves. Through the Farmers-General, Lavoisier found his wife (the daughter of another member) and made his fortune; but after the Revolution, the stigma of having been a tax collector for the repressive ancien régime was fatal, despite his liberal and reformist values.

Lavoisier associated with the philosophes in worldview as well as in politics. It was his insight that some portion of the air, not itself an element as the ancients and Aristotelians had thought, but made up (similar to Newton's white light) of a number of more basic elements—which, after Johannes Baptista van Helmont (1579–1644), he called gases—might actively enter into processes (of burning, roasting, and rusting) that were then puzzling the scientific world. Joseph Priestly, another associate from Holbach's salon, then working in America, had recently isolated an "eminently respirable air," which he called "phlogiston," thought to stream out of burning or roasted objects. Lavoisier inverted the theory, arguing that burning is an extremely rapid form of chemical *combination* of elements, the key being an invisible but ponderous material he named "oxygen." In 1777, he published his famous paper, *Memoir on Combustion in General*, and after winning key converts to his unification of such processes as breathing, rusting, and burning, he established a new analytic language for chemical compounds, in which the nomenclature reflected the new theory of composition, and thereby left (despite the guillotine) the legacy of a new science of chemistry joined coherently with Newtonian physics and astronomy.

A collaborator with Lavoisier, especially on his experiments to measure and mathematicize gas chemistry and respiratory physiology, was Marquis Pierre Simon de Laplace. Laplace, six years younger than Lavoisier, helped to design the essential instrument, the ice calorimeter, needed for their joint studies. But more important, the principal achievements of Laplace—who was another member of Holbach's circle and in particular the protégé of the mathematician d'Alembert, through whose influence he received a professorship at the École Militaire at age nineteen—were in mathematics and astronomy. Newton, we recall, had concluded that his planetary system was inherently unstable, tending to become disorderly and to require the intervention of the deity from time to time to correct the mechanism. Laplace adopted the problem once more, with the help of the mathematical achievements of Joseph Louis

Lagrange (1736–1813) and his own mathematical gifts, and showed that Newton was wrong. His system was better than even he had dared to conclude. Given the long run, the deteriorations Newton had considered destabilizing are actually periodic and self-correcting, Laplace showed. Saturn's orbit, for example, seems continually expanding; Jupiter's, continually contracting. But given a total cycle of 929 years, these expansions reverse themselves. To assume the perfection of the Newtonian world machine pays off. Here seemed to be mathematical confirmation of Holbach's ideas on the self-perpetuation of the "System of Nature." The results of Laplace's findings were published after the Revolution, during the years 1799–1825, in the monumental *Treatise on Celestial Mechanics*. It was during these years that Napoleon is reported to have asked Laplace what role was left for God in his world picture, and to have received the reply, "I have no need for that hypothesis."

It was with the same sense of perfect confidence in the regularity of the causal laws of the natural universe—unified, tidy, and mathematically intelligible—that Laplace also anticipated the possibility, in principle, of perfect predictability (and retrodictability) of every event, bar none. What would be required would be complete knowledge of all the relevant mathematical laws and all the positions and momentums of all the particles to which the universe can be reduced. This is obviously impossible in fact for human minds, limited as we are in our information; but, as a metaphysical statement about ultimate reality and as an ideal for guiding research, it shines with promise. Laplace embraced this ideal, and his achievements as "the French Newton" reinforced its power to win ever-wider allegiance in the world of science and in the educated public.

Laplace's public life was as prosperous as his scientific research. He was an active member of the Academy of Sciences from the time of his first election in 1773; during the Revolution, he was active in promoting the metric system; when the revolutionary government established the École Polytechnique, he was a founding professor; under Napoleon he became a member of the Senate and eventually its Chancellor, even named a Count of the Empire in 1806; and, after the restoration of the Bourbons, he continued to be honored and was made a marquis in 1817. Ten years later, he died peacefully in his bed.

During his time in the Senate, under the rule of Napoleon, Laplace was associated with another scientist-Senator, Pierre-Jean George Cabanis, who, though younger, was also a member of the circle of Condillac, Diderot, d'Alembert, Benjamin Franklin, Thomas Jefferson, and the others, at the Holbach salon. Cabanis was born in 1757, too late to participate for long in the fierce struggles against the ancien régime before it was overthrown. But his ideas were as fiery and his ideals the same as those of the older veterans. He insisted on mechanical explanations of all things. He thought of himself as performing on ideas the same analytical service Lavoisier had provided to chemistry. All ideas and ideals, he argued, are ultimately reducible to physiology. Therefore, we must turn more to teachers of medicine than to teachers of morals. In his most famous argument, the brain and the stomach are compared: just as the stomach digests food and secretes nourishing juices, so the brain digests sense impressions and secretes thought. He was "antimetaphysical," in intention at least. The deep causes in nature are unknown and must remain unknown; but whatever they are, they can be only physical, he contended.

Cabanis was true to his ideas of freedom and democracy. He was, at first, a supporter of Napoleon and became a Senator under his rule. But when Napoleon became as autocratic as the Bourbons had ever been, Cabanis protested. Napoleon was displeased and scornful, dubbing him and his friends with similar "outmoded" commitments, the "Idéologues." The name stuck to the shrinking band of true believers, who clung to the values of liberalism and materialism—now seemingly inseparably associated—even in a period of restoration and growing reaction. Perhaps Napoleon was right. In many ways, Cabanis was an idealogue. But there is no necessary shame in loyalty to ideals, even when they are inconvenient or out of fashion, as long as those ideals are fully acknowledged and well examined. Among mere human beings, alas, this is not always the case.

COMTE, MAXWELL, AND EINSTEIN

As I move from the beginning of the nineteenth century to our own time, I need to be ever more selective in my illustrations. They are just that, reminders intended to retell a story about one strand of modern metaphysics that should by now have awakened resonances of recognition. The remainder of this narrative can afford to be brief and impressionistic, therefore, and to count on the reader's filling in the large lacunae. It will skip from the classical expression of Positivism, with Auguste Comte at the start of the nineteenth century, to the classical expression of that century's physics, with James Clerk Maxwell, to the culminating achievements of Albert Einstein, in whose universe moderns still live today.

Comte, born in Montpellier in 1798, has the distinction of founding both a new school of philosophy, Positivism, and a new science, sociology. The two are intimately entwined, since Comte's Positivist understanding of the sciences led him to anticipate a science of society, and, reciprocally, since Comte's sociology was to be thoroughly Positivist in method and content. In addition, Comte believed from his youth that the progressive dynamic of history required deep reform in ethics, politics, and religion, to restore lost unities of thought and feeling. This led him beyond philosophy and science to the establishment of a new Positivist religion, the Religion of Humanity.

Ungainly and physically unattractive from childhood, Comte showed immense intellectual powers at an early age. At fourteen, he had rethought his religion and politics and had dismayed his ardently Catholic and royalist family by announcing his atheist and republican conclusions. At fifteen, he had achieved the highest score for all applicants on the entrance examinations for the École Polytechnique, the distinguished school of advanced science (where Laplace, we recall, had been a founding faculty member); but, because of his youth, he was denied admission until a year later. Eventually, departing his native Montpellier for Paris in 1814, he happily divided his time between intense study and rebelliousness. After only two years, Comte was sent home when a student demonstration, in which he played a leading role, resulted in the closing of the school for radicalism. Later, he was again excluded at the time of its royalist reorganization.

Against his family's wishes, Comte soon returned to Paris to study privately and to support himself (meagerly) by tutoring in mathematics. During this time, he read widely, taking a great interest in Marquis de Condorcet's writings on human progress, in David Hume, and in Adam Smith—all of whom, as mentioned, were welcome guests within the inner circles of the philosophes. After a year of virtual starvation, Comte accepted the position of secretary to the visionary social thinker Claude Henri Comte de Saint-Simon. Saint-Simon, forty years his elder, had already stated the "Law of the Three Stages" and was full of ideas on the restructuring and reform of society. After seven years, Comte, at first an admiring disciple, broke away with much acrimony.

In the next year, 1825, Comte married, despite extremely limited financial resources gained from tutoring. The marriage was stormy and ended in 1842, but during this period Comte gave the great course of private lectures, begun in 1826, that resulted in his six-volume *Cours de philosophie positive*. The complex course of seventy-two "*séances*," fully outlined from the start, was interrupted after only the third lecture, when Comte suffered a nervous breakdown requiring institutionalization and a slow, painful recovery (during which he attempted suicide by throwing himself in the Seine); but, in 1828, the thread was taken up and, in the years 1830–1842, the volumes appeared exactly as initially outlined.

The final period of Comte's life, following his divorce and the appearance of the *Cours*, was devoted to fulfilling his early commitment to the reform of society and religion, based on the intellectual foundations he believed his *Cours* provided. Despite growing fame, Comte never achieved a regular academic position and depended in large part on charitable subscriptions raised by admirers in England (including John Stuart Mill) as well as in France. In 1845, he met the beautiful, gentle, and educated Mme. Clothilde de Vaux and fell in love—so deeply that, after her untimely death in the next year, he gave homage to her with a ritualized trip each Wednesday to her grave, invoked her virtues aloud three times a day, and incorporated elements of feminine mysticism in his Religion of Humanity. The major books of this period were his *Système de politique positive* and his *Catéchisme positiviste*. He died of cancer in 1857, still at work on another attempt at reconciling religion and science, *La synthèse subjective*, of which only the first volume (1856) was completed.

The key to understanding Comte's ideas is the previously mentioned Law of the Three Stages, first enunciated by Saint-Simon but developed by Comte into a theory of historical progress and a framework for interpreting all human thought.

At the start, Comte argues, we think anthropomorphically, giving explanations in terms of qualities like our own. Just as the child kicks the toy that has tripped him and calls it naughty, so in early human history the seers and prophets invoked nymphs, demons, and divinities to explain their world. With the logical tendency for unification at work in all theory, the trend even in primitive theological thinking was toward monotheism; but the whole enterprise of thinking in such categories shows immaturity.

In youth, we discard the animist trappings of childhood, thinking instead in terms of "forces" and other impersonal, behind-the-scenes entities of abstract metaphysics. So, likewise, the best of ancient thinkers rose from the first, theological, to the second, metaphysical, stage of understanding. This was an advance, especially as abstract concepts became unified into ever more powerful systems. But it still allowed the obscurity and ultimate futility of unperceivable entities to enter thinking.

The fully mature stage of thought finally rose for Comte only when scientists, led by the example of Newton's rejection of "hypotheses" to account for the mathematical regularities of gravitation, resolved to think solely in terms of the lawful relations between observables. This rejection of any appeal to what cannot be "positively perceived" marks the attainment of the Positive—and highest—stage of human thought, whether in an individual, society, or sub-portion of society such as the élite community of scientists, philosophers, and other thinkers who take the sciences with sufficient seriousness.

Comte goes into much detail in his six-volume work to examine the sciences in their logical relations to one another. Shorn of this detail, his position is that the most general and inclusive sciences were required first, as the logically necessary preparation for the more particular ones. Mathematics, as the abstract or fundamental study of the forms of existence common to all things, is presupposed for the successful study of physics, which can be divided into celestial physics (astronomy) or terrestrial physics, either general (physics proper) or special according to the empirical elements (chemistry). Astronomy made important strides before terrestrial physics; but chemistry had to wait for its germination until general terrestrial physics had first come into bloom. In like manner, biology depended upon chemistry for its emergence as a lawful science. Biology is less comprehensive than chemistry, since the domain of living forms is less extensive than the domain of all forms exhibiting chemical laws. Correspondingly, biology, though logically depending upon chemistry, has positive laws of its own that are not merely the laws of chemistry; and this is just as should be expected, since living matter is observed to behave very differently from nonliving chemical entities. Thus, Comte rejected methodological reductionism of higher sciences to the lower, despite the fact that the higher presuppose the lower.

In the same way, human society is far less general than the biological realm as a whole, though society clearly presupposes and depends on the laws of life. This means the laws of human society, as they are uncovered, will inevitably have their own quasi-autonomy despite the complete grounding of sociology in biology, biology in chemistry, chemistry in physics, and physics in mathematics. This methodological uniqueness does not, for Comte, soften in the slightest the invariant character of social laws. Early in his *Cours*, "Social Physics" is what he terms the positive scientific study of society; only after several volumes does he introduce his newly invented word "sociology," for what he believed would be the "final science."

In Comte's classification of the sciences, it stands to reason that the rise of sociology had to await the establishment of all the prior disciplines. This centuries-long delay left the field of human society vulnerable to domination by the immature prescientific modes of thinking, theology, and metaphysics, as long as the benefits of the Positive mode in this area were unavailable. Thus, in Comte's analysis, adding the Law of the Three Stages to the classification of the sciences reveals that the moment is ripe—and inevitable—for radical social reform.

At least as early as 1822, during his association with the social reformer Saint-Simon, Comte had announced that he wanted to point the way to a better political, ethical, and religious order. In his mind, the great effort of developing the Positive Philosophy was largely a means for the sake of providing a responsible scientific foundation—something far beyond even Saint-Simon's aspiration—for a Positive Polity and a Positive Religion. No doubt Comte would have been disappointed in posterity for tending to take his efforts at social synthesis as less memorable than the preceding philosophic analysis.

The Positive Polity developed in his *Système de politique positive* was an élitist vision of a rational, harmonious society, with all members living generously for one another, the whole inspired and led by altruistic scientist-priests. Some have speculated that Comte's unconscious model was an idealized École Polytechnique, symbol of fond memories of youth filtered through rose-tinted glasses. On the other hand, if one grants Comte the inevitability of the Law of the Three Stages, then there is nothing fantastic about anticipating a much more rational society than anything hitherto encountered among humans. And if one is convinced, with Comte, that a fully determinate science of society is imminent, then all aspects of society, including ethics and religion, can in principle be engineered.

Comte took the domain of ethics and religion with utmost seriousness. Some commentators have criticized the absence of any science of psychology in his classification, leaving sociology as the "final" science; but it is not fair to charge that Comte ignored the individual person. Sociology was to be the overall name for what Comte called the "Study of Man," and this study was to include careful attention to the individual person as well as to people in relations. In his *Catéchisme positiviste,* Comte characterized the "individual" aspect of sociology as the study of *moral laws.* This emphasis on morality again illustrates what was on Comte's mind as he laid out the logical structure of the sciences: the whole edifice of science, rising from generality to particularity, finally focuses on human society—and within society, because of its still greater particularity, on morality.

Morality, however, needs to be motivated. The fundamental motivator in human life is religion. In reformed Positivist society, religion, though essential, will not remain at just the theological level of thinking: that is, it will dispense with the gods or with God. Instead, it will find inspiration in Humanity as the "Great Being." Comte developed a Positivist Calendar (with thirteen months of twenty-eight days, each dedicated to a hero of Humanity, e.g., Archimedes or Gutenberg or Shakespeare or Descartes) for use in veneration of human achievements of many sorts. A Positivist priesthood would preach rational truth and nurture social feeling and cooperation within society. The split between faith and reason, authority and autonomy, ritual and science, would at long last be fully overcome.

Comte believed that this Religion of Humanity, an intrinsically universal religion, would be especially attractive to those who, within the pre-Positivist stages of history, have been systematically marginalized or excluded. These are the various downtrodden proletariats of the world, and, of course, women everywhere. Comte concludes his *Catéchisme positiviste* with the following reflection on his hopes for Universal Positivist Religion: "Though it be yet very greatly hampered, especially at its centre, by the prejudices and passions which, under different forms, reject all wholesome discipline, its efficacy will soon be felt by women and proletaries. . . . But its best recommendation must come from the exclusive competence of the Positive priesthood to rally everywhere the honest and the thoughtful, nobly accepting the whole inheritance of mankind" (Comte 1891: 294).

There is irony in the fact that the principal actual inheritors of Comte's mantle, the Logical Positivists of the mid-twentieth century, adopted instead a disdainful attitude toward the value of ethics and religion, focussing rather on

Comte's rejection of non-empirical modes of thought and on his fascination by the sciences. We do well, however, to recall that Comte himself saw no necessary conflict between the sciences and religion, rightly understood.

A great exemplary figure of nineteenth-century thinking about natural reality is James Clerk Maxwell, a physicist who made lasting contributions to theories of matter, electricity, magnetism, and light, but whose views are far from what Comte would have approved as properly "mature." Maxwell was born in Edinburgh, Scotland, in 1831, when Comte's *Cours* first appeared in Paris. He was educated at the Edinburgh Academy and later at Edinburgh University, graduating in 1850. He proceeded to Cambridge where, in 1854, he obtained his master's degree from Trinity College, famed for its excellence in mathematics. His first teaching position (1856–60) was in natural philosophy at Marischal College in Aberdeen Scotland; and his second (1860–68) was in physics and astronomy at King's College, London. In 1868, he resigned to pursue his private researches at his Scottish estate in Kirkcudbrightshire. In 1871, he was called back to Cambridge as the first Cavendish Professor in experimental physics. There he supervised the design and building of the famous Cavendish laboratories, exhibiting the kind and unostentatious character for which he was affectionately known. He died in 1879, at only forty-eight years of age, having contributed two achievements, among many lesser ones, for which he is important to this narrative.

The first was his work on the kinetic theory of gases. We saw earlier that Robert Boyle had established, before the time of Newton, that the pressure of a gas in a closed container is proportional to its temperature. Later, in 1738, Daniel Bernoulli (1700–1782) accounted for Boyle's Law by hypothesizing (counter to Positivist preferences) that this pressure arises from the otherwise invisible collisions of gas "corpuscles" against the walls of the container. This idea was fruitful. The suggestion followed that the heat variable in Boyle's equation was nothing but these invisible collisions, something that James Prescott Joule (1818–1889) confirmed experimentally in 1843. In 1857, Rudolf Clausius (1822–1888), credited with establishing the field of thermodynamics, showed that the temperature of any gas will be directly related to the velocity of the corpuscles that comprise it, and that the rate of the collisions involved can be derived from the laws of classical Newtonian mechanics. At this point in the dialogue, James Clerk Maxwell, still at King's College, made his remarkable intervention. First, he showed that not all the molecules in the gas would be moving at the same velocity; that, instead, there must be some slower, some faster, in the mix. Boyle's Law and its successor statements must be in terms of averages and statistical probabilities, not certainties. Because the probabilities are very high, due to the large populations of molecules, the mathematical laws still describe accurately enough what Comte would have approved as the measurable data, but they must be conceived differently—something else is going on behind the covariation of variables.

In 1867, to illustrate his point, Maxwell proposed a thought-experiment: he explained it in terms of what might happen if one were, per impossibile, to introduce thought and purpose into the mechanism of gases. It is known from massive experience that heat never travels from a cooler to a hotter container; the hotter always cools as the cooler warms. But there is nothing *necessary* about this, Maxwell shows, if only purpose and intelligence were to defeat the normal probabilities. Imagine a tiny demon, a "door demon," in charge of opening and closing a hatch between a cooler and a hotter container. When the demon detects one of the relatively few faster-moving molecules in the cool container approaching its hatch, headed (according to classical mechanical laws) toward the hotter container, it could be let through; likewise, when it recognizes one of the fewer slow-moving molecules in the hot container approaching, the demon could obligingly allow it through to the cooler side. The result would be the "impossible" transfer of heat to a hotter body from a cooler body, with no violations of laws of classical mechanics but, instead, only cognition and steady intention changing the normal odds.

This was a powerful thought experiment. It convinced scientists working in thermodynamics that nothing but statistical probability—no inherent mechanical necessity—maintains the laws of thermal transfer, gas pressure, and the associated range of observable phenomena. This shift of loyalties from absolute calculations to statistical ones, from insisting on perfect determinism to accepting a range of likelihoods as adequate for explanation, was to be a fateful one.

Maxwell's other major contribution was to the field of electricity and magnetism. Here again he was far from Positivist in his approach to his problem. The problem was the irritating notion of action at a distance. In 1831, Michael Faraday (1791–1867) had shown experimentally that moving a magnet near a closed loop of wire can induce an electrical current in the wire. Likewise, an electrical current in a wire causes a distant magnetic needle to spin. Some scientists on the continent of Europe were beginning to accept sheer ("occult") forces between points of electrical charge in relative motion to one another, but this was deeply offensive to the English thinkers working on the issue. Faraday himself, William Thomson (later Lord Kelvin, 1824–1907), and Maxwell were not willing to do without "hypotheses" that could link causes directly to effects. Faraday employed the analogy of heat "fluxions"; Thomson, in 1846, used entirely different analogies to account mathematically for the same data; but, finally, in a paper to the Royal Society in 1867, and later in his monumental *Electricity and Magnetism* (1873), Maxwell produced a set of equations that could describe the stresses and motions of a material medium holding and joining the causes and effects in which electromagnetic influences could be propagated. The medium, the equations showed, needed to be an elastic, solid material. Maxwell calculated that propagation of electromagnetic influences in this medium would take place extremely rapidly, the elasticity of the medium allowing a wave form of propagation through it. This speed turned out (allowing for inaccurate data at the time) to be the same as the measured speed of light. Therefore, Maxwell hypothesized still further, light itself is an electromagnetic phenomenon, consisting in a small range of the frequencies constituting the visible spectrum.

Fourteen years later, Heinrich Hertz (1857–1894) showed experimentally that electromagnetic waves, travelling at the speed of light, could be generated and detected in his laboratory. In less than one more decade, in 1896, Guglielmo Marconi (1874–1937) had already improved and patented such techniques to send and receive messages; in 1901, he received a signal across the Atlantic Ocean, beamed between Cornwall, England, and St. John's, Newfoundland; and, thus, the present age of radio and television was on its way. But Maxwell's lasting influences, though institutionalized by powerful broadcasting industries, went far deeper still. His commitment to the values of simplicity, coherence, and unity for thinking about the universe had been rewarded up to this time, with a tying together of some of the most mysterious phenomena puzzling thinkers over the ages: magnetism, electricity, and light. His commitment to mathematics as the proper way to think about the universe and to matter as the only acceptable framework for understanding the events—of all sorts—occurring around us had brought results, both theoretical and practical, beyond the wildest dreams of Pythagoras or Democritus.

It is true that Maxwell's demon remained for him a haunting mystery. The thought experiment had shown the utterly alien character of cognition and purpose in the great, colliding domain of statistical mechanics. While it showed, as he intended, the strictly probablistic character manifested by events reducible to huge numbers of collisions between the tiny corpuscles that make up the kinetic universe (gases only or perhaps all of matter?), it also showed how out of place mind is in the material cosmos pictured in this experiment. The argument functions as a reductio ad absurdum. There are no demons to recognize molecules and purposefully open and close doors for them. Hot gases, liquids, and solid bodies do not gain heat from cooler ones. Where then is mind in nature? Each of us seems to be an example, larger and more complex, of Maxwell's demon: we recognize our immediate environment, we influence our world (using natural laws) to upset the odds and to realize our otherwise improbable purposes for the future. But how can this be? There seems to be a radical discontinuity between a kinetic theory of reality and the most obvious facts about our human mental activities in it. Granted, it was no part of Maxwell's function *qua* scientist to "hypothesize" about this problem—how *actual* demons like ourselves fit coherently into the ultimate understanding of reality—but without some such hypothesis, the commitment of the scientific thinker to simplicity, unity, coherence, and adequacy—to the full range of data—remains partial, its comprehensive scope arbitrarily blocked. The very idea, itself, that thought about reality should be split into "scientific" specializations and stop there looks odd from this perspective. Either give us Positivism, with its consequent foreswearing of all attempts to "hypothesize" beyond the given regularities of experience (foreswearing thereby the attempt, precious to Maxwell, of understanding what is going on behind the scenes) one might conclude, or continue the search for a fully coherent theory of reality, inclusive also of the reality who is doing the theorizing.

Albert Einstein, who for a large part of his adult life was on both sides of the decision between Positivism and a realist theory of reality, was born in March in the same year that Maxwell died (in November). After a year in Ulm, where he was born, he moved to Munich, where his father and uncle ran a small factory. His uncle supplemented his formal education (which he disliked) with an introduction to algebra and geometry, by means of which he amused himself, but at the time young Albert showed little aptitude for studies. At fourteen, he became enthralled with popular science and attempted, at age sixteen, to win admission to the Federal Polytechnic in Zürich. He failed on his first try, succeeding a year later, in 1896. As a student, he was inattentive to his formal assignments, but in his private reading he read theoretical physics voraciously; his favorite was Maxwell, on electromagnetic theory.

Having become a Swiss citizen during his student days, Einstein looked for work in Switzerland after graduation in 1900, but found few suitable openings. Finally, in 1902, he located a position in Bern, at the patent office, and married a classmate from the Polytechnic. Suddenly, as it seemed, he exploded into publication in 1905 with a set of papers in *Annalen der Physik* that were, as we shall see, to shake the Newtonian world picture to its foundations.

The papers won him deserved attention, and he began an apparently frantic series of professional moves. In 1909, the University of Zürich offered him his first academic position; in 1911, he became Professor of Theoretical Physics at the German University at Prague; in 1912, he returned to Switzerland as a professor at his alma mater; and, in 1913, he was appointed to a chair at the University of Berlin and a research position at the Kaiser Wilhelm Society, also in Berlin. Once in Berlin he obtained a divorce from his first wife, by whom he had two sons; six years later, he married his cousin Elsa. In May of the same year, 1919, the prediction made on the basis of his theory of general relativity—that light close to the gravitational field of the sun would be bent from its straight-line path—was dramatically confirmed by British expeditions sent to observe the total eclipse. The general public started to hear about Albert Einstein and the strange world he had described. His fame grew in 1921 with the

Nobel Prize (not for his theories of relativity, but for work with the photoelectric effect, whose significance we shall note later), and he lectured far and wide during the next decade. He was on one such lecture trip to the United States when Hitler came to power in 1933. He never returned to Germany. Princeton's newly established Institute for Advanced Study became Einstein's home for the rest of his life. There, he supported various anti-war and Zionist causes but also wrote his famous letter to President Roosevelt urging nuclear research to counter the threat of a Nazi atom bomb. It was there, too, that he received (and declined) the invitation to become President of Israel; argued quietly with colleagues about what he felt were the inadequacies of quantum physics; played his violin in the evenings; and worked to the end of his life to find the unified field theory that always eluded him. It was also there that he died on April 18, 1955.

Einstein blew hot and cold until late in life on the issue of "hypotheses" versus Positivism. At the end, he came down firmly for "hypotheses," as needed, free constructs of the mind, although finally—because they purport to tell us about an objective reality beyond the mind—in need of empirical grounding; but the story of his contributions to theory of reality contains many conflicting currents on this score.

One of his first topics was the question of the objective reality of the colliding "molecules" central to the "hypotheses" of the kinetic theory. In this case, his influence leaned toward establishing the physical reality of these theoretical entities. This he did by reflecting mathematically on one of the anomalies of observation left unexplained since 1827, when Robert Brown (1773–1858), a Scottish botanist, had observed under a microscope the continual agitation of tiny bits of pollen in a beaker of water that was otherwise completely still. This "Brownian" movement, Einstein showed, could be retrodicted mathematically as the visible result of collisions between invisibly small molecules and microscopically visible pollen grains. Far from an anomaly, the Brownian movement became instead a direct empirical confirmation of the kinetic theory of matter. Although in themselves still unobservable, molecules became nevertheless more than "mere" hypotheses, thanks to Einstein's 1905 paper on the topic.

However, another 1905 paper on special relativity wielded a positivist scalpel against the hypotheses of "ether" and "simultaneity." The supposed solid, elastic medium Maxwell thought was needed for the transmission of electromagnetic waves simply had no mathematical meaning (this may have been enough for Einstein) and, in the famous (though perhaps not known to Einstein in 1905) experiment in 1887, performed by the American scientists Albert A. Michelson and Edward W. Morley, there turned out to be no empirical meaning either. If the earth were drifting through a sea of this ether in some direction, and if light waves were propagating at a definite rate through this sea, then the speed of light should depend on the direction and velocity of the earth's motion. This simply did not prove true, when measurements were carefully taken. The speed of light was the same, no matter what the direction of its propagation.

Einstein's special theory of relativity could make sense of this as no other theory could. For years, the young Einstein had been fascinated by the thought of what a light wave would "look" like from the perspective of someone moving ahead of it, at just the same velocity. It should, on Newtonian principles, appear to be a spatially oscillating electromagnetic field apparently at rest. But this makes no sense at all in Maxwell's equations. It is an absurdity, a contradiction. Therefore, Einstein had to postulate that one's motion is irrelevant to the speed of light as it is received at one's special reception point, one's own "inertial frame" (this restriction to special inertial frames, in which gravitation is negligible, is what makes this the "special" theory of relativity). No matter what one's motion, relative to other inertial frames, the laws of physics, definitely including the speed and character of light as expressed in Maxwell's equations, will continue to hold. This in turn means there is no meaning to the notion of travelling "at" or "greater than" the speed of light. The phrases become logical contradictions and have no place in the conceptual geography of the theory.

Similarly, with regard to the notion of "simultaneity," Einstein saw that to measure it in a universe where Maxwell's equations obtain, one needs to keep in mind the finite constant of the speed of light. In Newton's infinite, homogeneous, equable space and time, assuming God's sensorium to be coextensive with the whole expanse, it might make sense to talk about two absolutely simultaneous events at great distances from one another. God, at least, would know they were occupying the same moment in time. But measuring simultaneity in a world where every special reception point will detect light arriving at the same speed, regardless of other relative velocities, becomes deeply problematic. Clocks, by which alone time can be given an operational meaning, will have to run more slowly as their velocity increases, so that the speed of incoming light will turn out the same. Two events that are effectively simultaneous within one inertial frame may not be so when time is measured by clocks in another inertial frame moving rapidly in relation to the first. Einstein's theory also connects the slowing down of moving clocks directly with a gain in their massiveness. At the limit velocity of light this massiveness would become infinite—another argument from absurdity against any material entity aspiring to break that speed limit. But velocity implies energy; seeing velocity and mass varying together, Einstein inferred that mass (m) is a form of energy, equivalent in principle to energy (E) under the limit of the constant (c) speed of light. From this relationship, the portentous equation, $E=mc^2$, emerged.

Under Einstein's formula, the matter of our universe should no longer be pictured as inert or passive, merely pushed around by "forces." Material is energetic; conversely, it is energy made massive. A third paper, published in 1905, deals with this duality of energy and massiveness in another way, by relating the wave character of radiation, particularly light waves, to a corpuscular character more typically associated with matter. Assuming a real corpuscular nature for light radiating from hot bodies—so that it comes only in a limited number of specific "quanta" of energy rather than in a continuum of mathematically possible quantities, as should be the case if it were only a wave motion—Einstein was able to retrodict the actual empirical findings described by Max Planck (1858–1947) in 1900. Planck's Law had given mathematical form to all the observations, just as Comte would have considered the whole and complete task of scientific thought; but Einstein went much further, hypothesizing that all radiation must have a real corpuscular as well as a real wave character. Then, with the aid of this quite nonpositivistic hypothesis, he went on to show that a further deployment of this theory of the microscopic world could effortlessly account for the hitherto puzzling emission of electrons from a metal plate on which light is shone, the "photoelectric effect." Einstein was awarded the Nobel Prize in 1921 for this vital discovery about the duality of the world of radiation, which contained the beginnings of quantum physics.

It is hard to categorize the theory of general relativity as positivistic or nonpositivistic. On the positivistic side, one of the principal achievements of Einstein's theory is to eliminate the concept of some "force" of gravity somehow slipping through all shields to grasp helpless entities in invisible tentacles, accelerating them remorselessly toward one another. Einstein's solution was to return to the mathematical ideal of perfectly straight-line motion, but to redefine the geometry of space and time in such a way that gravitational accelerations could be treated mathematically as straight lines in a four-dimensional space-time continuum. In this way, the "special" restrictions of special relativity could be removed and all inertial frames, no matter what their motions relative to each other, could be included in one grand vision of the universe. This general theory, published in 1916, was less immediately useable (or testable) than the special theory, but among the few empirical predictions it afforded was the lens effect light rays should show when passing through the more tightly curved space near massive bodies like our sun. This accounts for the great excitement in 1919 when this bending was indeed observed. In addition, Mercury, which, as the closest planet to the sun always moves through the more deformed space nearby, should show corresponding deformations in its orbit. These anomalies had indeed been observed for many years, and had puzzled astronomers working with Newtonian assumptions about homogeneous, Euclidean space. Once again, an Einstein theory could provide a retrodiction of known but unexplained data—this time by applying a non-Euclidean geometry to space-time.

Little wonder, therefore, that in his later years Einstein put positivism aside. In old age, reflecting on the quest that moved him from the start, despite many intervening positivistic moments, he wrote: "Out yonder there was this huge world, which exists independently of us human beings and which stands before us like a great, eternal riddle, at least partially accessible to our inspection and thinking" (Einstein 1949: 5). There is an objective world "out yonder," whose character we can discover by free speculation, mathematically led and empirically confirmed. And this objective world is in itself perfectly ordered, Einstein insisted. Nothing is left to chance; nothing is, in the end, merely statistical or probable. If we need to cast our laws in probablistic mathematical forms, this is only a sign of our ignorance of the underlying, perfect laws of "the Lord." This was the basis for his unrelenting criticism of the direction taken by quantum mechanics and virtually the whole profession, which became convinced, despite his passionate contrary advice, that quantum physics reveals a world that contains, at the microcosmic extremes, fundamentally indeterminate features. Max Born, a physicist sharing the majority view, received a famous letter from Einstein putting the matter in a theological metaphor: "You believe in God playing dice and I in perfect laws in the world of things existing as real objects, which I try to grasp in a wildly speculative way" (Einstein 1949: 176).

Was it a metaphor to speak of God? Perhaps. But it was no "mere" metaphor for Einstein, who was fond of such expressions. He wrote feelingly of his "cosmic religion," consisting in a highly Spinozistic adoration of the whole of nature in its perfection, mystery, and impersonal splendor. When he was twelve, he reports, he turned away, as did Spinoza, from the traditional religious ways of thinking, in which prayers and pleadings of a personal sort are supposed to occasion the intervention of another Person who, arbitrarily or sentimentally, is thought to respond. For Einstein, the key to cosmic perfection was in its causality. Thus:

> For any one who is pervaded with the sense of causal law in all that happens, who accepts in real earnest the assumption of causality, the idea of a Being who interferes with the sequence of events in the world is absolutely impossible. Neither the religion of fear nor the social-moral religion can have any hold on him (Einstein 1930: 1).

Sacred value is at stake then in the dispute over the indeterminacy principle. This is for Einstein a matter of commitment, not preponderance of currently-available evidence. As Born put it, reflecting on Einstein's letter to him that rejected the idea of God as gambler: "That his opinion in this matter differs from mine is regrettable, but it is no object of logical dispute between us. It is based on different experience in our work and life" (Einstein 1949: 176).

Albert Einstein was a deeply committed man. His values—mathematical simplicity, unity, and intelligibility; perfect causal determinacy; and exclusive reliance on efficient causality—are familiar and fundamentally modern. He transformed important aspects of the modern world picture, of course. He modified the geometry by which space and time are to be interpreted; but space and time are still primarily to be conceived through the abstractions of geometry, not through first-hand experience of distance or becoming. He altered the understanding of matter from the "hard, impenetrable, and massy" corpuscles of the seventeenth century to packets of enormous energy, every corpuscle having its wave-like vibratory frequency and every wave having its particle-like discreteness. But within the new understanding, the space-time universe, however shaped, contains nothing more than "wavicles" of matter-energy laid out in four-dimensional "time lines" of eternal necessity. His own answer to what I have called the modern agenda, defining the appropriate place in reality for mind, purpose, quality, and value, was to "transcend" these features of experience as merely "personal" and therefore petty. After he renounced traditional religious faith at age twelve, he turned to physical theory for even greater solace. "It is quite clear to me that the religious paradise of youth, which was thus lost, was a first attempt to free myself from the chains of the 'merely-personal', from an existence which is dominated by wishes, hopes and primitive feelings" (Einstein 1949: 5). There is no intelligible place for wishes, hopes, purposes, or values in the world he eventually conceptualized. For him, contemplation of it was a liberation from the small to the sublime.

Of course, Einstein lived his whole life as an appreciator of value and as a moral agent. He felt strongly the obligation to work for causes he judged worthy and to throw his influence against war. He considered it important to warn President Roosevelt against the danger of a Nazi nuclear weapon and to do what he could to stimulate countervailing research. He deeply sympathized with Zionism and with the suffering and hopes of his fellow Jews. He enjoyed good music, good conversation, and the miracle of self-aware thinking. He was not only a mathematical genius, he was a wise and moral man. But none of this can be interpreted through the theoretical fruits of his genius. Sadly, at the pinnacle of its cosmological achievement, the modern quest for understanding reality continues to leave the quest itself, its importance, its purposes, its joys, its obligations, its qualities and values, entirely out of the account.

7

THE PRIMACY OF MIND

Dropping back from the twentieth century, but remembering the major branch represented by the modern majority view, we find ourselves starting our climb again in the seventeenth century, soon after Descartes. This time my narrative will follow the minority who attempted to deal with the modern metaphysical agenda—Descartes' bifurcation of mind from matter, values from nature—by making mind, not matter, primary.

Arguing for the primacy of mind can take different forms. Not everyone whom we shall encounter on this second branch will share all fundamental values with one another; but one commitment they do share: the commitment to the values of experienced qualities. These will not be bargained away or ignored as someone else's problem. Nor can they be "transcended," as though opting for wider, less individual values somehow eliminated the problem of the valuer's relation to the rest of reality. Higher, wiser, more benign subjectivity does not eliminate the problem of subjectivity. What is it? How do minds relate to brains and to bodies and to other persons and to the wider world of animals and mountains and stars?

We shall reflect on the answers of one seventeenth-century genius who is often located in the same firmament with Isaac Newton (and who was often, to his detriment, embroiled in fierce conflict with Newton and followers); next, we shall examine the alternatives of two eighteenth-century philosophers who had even greater immediate influence on the course of thought; and, then, we shall choose one exemplar from the late nineteenth century before ending our narrative in the early twentieth century. Our treatment will be appreciative, but we shall see that it must be critical, too.

LEIBNIZ AND BERKELEY

Gottfried Wilhelm von Leibniz was another authentic genius of the seventeenth century, an age rich with intellectual brilliance, as we have seen. He was born in the summer of 1646 in Leipzig, Germany, the son of a professor of moral philosophy at the University of Leipzig. Gottfried was only six when his father died, but his library remained open to his child, who voraciously read through it from an early age, teaching himself Latin and Greek as he went along. By age fifteen, Leibniz was admitted to the University where his father had taught. He studied for a career in law, completing his undergraduate degree swiftly, but moving to Altdorf (near Nürnberg) for his doctorate, which he received at age twenty-one. (Leipzig would not grant him this advanced degree because of his youth.) Settling in Nürnberg, he became a friend of the former Prime Minister of the Prince Bishop, the Elector of Mainz, who put his legal talents to work in redrafting the legal codes of Nürnberg. Through this contact and because of the excellence of his work, he won a position with the Prince Bishop himself, Johann Philipp von Schönborn, Elector of Mainz. This initially involved legal work but soon evolved into diplomatic service. At Leibniz's own suggestion, he was sent, in 1672, to King Louis XIV in Paris to persuade the Sun King to attack Egypt. It was to be a latter day Crusade with multiple benefits, commercial and political (not least for Germany, seeking to deflect aggressive attentions from powerful France). The mission failed to persuade King Louis, but it gave Leibniz sustained entrance to the intellectual society of Paris, which at that time included besides assorted Cartesians, the philosopher Nicholas Malebranche and the mathematician Christiaan Huygens, from whom we have already heard. Leibniz advanced his earlier mathematical studies with Huygens and, while in Paris, invented a calculating machine that could add, subtract, multiply, divide, and even extract roots. During the early months of 1673, Leibniz travelled from Paris to London on another diplomatic mission for the Elector of Mainz; while there, he demonstrated his calculator to the Royal Society and soon after was elected to membership. While there, Leibniz also established lasting links with Robert Boyle.

Back in Paris and after the death of the Prince Bishop of Mainz in 1673, Leibniz advanced to a new post with the Duke of Braunschweig-Lüneburg. In 1675, at the Duke's request, he established residence in Hanover, the Ducal seat, travelling from Paris by way of Amsterdam, where, as we noted earlier, he visited Benedict Spinoza and was allowed to read and take notes on the unpublished manuscript of Spinoza's *Ethics*. For the rest of his life, Leibniz worked for the Dukes of Hanover in various positions of usefulness, including supervising the mint and the deep silver mines in the Harz region under Hanoverian control. His legal arguments succeeded in winning Hanover the important status of Elector. Elector George Louis, who acceded to this title in

1698 while Leibniz remained a member of his Court, moved to England in 1714 as King George I. This Duke-Elector, George, age thirty-eight at his accession, did not hold "old" Leibniz (then fifty-six) in high regard as had the previous Dukes. Leibniz responded by widening his horizons, becoming a member of the Académie des Sciences in Paris in 1700, President (for life) of the Berlin Academy (also in 1700), and privy councillor to other monarchs, the Elector of Brandenberg and Peter the Great of Russia. In addition, he was named Baron of the Empire in Austria.

These were years of great obloquy, however, against Leibniz. Beginning in 1684, he had published papers from Hanover dealing with a new mathematical technique, the calculus of infinitesimals, invented in the years following his first trip to London in 1673, when these ideas first occurred to him. Newton, as we remember, had developed his "method of fluxions" as early as the plague years, 1665–1666; but with his penchant for secrecy, he had held back from publication. Though privately circulated, his treatise *On Analysis* went unpublished until 1711. Therefore, he was furious at Leibniz's claim for priority, and with the aid of associates in the Royal Society, which formally took his side, he orchestrated a bitter controversy during which accusations of plagiarism were forcefully made against Leibniz. Scholars today generally conclude that the two geniuses each had indeed worked independently in their inventions. Newton had priority of discovery, but Leibniz had legitimate priority in publication and was innocent of plagiarism. Today's exoneration did not help Leibniz's reputation at the time of course; he shot back, but his was a lone voice and he was clearly injured as the attacks continued into his later years.

The later years were lonely. Many of his best associates had left for England with King George. He continued his writing, summarizing his views in the *Monadology* in 1714. Most of his philosophical work, however, (including the *Monadology*) remained unpublished for extended periods. Of his philosophical books, only the *Theodicy* appeared in print during his lifetime, published in Amsterdam in French (as *Essais de Théodicée sur la bonté de Dieu, la liberté de l'homme et l'origine du mal*) in 1710, when Leibniz was already sixty-four. Although his other manuscripts and correspondence, when eventually published, revealed one of the most powerful and advanced minds of his century, his death, when it occurred in 1716, went unnoticed by the world of learning.

Since Leibniz's thought took shape gradually through many phases during his long career as a diplomat, courtier, and government minister, and since much of his writing was discovered long after his death—some only in the twentieth century—a general synoptic overview is the approach best suited for a values-based narrative like this one. We shall see that Leibniz blended profound premodern commitments with characteristically modern ones. My account will focus on four: unity/coherence, mathematics/analysis, quality/ subjectivity, and divinity/perfection.

As a metophysical thinker, one of Leibniz's most compelling values was unity-making. There was no apparent dualism he was not eager to make coherent, no either/or he did not long to turn into a both/and. This was as true of his efforts in practical affairs—in his "win-win" proposal to Louis XIV, for example, designed to help both Germany and France, in his efforts to promote institutions for easing cooperation among scientists, and in his labors for effecting reconciliation between Catholics and Protestants—as it was in his theoretical work.

Such values could never find ease intellectually on the Cartesian dualism between matter, res extensa, and mind, res cogitans. First, regarding matter, Leibniz argued that it cannot possibly, as Descartes and Spinoza had held, be *merely* extension. Extension in itself is impotent, just a geometrical fiction; but matter is characterized by force—at bottom the force capable of excluding every other bit of matter from occupying its locus. Matter, that is, has a primary power of impenetrability. No two bodies can occupy the same space at the same time. Even Descartes had admitted that matter has inertia, the capacity to persist until impressed with a motion or change in motion. This is nothing merely passive; it is a force, a resistance power. This force possessed by, and constituting, every particle of matter—to exclude every other—is essential for, and prior to, mere extension. Without it, the whole spatial realm would slide together, collapse, and extension itself—made up of infinitely many "heres" and "not-heres," "theres" and "not-theres"—would disappear.

Similarly, mind is unfortunately characterized by Descartes and Spinoza as *nothing but* consciousness. "Thinking substance," however, comes in many degrees. Sometimes mind is fully awake, alert, and concentrating; but these moments are the rarities. Much more often we experience mind at a lower pitch: sleepy, wandering, fuzzy, dazed. It seems better, closer to the facts, to think of mind as the force or power of having subjective qualities of different degrees ranging from extremely alert and rich, at one end of a spectrum, to extremely dopey and minimal, at the other. At the low end, mind could exist in an unconscious state, rising into and falling below cognitive awareness. The higher end can be called "apperception," awareness of perception or self-consciousness, while the lower can be called mere "perception," or, even further down the scale, *"petite perception,"* as Leibniz called it in the French he preferred for his philosophical writing. In any case, and for any level, it is certain that something prior to the various qualities of mental existence must exist to support these qualities—a force of "minding" (which also excludes the subjectivities of other centers of "minding")—and that this force must be present through all the changes of quality that we know to be a normal part of the sort of thing minds are.

Mind, defined as nothing but self-conscious apperception, can of course have nothing to do with, and can never, in principle, interact with, matter defined as nothing but extension. But this Cartesian dilemma is based on a false either/or. Mind is more than its conscious qualities; matter is more than its spatial spread. Significantly, both are grounded in a force that must be appealed to for their respective essential characters. Perhaps, in this way, can lie a fruitful both/and.

At this promising point, let me introduce another value of intense interest to Leibniz, what I earlier called the value of mathematics/analysis. It has already implicitly appeared in the discussion of the continuous spectrum, from wide-awake to different degrees of unconsciousness, the different qualities mentality can experience. Leibniz found essential clues to reality through his invention of the infinitesimal calculus. From this mathematical viewpoint everything is continuous, a question of infinite gradations tending toward the limit, zero, that is never reached in actuality.

Even at an early age, Leibniz had been fascinated by the possibility of what the twentieth century calls symbolic logic. As a youth, he contemplated the advantages of translating all questions into their smallest, most elementary parts, in a universal vocabulary. Then, when opinions differed, it would be possible to cut through the fog and dust of rhetoric by logically deducing the answers to universal rational satisfaction. Instead of debate, scholars would say to one another, "Come, let us calculate." Leibniz's calculating machine, his ticket of admission to the London Royal Society, takes on a new, wider significance in light of this youthful commitment combining the age-old values of coherence and unity with the characteristically modern ones of analysis and mathematics.

Further, it was his grand achievement of the calculus, with its stress on continua of infinities, that shaped Leibniz's positive answer to Spinoza's monism on which he had taken careful notes in Amsterdam. Leibniz's negative reservations were not especially mathematical. They were mainly qualitative. For example, he was not satisfied at the explanatory power of Spinoza's simple assertion that extension and consciousness are two of the infinite attributes of Substance (and the only two we know), since calling them "attributes" of a single reality—a reality which, according to Spinoza, is nothing more than its infinite attributes—fails to show in the least *how* the irreconcilable qualities of mere extension and pure consciousness can be coherently related.

Leibniz's affirmations, however, contrasting his stance with Spinoza's, clearly reflect his high regard for the infinitesimal calculus and his religious commitments, working in harmony. First, it is theologically impossible, he noted, to hold that there is nothing besides God; this would overvalue the world, making it divine, and undervalue God, denying the activity of creation. But beyond this, we have already seen that for the "attribute" of extension to be real, there must be many centers of impenetrability. How many? The calculus demonstrates the number must be infinite. These material particles must not be confused with mere geometrical *points*, which are empty abstractions, devoid of force; but like points, they can have no extension themselves, since atoms are constituted by the power of impenetrability—stubborn otherness— on which extension is based. Having no extension, they are indivisible, in reality as well as in concept. This distinguishes these smallest real bits of matter from the traditional atoms of Democritus and Gassendi, since they have some size and therefore are at least in principle divisible by the same process that allows any spatial extent, however small, to be halved. Therefore, Leibniz, to distinguish his proposal for the smallest real entities from both points and atoms, calls them *monads*, the analytically necessary units that cannot further be divided (without which primary units nothing secondary could be built up) and cannot have space as part of their real natures (or they would not be the impenetrable, indivisible units required).

Such monads, necessary for the "attribute" of extension, are also needed for understanding the "attribute" of mind, as long as mind is not gratuitously defined as nothing but pure, self-conscious cognition. Since one consciousness does not and cannot overlap with other consciousness, there must be a force for otherness, "impenetrability," in the mental domain as well as the material. And since, as we have seen, there must be an infinite number of degrees of mentality, the world of mind turns out to be a world of minds: unextended, unmixed, unconfused with their qualitative contents which vary from time to time. But this is the very same world, seen from within, that analysis of extension gives us, seen from without.

Spinoza was not wrong, Leibniz acknowledges, in his definition of "substance," which, as in Descartes' definition, requires that a substance must be that which exists in itself and can be understood through itself. He was wrong only in supposing that on this definition there can be but one Substance. In fact, there must be an infinity of substances, each existing in itself, each fully understandable (once created by God) in terms of itself.

At this point we need to note another of Leibniz's commitments—to the values of quality/subjectivity. To understand a monad adequately—as to understand a person truly—is to think in terms of inner reality. Only such an intimate viewpoint gives access to the genuine uniqueness of a given reality. Its qualities (including its spatio-temporal qualities) are not and logically cannot be exactly replicated. Leibniz's "Principle of the Identity of Indiscernibles" is based on this insight. Any "two or more" "things" that share precisely "their" full set of qualities, including exactly the same qualities of space and time, "are" just the same thing. There is nothing by which "they" could be distinguished. As Duns Scotus held much earlier, every individual thing has its own "thisness." Nevertheless, as William of Ockham insisted, everything that is real is an individual.

(Here Leibniz hopes to reconcile Realism and Nominalism in a principled "both/and.")

Now we can put this together. First, each fundamental reality must be understood entirely through itself. It can suffer no significant influences from, enjoy no real interactions with, other fundamental realities. Otherwise it would not qualify as true "substance," intelligible in itself. But, second, each fundamental reality is distinguished by its unique interiority of qualities. Therefore, the monads' distinguishing internal qualities must be understood as developing entirely independently, in complete subjective autonomy. Monads, as Leibniz put it, have no "windows" to each other. From eternity (or from its creation *ex nihilo*) every monad—to qualify as "substance"—must be conceived as unfolding according to its own internal *telos*.

Still, we find ourselves in a kosmos in which the infinitely varied parts are delicately attuned; conscious minds (like our own) are closely associated with organic bodies that feel and move and are united in their identities through association with their ruling monads; more generally, in the physical world, mathematical laws reflect the regular motions of macroscopic entities comprised of "slumbering" monads organized into unities by higher, though far from conscious, monads. How can this apparent interaction be accounted for in the face of the necessity that every monad is developing according to its own interiority alone? Leibniz's answer is to invoke the infinite intelligence of the Monad of monads, God the Creator. The world appears to work by a web of interactions but this cannot be; therefore, each fundamental reality must be internally preordained to develop as though it were engaged in harmonious interaction. In reality, Leibniz concludes, the world simply manifests God's preestablished harmony. Every detail is foreseen. Nothing happens by chance; nothing happens by "impressed" forces. The laws of physics are simply descriptions of the coordinated outworkings of previously designed mental interiors of monads. Matter is real, reflecting the reality of monads considered externally, but mind is primary. Mind is what constitutes the infinite numbers of finite entities (low in mental quality though most may be) that are preordained in their subjective development; and infinite Mind is what creates and preordains all.

Finally, we are brought to explicit notice of Leibniz's commitment to the value of divinity/perfection. This is a value of kosmos we have observed as operative from the pre-Socratics to Einstein. No one held it more intensely than Leibniz. Absolute perfection is beyond our conceiving of course; but Leibniz points out that taking it with full seriousness has compelling implications. Nothing is impossible for such a being except for what is logically meaningless; that is, except for whatever must be eliminated by the actualization of some mutually exclusive possibility. Just as the "impenetrability" of bodies (two of which cannot be at the same place at the same time) rests ultimately on the Principle of the Identity of Indiscernibles, which shows that "two" entities, identical in all respects, cannot possibly be "two" but must be one only, so many other things are not "compossible" (possible together). Absolute perfection of power is not less absolute because of the exclusion of what is not compossible. God chooses among compossibles—the only meaningful choices, after all—and has the entire range of internally compossible worlds from which to choose . For example, a possible world would be one in which Adam and Eve refrain from disobedience; but in that world there is no compossibility of redemption, through Christ, from a Fall that did not happen. Absolute perfection, having unlimited power to choose one actual world from all the internally compossible ones, will act only for the total best. This does not mean the chosen world will be spared evil, pain, and frustration. In the world actually chosen, as we can see, there is much of that; Leibniz interpreted this as resulting from the Fall. The possible world-with-Fall-and-Christ must have been judged better by standards of absolute perfection, therefore, than the possible world-without-Fall-or-Christ. Thus, the pains and evils of the actual world must have been foreseen by God and judged on the whole better to endure than to avoid by forsaking the world altogether, including Christ and other lesser but evil-overbalancing goods. In this sense, realistically aware of evil but confident—despite all—in God's perfect judgment in having chosen this rather than any other world, Leibniz deems this the "best" of all internally compossible worlds. The lampoonings his views have suffered on this matter, from the brilliant sarcasms of Voltaire's *Candide* (published nearly one-half century after Leibniz's lips were sealed against reply) to the present day, have been fun but hardly philosophically fair.

Still, it is fair, I suppose, to register common-sense incredulity about Leibniz's proposals, despite the logical sophistication and the mathematical genius that undoubtedly lies behind them. What his worldview lacks is fundamental plausibility. It makes everything radically other than it seems. Our experience is of a world that seems to be full of causal interactions, not only between minds and bodies but between things and other things. Leibniz would have us believe that there are no causal interactions between anything at all, only an unwinding of an infinite number of subjective plot lines in orchestrated unison. Our experience seems to indicate that there are genuine alternatives open in the future that make the future different, in principle, from the past. But Leibniz contends that the outworkings of God's preestablished harmony are as determinate for the future as they are for the past; there is nothing to do, as it were, but walk through our parts. For any who have struggled with a hard personal decision or wrestled to create a new thought or painting or melody, this feels wrong. We seem to feel the powers of other things, as though our organisms were in direct touch with other organisms and as though we were open to influence in our perceptions (conscious and semi-conscious). But Leibniz would have it that we are only viewing our perceptions on the interior screens of our windowless selves.

All these grounds for incredulity stem from Leibniz's theoretical commitment to the Cartesian-Spinozistic ideal of "substance." It tempts one to wonder what his philosophy would have been able to contribute to modern thinking if he had not been mesmerized by the powerful sense that true substances need to be above dependence on relations, either in fact or in concept. Later, we shall see what happens when, as in the philosophy of Alfred North Whitehead, the postulated primitive units of reality are given "windows," and essential connectedness with one another is affirmed as a great value.

Another ground for incredulity may lie in the realization that if all our perceptions are limited to our windowless interior, we have to wonder why we need to postulate a physical organism for ourselves (our bodies) at all—or indeed a physical world of bodies impenetrably resistant to one another, even if they are supposed to have a tiny amount of interiority of their own. If windowlessness is to be taken strictly, our mental perceptions are not "of" or "from" our bodies, our kinesthetic insides, our sense organs, or even our brains. Our private awareness, as "dominant monad" is (like all monads) supposed to be entirely unextended and causally uninfluenced. If God's preestablishment of our unfolding mental qualities is quite capable of simulating input from "virtual" stomach rumblings, pin pricks, musical sounds, the chatter of other persons, and so on, why bother with creating real stomachs, pins, violins, or people?

This rhetorical question becomes quite central to the immaterialist philosophy of George Berkeley, a younger contemporary of Leibniz, who was aware of some of Leibniz's work. Berkeley, though of English parentage, was born in Ireland in 1685 and was educated at Trinity College in Dublin. Elected a Fellow at Trinity in 1707, and ordained a deacon in 1709, he published his first book, *New Theory of Vision*, in the latter year, already (as we can tell by notes he made at the time) convinced of the immateriality of the world, though not arguing for it directly in that book. The following year, however, he published his radically empiricist *Treatise Concerning the Principles of Human Knowledge*, Part One; and on an extended trip to London in 1713 he published the popular *Three Dialogues Between Hylas and Philonous*. On this trip he met and conversed with the intellectual lights of London, including Joseph Addison (1672–1719), Richard Steele (1672–1729), Alexander Pope (1688–1744), and Jonathan Swift (1667–1745). From London, in 1713, Berkeley, then age twenty-eight, made a year-long trip to the Continent, just in time to meet and converse with the aged Malebranche, who died in 1715. At thirty, Berkeley began a second visit to the Continent, the same year in which Leibniz met his lonely end and young Voltaire, back from exile in Holland, was on the brink of an involuntary visit to the Bastille. During this four-year tour, Berkeley, distressed by the implications of the scientific world picture then taking hold in England and France, wrote his critique of Newton's philosophy of nature (and of Leibniz's theory of "force") in *De Motu*.

From 1728 until 1731, Berkeley lived in America in pursuit of his dream college to be founded in Bermuda, wherein all races and backgrounds—most notably American Indian youth—would receive first-rate education together. This college, approved (and ostensibly funded) by Parliament, was to be provisioned from Rhode Island, where Berkeley took up residence while waiting for the money to arrive. During his residency in Newport, he wrote *Alciphron*, another sharp critique of the "freethinkers" riding—for a fall, he thought—the current scientific revolution. This was published in 1732, after his return to London, as Berkeley was disappointed by Parliament's failure to honor its funding pledge. Still another broadside against Newton (and by implication Leibniz) appeared in *The Analyst* (1734), attacking the conceptual foundations of the calculus (Newton's theory of "fluxions") by challenging the intelligibility of infinitesimals. This book was followed the next year by another work in the philosophy of mathematics, *A Defence of Free-Thinking in Mathematics*.

In 1734, the year of *The Analyst*'s publication, George Berkeley, who in the decade since 1724 had been the Dean (largely in absentia) of the Anglican Cathedral at Derry, became at last "Bishop Berkeley," elected Bishop of Cloyne, Ireland. The final two decades of his life were spent mainly on administrative duties and on concerns about unemployment and public health in his diocese. His last book, *Syris*, which dealt with these issues (and extolled the public health virtues of tarwater) was published in 1744. In 1753, Bishop Berkeley, at the age of sixty-eight, died on a visit to Oxford.

This minority thinker, though doggedly resisting the Newtonian bandwagon, was not in all ways an outsider to modern values. On the contrary, Berkeley was modern to the core in his enthusiastic empiricism and his uncompromising nominalism. Not a positivist, of course, because of his insistence on explaining all phenomena by reference to God's direct activities, Berkeley nevertheless gave ammunition to later positivists who were ready to use his arguments against scientific "hypotheses" but to abandon references to God.

Berkeley's commitment to the cleansing values of empiricism is as total as anyone's, including Comte's. The meaning of every term that has meaning must be found in a prior experience—for the most part, in sense perception. The most radical application of this empiricist principle becomes clear in Berkeley's unflinching analysis of the expression "to be." What does it mean "to exist" or "to be"? It means something is either being experienced (perceived) or is experiencing (perceiving). Berkeley's famous shorthand slogan, *esse est percipi*, points to this logical link between the meaning of existence and the presence somewhere of a perceiving mind. In the absence of such a mind, there is literally no meaning behind the assertion of the existence of anything. Even when we think of something existing "unperceived" (say) on the far side of the moon, we are thinking and imagining ourselves perceiving this object, thereby supplying the missing mind. We forget to include ourselves and our imaginings in describing the total picture. In some contexts, self-forgetfulness may amount to commendable modesty, but here it is a logical oversight that leads to a meta-physical mistake. The mistake is in supposing that existence can be made sense of without reference—overt or covert—somewhere to mentality.

What is a "thing" on this radically empirical analysis? A "thing," Berke-ley replies, is nothing other than the collection of perceptions we have of it. The meaning of the "thing" is nothing more than the collection of ideas we can remember later from having had these perceptions. The meaningfulness of talk about something "more" than what can, in principle, be experienced is ruled out by the empirical principle. What an object "is," therefore, is exhausted by its perceptible qualities in their entirety.

What are these qualities? First and most striking are the colors and scents and tastes and sounds and touches of the variegated world of experience. But as Berkeley is quick to acknowledge (as with Galileo and Descartes), these are all dependent on mind. All the modern arguments skeptical of the "secondary" qualities—the obvious facts that pain is not in the pin nor tickle in the feather, the relativity of felt temperature to the prior condition of the perceiver, the illu-sions of vision and taste due to illness or other circumstance—all these are embraced heartily by Berkeley and restated with vigor. None of these can pos-sibly be conceived without a mental receiver on which they are completely dependent. Then Berkeley springs his empiricist attack on the independence of the so-called "primary qualities." We have never experienced "number" with-out *somethings* to count; we have never experienced "extension" or "figure" unqualified with one or another actual color or texture or felt temperature; we have never experienced "motion" except in the context of, and by means of, all the mind-dependent qualities through which (alone) we experience moving things. If the "secondary qualities" are totally dependent on mind, so are the "primary qualities." It is wholly unempirical to suppose otherwise; and to the extent that it is unempirical, it is meaningless.

Berkeley's early theory of vision reinforces the general point. What we see are perceptions, not physical things in themselves. Sight enables us to coor-dinate other perceptions, especially the perceptions of touch. A visual field is fundamentally a resource for innumerable predictions of what we would be able to touch if we reached in certain directions or walked in others. A complete account can be given without reference to independently existing material things. All we need is an interlocking and regular set of perceptions from the various senses. These senses are completely different from one another and completely arbitrary in their qualities. But as we learn from the experiences of life, their radically incommensurable deliverances to awareness are for the most part regularly related. When they are not, we speak of "illusions" and seek to understand them in other ways.

In the same way, Berkeley interprets the findings of the natural sciences. The "objects" of the sciences are all (and only) perceptions carefully observed, measured, and related to other perceptions in regular ways. There is no need—it reaps only confusion—to suppose there are unperceived, unperceiving, passive material entities pushing or pulling, bouncing or blocking, "behind the scenes" in nature. The predictable fruits of scientific observation are wonderful, and enough.

Why is nature so wonderfully regular? Why do scientists find constant correlations, reliable laws, between various ever-finer perceptions in ever-enlarging domains? Berkeley's answer points to the magnificent intelligence and faithfulness of God, the infinite Spirit whose activity is manifest directly to our finite spirits through our individual perceptions of a common world that permits human community and rewards responsible predictive behavior.

Many critics at this point raise an empiricist objection to Berkeley's invocation of God as an explanatory principle. We have no perceptions of "God"; how can this word have any more meaning than the phrase "unperceived matter"? Berkeley has a reply. True, God is not a sense-object among our other perceptions, but our experience is not only of perceived objects, it is of the activity of perceiving, that is, we experience *ourselves* in the act of receiving perceptions, manipulating ideas, and expressing purpose. We do not have perceptions of our minds (and thus we do not have, in the technical sense, "ideas" of spirits), but we experience mentality in our own inner actions and thus have meaningful *notions*, based on the empirical principle, even where we lack *ideas* derived from perceptions. There is more meaning behind assertions about God, therefore, than about inert matter. God can be thought of like ourselves, active—but far more so—and purposive and perceiving. Regarding unperceived and unperceiving matter, in contrast, we have neither idea nor notion.

Berkeley's commitment to empiricism coheres with his uncompromising nominalism. "Universal forms," apart from individual things, can no more be perceived than "unqualified matter"; and even "concepts" are suspect if they are taken as more than specific images drawn from experience and taken actively by our minds to represent a range of particulars. There is no such thing as "triangularity," for example. Nor can "it" be thought. Every triangle must be of a particular sort, either right or equilateral or scalene or obtuse. Any one sort excludes the particular characteristics of the others. We never have seen, cannot imagine, and thus cannot think of "triangularity in general." But we can (and do) take one particular, experienceable sort and by a mental effort, let it *stand for* the others that qualify on the more minimal grounds of being a plane figure with three sides.

Berkeley's polemic against abstract ideas, from which in his view come most errors and confusions, led him, as part of his antirationalist campaign, to an antimathematical stance, as we noted earlier. This required his opposition to Newton's and Leibniz's obsession (as he saw it) with infinitesimals and other fictions of calculus. The key to this form of mathematical thinking is in its supposition that it is meaningful and useful to talk about "points" and "instants" and about the "infinite divisibility" of spaces and durations. Berkeley counters that this is an ungrounded assumption leading to serious mistakes. If existence applies only to what is perceptible, then no line is in reality infinitely divisible. Every line will have a finite capacity for division, down to its smallest perceptible segment. It is meaningless to speak of smaller segments than that and foolish to fall willingly into Zeno's mental snares. A mile-long line may well be divisible into 10,000 equal parts or even more if one has the patience to do it, but an inch-long line is not hospitable to the same process. The mistake is for mathematicians to generalize from what is really possible in one case to what is not possible—thus, not clearly imaginable or thinkable—in the other. They leave the realms of reality behind and substitute fiction. Perhaps this might not be so bad if left at that, but then they attempt to persuade us to take their empirically empty fiction as fundamental to meaningful explanations about the real world.

Berkeley's treatment of the concepts of "space" and "time," "motion" and "natural law" are no less radically in opposition to the Newtonian majority view. Space cannot possibly refer to some (utterly unexperienceable) Void, as in the ancient Atomists, nor to the infinite absolute "container" defined by Newton. Our only ideas of space grow out of the perceptions we have of free or obstructed movement of our bodies: getting from place to place, moving from touch to touch, texture to texture, temperature to temperature, visual field to visual field. "Time," if meaningful, is always experientially filled. It is rooted empirically in the experiences of succession in our thoughts and our perceptions. "Motion" (like "rest") is therefore always related to one apparent bodily state and some other apparent bodily state, observed in the context of empirically meaningful space and time. If there were no second body, there could be no meaning to motion since "absolute motion" would be forever imperceptible. Rest is meaningful only in contrast to motion. "Natural law," finally, is always descriptive, never prescriptive. "Laws" do not force or determine events. God acts regularly, though freely (and is quite capable of miraculous suspensions of normal rules, for good enough reasons); thus, events are primary, laws are secondary, though important for our normal planning purposes. Above all, laws by themselves do not "explain" anything. They only describe how God's purposes are normally executed. To understand the cosmos rightly is to explain by ultimate reference to the only active causes, minds or spirits, and above all by reference to their purposes. In the end, for Berkeley, only final causes can genuinely explain.

George Berkeley's views are notoriously difficult to refute. They take into consideration all possible evidence that might be brought against them. Everything remains experientially unchanged when "inert, unperceiving" matter is dropped, since the sense of a common world and its massive, independent stability is ex hypothesi, inspired directly in each finite center of perception, on Berkeley's account, by God. And yet—ever since Samuel Johnson's famous kicking of a stone in his futile attempt to refute Berkeley—many (who know perfectly well that simply appealing to what amounts to more perceptions cannot in principle shake Berkeley's idealist proposal) have simply felt unconvinced that perceptions and perceivers *alone* can adequately account for the cosmos. One implication of this view, that there are no genuine causal interactions directly between the things that make up our experienced universe, is deeply counterintuitive. The further implication that things are nothing in themselves but collections of perceived qualities, arbitrarily linked by fiat of a Spirit whose sole concern is with the education and nurture of human spirits—using the great world of nature simply as an elaborate stage on which our species can act out our moral drama—seems reductionist, albeit in an anthropocentric direction, and is hardly more palatable than the reductionist antihumanisms of the majority path.

What of the animals, perceivers (as it seems) but not language-using human spirits? Do they exist in their own right by virtue of their active perceivings? Does God present to them a common world suitable to their apparent sense organs? Do they represent other sorts of spirits? How many sorts are there? Is there a lower bound below which there is no "there" there, as would be provided by Leibniz's monads of varying mental quality, but only God at work in our (and others') minds? Further, if God works in various minds relative to their finite capacities to perceive, what happens to the hope that a "representational" theory of ideas can be avoided? If God's idea of an object, a chair, for example, is freed from the limitations of this or that perspective, this or that ambient lighting condition, and so on, how can it at all resemble what our ideas, always limited by and reflecting such conditions, must be? Are God's ideas exempt from the nominalist logic of particularity? If "triangularity in general" is not nonsense for God, why must it be nonsense for us? If, however, good logic requires that it be nonsense for us, how can we then meaningfully propose that God's archetypical ideas support the stable universe from all possible perspectives at once?

George Berkeley's comprehensive challenge to the Newtonian worldview, from material particles to the infinitesimal calculus, is an impressive modern counterattack on behalf of the values of mentality against their neglect or violation. The majority bandwagon had too much momentum for one shoulder—however determined and inventive—to stop, of course; it simply rolled on, leaving Berkeley's idealistic theism by the side of the road, a philosophical curiosity. It makes one wonder what would have happened if Berkeley's opposition had not been so total. What if one were to accept the Newtonian picture in general, only supply a mentalistic foundation for it, one that would protect moral experience, purpose, and all the humane qualitative values from scientific elimination, while leaving all the modern values of mechanistic determinism intact or even stronger? This sounds like a tall order, yet it is exactly the project undertaken by the formidable Immanuel Kant, whose proposal we will next review.

KANT

The infant Kant, who was to grow into a thinker rightly ranked with the great Hellenes, was born in 1724 (the year Berkeley became Dean of Derry) into the modest home of a saddler in Königsberg, a Hanseatic League city, founded by the Teutonic Knights in the northeastern part of Prussia that today is Kaliningrad, located in what is now extreme western Russia near the Polish border. He claimed a Scottish grandparent, but otherwise was intensely a "local" person, never in his long lifetime having left the area. His early education was taken at a nearby pietistic Protestant school, Collegium Fredericianum, in accordance with the strict values of his devoutly Protestant home. At sixteen, Kant began his studies of physics, mathematics, philosophy, and theology at the University of Königsberg, from which he graduated in 1746, the year Diderot joined the *Encyclopédie* project in Paris and a year before La Mettrie fled to Holland for refuge in Berlin after publishing *L'Homme Machine*. At this time, because of his father's death, Kant was obliged to break off his formal studies to support himself by tutoring with several families in the region; after nine years of self-education and private writing, he completed his doctoral dissertation, received his degree from the University of Königsberg, and began steady employment as *Privatdozent* (lecturer) at the University. In the same year, 1755, he published his Nebular Hypothesis on the formation of the solar system, a strictly Newtonian deduction of how gravitational forces, starting with evenly distributed matter at the outset, would bring about the formation of planets with the positions and motions we observe today. Physics and mathematics, as well as philosophy, formed an important part of his lecturing responsibilities during these years. He was entirely at home in the Newtonian mechanical world picture and outstandingly adept in its mathematical expression. At the same time, his early philosophical background and convictions tended to be Leibnizian, though with increasing disenchantment—fostered by his reading of the British empiricists—with the rationalist assumption that the nature of things can be penetrated by thinking alone. One of his works from this Privatdozent period,

Dreams of a Spirit-Seer, Explained Through the Dreams of Metaphysics (1766), mocks the pretensions of mere conceptual manipulation in building a plausible worldview, taking the florid claims of Emanuel Swedenborg as his target.

At age forty-five, Kant fully realized for the first time the problem of understanding how the necessities of pure mathematics can be determinative for the world of experience that science investigates. Why should the world of contingent things follow the ideal dictates of mathematical laws? In the next year, 1770, he presented an early version of his solution to this problem as his Inaugural Dissertation for the Professorship of Logic and Metaphysics at the University of Königsberg. The solution was revolutionary. Later, Kant himself compared it to Copernicus' reversal of the positions of Earth and Sun. For the rest of his life he was busy spelling out the details, correcting and extending his revolution. For ten years after taking his Professorship, Kant published nothing; then came a series of epoch-making books: the *Critique of Pure Reason* (1781), its clarification in *Prolegomenon to Every Future Metaphysics* (1783), his *Groundwork for a Metaphysics of Morals* (1785), an alternative (in terms of motions and forces) to the atomistic theory of matter (in which all the Newtonian laws are still preserved) in his *Metaphysical Foundations of Natural Science* (1786), a second edition, with considerable rewriting, of the *Critique of Pure Reason* (1787), his *Critique of Practical Reason* (1788), and the *Critique of Judgment* (1790). By this time, Kant had reached what we think of as normal retirement age, but his stream of publications continued, including *Religion within the Limits of Reason Alone* (1793), an effort that was sternly rebuked by the conservative King Frederick Wilhelm II of Prussia, and the *Metaphysics of Morals* (1797), published at age seventy-five. Kant persisted—attempting to rectify misunderstandings and what he considered misapplications of his great proposal, and working tirelessly on a "Transition from *Metaphysical Foundations of Natural Science* to Physics," where he hoped to show that the fundamental laws of Newtonian physics can be deduced as a priori necessities of reason (notes published later as his *Opus Postumum*)—until his death, which came a few weeks before his eightieth birthday.

The vast range of Kant's thought, of which I have mentioned only highlights, is obviously beyond the scope of this swift narrative. I shall be content to reflect on his intervention on behalf of just three commitments, which characterize and illuminate his entire work: the values of mathematics, mechanism, and mind.

Kant's veneration for mathematics, both in its algebraic form and as Euclidean geometry, is for him a foundation stone of all his thinking. Mathematical truths are paradigms, not only for scientific understanding but for what metaphysical and ethical pronouncements should be. They are certain. They are universal. And Kant believed they are informative. In other words, they are both a priori and synthetic.

It is easy for a statement to be a priori and true if it is a mere tautology, that is, if its truth is assured by the presence in the subject's definition of what is merely drawn out, analyzed, and made explicit in the predicate. "My sister is a sibling," is an example of this easy kind of a priori truth, since understanding what "sister" means will reveal that "being a sibling" is part of the definition of the relationship. This is the logical character of a priori analytic truth, which depends on clear analysis of the meanings of the concepts involved.

It is also easy for a statement to be synthetic and true if it is only contingently true, a posteriori. "My sister is blue-eyed" is such a statement. There is nothing in the concept of "sister" that guarantees the truth of this predicate; therefore, the statement adds something to the subject. Subject and predicate synthesize a new truth. But of course the statement can be false; and it is false whenever it is asserted of a subject with nonblue eyes. This is no paradigm for the certainty required for genuine knowledge.

Mathematical assertions, however, are both certain in themselves and not merely analytic. To assert "7 + 5 = 12," Kant argues, is to say something that is always and necessarily true. This can be demonstrated. At the same time, the concepts involved are all distinct. Neither 7 nor 5 covertly includes the concept of any other number than themselves. And 12 has its own qualitative meaning. The mathematical assertion is synthetic, therefore, though entirely necessary and universal, thus also a priori.

The wonderful character of the synthetic a priori propositions of mathematics inspired Kant to ask himself how such necessary but informative truths can be possible and how they can be related, as they clearly are, in the findings of mathematical physics. This turn, to the search for the *conditions of the possibility of what is indubitably the case*, marks what Kant called the "transcendental" method. His answer, as we shall see, marks the beginning of what he called his "critical" philosophy—"critical" because its first priority is to subject the powers and limits of the mind itself to radical criticism. It was the 1769 insight into the need for this critical move that was first expressed in 1770 through Kant's Inaugural Dissertation. Kant's "Critical Period" dates from this, and the essence of his Copernican Revolution is revealed in it.

Intimately related to Kant's veneration of mathematics is his complete commitment to the absolute laws of Newton's mechanical world picture. This does not mean there is no room for differences of interpretation, especially over the character of matter itself, which Kant prefers to conceive in a more active (Leibnizian) modality than in terms of the inert atoms of then-current fashion. Matter, for Kant, is simply the capacity to move in space. But we must not be distracted by details. The key question in any interpretation of matter is to understand how its motions in space—indeed, how space itself and time—can be so perfectly described by our algebraic formulae and by our geometry. Mathematics is knowable a priori; this secures its certainty. But space? If space is merely empirical, given to us only a posteriori, then assertions about it should be as contingent as those about blue-eyed sisters; but then the security and perfection of scientific knowledge ought to vanish into mere mystery or (amounting to the same thing) good luck. What are the necessary grounds for the possibility of secure mathematical knowledge—which for Kant we undoubtedly have—of spatial and temporal phenomena?

The answer rests in mentality. Space and time cannot be merely the deliverance of experience a posteriori. This would be unworthy of the certainty of mathematics and the laws of mechanics. Besides, to begin having an experience of any particular spatial extent or other, or of any particular temporal duration, is already to presuppose *spatiality* or *temporalty*. If the original ideas of space and time really had to be built up inductively out of particular empirical encounters with spaces and times, they could never arise. Such encounters could never even get started without some prior reception-capacity that presupposes acquaintance with or receptivity to spatiality and temporality. Space and time are not features of the preexperienced world so much as the forms that minds bring a priori to the experience of anything.

This is a radical turn no doubt, but one with the exciting consequence that the applicability of geometry to space—if *both* are now considered to belong to the domain of the a priori—is no longer a matter of dumb luck or sheer mystery. They belong together. The possibility of the certainty of what Kant already took as certain is established.

At the same time, Kant's "Copernican Revolution"—his placing the mind at the center of all spatio-temporal experience as boldy as Copernicus placed the sun in the center of the universe—will have other consequences no less startling than those that flow from replacing the Earth by the Sun in astronomy. Both revolutions are disturbing; both are counterintuitive; both shatter firmly held presumptions. As Kant realized at the time of his Inaugural Dissertation, making this change changes everything. We can no longer suppose that the world we see and walk through—the world investigated by scientists—is at all like the world as it is in itself. If space and time are provided by our minds, not found as given features of the preexperienced universe, then we can have no ideas that really resemble the universe as it is apart from our mental activity. We can have knowledge, secure and mathematically perfect, but only of the "phenomena" that have been processed through experience. In contrast, what Kant calls the "noumena"—the realities that lie behind and are coresponsible with our minds for our experienced world—are forever beyond our cognition.

A major consequence of the "phenomena"/"noumena" division, and a highly desirable one for Kant, is the ability on its basis to affirm *both* complete determinism for the world science investigates *and* complete freedom for human moral agents. The truth that La Mettrie affirmed in *L'Homme Machine*, that there is no part of the empirical world—including the empirical human self—not completely determined by prior causes is a required assumption adopted for the sake of the high values of scientific knowledge. It can be maintained *for the phenomenal domain*. At the same time, since there is no way of knowing what the self is like *in the noumenal domain*, there is no way of proving that the self, as it is "in itself," is not entirely free, a required assumption adopted for the sake of the urgent values of moral responsibility. Kant is committed to both.

His argument, developed in the two decades following his Inaugural Dissertation, flows from the critical turn. Not simply space and time are provided a priori as forms of sensory experience (for space) and all experience (for time). The solution to the widespread skepticism about real causal connections between empirical things, found as we have seen in Malebranche and Spinoza, Leibniz and Berkeley, but recently raised to a fever pitch by Kant's contemporary, David Hume, can be obtained through the same appeal to a priori mentality that answered the problem of the mathematical character of space and time. In the *Critique of Pure Reason*, Kant deduces the category of causality as one of the necessary elements presupposed for thinking a world. The transcendental method is employed again: what must be presupposed for the possibility of having what we most certainly do have? We certainly have the conception of an orderly world. For that to be possible (as it certainly is), we must think all events through the category of lawful sequence. But that is causality as it relates to phenomena. We can be sure *in advance* that whatever happens has a regular cause. If we do not find it right away, we may stake everything on the certainty that it will be worthwhile to keep looking. What assures us that such commitment—which amounts to affirming the research program of all the sciences—is worth investing unlimited time and treasure? The assurance, Kant replies, is perfect: it rests in the necessities of pure reason itself. Our minds, at least in their cognitive mode, bring with them the determinations of total causality wherever they operate. We cannot, therefore, cognize any subject matter of actual or possible experience without attributing to it full causal determination.

What then of freedom, so important for the sake of values other than scientific ones? Kant offers the phenomenal-noumenal distinction as a barrier against any encroachment on the precious reality of moral responsibility. Persons examined scientifically will inevitably be found to be fully determined in their choices and activity, he acknowledges, since that is an a priori of pure reason. But there are values other than cognitive ones and reality other than the world of actual or possible experience. True, we can never *cognize* ourselves as free to take responsibility for our decisions, since cognition brings determinism with it. But *if* there are strong reasons to believe that we must be free, as we are *in ourselves*—moral agents involved in a world of practice—then (since freedom cannot be *dis*proved of the noumenal realm) we are justified believing what we cannot know.

There are indeed such strong reasons, Kant shows—the strongest. By a transcendental argument it is clear again that whatever is necessary for the possibility of what manifestly is the case may be postulated. As rational agents we are manifestly beings under moral obligation. This is not merely a matter of moral intuition as the pietists of Kant's youth might have held. It is the logical consequence of knowing what "duty" means. To understand "duty" is to realize that it means acting lawfully, that is, under the law of reason. Pure practical reason demands practical consistency and coherence, acting on principles or maxims that can be willed to be universally applicable. This is what we *ought* to do, and to understand the concept of duty is to find ourselves under its rule. It is a categorical command, the essence of "ought" with no "ifs" or "buts" allowed.

Whatever is presupposed for the possibility of what manifestly *is* needs to be postulated. We are manifestly under the rule of "ought." What is presupposed for its possibility? Most fundamentally presupposed is that we *can* do what we *ought*. Without this "can" the "ought" disappears. No one can meaningfully hold that I "ought" to do something that is manifestly impossible for me to do, for example, to leap unassisted over the Moon. Take away the "can" and the "ought" evaporates into meaninglessness. Therefore, *since* we find ourselves obliged by the categorical imperative to behave morally, we must in ourselves be free moral agents, however different matters may look from the phenomenal perspective of science. This freedom cannot be *cognized*, since pure theoretical reason will always bring along its deterministic category of causation, but it can (and must) be *postulated* by pure practical reason. For Kant, the solution is to have both: the values of mathematical physics and determinism, on the one hand (for rational thinking), and the values of freedom and moral responsibility (for rational living).

Another "both" made possible, Kant believes, by the hermetic seal between phenomena and noumena resolves the old debate between efficient and final causes in the universe. Galileo's emphasis, as we saw, on efficient causality as the only one appropriate for scientific thinking, quickly led to the modern downgrading or denial of final causality as a significant factor in things. For Kant, this elimination is certainly appropriate for the phenomenal world with which science works. Only mechanical accounts are allowed. Still, there are two levels (beside our own purposive moral intuitions) on which the attribution of final causality in nature is attractive.

One level has to do with organic life in general, which Kant, from his earliest "pre-critical" days, saw as inexplicable through purely mechanical categories. We are drawn to teleological ways of thinking when we observe organisms, just as Aristotle was so drawn. These ways of thinking are not properly scientific, but they are hard to resist; and they can be heuristic, leading to more scientific ways of understanding.

The second level is more comprehensive: it is to look at the whole of nature as organized by a great Planner, whose purposes give meaning and unity to the universe. Kant is never willing to consider such ways of looking, which he acknowledges as attractive, legitimate theoretical speculations. None of the theoretical arguments for God are adequate. The argument from design, which is closest to this way of viewing the universe, fails to determine a full concept of God, at most a finite Demiurge, like Plato's; and such a Maker would not necessarily be of moral interest or worthy of religious impulses. No, God as unified cause and purposive designer is at most an Ideal of Pure Reason, never to be proved or cognized. Thus a place-mark is established in the domain of speculative reason, even though it cannot be filled by cognition. And given the obligation of the practical life to morality and the implicit promise of happiness embodied in our empirical makeup as organisms craving happiness, it is reasonable to postulate God as the guarantor of the highest good, the union of *deserved happiness with moral excellence* as the goal of life. This postulate is a necessity only of practical reason, of course, not a logical necessity. But nothing in the range of speculative knowledge can possibly gainsay it; and practical reason needs it. It is, therefore, a reasonable faith.

It is impossible not to admire Kant's commitments to all the great ideals he was determined to acknowledge, and his genius in turning the world upside down, as it were, to achieve his demands for "both" the values of scientific precision and prediction "and" the values of human freedom, morality, and purpose. In the end, he achieved a theoretical basis for the security of scientific knowledge in his strong sense, though at the loss of any possibility of having knowledge of reality as it is in itself. Likewise, he mounted a heroic defense of freedom and the qualitative life of moral excellence, but at the loss of any way of understanding *how* it is possible, or how it can conceivably be true of people at the same time that they are scientifically knowable as completely determined and (in principle) fully predictable in every detail through the powers of theoretical reason. The inconceivability of the connection remains a blank and must remain so.

In accepting this result, Kant admits an incoherence through the heart of his attempted synthesis. It is an incoherence at several removes from the relatively straightforward mind-body problem that sets the modern agenda, but in many ways it is only a different version of it. For Kant, mind is the domain of freedom, quality, and purpose; mind also is the imposer of mathematics, space, time, and causality on the realm of the known. But mind as free and responsible agency cannot know itself with its own categories—categories it cannot escape. The connection between the way we know our bodies and the way we intuit our moral life is swallowed up in the different powers of mind and never reemerges. It remains a mystery, craving but forever defying solution on Kantian grounds.

Similarly, Kant's great vision respects purpose and has room for faith in a God who measures out happiness in proportion to moral desert, fulfilling the promise of the practically necessary *summum bonum*. But how are we to *think* such an "ethico-theological" solution to our human quest for ultimate meaning? Putting aside all pretensions of *cognizing* this postulate of pure practical reason, the very concepts necessary to describe God's practical functions are fatally tainted by the inevitable categories of all thought. To function as the postulate of practical reason, God must be thought of as an entity, a substantial being of some sort who understands everything about us, accomplishes things, is the cause of our states of happiness, adjusting conditions in perfect accordance with our moral qualities. But central to Kant's entire revolution is the insistence that categories such as these—substance, cause, etc.—are wrongly used with reference to what is supposedly outside the empirical world. They are held to be utterly inapplicable to the noumenal world which God by practical postulate inhabits. True, Kant attempts to distinguish between "thinking" and "cognizing" beyond the great divide, appealing to analogy, but a severe problem of logical consistency seems to pursue him down this path. In the *Critique of Judgment* he writes:

> However, if I wish to *think* a supersensible Being (God) as an intelligence, this is not only permissible in a certain aspect of my employment of Reason—it is unavoidable; but to ascribe to Him Understanding and to flatter ourselves that we can *cognize* Him by means of it as a property of His, is in no way permissible. For I must omit all those conditions under which alone I know an Understanding, and thus the predicate which only serves for determining man cannot be applied at all to a supersensible Object; and therefore by a causality thus determined, I cannot cognize what God is. And so it is with all Categories, which can have no significance for cognition in a theoretical aspect, if they are not applied to objects of possible experience.—However, according to the analogy of an Understanding I can in a certain other aspect think a supersensible being, without at the same time meaning thereby to cognize it theoretically; viz. if this determination of its causality concerns an effect in the world, which contains a design morally necessary but unattainable by a sensible being. For then a cognition of God and of His Being (Theology) is possible by means of properties and determinations of His causality merely thought in Him according to analogy, which has all requisite reality in a practical reference though *only in respect to this* (as moral) . . . (Kant 1914: 428–9).

What, however, is "thinking" God as an understanding causal agent if not "cognizing" without meaning it—that is, without taking cognitive responsibility for the thought? But *thinking* something without *meaning* it would seem to cancel itself out, leaving behind nothing but a disavowed mental image. This is not even "analogy" as Kant suggests. It resembles more the act of a shell-game artist: "Now you see it, now you don't."

HEGEL

Despite the originality, comprehensiveness, and depth of Kant's proposed revolution, it was deeply disturbing to most of his more significant successors. Indeed, perhaps Kant's thought gained its immense historical importance mainly because of the stimulus it gave to those who were unsettled and dissatisfied with it. Were I attempting a full history of philosophy, this would be the occasion to discuss the many waves of response spreading in different directions that Kant's ideas set in motion, especially (at first) among German-speaking thinkers of the nineteenth century. After Kant's intervention in the discussion, his revolutionary proposals demanded to be addressed in one way or another. After him, in a more than trivial sense, all philosophy became post-Kantian.

This narrative, however, is not so intended. It is a selective story of values interwoven with theories of reality—theories bearing in turn on the status of values themselves. With that in mind, let us ride just one of the crests of the post-Kantian tsunami: the mountainous wave represented by the thinking of Georg Wilhelm Friedrich Hegel.

Hegel, the son of a minor official, was born in Stuttgart in 1770, the same year in which Kant, making his Critical turn, presented his *Inaugural Dissertation*. After theological studies (1788–1793) at the University of Tübingen, where Hegel enjoyed the close friendship of fellow students Friedrich Hölderlin (1770–1843) and Friedrich Schelling (1775–1854), he supported himself by tutoring for a wealthy family in Bern (1793–1796) and another in Frankfurt (1796–1800). During those years, he was engaged privately in studies of Christianity, which he composed (unpublished) as "The Life of Jesus" (1795), "The Positivity of the Christian Religion" (1796), and "The Spirit of Christianity" (1799)—studies that emphasized ethics and minimized the importance of miracle or specific historical events for Christian faith. In 1800, Hegel moved to the University of Jena where his friend Schelling was then Professor of Philosophy. At Jena, Hegel wrote his dissertation, *De Orbitis Planetarum* (1801), which criticized Newton's abstractions and attempted to establish Kepler's Laws on a priori grounds. On the strength of this work, he was invited to teach at the University of Jena, where he collaborated with Schelling on editing the *Kritisches Journal der Philosophie* and published his own book comparing the philosophical system of Schelling with Schelling's Kantian predecessor, Johann Gottlieb Fichte (1762–1814).

Hegel's life was disrupted in October, 1806, by Napoleon's victory over the Prussian-led coalition in the decisive Battle of Jena. Suddenly unemployed when his university closed, Hegel left to become editor of a daily newspaper in Bamberg. Having brought with him an extensive manuscript containing his first major answer to Kant, he published it, while in Bamberg, as the *Phenomenology of Mind* (1807). The newspaper job held Hegel's interest for only one year, after which he took a position as headmaster of a high school in Nürnberg, where he remained for eight years, from 1808 to 1816. During those headmaster days, he managed to write his two-volume *Science of Logic* (1812–1816). On the strength of these publications, Hegel was called to professorships at Heidelberg and Berlin. Choosing Heidelberg first, he remained for only two years (1816–1818), but while there published the first version of his *Encyclopedia of the Philosophical Sciences in Outline* (1817). Then, on the renewal of the Berlin offer, he became Philosophy Chair in 1818 at Berlin, where he taught to ever-mounting acclaim. His fully developed lectures on aesthetics, philosophy of history, philosophy of religion, and the history of philosophy, were preserved and published posthumously. Before his death at age sixty-one (in the cholera epidemic of 1831), he published his *Philosophy of Right* (1821) and an enlarged version of his *Encyclopedia* (1827). Following his death, students and friends gathered his many writings, published and unpublished, into an eighteen-volume edition. Hegel's students and admirers also continued to meet in self-consciously Hegelian discussion groups. Some, who had met under Hegel's influence during his lifetime, continued as the "Old Hegelians." Others, including Karl Marx and Friedrich Engels, "Young Hegelians," gathered in years after Hegel's death to advance more radical interpretations of the master's meaning.

Hegel's meaning remains to this day complex, convoluted, and controversial. My present narrative is no place to argue—or even display—the details of thousands of pages of intricately interwoven ideas that cover quite literally every topic from phrenology to the world-historical transmorality of Napoleon. Rather, I shall limit myself to just a few pages reflecting on the "big picture" represented by this painter of the biggest of big pictures.

Hegel's deep preferences, expressed in his methods and findings, are an interesting mix of previously encountered values. His commitments were above all to *reason* and its ultimately successful capacity to know absolute truth; to *unity* and the coherence brought by final wholeness; and also to *competition* or "strife"—even war, quite literally between nations, as well as more figuratively—through which the final wholeness of reason is winnowed and enlarged. Regarding the valuing of competition, we recognize distant echoes of Heraclitus (Chapter 2), with his praise of Strife within the Logos of constant change. But also we should recognize the mounting chorus of eighteenth-century liberal economists, especially Adam Smith, whom Hegel greatly admired. The surge of capitalism, with its firm faith in private competition for advancing the general betterment of all, and its comforting master-image of the Invisible Hand, was well under way in Europe. Hegel's attitudes were not immune to its context, even though, ironically, his praise of negativity, contradiction, and the dialectic struggle was to inspire capitalism's fiercest nemesis.

Hegel's first major commitment, to the comprehensive competence of reason, led him (in agreement with virtually all the post-Kantian German philosophers) to discard Kant's "thing-in-itself," the so-called noumenal world "behind" the world of phenomena, the merely "problematic" world (Kant's term) forever in principle inaccessible to theoretical approach. To jettison the "thing-in-itself" by Hegel's time was not a difficult move. Johann Fichte, at first warmly praised by Kant for understanding him so well, had been the first to do so, urging that this was the proper development of the Kantian spirit. Horrified, Kant repudiated the very suggestion and broke with Fichte. However, Hegel's friend, Schelling, had also followed Fichte. There was little to be said on behalf of the noumenal world. It was retained by Kant as a shadowy, unknown realm in order to avoid Idealism, so that something other than mind could be held "responsible" for the world of experience. But how "responsible"? It could not in all critical consistency be thought to be *causally* responsible, since the concept of causality is one of the a priori categories of pure reason, on Kant's holding, inapplicable in principle to anything outside phenomena. To bend on this would be to jeopardize the wedge between phenomena and noumena that allows the postulate of freedom for noumenal selves to breathe, unsuffocated by the complete determinism required by empirical science.

But if things-in-themselves are not capable of being causally responsible for experience—if they are completely outside the a priori forms of experience provided by space and time, thus unimaginable, and, if they are not in principle cognizable by any of the categories of reason, thus unthinkable—then why are they needed? What positive function do they continue to perform? What can "they" possibly signify to us? "They" are an incoherent residue left from a different metaphysics, a tribute to the ghostly influence of Newton. If we were able to penetrate to the "other side," Hegel points out, what we would find there would be ourselves thinking, that is, mind. Therefore, let it be acknowledged that wherever we search, only mind is found. There is no getting away from or flying beyond *Geist*: "spirit," which—if it is always remembered that this word indicates something active, not merely contemplative—we can render "mind." All is mind; mind is all. In principle, what is real is rational and what is rational is real. Therefore, since mind can know itself without external limitation, reality is ultimately knowable and knowable absolutely.

Hegel's second and third primary values, of unity and competition, may be taken together. I shall simply illustrate them through thumbnail reflections on Hegel's first two major works, the *Phenomenology of Mind* (1807), written at Jena before Napoleon's rude interruption, and the *Science of Logic* (1812–1816), written while running his *Gymnasium* in Nürnberg. The former, more youthful (and hurried) work, has imperfect structure, rougher transitions, and makes less use of the famous "dialectic" than following works. It is, nonetheless, enormously insightful and influential. The two-volume *Logic*, immense and magisterial, complements the earlier publication. Together, these great products of speculative thought laid the foundation not only for Hegel's professional career, which led to his professorships at Heidelberg and Berlin, but for his many further ventures into the philosophy of history, religion, aesthetics, and the like, which for our purposes may be left aside.

If all is mind and mind is one, then absolute knowledge must be of nothing less than the whole. Partial truth, insofar as it is partial, is error. But error, conversely, can by the same token be appreciated as partial truth. Mind at its most primitive and partial is mainly in error, but fortunately errors conflict with other errors and force a larger formulation embracing what is true in both. The larger formulation, as long as it is still partial, is still in error; but the process of conflict and resolution continues. In this way, mind unfolds itself toward larger and larger realms of adequacy. The unfolded truth, though larger, carries the lesser along. Hegel relies on the German word *aufheben* to express this relationship. In one sense, the word means to "cancel," as in the adage, "*Aufgeschoben ist nicht aufgehoben*," ("Postponed is not cancelled"); but in another sense the same word means to "keep," "preserve," or "secure," as in "*Dein Geheimnis ist gut aufgehoben*" ("Your secret is well kept"). Hegel intends both meanings. Prior, competing stages are cancelled when they are overcome in larger, more adequate syntheses, but they are not eliminated in their partiality. The partial, less adequate is preserved even as the fuller, more adequate is added.

Phenomenology of Mind begins with what I shall term "mere-consciousness," then moves to "self-consciousness," and finally to "reason." Reason transcends self-consciousness, just as self-consciousness transcends mere-consciousness; but none of the higher unfoldings of mind eliminates the lower. In fact, it is only through the continuing presence of the lower that the higher can concretely be expressed. Sense-perception, as exemplar of mere-consciousness, is an early act of mind. As Plato pointed out in his allegories of the Cave and the Divided Line, this is a primitive level, requiring something more to provide stability and unity—a "something" to believe. Hegel specifies this addition as the functioning of real forces "out there"; his is no subjective idealism in danger of solipsism, but we have seen that real forces are not separate from mind, they are more mind. We rise from the welter of sense to the recognition of many centers of mind-activity, each desiring, shaping, wanting to subdue—each according to its internal vector.

Mere-consciousness is transcended and unified by the next stage, self-consciousness (though sense-perception is preserved). Here lies the domain of interpersonal relations, where each self needs acknowledgment by another self in order to be itself. Self-consciousness, in other words, essentially needs a social context and is initially realized as such. Yet such a realization is necessarily unstable. In early stages of human emergence, when a few unusually daring or lucky selves made bondsmen of others, a contradiction emerged. The masters need the acknowledgement of other real selves to be the selves they yearn to be. But bondservants are depersonalized by their condition; thus, while in this relationship they cannot give their masters the personal confirmation they need. While the frustrated and indolent masters consume the fruit of their servants' labor, the servants learn from interaction with the objective forces of nature how to create goods through technological effort. Driven by fear of the death their masters can inflict, these servants are (paradoxically) strengthened by being forced to deal with the negativities of nature. One of the attitudes that rises from this painful but fortunate conflict is that of stoicism. Here one hopes to find freedom from within oneself alone. But once thinking is unleashed in such solitude, it becomes entangled in its own nets and becomes skeptical. The individual becomes divided internally; the low, finite, part is accepted as one's own character, while the eternal, absolute aspects of mind are attributed elsewhere, beyond the self, in an external God blessed with all perfections, contrasted with "a worm like me." This state of "unhappy consciousness" is the one found in Judaism and Christianity, inheritors of the skeptical disintegration of classical culture.

From unhappy self-consciousness, mind is driven to its next stage in search of reconciliation: to reason. At the beginning of this stage, scholars of "objective truth" grind their knives ever sharper to carve their ever smaller bits of information from the entirety of truth—but then they start to use them on each other. Morality is required to save the competition from becoming a massacre. Different modes of morality ensue. First comes the unreflective morality of natural communities, perhaps the "unexamined" type of morality stung by the gadfly of Socratic questioning. Once examination is embraced, however, community tends to be lost, as in the self-aware but deadly morality of the Jacobin Terror, in which ideals of abstract freedom violate the cohesiveness of concrete human society. Finally, however, these two competing forms of morality are taken up and unified (aufgehoben) in the ideal of freedom-in-community, where individual persons cooperate for the larger general will. Such an ideal transcends morality itself and rises to the level of religion. At first "natural" religion is highly objective, worshiping volcanoes and idols made by human hands; but even such objects, which can be beautiful, give rise to religions of art, highly subjective, as in the magnificent art-religions of ancient Greece; therefore, finally, transcending and uniting both the objective, out-ward-oriented, and the subjective, inner-oriented forms of religion, rises abso-lute religion—Christianity—in which both the competing lower varieties are united and given their due through the images of Creator God, Suffering Son, and Pervasive Holy Spirit. Absolute religion, however, is still dependent upon images. Images are too particular and imprecise for the telling of absolute truth. Absolute religion demands to be aufgehoben in philosophy.

When philosophy at last rises to the level at which philosophers begin to reflect back on this long journey taken by mind from its lowest and most par-ticular sense perception to the highest realization of the Absolute Mind, unfolded from all the nested levels of particular things precisely *as* Mind, including all and illuminating all, this is the triumphant moment in which Absolute Mind starts thinking self-consciously about itself. Here is philoso-phy's cosmic importance. It is only through the thoughts of human minds, lifted by this exhausting but infinitely rewarding exercise of reason, that the Absolute Mind comes to know itself. When finite thought momentarily leaps out of its finitude in such philosophical moments, it literally becomes Infinite Thought thinking Itself.

Little wonder that Hegel's students in Berlin were thrilled at his lectures. They felt privileged, in thinking his thoughts with him, to share in the historic moment when the Absolute first became conscious of itself through them. They, as incarnate fragments of Absolute Mind, could think of themselves as experiencing union with the kosmos and with each other, lifted to an unprece-dented plane of knowledge and reality.

All of the preceding has been couched in terms of "process." The clash of earlier states leads in time to a later state, which transforms everything, even though earlier states continue to make themselves felt. Hegel's next major pub-lication, *Science of Logic*, however, approaches the dialectic between the lesser and the greater, the more abstract and the more concrete, nontemporally. Logic is the study of Absolute Mind in itself. Since the rational is the real, logic will involve laying bare the lineaments of reality as the Absolute is (in a nontempo-ral sense of "is"), quite independent of any unfolding in history. History is the domain in which Absolute Mind realizes itself, certainly, but that is not the point in logic. Philosophers need time to explicate the logical relationships within the Absolute, of course, but this is a reflection on the finite human con-dition, not on the Absolute as it is for itself.

The *Logic* is divided into Hegel's familiar three-part design: the Logic of Being, the Logic of Essence, and (transcending and completing both parts) the Logic of the Concept. It is not possible to summarize his many-levelled argu-ment—and unnecessary for our purposes. Instead, a sense of what is provided by Hegel in this great work is enough to show the applicability of his key commitments to the competence of *reason*, to the vital role of *competition*, and to wholeness through final *unity*, in the nontemporal realms of logic no less than in the domains of time and change.

The Logic of Being begins at the most abstract possible level. Consider "pure being" apart from any determinations whatever. What is it? In its total indeterminateness it is utterly indistinguishable from nothing at all. Mind contemplating mere Being wanders back and forth between Being and Nothing. Nothing is the opposite of Being, its ultimate competitor, as it were, but nevertheless they are conceptually inseparable. This logical (eternal) movement between Being and Nothing is aufgehoben by—and constitutes—Becoming. To try to think Being at its most abstract level is necessarily to think Becoming. In other words, at the very heart of Absolute Mind (Being) is generated the logical necessity of unfolding (Becoming). This beautifully coheres with the *Phenomenology of Mind*, but is as logical necessity even more fundamental. Other similar discoveries unfold in the Logic of Being, could we but stay to share them. One more sample must suffice: Indeterminate Becoming is not intelligible alone; it requires for its very concept that something determinate be added—this is *quality*. But quality in general competes with, while yet demanding, *quantity*. How much of whatever? That is the question that inevitably calls forth the opposite category. How to reconcile pure quantity with pure quality? The two rivals are aufgehoben in the higher unity of *measure*. Measure tells us *how much* of *what sort* and thus reconciles quantity with quality. And so on.

The Logic of Essence picks up the logical implications of what it means in itself for Pure Being to Become. It must differentiate itself into quanta of qualia. But as it does so, in increasing tension with the pure abstractness of the Logic of Being, it finds itself broken into competing categories that still require each other—though quite different—in order to be themselves. For example, we find *cause*, which is opposite from, yet requires *effect*. Cause can only be understood from the standpoint of its having some effect; effect can only be understood from its having been caused. They are poles apart, yet they "mediate" each other's meaning; that is, each can mean what it means only *through* reference to the other. The same is true for action and reaction, substance and accident, essence and existence.

The only satisfactory solution is that the competing realm of the Logic of Essence, which itself is in contradictory relation to the perfectly abstract Logic of Being, be entirely aufgehoben into a new level of logic, the Logic of the Concept. The Concept mediates not through some *other* (as in the dual categories of the Logic of Essence) but finally through *itself*. It provides self-mediation to conflict because Concepts can illuminate, "pass mind into," their opposites without ceasing to be what they are. This can be done subjectively, through the "internal" rules of formal logic that explicitly apply to mentality. Hegel contrasts the unity of a premise, taken as an unanalyzed element in formal logic, with the diversity represented by the "subject-copula-predicate" form of the judgment that makes up premises themselves, and how both these competing subjective logical forms are transcended and made to work together in the syllogism that contains them. It can also be done objectively through the "external" manifestations of Absolute Mind in nature, showing itself first as mechanical (physics), then as possessing other nonmechanical properties (chemistry), and—combining both, using but transcending them—as teleological organic nature (biology). But formal logic, in its subjectivity, and natural science, in its objectivity, clash until they are themselves aufgehoben in what alone can transcend and unify the subjective and the objective, viz., the Absolute Idea, human history, art, religion, and philosophy.

Hegel has made the cycle via logic from Absolute Being in its most abstract conception to Absolute Being in its most concrete and proliferated character. Every detail of nature and of human history stands implicit in—and logically presupposes—Absolute Mind.

BRADLEY

Clearly, Hegel is happy to devour even the smallest, delicious morsel of his cake and to have it too. For him, the temporal recital of the Absolute's unfolding is as important and true as the nontemporal unpacking of the fully determinate Absolute out of the necessities of logic. Hegel takes history with full seriousness. His later works, not just the early *Phenomenology of Mind*, make this abundantly clear. Time is no illusion. History is for him the field within which Absolute Mind manifests itself in the only way it can be actual—that is, concretely.

Only fifteen years after Hegel's death, however, a child was born who later would strongly challenge this attempt to have the Absolute both in and out of time. Francis Herbert Bradley, who entered the world in Glasbury, South Wales, in January 1846, one of twenty children in the family of an Evangelical minister, was to become both inspired by and critical of the Hegelian vision.

Bradley's life after Wales was spent almost entirely at Oxford, where he died in 1924. He attended University College as an undergraduate; then, in 1870, was awarded a Fellow's position at Merton College, where he spent the rest of his years. His poor health required nearly unbroken seclusion, which he put to use in an intellectually strenuous regimen of regular writing. He wrote with such acerbity, brilliance, and power that his sickly body paled into insignificance. He was, as he saw himself, a gadfly. His mission was to sting sleepy English philosophy into wakeful awareness of its many shortcomings. One favorite target was British empiricism, the bluff and hearty trust in the senses without awareness of their many failings as avenues to knowledge. Others were unreflective individualism in political attitudes and utilitarianism in ethics. John Stuart Mill (1806–1873) was one of his favorite opponents. He attacked Mill not only in his *Ethical Studies* (1876), where utilitarianism falls under his lash, but in *The Principles of Logic* (1883), in which Mill's empirically grounded logic and psychology are roundly condemned.

Bradley's principal contribution to metaphysics also opens with a polemic. *Appearance and Reality* (1893) is divided into two unequal parts. The first, shorter part is entitled "Appearance" and seeks to torpedo all the comfortable beliefs of British common sense. The whole domain of empirical science also is exploded. "Reality," his second, much longer part offers Bradley's own metaphysical alternative, with a challenge that his readers think—*really think* (without allowing contradictions to muddle and destroy meaning)—any alternative. This, he assures us quite firmly, with a serene confidence grounded in the Law of Noncontradiction, is not a logical possibility at all.

Here is the clue to the major quarrel between Bradley and Hegel. Hegel, as we saw, valued strife between ideas. He saw contradictory judgments as partial truths in competition, capable of forcing higher synthesis for the betterment of all—a sort of Invisible Hand of the mental marketplace, creating more wealth through struggle. Bradley took an entirely different attitude toward contradictions. He disvalued them intensely. Contradictions for him are always signs of theoretical failure. One thing we know for certain is that ideas infected with contradiction cancel themselves out and thus state no possibility. To let the camel's nose of contradiction under the tent of thinking is to abandon everything that makes theory intelligible, thus worthwhile at all. Bradley acknowledges this assertion is unnegotiable, that in making it he is in effect claiming infallibility as his starting point. But, he counters, everyone at some point must make a similar claim (whether aware of it or not), since theory itself depends on it. The Law of Noncontradiction is the necessary condition of intellection even for skeptics, if they want to assert anything rather than nothing. As Bradley writes:

> Outside theory take whatever attitude you may prefer, only do not sit down to a game unless you are prepared to play. But every pursuit obviously must involve some kind of governing principle. Even the extreme of theoretical scepticism is based on some accepted idea about truth and fact. It is because you are sure as to some main feature of truth or reality, that you are compelled to doubt or to reject special truths which are offered you. But, if so, you stand on an absolute principle, and, with regard to this, you claim, tacitly or openly, to be infallible (Bradley 1893: 454).

There may be good reasons for expressing feelings of modesty about one's intellectual powers—even one's low estimate of intellection in general—"but such an estimate or such a feeling must remain outside of the actual process of theory. For, admitted within, they would at once be inconsistent and irrational" (Bradley 1893: 455).

In agreement with Hegel, Bradley is completely committed to the value of *wholeness*. This value is in fact his dominant concern, as though "wholeness" and "health" remain for him the synonyms they once were for our Indo-European ancestors. Even the Law of Noncontradiction, though a theoretical absolute in its own right (as we have seen), is further embraced by Bradley because it defends against the unhealthy fragmentation of thought into incompatible bits.

What about the value of the intellect itself, the competence of reason? Hegel was unrestrained in his embrace of the ideal and the real possibility of absolute knowledge—the sort of knowledge (ironically) that Kant's "Critical turn" had attempted to preclude. On this point, Bradley is more guarded. At one level, Bradley sides (against Kant) in favor of the possibility and importance of metaphysical thinking. Metaphysics cannot be known to be impossible in principle, he argues, since to know that would require one to know reality well enough to know that it cannot be known—but that is a contradiction! Such a claim can only be made by "a brother metaphysician with a rival theory of first principles" (Bradley 1893: 1). Further, it is not useless, even if it fails, since at the very least it brings satisfaction akin to writing poetry.

> And so, when poetry, art, and religion have ceased wholly to interest, or when they show no longer any tendency to struggle with ultimate problems and to come to an understanding with them; when the sense of mystery and enchantment no longer draws the mind to wander aimlessly and to love it knows not what; when, in short, twilight has no charm—then metaphysics will be worthless (Bradley 1893: 3).

At another level, however, we had better not deceive ourselves into expecting absolute knowledge, à la Hegel. Knowledge itself with thinking itself suffers from an ineradicable contamination by appearance, as we shall see. We can know for certain what *cannot* be the case for reality; we can even know for sure what *must* be the case in a general way for reality. But to know reality itself is a different matter, for reasons resting on our knowledge of what reality must exclude.

To begin, we need to know how to recognize appearance in order to know what reality cannot possibly be. Whatever cannot consistently be thought must be appearance. This does not mean appearances do not really appear; they do. It means we must go beyond such appearing in our *thought* about what is ultimately the case, if we are to avoid entrapment in bad theory.

One bad theory, for example, is the common view (held by Galileo and his followers) that there is an important difference in reality between primary and secondary qualities. This is simply sloppy thinking, Bradley argues, for many of the reasons familiar to us from George Berkeley's critique. If secondary qualities are mere appearance because of their relativity to our perceptual apparatus, then so-called primary qualities (the numerable qualities of spatial extension) must be condemned on the same grounds. "The extended comes to us only by relation to an organ; and, whether the organ is touch or is sight or is muscle-feeling—or whatever else it may be—makes no difference to the argument" (Bradley 1893: 12–13). Moreover, the "primary" qualities never are experienced, or even imagined, without some "secondary" (which therefore may rightly qualify as more primary than the "primary" ones). Therefore (to share a sample of the Bradleyan pen-lash):

> I can appeal to what is indisputable. Extension cannot be presented, or thought of, except as one with quality that is secondary. It is by itself a mere abstraction, for some purposes necessary, but ridiculous when taken as an existing thing. Yet the materialist, from defect of nature or of education, or probably both, worships without justification this thin product of his untutored fancy (Bradley 1893: 14).

If it is objected that scientists find it useful to work with characteristics of things that are subject to mathematical treatment, Bradley will concede only the practical, not the theoretical, benefit. "It is doubtless scientific to disregard certain aspects when we work; but to urge that therefore such aspects are not fact, and that what we use without regard to them is an independent real thing—this is barbarous metaphysics" (Bradley 1893: 15).

All this is mere warm-up. Other concepts, much more precious to common sense than "primary" qualities, are contaminated with logical contradiction. For this reason they must be scrapped. No theory that hopes to approach reality even in a modest, general way can have use for them. They include the common notions of substance and adjective, relation and quality, space and time, motion and change, causation, activity, thing, self, and, of course, things-in-themselves.

I shall simply illustrate Bradley's method of argument in respect to relation and quality, space and time. The other arguments are essentially similar.

It seems the world is full of things in relation and possessing qualities. Bradley does not dispute this. Of course, the world seems that way; and, of course, it is practical to act in terms of the implicit theory of reality that these words imply. But practice is one thing; understanding is another. "The arrangement of given facts into relations and qualities may be necessary in practice, but it is theoretically unintelligible. The reality, so characterized, is not true reality, but is appearance" (Bradley 1893: 21) Why unintelligible? Bradley's answer is to draw out contradictions implicit in the very concepts.

First, qualities must rest on relation. Quality P must necessarily depend on the relational property of being *different from* quality Q (and all other qualities not identical to itself). If a certain shade of red is not different from all other hues, then it is nothing determinate and is no quality. But the moment you have something *distinct from* something else, you find you already have relations. Also, quality P must depend on the relational property of being *identical to* itself, wherever and whenever encountered. But, second, qualities must not rest on relation. If there is to be a relation, for example, a certain shade of red to others not that shade, there must first be something distinct (those shades) to be related. Relations require terms to be related. Here is a strict contradiction: a quality both *is* made what it is by virtue of its relations *and is not* made what it is by virtue of its relations.

Relations themselves are equally unintelligible when examined. First, there can be no relation without prior terms. This is obvious; a relation without terms to relate is an empty absurdity. But what relates the relation to its terms? If relations are supposed to be metaphysically real, they must bear some relation to their terms; but relating the term and the relation requires still another relation—and so on to infinity—if all relations require a relation to what is related. Alas, an infinite series, never completed, never succeeds in finally relating. Therefore, at the root of the concept of relation we find the contradiction: a relation must be related to its terms and a relation cannot be related to its terms.

It will be obvious that a real world bereft of all relations, all qualities, will be completely different from anything we can experience or imagine. It is hardly necessary to go any further toward demolishing familiarity, since if there are no real qualities or relations there certainly can be no real time or space. But Bradley does proceed to do this anyway, for good measure. The contradictions can briefly be paraphrased: Space is more than a relation and space is not more than a relation. Likewise for time. Consider the first assertion. Space must be more than relation, since relations require terms. Therefore, parts of space, extents, must be first, to be related. If they are extended (and they must be, to be parts *of space*), these extended parts are made up of infinitely many over-heres rather than over-theres, that is, composed of relations. When examined, these little extents cannot be thought to exist in themselves; they disintegrate into relations. Likewise for time; the parts of time must be finite durations or time as a whole will not be temporal. These parts must be prior to any relations of earlier or later between them. Yet these durations are made up of nothing but relations of earlier and later—what else is meant by a duration?—therefore, the relations are necessarily first. For both space and time, relations are first and are not first. Quite aside from the familiar paradoxes of space and time, rejecting all boundaries and yet defined only by boundaries—antinomies also rehearsed by Bradley—the ideas of space and time are riddled with contradiction and therefore present no possibilities for inclusion in an adequate theory of reality.

It is equally evident a fortiori that if space and time are merely appearance, so must "motion" and "change" be excluded from reality, since they essentially depend on space and time. Similarly, "causality" must be abandoned, since causes and effects are relations, and relations have been shown to be unintelligible. "Activity" too may be mown down, since it is nothing but self-caused change and thus is infected by not one but two contradictory ideas at once. "Things," once qualities, relations, space, time, and causality have been excluded from reality, have no place on Bradley's logical map. And individual "selves," centers of causality (mere appearance) supposedly retaining some self-identical qualities (mere appearance) over time (mere appearance), drop out as self-evident absurdities. None of these common ideas can be candidates for inclusion in a self-consistent theory of reality.

What then can be thought about reality? Is there anything left? Yes, replies Bradley, there is much to be said that can certainly be known. First, there are the appearances! Appearance really appears. This is important in two huge respects. (1) There is no sense at all in looking for a reality that hides somewhere outside or behind the experience that appears. As Hegel also insisted, the Kantian "things in themselves" sealed away from all possibility of cognition are utterly without meaning, a blank embarrassment for any meaningful theory. "The assertion of a reality falling outside knowledge," Bradley affirms at the very close of his section on Appearance, "is quite nonsensical" (Bradley 1893: 114). (2) We know with certainty that appearances exist, and whatever exists must *somehow* belong to reality. There is nothing except reality to which they can possibly belong. Whatever is thought to be reality cannot possibly be *less* than the appearances.

At the start of his large section on Reality, Bradley takes inventory of the positive results he has attained so far. He has an infallible criterion of reality: the Law of Noncontradiction. Thus far he has used it negatively, to thresh out the chaff, but it can be used positively, too. "Ultimate reality is such that it does not contradict itself" (Bradley 1893: 120). That is, it is whole. Unity of ultimate reality is thus guaranteed by the one ultimate criterion, whose *absoluteness* is manifest by the fact that to doubt it (meaningfully and consistently) requires that it be assumed, and whose *supremacy* is assured by the fact that if there were several criteria of reality, they would all need to be consistent, thus enthroning Noncontradiction as primary. Added to this criterion of criteria, Bradley also has positive information about reality. First, if reality is without contradiction its nature is harmony. Second, since appearance has existence it must belong to reality. Third (combining the first and second items), since appearance belongs to an ultimately harmonious reality it must be "somehow real in such a way as to be self-consistent" (Bradley 1893: 123). Fourth, since reality is ultimately harmonious it must be one also in the sense of singularity—there can be no second reality, much less many.

In sum, there is one and only one nonrelational reality, a system in which everything fits. As such—single, perfect, and nonrelational—it may for the first time be called the "Absolute," as Bradley begins to do only after establishing this much. What is the content of the system that comprises the Absolute? There is only one choice, given what has been proven. The content must be appearance, and appearance only appears to experience, to mentality. The Absolute is therefore sentient experience; it must "hence be a single and all-inclusive experience, which embraces every partial diversity in concord" (Bradley 1893: 129).

Immediately, and significantly from the viewpoint of the thesis of this book, Bradley turns from the question of the theoretical perfection of the Absolute, which is now established to his satisfaction, to the much more problematic issue—for him—of practical perfection. That is, is the sentience of the Absolute *pleasant,* reflecting health and well-being, or is it a system theoretically perfect but still admitting "defect and misery" (Bradley 1893: 130)? This is important for Bradley but difficult to answer. There is no direct proof possible. The Ontological Argument for the necessity of perfection will not satisfy, since there is no logical passage allowed from "ought" to "is." Perhaps theoretical perfection *ought* to entail pleasure, but that, alas, seems out of reach of any purely rational argument. Still, an indirect proof may work. The practical demand that the Absolute's experience be dominantly pleasant will not be silent. Therefore, if this genuine element of our nature should forever be discontented, it would entail that no full harmony in the Absolute would be possible. The clash of the ideal with the actual would in the end destroy the perfection of the system we know must somehow be perfect. Thus, indirectly, we may be assured, Bradley tells us, that on balance the Absolute's experience *must* be satisfactory. Pain will need to be present in the Absolute, since pain unfortunately is experienced—and all appearances must finally be acknowledged in reality. But this need not simply be *as* these pains are experienced. Somehow the Absolute will take up the pain of the sentient world and overbalance it, relate it, triumph over it.

How can we possibly conceive of such relationless reality? Is this an idea entirely ungrounded in experience and therefore as much condemned to nonsense as the ideas Bradley has already so severely chastised? No, Bradley offers four empirical grounds for reference toward (though of course not adequate comprehension of) his proposal of nonrelational sentience as Absolute reality. The first is what we might call "mere feeling," the state of mind just before wakefulness when there is differentiation in experience but yet no clear relations between one thing and another. Obviously we cannot give clear, crisp descriptions of this state, since it lies below the level of clarity and crispness. Once we are fully enough awake to begin the task of description, we have emerged out of mere feeling and are in the world of qualities, relations, space, time, cause, and all the other contradictions the Absolute must reconcile. Still, there is a reference to this idea of rich diversity before qualities and relations; that is the sort of reality—but at an infinitely higher level of complexity and awareness—that the Absolute is. Second, we experience an inchoate hunger to get beyond disunity; we feel, Bradley says, "hostility" to distinctions. That feeling is another reference, poor and weak though it may be, to the Absolute's consciousness. Third, all relations, though they fail to overcome the infinite regress that makes them fall into incoherence, presuppose—in the sense of tending toward—a unity on which they would stand if they could. If relations are experienced as vectors toward the unity they struggle vainly toward, they can hint at the character of the Absolute. Finally, the experiences of goodness and beauty, in their yearning toward overcoming the fragmentation of moral and aesthetic experience, respectively, can direct us imperfectly but helpfully toward the Absolute.

The Absolute must reconcile in itself all the contradictory appearances of experience. Is this thinkable? No, Bradley answers, necessarily not. Thinking essentially divides "whatness" from "thatness." Even true judgments predicate something (a "whatness") of a subject (a "thatness"), thereby attempting to unite a character with a subject. Unfortunately, the union is never complete because the estrangement of "what" from "that" would never have been allowed in the first place, had we remained in reality. Thought desires the primal unity of the Absolute, but this is a hopeless desire, like the desire of lovers to transcend selves. To be a lover is necessarily to be a self; to be thought is necessarily to remain partial in the realm of subject and predicate. As Bradley says, "in desiring to transcend this distinction, thought is aiming at suicide" (Bradley 1893: 148). Even if the cognitive aspect could, per impossibile, perfectly unite its subject again, the additional mental aspects of will and emotion remain part of the yearning mix of what it is to be a thinker. Only the whole universe would be finally the truth.

> Such a whole state would possess in a superior form that immediacy which we find (more or less) in feeling; and in this whole all divisions would be healed up. It would be experience entire, containing all elements in harmony. Thought would be present as a higher intuition; will would be there where the ideal had become reality; and beauty and pleasure and feeling would live on in this total fulfilment. Every flame of passion, chaste or carnal, would still burn in the Absolute unquenched and unabridged, a note absorbed in the harmony of its higher bliss. We cannot

imagine, I admit, how in detail this can be. But if truth and fact are to be one, then in some such way thought must reach its consummation. But in that consummation thought has certainly been so transformed, that to go on calling it thought seems indefensible (Bradley 1893: 152).

Therefore, truth as we know it remains on the side of appearance, not reality. The same is true of goodness. Evil and good, for Bradley, are certainly not illusion; but they are both appearance. They both imply the division between fact and ideal. Evil rests with the separation; goodness attempts to reunite them, but with the same impossible—suicidal—desire as truth. The main difference is that truth is theoretical, a matter of "being," while goodness is practical, a matter of "making." Acts of will are essential to moral goodness, and discrepancy in the latter case is a challenge to reform rather than to theoretical synthesis. But neither is to be taken as ultimate, nor is religion, which by postulating both a God and a world, divided by finitude and sin, violates the unity of the Absolute. Bradley regrets spending so much time on these subjects. "It is mainly the common prejudice in favour of the ultimate truth of morality or religion, that has led me to give to them here a space which perhaps is undue" (Bradley 1893: 355).

With this we need to take leave of Bradley and of the branch in modern thought leading to his absolute idealism. Bradley was of course not the last of the Idealists. In America, major thinkers, including Harvard's Josiah Royce (1855–1916), whose thought dominated American philosophy until the First World War, Borden Parker Bowne (1847–1910) and his successors at Boston University, the admirable Edgar S. Brightman (1884–1953) and Peter A. Bertocci (1910–1989), as well as Yale's Brand Blanshard (1892–1987), continued to explore the consequences and possibilities of beginning with the primacy of mind. But no one followed the path more unswervingly than F. H. Bradley. More than anyone, Bradley accepted the full consequences of taking Hegel's nontemporal interpretation of mind under the aspect of the *Logic*. And, more than anyone, Bradley refused to swerve, even when it looked increasingly clear to others that his path was leading to a dead end.

There is much of value to glean from Bradley's path. One of his signal contributions was in his drawing attention to the importance of feeling as a mode of experience largely overlooked by orthodox empiricists. This hint will be picked up and greatly elaborated in the metaphysical proposals of Alfred North Whitehead, as we shall see. But Bradley's thirst for coherence, matching only Parmenides' and Spinoza's in intensity, was purchased at a huge price in adequacy to fundamental intuitions of normal healthy life. What he lost, timelessly digested in his unthinkable Absolute, was the stuff of fundamental social intercourse: recognition of the finite reality of indissoluble selves and other interactive entities in a world making itself—and inviting us to join in the making. He lost plurality, change, and any point for purpose. "And thus the native hue of resolution/ Is sicklied o'er with the pale cast of thought" (Shakespeare 1974: Act III, Scene 1, lines 83–84).

From a values perspective, Bradley's vision is hardly an improvement, though offered on behalf of mind, over the vast frozen space-time kosmos of Einstein and his modern materialist admirers. To retrieve a universe of real becoming, we now need to step back half a century to the moment after Hegel's death. There we can pick up once again the other (temporal) side of the grand dialectic.

8

THE PERVASIVENESS OF CHANGE

By the end of this chapter we shall have concluded a long trip, from the great premodern pioneers of speculation, through modern theories of reality, toward an agenda for the metaphysical needs of the future. In Part Three, my narrative approach will need to be replaced by another form of exposition, one better suited for the uncertainties and opportunities of the transitional present.

But for the subsequent pages we have one more branch of modern thinking to follow, defined by commitment not to the values associated with matter or with mind—both sorts of thinkers are involved—but to development and change. Descartes' modern agenda is still unaccomplished, as we have seen. What we had hoped for was a theory of reality capable of embracing and making coherent all of physical nature in its obdurate objectivity, its massive regularity, its hospitality to mathematical portrayal, and all of our first-hand experience of purpose, moral responsibility, love, appreciation of beauty, and religious exaltation. Instead, we have been offered an unwelcome choice: take matter/energy and forget (quite literally) about mind, or take mind and lose nature.

I hope it is clear from the story I have told in the foregoing pages that this is a dramatic simplification. There are more nuances in every major attempt to address these issues than this stark disjunction reflects. Nevertheless, the modern agenda has been stymied. Whether we start from values conducive to quantification and mathematics or from those hospitable to the qualitative texture of personal experience, we seem unable to reach across the gulf to give fair and full treatment to the other side.

Could the problem be located in the implicit supposition, during most of modern times, that we must reconcile two "adult forms," as it were, that may have grown far apart? Might we do better if we were to emphasize the *process* that has given us both mind and matter more than these finished *products* as they now intractably stand before us?

MARX AND DARWIN

This chapter explores such a possibility. For this, we step back to Hegel, or to the period just after Hegel, during which his thought, even in death, "weighed heavily upon the living," as Karl Marx later said (McInnes 1967: 172). I begin with Marx and Charles Darwin, not because they were outstanding metaphysical thinkers, but for other reasons. If we wanted a "real metaphysician," we could hardly do better than F. H. Bradley, a secluded academic all his days, thinking ultimate thoughts for a living—and having no other life—who could be taken as a prototype of that. Rather, Marx and Darwin are both men of other affairs. Marx of course was greatly influenced by that earlier "real metaphysician," Hegel, but was influenced more as a would-be world-changer than as a world-thinker. Still more important, both Marx and Darwin left enormous legacies of change—on behalf of change. The "real metaphysicians" who follow breathe a new air. It is moving, flowing, and filling their sails as they set out for new destinations.

Karl Heinrich Marx was born in May 1818, the year Hegel moved from Heidelberg to the University of Berlin to begin his reign of triumph. Young Marx, who grew up in Trier, Rhineland, was a first-generation Christian, baptized into the Evangelical Church after his family converted from Judaism early in his life. This was a coerced conversion, required so that his father, a distinguished lawyer, could continue to practice under Prussian autocracy. Under the circumstances, Marx did not long remain a Christian. After a year of study at Bonn, he transferred to the University of Berlin, where he turned his attention to philosophy and history in 1836, five years after Hegel's death. Already known as a militant atheist to his undergraduate friends in the Young Hegelians group (led by a junior faculty member, Bruno Bauer), which took principal delight in attacking organized religion and Prussian autocracy, Marx gravitated readily toward the materialism of ancient Atomists. In 1841, at the age of only twenty-three, and anticipating an academic career, he received his doctorate from the University of Jena, where he presented his thesis on Democritus and Epicurus. Meanwhile, the dismissal of Bauer for radicalism made it clear to Marx that he had better seek some other line of work.

In the next year he moved to Cologne, where he was offered the editorship of the liberal newspaper, *Die Rheinische Zeitung*. His fiery editorials sufficiently provoked the Prussian authorities to close the newspaper down within the year. Out of a job and newly married to his childhood sweetheart, Jenny von Westphalen (whose father, the Baron von Westphalen, was an early socialist influence in his life), Marx then moved to Paris, where in 1844 he met Friedrich Engels, with whom he would remain in closest literary and philosophical partnership for the rest of his life. Fellow materialist Ludwig Feuerbach's book, *The Essence of Christianity* (1841)—arguing that human beings create God in their own idealized image in an act of self-alienation that sunders the noble from the low and (falsely) requires control by church and state—inspired Marx. In Paris (in manuscripts published long after his death as his *Economic and Philosophic Manuscripts of 1844*), he transposed the concept of alienation from Feuerbach's religious key into an economic one. By the end of 1844, Marx found himself expelled once again for political radicalism, and with Jenny and Engels he moved to Brussels for an important three-year period. During these years Marx and Engels together expanded some "Theses on Feuerbach" that Marx had written in Paris into a book-length manuscript, "The German Ideology," in which a clear and original materialist view of history, combining Hegelian with British economic thought, was worked out, maintaining that the nature of the individual depends on the material conditions determining economic production. In these years Marx and Engels also wrote "The Poverty of Philosophy," predicting the dialectical breakdown of capitalism from internal material contradictions and attacking the excessive trust in ideas manifested by such as the French socialist-anarchist, Pierre Proudhon (1809–1865). While in Brussels, Marx joined the League of the Just, a group organized mainly by radical German émigrés and headquartered in London. Marx and Engels travelled to England, both to visit the prosperous Engels' family spinning factories in Manchester and to attend a conference of the League of the Just in 1847. The conference listened with admiration to the ideas of Marx and Engels, renamed itself the Communist League, and commissioned the two theorists to draft its platform. This commission was accepted by Marx and Engels, their work was adopted by the League, and the *Communist Manifesto* was published in 1848.

Simultaneously, a wave of revolutions broke out in Europe. The first occurred in Paris, and Marx immediately moved back to France from Brussels. Soon the risings spread to Prussia; King Friedrich Wilhelm IV was forced to accept parliamentary government and allow a free press. Again, Marx moved swiftly, returning to Cologne where he established the *Neue Rheinische Zeitung*, hoping to pick up where he had been required to break off five years before. All too soon for Marx, the revolution failed and repression returned. The infant newspaper was closed by the authorities; Marx was tried for sedition; and, though he was acquitted, he was forced again to leave German soil, never to return. He repeated his exile by way of Paris, then left for London where he settled in the poor district of Soho in 1849.

Life in Soho during the next decades was terribly difficult. Marx had arrived with Jenny and their four children. They then added two more to their household. There was no regular source of income. Three of the children died. Engels' factories were thriving in Manchester, and the old partner was generous with his gifts, but Marx found it impossible to manage his affairs, especially while "keeping up appearances." Some income was added sporadically by Marx's foreign correspondent columns for the *New York Daily Tribune*, a large-circulation radical newspaper. At the time of the American Civil War, Marx leaned strongly toward the industrialized North. During these years, Marx determined, as he said, to study the "laws of motion" of the capitalist society as a whole. He spent his days in the British Museum, wrote an enormous "Outline" (the *Grundrisse*, unpublished) for this project, studied Adam Smith's and David Ricardo's economic theories closely for their theories of surplus value, and finally brought his Volume I of *Capital* to publication in 1867. The remaining two volumes, largely written, were left for twenty years for posthumous editing and publication by the faithful Engels.

Marx was distracted in his later years by many things. He spent much of his energy on the leadership of the International Workingmen's Association (the so-called "International"), of which he was founder (in 1864) and leading spirit. A great deal of his time was spent preparing for the annual congresses and in fending off the anarchist wing of the Association led by Mikhail Bakunin. He was also distracted and dragged down by his health. In later years he was covered with boils, an affliction with Biblical resonances from which he sought relief in spas throughout Europe, as well as in Algeria, to no avail. He may also have suffered a stroke or at least loss of self-confidence. A final blow came with the death of his beloved Jenny in 1881, and of his elder daughter, after which life lost its savor for him. He died in March of 1883.

This was a man with "heart." He wore his values on his sleeve. He was obviously and consistently outraged, from youth to death, at tyranny, repression, and injustice. His father and family were coerced into their conversions to Christianity; his undergraduate mentor in the Young Hegelians was dismissed by repressive authorities; his own academic career was aborted by the thought-police, as was his alternate editorial career; and, likewise, was his attempt to regroup in Paris with fellow exiles. All this to have endured while only twenty-five years old!

We are not surprised, therefore, to find Hegel's high regard for conflict, negativity, and struggle strongly shared by Marx. His attraction to materialism, as well (though a complete reversal of Hegelian values), should be seen in the context of the heavy, self-righteous, religious coloration of the status quo. The almost automatic recoil from confrontation with repressive Church-State alliances to materialist worldviews—something we noted a century earlier among the philosophes and idéologues opposed to tyranny before and after the French Revolution—is familiar and wholly understandable under the circumstances. Metaphysics became a weapon of opposition. *Écrasez l'infâme!*

The combination of commitment to Hegel's dialectical change with Feuerbach's anticlerical materialism was an explosive mixture. "Historical materialism," as Engels called it, or "dialectical materialism," as most followers preferred, was "materialist" in two respects. On one hand, it was metaphysical materialism of the standard form we recognize from the classical Atomists through Baron d'Holbach; on the other, it was a new interpretation of materialism stressing material economic interests as determining all else. Thus, it was doubly important for Marx to criticize (demolish) religion as the "opiate of the people." First, in order to end the alienation of workers from themselves and each other, they need to be alerted to the real absence of God, soul, and spirit, from the universe; the kosmos needs cleansing of Christian drivel. Second, they need to realize how religion is used to poison their economic interests, dulling their awareness of present sacrifice in return for supposed future "pie in the sky," while their surplus labor is systematically stolen from them by the capitalist system.

One of Marx's most important contributions to the unfulfilled modern agenda comes here. He generalizes from his critique of religious belief to all belief-structures and ideational forms of culture. These, he declares, are mere superstructure, generated by the economic realities beneath. They are "ideologies" which do not precipitate but only follow changes in material circumstances. The real place of mind in the kosmos, therefore, is as an epiphenomenon, a fickle wraith changing as material forces of production create their own contradictions and are supplanted by new ones. Each social system generates forces within itself (as thesis calls forth antithesis in Hegel)—economic forces that will eventually result in the destruction, probably sudden, of the old forces, replaced by a new set with their own relations of production, including their own ideas, beliefs, arts, and philosophies.

Critically, if this were my aim, there would be much to examine. The empirical reliability of Marx's claims, for example, is in many cases weak. It seems simply not the case that ideas are always the by-products of economic interests, either in individuals or in whole societies. The phenomenon of prominent "class traitors" among the wealthy, working in support of policies benefitting the less fortunate classes, for example, is too well known to be ignored. The motive power of nationalism and religion, too, is a reality that often eclipses economic interests. The predictive accuracy of Marx's expectations, for another example, is notoriously poor. In his lifetime, as after, theoretical expectations were repeatedly disappointed; in contrast, the Russian Revolution "should" not have happened in the absence of far greater industrial development through which the "dialectic" could have matured its contradictions. Even the logical tightness of Marx's predictions, such as they were, seems inadequate. He never considered the possibility of capitalism's being only one in an indefinite future sequence of oppressive systems that might have to be worked through. Somehow, capitalism's demise was supposed to bring about the end of the entire dialectic process. For a lover of contradiction and struggle, this seems odd.

But these problems are not the main point for this narrative. Rather, we are left wondering about the real status of mind and values in the universe. What does Marx think he is doing when he proclaims his theories? Are these, the fruit of his sacrificial lifetime labors, to be taken as the mere ideological panting of a man struggling with poverty and boils, mere warm air to be blown away by larger stipends from Engels' capitalist spinning machines and by the price of more effective medical services? Certainly not. But on his theory of reality how can his—or any—ideas be other than ideological? How can mind generate truths that are independent of the material substructure of which, on his atomistic metaphysics, they are entirely the product?

Likewise, we are left wondering how Marx's predictive determinism (obtained from studying the "laws of motion" of capitalism) relates to his ethical prescriptivism. How can moral appeals work to change the course of history if morality is mere epiphenomenon and if history is implacably run by material forces? He needs a theory of mind—for himself, at least, and for the people he aims to rouse to the barricades—that is not permitted by his adopted materialism.

What he has succeeded in doing, as no one else, is alerting us to the dangers of "false consciousness" based on factors of which we would prefer not to be aware. And, like no one else in history, he has drawn attention to the self-deception and hypocrisy that masks group-selfish systems of exploitation and injustice in the world of affairs. This he has done by combining an Old Testament prophet's sense of justice with a thoroughly temporalized vision of the universe—a universe open to radical change for the better. These are great achievements justifying his enormous influence in the twentieth century. But they are not answers to Descartes' modern agenda. If anything, his stern cry for justice, combined with his theory of reality—in which there can be no place for justice or injustice, purpose, or value of any kind—has exacerbated more than anyone else's the painful problem of modern mindlessness.

The person who was to do more than any other to advance the awareness that change is fundamental in the universe, not only (as Marx had held) for human history but also for all life and the physical world itself, was Charles Darwin. Darwin was born in Shrewsbury, England, in 1809, the son of a wealthy physician and grandson of the pleasantly eccentric poet-philosopher Erasmus Darwin (1731–1802). Charles' mother was Susannah Wedgewood Darwin, the daughter of Josiah Wedgewood (1730–1795), founder of the great pottery enterprise still bearing his name. Despite his good family, young Charles did not show early promise of greatness. He was poor at his schoolwork at the Shrewsbury School, from which he was removed at age sixteen by his irritated parents and sent to Edinburgh to become a physician, following in his father's footsteps. Darwin proved not merely undistinguished at these studies, however; he was downright squeamish. Operations (without anesthesia, of course) revolted him. As a last resort, he was sent to Cambridge at age eighteen to become a cleric. But theology did not spark his interest either. Instead, he enjoyed sports and natural history. One friendly Cambridge botanist, John Stevens Henslow (1796–1861), encouraged Darwin, trained him, and salved his badly bruised self-confidence. When, at twenty-two, Darwin received his undergraduate degree (in the year of Hegel's death), Henslow arranged for the great adventure of Darwin's life: a five-year trip as an unpaid (but official) naturalist on the research vessel, H.M.S. *Beagle*.

This voyage was the making of Darwin. It honed his observational skills and provided him hints and data he would use in years to come when formulating his theoretical work. Unfortunately, it also exposed him to bites by a South American insect (*Triatoma infestans*), which carried the parasite that made the rest of his life miserable, as he suffered from the incurable Chagas' disease, resulting in unsettled bowels, vomiting, and fatigue.

He returned to England at age twenty-seven and began writing his reports. At thirty, he married his cousin Emma Wedgewood, settling in London at first; but his health problems made society unbearable. After two years the Darwins moved to the country, at Downe in Kent, where Darwin lived and worked with his wife and ten children (of whom seven survived to adulthood), until his death at age seventy-three.

Darwin's quiet life was as the eye of the hurricane of change his thought inspired. Indeed, the grand theme of his work on all fronts was—at bottom—*change*: change in the rocks under our feet; change in the species around us—and change in our own human nature. It seems hard now, so complete has been the change his impact brought about, to imagine the thought-world he entered only a century and a half ago. The emphasis was fixity. Mountains, continents, islands, and seas were simply there as God had made them not so very long ago (Archbishop James Ussher's [1581–1656] careful estimate, on Biblical evidence, dated creation at 4004 B.C.); and all the species were fixed too. Both the Bible and Aristotle agreed on that.

There had been occasional dissenting voices. In ancient times, as we recall, Heraclitus was the great apostle of change, Empedocles offered a crude theory of natural selection, and the Atomists attributed all present structures to chance configurations of atoms falling in the void. Closer to home, Jean Baptiste Pierre de Lamarck had proposed in *Philosophie Zoologique* (1809) that animals adapt to changes in the environment with new behavior, inducing changes in organs or parts, and that such acquired traits are passed on to offspring. Charles Darwin's own eccentric grandfather, Erasmus Darwin, had proposed something similar to an evolutionary theory. But the vast consensus of the age was against this. Species do not interbreed. They constantly replicate themselves in their young. They were designed, most sensible people thought, by the benevolent (though sometimes inscrutable) intelligence of the Divine Maker. While at Cambridge, Charles Darwin, along with all other undergraduates, had been required to read *Natural Theology* (1802) by Archdeacon William Paley, the *locus classicus* of such reasoning. It was the accepted wisdom of the age.

On the *Beagle*, however, young Darwin was driven to other ideas. These included geological reflections, part of his assignment. One of the anomalies to be understood was the existence of coral reefs and atolls, rings of coral surrounding sometimes an island, sometimes just a lagoon. Since the animals creating coral shell are unable to live under conditions deeper than 120 feet below the surface, but since empty coral shell structures supporting the living portions of the reefs often extend much further down, it occurred to Darwin that this gives strong indication of gradual sinking of volcanic islands. Sometimes, the volcanic peaks constituting the islands disappear entirely below the surface, leaving empty lagoons encircled by upward-growing reefs built on their submergent shoulders. Elsewhere, young volcanic islands rise, Darwin theorized. More, at high altitudes in the Andes Mountains of the South American continent, he found fossils that once had been beneath the sea. Earthquakes and volcanoes raise and lower the land. Sediments crystalize under the enormous pressures of overlying rock. Everywhere there is flux. The solid stone itself bears messages of change. Darwin's books on geology, *Coral Reefs* (1842), *Volcanic Islands* (1844), and *Geological Observations on South America* (1846), were enough alone to assure his eminence as a messenger of change.

But of course it was his then-radical ideas about biological change that fueled the greatest storm. There were three areas of convergent evidence that struck him on his voyage. One area came from fossils he found of closely related species separated in *time* from one another. Giant sloths once roamed South America. Today, the species is extinct but closely related sloths roam in their place. Could one have descended from the other? How? Why? Second, another area of evidence came from current species, different but closely related, separated in *space* from one another. This was especially noticeable in the Galápagos Islands, where Darwin found each island has its own distinctive species of tortoise, its own species of birds, and the like. Why? Climate and other conditions—identical among the islands—could not account for the variety of species. Special creation of such variety in such a limited area seemed a strained, implausible hypothesis. Darwin made a special study of the various species of ground finches in the Galápagos chain and found the one correlation observable was between the type of food available and the structure of the beaks of the differing species. Where large seeds were plentiful, finches with large, powerful beaks were found; where there were small seeds, there were finches with smaller beaks; where insects abounded, finches had fine, insect-catching beaks. Each species of finch was well-adapted to the food available in its environment. How had that happened? A third area of evidence for the possibility of change came from the familiar human practice of cultivation of plants and domestication of animals. When certain traits are wanted, humans deliberately select parents that have these traits and breed them to produce offspring with even more pronounced traits of the desired sort. Then these offspring are in turn selected, so that over generations of guided reproduction, the desired trait can be established in a population. Change, over time, can be produced by steady, conscious selection in a given direction. But this involves human purpose, requiring the activity of horticulturists or animal breeders. What in unaided nature—as in the Galápagos Islands—could play the part of deliberate selective agent? Darwin returned to England with his mind full of hints and theories, but at first he could not answer the last question on selection.

Two years after his return, at age twenty-nine, he read *An Essay on the Principle of Population* (1798, second edition, 1803) by Thomas Robert Malthus (1766–1834), which gave him the answer to the question of "natural selection." Malthus was worried about the future of the human race. He noted that food supply can be increased, but only additively, in arithmetical progression, while people, if unconstrained, continue to have babies who grow up to have more babies in geometrical progression. No matter how much food can be supplied by the farmers and fishermen, it will be a finite quantity; and, in a comparatively short time, populations will multiply to devour it all. Therefore, Malthus was pessimistic that social programs, like the Dole and the Poorhouses in England, were ever going to solve the problem of poverty and hunger. Constraints on reproduction, including moral suasion, were called for (as he emphasized more in the second edition), but really only misery, overcrowding, disease, war, vice, and near-starvation would be likely to keep populations in balance over the long run.

Darwin saw immediately the application of this argument to the problem of steady selective pressure on populations of plants or animals in nature. The food supply being fixed, since no species but ours can deliberately control their own food production, populations will always expand to the point of starvation. Those which happened to have traits helpful to survival amid scarcity will succeed more frequently in breeding and passing on their traits; in the next generation, there will be more of those traits in the feeding population, crowding out the less well-adapted; and, soon, those unfortunates will disappear altogether from the breeding pool. Over time, and given spatial separation, different species will descend from a common ancestor species, specific traits to depend on differences in the isolated environments. The mystery of the Galápagos could at last be solved. Species should no longer be considered fixed but changing, no longer designed by divine purpose to fit their circumstances but "selected" automatically by chance variation coupled with population pressure.

Darwin, surprisingly, did little about this discovery. Could it have been too large and unsettling a notion for a young man in ill-health to handle? He wrote an outline of his theory two years after reading Malthus, then a more complete essay, unpublished, stating it two years after that, when he was thirty-three; but he showed it to only one person, the botanist Joseph Dalton, and then dropped the matter while he returned to his exhaustive study of barnacles, which occupied him for more than a decade. Finally, at the urging of friends, he returned to his "species work," after fourteen years of inattention. He was still working on it two years later, at age forty-nine, when he received an upsetting letter from Alfred Russel Wallace, describing to him the very same theory as his own, developed independently by Wallace in Malaya. This was a crisis requiring swift measures, if credit was to be fairly given. Therefore, on July 1, 1858, Darwin and Wallace presented a joint paper stating their theory of evolution to the Linnaean Society in London.

Darwin's *On the Origin of Species*, a very large and detailed book, was published in November 1859, the next year, when he was fifty. Immediately, the hurricane began to swirl. Darwin himself took little part in controversies stimulated by his findings. Conservative thought, however, was outraged, especially at two points important to this narrative.

First, the evolution of species, as described by Darwin, not only introduced change where stability had been assumed but characterized it as automatic, mindless change. The Newtonian world picture had been largely accepted for physics and astronomy. These fields, even for thinkers like Paley, were domains of mechanism. True, Newton himself, and poets like Joseph Addison (1672–1719) saw God's intelligence manifest through the "spacious firmament on high," but at a distance in both time and space. Biology was different. Living species are close and active; they were thought to show with special intimacy and force the particular providence of the designing mind of God. As Paley says of the difference, one might strike one's foot on a stone in a heath and think, without obvious absurdity, that it had lain there forever. But finding a watch lying there is entirely different: it demands a watchmaker sometime in its past. The living species were like watches running everywhere, all insisting—by virtue of their wondrous adaptation—on purposive agency as their only rational explanation.

Now, however, Darwin has shown that the adaptation of living things to their environments can be explained, instead, as products of nonpurposive processes. Natural "selection," despite the original mentalistic associations of the word, is a mindless *mechanism*. The mechanical world picture has swallowed life itself. Final causation is squeezed still further out of nature. Its last refuge is in the human mind.

After Darwin's revolution, the human mind is just one more part of the biological order that is mindlessly run. This is the second great outrage expressed by Darwin's opponents. The logic of Darwin's evolutionary vision is clear and compelling. *Homo sapiens*, as a species, is in countless ways—embryologically, structurally, etc.—similar to other species of primates; primates share many traits with nonprimates, and so on, "all the way down." In the sweep of evolutionary change, humankind itself must be descended from ancestors that were prehuman. The minds of which (and with which) we boast are simply variations on animal powers of sensation, anticipation, and motivation. Some of these traits, by virtue of their quantity and quality, must have been "selected" as giving competitive advantage in the battle for survival.

Darwin accepted this logic. It does not entail that our minds are today on all fours with the minds of prehuman organisms. Darwin never said it did. It does entail that our mental powers are biologically grounded and intimately related to mental powers of other magnitudes and qualities within the biological universe.

Darwin's shriller critics were mistaken. Evolution does not entail that conscious purpose and deliberate agency in humans are illusions. It does suggest that homologues of purpose and agency should be expected elsewhere in the biological kingdom, since all our powers descend from common ancestors. The Darwinian vision of pervasive change, however, offends deep values of some critics in multiple ways. One is simply the challenge to long-treasured worldviews enshrined in authoritative scripture and ecclesiastical institutions. More obviously, more intractably even than Galileo or Newton, Darwin cannot easily be harmonized literally with the creation stories of the Bible. If one treasures the Bible as inerrant, this is a mighty insult. But even apart from formal religious values, the Darwinian vision of human descent challenges species' pride. Inaccurately (but to many cartoonists' delight) Darwin was accused of saying the human race is descended "from monkeys," or (even more inaccurately) that we are "merely" monkeys. Nothing could be further from Darwin's careful methods than to confuse quite distinct species one with another. It is only rhetoric (whether used for or against the higher human values), not science, that rides on metaphors like "the naked ape," as though such phrases accurately or completely characterize human being.

Darwin himself never publicly claimed to be a metaphysician, a theorist of reality as a whole, or even to have all the answers to the biological questions relevant to his revolution. He could not, for example, explain where the variations come from that nature "selects" in its impersonal way. This question had to await the application of Gregor Mendel's (1822–1884) law of genetic inheritance, not generally appreciated until after 1900, when Hugo De Vries (1848–1935), a Dutch botanist, discovered and drew attention to Abbot Mendel's monastic experiments.

In private, however, Darwin carried on extensive discussion of metaphysical themes in notebooks, particularly Notebook M, in which he licensed himself to ponder issues on which his public lips were sealed. In the notebooks he argued strongly for the complete continuity between mind or "reason" in nonhuman nature and in *Homo sapiens*. In all these personal reflections, Darwin maintains a thoroughgoing naturalism which he sometimes acknowledges as amounting to downright materialism. In Notebook C, after a reductionist consideration of religion, he high-spiritedly exclaims: "Love of deity effect of organization, oh you materialist!" (Herbert 1977: 202).

Still, apart from Darwin's private opinions, it is still necessary to ask about the ultimate status of mind in the universe. Is it a mere byproduct of matter, an epiphenomenon determined entirely by its material substrate? Is it, rather, independently real and equipped with unique powers of its own but a sudden "emergent" from biology in the vast history of evolution? Is it, as Pope Pius XII declared in his encyclical, *Humani generis* (1951), something divinely created for each human being and infused into the embryo at conception? (The Pope, contrary to Darwin's private opinions, held this dualistic view compatible with Darwinism if evolution is considered simply a hypothesis accounting for the human body alone.) Or is mind, as Darwin held, found on a continuous scale in nature (Herbert 1977: 203), undergoing amplification, enlargement, and enhancement by cosmic pressures of pervasive change?

All these questions and more are left open for debate, despite Darwin's materialist interpretation of his contribution to the modern worldview. To address them became a primary concern of the philosophers of change with whom we now engage.

BERGSON

Henri Bergson was born in 1859, the portentous year in which Darwin's *Origin of Species* was published. His parents were both Jewish: his mother came from an English family and his father had a Polish background. The Polish family name was Berek, and "son-of-Berek" turned into the French "Bergson." Bergson's father was a distinguished musician, the former director of the Geneva Conservatory of Music.

Bergson was born and raised in Paris, attending the Lycée Condorcet where he was drawn to science and mathematics as well as to classical studies. At age nineteen he enrolled at the École Normale Supérieure with a teaching career in view. While there, he distinguished himself, among other distinctions, with a remarkable essay on a problem in Pascal's geometry. After graduation, and with his teaching credentials in 1881, at the age of twenty-two, Bergson began to teach at lycée outside Paris, first for two years at Angers, then for five years at Clermont-Ferrand. During these years he concentrated his studies in philosophy of science, in particular, through the evolutionary categories of the English author Herbert Spencer (1820–1903).

Spencer was a thoroughgoing mechanist. Lacking formal education, Spencer was not at first taken seriously by many academics, but his books drew much attention and were soon adopted widely at academic institutions, from Oxford to Harvard and Yale. His early views on evolution, first enunciated in *The Principles of Psychology* (1855), were published before Darwin's (we may recall that Darwin long delayed going to press with his ideas of 1842). Then, Spencer's *The Principles of Biology* (1864–1867) fanned the evolutionary winds that began to blow after the appearance of *The Origin of Species*. And, finally, in his three-volume *The Principles of Sociology* (1876–1896), Spencer coined the key phrase "the survival of the fittest" (which does not appear in Darwin's work) for the first time in the great debate. Spencer's philosophical orientation was enthusiastic in embracing the pervasiveness of change. He equated change with progress. The automatic selection of nature must result in better and better states of affairs. This wonderful mechanism must be allowed to work its way into human society. The rich and powerful have shown themselves to be more "fit" than the poor and weak; therefore, they are more worthy—in nature's sense—of enjoying and retaining the fruits of their success. It would be wrong to interfere with nature's universal winnowing process by restraints on the rich or artificial "safety nets" for the poor, according to Spencer.

Bergson reflected on such ideas, in particular on the logic of the mechanistic philosophy of science behind them, and at first was convinced of their adequacy. But while still in his twenties, while teaching at the Lycée Clermont-Ferrand, he realized with a start what mechanical science systematically excludes: *time*, defined as real *duration* rather than as abstract clock-readings leading to an ineffectual formal variable, t, that has no thickness and makes no difference. The mathematical concept of t can be reversed by simply changing its sign from a plus to a minus. Real time, experienced as duration, is irreversible. In human experience, the sheer passage of time is important and cumulative. In fact, in human experience, nothing can ever happen "again," in exactly the same way, by virtue of the sheer fact that it has already happened—and this temporal reality changes the total context. Nothing can ever be done twice for the first time. In mechanistic science, however, time is external to what happens, making no difference. Mechanics is utterly unhistorical in this sense; every stroke of a pendulum, considered mechanically, is qualitatively indistinguishable from its predecessor or its successor. Direct human awareness—our only first-hand access to time—is entirely historical. There is a profound inadequacy in any scheme of thought, no matter how magnificent, that leaves immediate intuition out of account.

This insight, which was to underlie all Bergson's future contributions to metaphysics, was published in his first book, *Essai sur les données immédiates de las conscience* (1889), which also was accepted for his doctoral degree in the same year, while Bergson was thirty. The English translation of this title, as

Time and Free Will (1910), is misleading without its subtitle, *An Essay on the Immediate Data of Consciousness*, which alone expresses the French title and with it the essence of Bergson's method. This method is to draw attention to direct experience, as contrasted with concepts and theories. More will be said about this soon.

Meanwhile, after completing his manuscript and submitting it, Bergson moved back to Paris in 1888, accepting a teaching position at the Lycée Henri IV, where he taught while thinking through the positive relationship between mind and body. In *Time and Free Will,* he had attempted to show what *cannot* be concluded about reality from abstract mechanistic science: the determinism of concrete, immediate acts of mind by material circumstances. Next, he turned to thinking through the actual relations between mind and body in a second major book, *Matière et mémoire: Essai sur la relation du corps à l'esprit* (1896), translated into English as *Matter and Memory,* in which he overcomes the dualism of his first book by interpreting matter (as we shall see below) as having within it at least a small degree of "memory." In the next year, this remarkable book resulted in a professorship for Bergson, who was now back at his alma mater, the École Normale Supérieure. But his career was on an even steeper upward trajectory. In 1900, he was appointed to the chair in philosophy at the Collège de France, his nation's most prestigious institution of higher learning. During the next fourteen years, until the outbreak of the First World War, Bergson's intellectual influence was at its pinnacle. His lectures were ecstatically received. He continued to publish with great success: first, a book on laughter, *Le rire* (1900), then his important *Introduction à la métaphysique* (1903), next his immensely influential *L'evolution créatrice* (1907), (*Creative Evolution*, 1911), and, finally, a work on the perception of change, *La perception du changement* (1911). His marriage in 1891 to the cousin of the novelist Marcel Proust (1871–1922) led to much interaction with leaders in the arts and influenced Bergson's ideas on French culture in general.

In 1914, at the outbreak of the First World War, Bergson retired from his active duties at the Collège de France to pursue diplomatic activities, including missions to Spain and the United States. In the next year he was honored, as only a tiny few are, with election to the Académie Française. After the establishment of the League of Nations in 1920, he was made president of the League's Commission for Intellectual Cooperation. In 1921, suffering from disabling arthritis, Bergson resigned his Chair at the Collège de France; and, as his health deteriorated still further, he resigned from the League Commission in 1925. In 1927, when he received the Nobel Prize for Literature, his arthritis prevented his attending the ceremonies in Norway.

During his years away from publishing and lecturing in philosophy, Bergson continued to think. In his latter years he meditated, especially on ultimate questions of ethics and religion. At last, after a long gap, in the year before Hitler's rise to power, he published the result of his thoughts in *Les Deux Sources de la morale et de la religion* (1932), (*The Two Sources of Morality and Religion*, 1935), to which we shall return. His spiritual journey, reflected in that book, allowed him to appreciate, above all, the insights of the Christian mystics. In his will, written in 1937, he stated that he found in Catholicism the "fulfillment of Judaism." But he refrained from making a formal conversion to Christianity. The times were wrong for deserting, or seeming to desert, his Jewish heritage. In 1940, after the defeat of France, the newly installed Vichy government of France, under the effective control of Hitler, required the registration of all Jews, but offered Bergson an exemption. Bergson, at eighty-one, foreseeing "a formidable wave of anti-Semitism about to break upon the world" (Bird 1974: 844), rejected the exemption and rose arthritically from his bed to stand in line for registration with his fellow Jews. A few weeks later, in January of 1941, he was dead.

Underlying Bergson's entire vision of reality, as I noted earlier, was the contrast—amounting to a dualism—between immediate intuition and intellectual abstraction. The latter, which in his *Introduction to Metaphysics* he calls "analysis," is for Bergson always something external to what is intimately the case. Analysis depends upon being built up out of various points of view, constantly circles about the subject for additional vantage points, depends on concepts applicable to infinitely many other similar subjects, and requires endlessly many representations of the subject—analysis is, in a word, always *relative* in its approach to reality. Intuition, on the other hand, knows its subject matter from within. Intuition provides union, penetration into reality; intuition is internal, has no point of view, and needs no representation—intuition is, in contrast, *absolute* in its grasp of what is intuited.

Bergson offers a simple example:

> When you raise your arm, you accomplish a movement of which you have, from within, a simple perception; but for me, watching it from the outside, your arm passes through one point, then through another, and between these two there will be still other points; so that, if I began to count, the operation would go on forever. Viewed from the inside, then, an absolute is a simple thing; but looked at from the outside, that is to say, relatively to other things, it becomes, in relation to these signs which express it, the gold coin for which we never seem able to finish giving small change (Bergson: 1955: 23).

Science clearly works through analysis. This is of enormous practical use. Measurements, translations into mathematical formulae, and calculations allow for predictions; and predictions allow us to anticipate external events, to defend ourselves against unhappy surprises, and to control the material world. Natural science gives us relative information about what to expect, just as August Comte proclaimed: "*savoir pour prévoir.*" But metaphysics is not interested in relative information; it is in pursuit of absolute grasp of reality itself. Therefore, metaphysics must abandon analysis, quit applying ready-made concepts to unique events, and take up the cultivation of intuition.

> If there exists any means of possessing a reality absolutely instead of knowing it relatively, of placing oneself within it instead of looking at it from outside points of view, of having the intuition instead of making the analysis: in short, of seizing it without any expression, translation, or symbolic representation—metaphysics is that means. *Metaphysics, then, is the science which claims to dispense with symbols* (Bergson 1955: 24, emphasis in the original).

Such cultivation is not an easy task. Intuition is not the way we are accustomed to approaching our world. Our evolutionary history has accustomed us, as a survival skill, to analyze everything. Natural selection does not favor metaphysicians who care about absolute grasp of reality; rather, it favors clever calculators who can get practical questions solved long enough to reproduce. But intuition is still possible for us. If we work very hard against our analytical grain, our powers of immediate sympathy can be cultivated into a method of "*intellectual auscultation*" (Bergson 1955: 36–37, emphasis in the original); that is, into a method of intently listening to the throbs of reality as they directly present themselves to us.

The one reality that always is directly available for such intuition is our own self. Here is at least one subject for absolute grasp. We are vaguely aware, nearly constantly, of our internal flow of thoughts and actions through time. Even here our habits of analysis are strong. We tend to focus on our perceptions: clear and distinct sense-images, particular memories and abstract thoughts, juxtaposed with one another in a complex way. But this is just the surface of the self. If we attend more carefully, we find, at a deeper level, memories attached to our perceptions. These make the perceptions rich with meaning, but these meanings are not found on the surface; they rise out of something that holds the present together with the experiences of the past; they rise out of the enduring self, deep underneath all these specific memories, even underneath the motor habits we have learned and unreflectively perform. At the center of our self, if we feel deeply enough and listen carefully enough, we find the continuous duration that our self most really *is*. This duration holds everything together. And we find that what on the surface seems like just a swarm of individual percepts is in reality a unity of temporal duration in which everything interpenetrates. Only retrospectively, and by virtue of our powers of abstraction, can we say these are even "multiple" states.

There is a succession of states, each of which announces that which follows and contains that which precedes it. They can, properly speaking, only be said to form multiple states when I have already passed them and turn back to observe their track. Whilst I was experiencing them they were so solidly organized, so profoundly animated with a common life, that I could not have said where any one of them finished or where another commences. In reality no one of them begins or ends, but all extend into each other (Bergson 1955: 25).

To describe this sort of inner reality in words is not just difficult but literally impossible. Analysis spoils such duration by chopping it up into timeless concepts and therefore *must* fail. Still, Bergson tries to point our attention to our own intuited experience by use of metaphors. First, consider that the self is a coil being unrolled—or, equally good, rolled up: like "a thread on a ball, for our past follows us, it swells incessantly with the present that it picks up on its way; and consciousness means memory" (Bergson 1955: 26). No, Bergson says, these are both poor metaphors, since they make too much of lines and surfaces, suggest homogeneity, and are subject to mathematical abstraction leading to Newtonian treatment. Try another: the self is a spectrum of colors, with different hues insensibly leading to each other. But again no. In a spectrum, the colors are spatially separate and really do not interpenetrate. Transition between colors in a spectrum is subtle, but every shade of color still excludes every other from the same space at the same time; "pure duration, on the contrary, excludes all idea of juxtaposition, reciprocal externality, and extension" (Bergson 1955: 26). Here is a third metaphor: The self is an infinitely small elastic body contracted to a mathematical point, then drawn out in a smooth continuous action. The *action* of drawing is the self, the trail drawn out is just its track in space. This may be a somewhat better metaphor but it cannot show how the self both unfolds and grows. And it leaves out the richness of subjective experience. The lesson is that duration can be intuited but not expressed in concepts, even in images. The best we can do is use these inadequate images to help us see for ourselves. If we have had the basic intuition of our duration, the conceptual hints will help remind us of it and will make sense; if not, there is nothing to be done.

This is how science needs to be complemented and completed by metaphysics. The science of psychology, for example, gives us concepts of the self which, to the extent that they stimulate an intuition, come to life for us. Without these intuitions, reality slips away. To take another example: the concept of "time" is practically important. Physicists like to predict; businessmen like to be able to meet for appointments. Therefore, we convert duration into clock time in order to *quantify* what is essentially a *qualitative* experience of passage. The breaking up of time into hours and minutes and seconds turns duration into homogeneous units that allow counting and coordination. That is their function. Abstracting these qualitatively empty units allows us to draw up calendars—one sort of spatialization of time—and create time lines of all sorts. But we should not fool ourselves into the supposition that this useful quantification gives us real time. These units, defined as lacking any qualitative becoming of any particular thing, are simply conceptual containers for any qualitatively real duration that might concretely fill them. So-called temporal units, like minutes, are therefore themselves immobile and unchanging. They have no becoming in themselves. There is little wonder then that paradoxes of time arise. Analysis tries to obtain *passage* from multiplying *stoppage*. This is as absurd as trying to get a positive number while multiplying by zero. No matter how many zeros, the total is zero.

One's self is a duration. Real time, the qualitative becoming we experience through intuition, is at the heart of what it is to be a self. But what of the rest of the universe? Can we ground in intuition anywhere the presence of cosmic duration?

Bergson replies through a very simple illustration. In *Creative Evolution* he turns outward to the world around us, while using the same tools of thought laid out in *Introduction to Metaphysics*.

> If I want to mix a glass of sugar and water, I must, willy-nilly, wait until the sugar melts. This little fact is big with meaning. For here the time I have to wait is not that mathematical time which would apply equally well to the entire history of the material world, even if that history were spread out instantaneously in space. It coincides with my impatience, that is to say, with a certain portion of my own duration, which I cannot protract or contract as I like. It is no longer something *thought*, it is something *lived*. It is no longer a relation, it is an absolute. What else can this mean than that the glass of water, the sugar, and the process of the sugar's melting in the water are abstractions and that the Whole within which they have been cut out by my senses and understanding progresses; it may be in the manner of a consciousness (Bergson 1944: 12–13).

Here Bergson proposes that the whole cosmos should be considered a grand Duration.

This suggestion helps in understanding the relationship between time (real time, qualitative becoming) and space, Bergson says. If we also adopt from Descartes the understanding of matter as ultimately pure geometrical extension, the relationship between mind (which is fundamentally memory or unified duration) and matter (the local filling of mathematical extension) can at last be clarified. Extension, as we intuit our own selves, is experienced as the opposite of intension, that is, the vivid, variegated-but-unified, enduring, swelling reality of selfhood. Things become "spread out" in experience when we relax the intensity of our consciousness. If we are listening to a speech and start to drowse, the sentences begin to float off by themselves, phrases fragment into mere words, words splinter into earlier and later sounds, distinct and separate from other sounds to which they are no longer connected, and become meaningless babble. The higher our mental intensity, the more unified (and less extended) our awareness: we can hold whole sentences in mind and even grasp the unified meaning of complete paragraphs. It is said that Mozart could grasp whole movements of his symphonies together in one magnificent moment of musical meaning.

Space is the *detension* of time, understood as qualitative mental duration, Bergson ventures. The limit of detension would be pure geometrical extension. But here, as noted earlier, Bergson overcomes his heritage of Cartesian dualism. On the spatial side, material things (like sugar crystals) are extended but still retain some small degree of inner qualitative particularity, some duration. On the temporal side, minds tend to relax toward extension and materiality.

It is the extension of matter that allows material systems to be isolated, at least provisionally and enough for abstractions to apply. Thus,

Matter has a tendency to constitute *isolable* systems, that can be treated geometrically. In fact, we shall define matter by just this tendency. But it is only a tendency. Matter does not go to the end, and the isolation is never complete. If science does go to the end and isolate completely, it is for convenience of study; it is understood that the so-called isolated system remains subject to certain external influences. Science merely leaves these alone, either because it finds them slight enough to be negligible, or because it intends to take them into account later on. It is none the less true that these influences are so many threads which bind up the system to another more extensive, and to this a third which includes both, and so on to the system most objectively isolated and most independent of all, the solar system complete. But, even here, the isolation is not absolute. Our sun radiates heat and light beyond the farthest planet. And, on the other hand, it moves in a certain fixed direction, drawing with it the planets and their satellites. The thread attaching it to the rest of the universe is doubtless very tenuous. Nevertheless it is along this thread that is transmitted down to the smallest particle of the world in which we live the duration immanent to the whole of the universe (Bergson 1944: 13–14).

The important point is that "the universe *endures*" (Bergson 1944: 14). It both unwinds, detends, relaxes (though never completely, to the point of zero duration) into matter; and invents, creates, and evolves through the matter it has thereby produced.

This is the proper metaphysical understanding of biological evolution. The mechanists try to understand evolution by breaking the problem into specific parts: postulating tiny accidental changes in a material substrate that then is selected by nature's blind push toward elimination of the comparatively ill-adapted. They worry about whether these mutations are sudden or gradual. What they should worry about more deeply is whether the whole can be put together out of many bits, at all, or whether the entire approach is corrupted by the analytical method of thought. The finalists, just as misled by analysis as the mechanists, also conceive evolution as a complicated matter of putting an infinite number of parts together to make functioning organs. They correctly chide the mechanists for failing to see how implausible it is that an organ like the eye could have been built up gradually, thanks to merely mechanical pressures for survival, out of many parts working together. For there to be any survival advantage, the whole organ must *function* in an advantageous way; but there is no advantage to having an "almost"-functioning eye. Until all the parts are together and working, there is no basis for natural selection. Seeing this, the finalists err by postulating some guiding purpose that constructs organisms the way Paley's watchmaker constructs watches. This postulate does not seem in any way supported by the apparently aimless proliferation of forms of life. A purposive maker should have assured more harmony in the biological world. There is plenty of diversity but no sign of purpose.

Instead, a proper metaphysical approach, understanding from within what is involved in creativity, will see this evolutionary universe as manifesting simplicity of action where both mechanists and finalists find complexity and puzzlement. The Duration that is the Whole simply expresses itself in and through the variety of organic forms. In this function, the cosmic Duration can be called the Life Force or Vital Impetus—in French the *Élan Vital*. The Life Force pushes for higher levels of quality through its own debris (i.e., matter), and when its spurt of creativity is done, there are complete organisms, wholly functioning, created in a simple act like the moving of a hand through space. If the hand were moved not through empty space but through iron filings, and if these iron filings were alone available for analysis, the arrangement left by this simple act would have to be explained in terms of great complexity, each motion of each tiny metal bit needing mathematical description begging for the derivation of some general law of change. This is what mechanists do, to their unending frustration. It is much simpler to look at quality-enhancing functions, such as sight, as simply produced by a Life Force streaming through matter, a Force that leaves various life forms—whether insects or octopi or horses—with complete, functioning eyes, even though in the details of structure and ontogeny these organs may be completely different.

In this vision of reality, grounded in creative temporality, the ultimate significance of the evolutionary process stands out in bold relief. Bergson divides the life-story of our planet into two streams, the plant and the animal; the animal he divides again into two main streams. The great stream of plant life exists in a condition of mental torpor, to the extent one can speak of vegetative "mind" at all. But the animal stream, while divided into innumerable rivulets, shows two main ways that Life has established society—and thereby multiplied mentality—beyond individual organisms. The first of these ways is through insect life ending with the hymenoptera: the bees and ants. The second is through mammals and primates leading to Homo sapiens.

Interestingly, the two contrasting streams of animal life have inverted orders of subjective duration. The social insects construct their elaborate nests and perform their intricate activities simply on the basis of instinct. The Life Force assures survival for these organisms by cooperation based on dull but powerful necessity. In contrast, the Life Force, effecting itself through human society, preserves itself through intelligence. Intelligence is our principal weapon for survival. It can also get us into great trouble as we shall see in a moment; but above all it is practical. Its function is not metaphysical truth-telling. For that, as we have already noted, we need something else—intuition—which functions analogously to instinct in animals with intelligence.

Intuition is not instinct. Unlike instinct, but like intelligence, it is free and creative. Unlike instinct, but like intelligence, it is open to conscious inspection. Conversely, unlike intelligence, but like instinct, it is fluid, deep, and direct. A wasp lands on a caterpillar and stings it in its tiny brain ganglion so that it survives, paralyzed, long enough for the eggs the wasp then lays on the caterpillar's back to hatch, thus providing the emerging larvae fresh food. For the wasp, this routine is purely instinctive, no problem at all: just a smooth, direct act of landing, stinging, and laying eggs. For a human equipped with intelligence and lavishly outfitted with tools previously designed by applications of intelligence, accomplishing the same task would require a very different technique; namely, precisely measuring to the key ganglion from some surface reference point (an inductive inference based on a history of many prior measurements and dissections), inserting a hypodermic needle, carefully gauging the amount of poison needed for paralysis rather than death, timing the injection, and so on. Intelligence makes everything complex. Instinct—and intuition—find everything simple.

When Bergson returned to philosophical writing, after decades of public service, the life-affirming simplicity of the intuitive had become the clue to his understanding of both morality and religion. The presence of felt moral obligation is, after all, both a primary fact in all human cultures, and a mystery. Why should creatures with intelligence feel strongly pressed somehow to sacrifice what may be obviously in their private interest for the sake of community standards?

Organisms directed by instinct regularly give up their lives for the good of the herd or the nest, and we understand this is the way life has found to protect the species, what might today be considered a form of genetic-based "altruism" directed toward kin. Buffalo males draw themselves into a circle against a predator to fight—perhaps to die—for their young, although the healthy bulls might otherwise escape and leave the vulnerable to their fate. Army ants on the march throw themselves selflessly into ditches until their bodies make a bridge for those behind to cross safely over. The needs of the species are met and life is advanced.

Imagine one of these ants suddenly equipped with intelligence and the freedom that comes with it. Approaching the watery ditch it can easily foresee what will happen. It can count the numbers of colleagues ahead and calculate the volume of bodies needed for sacrifice to the entire column's long-term needs. There is no good reason, it reflects, why its mere position in line should doom it to an early drowning. It steps temporarily out of the march, politely murmuring, "After you!" Later, it crosses on the backs of the others, ready to march another day.

This is the danger of intelligence to life. If all the ants were as intelligent as our exception, the species could never survive. But we humans are intelligent. Analysis is our biological secret weapon, with which we (in reverse parallelism with the ants) have dominated the earth. How then has human community, necessary for the survival of helpless infants and the great superstructure of complex civilization, been spared the "After you!" syndrome? The answer is provided by the pressures of moral obligation, life's way of defending itself against the corrosive potential of free, self-regarding intelligence. Moral obligation is not instinct. Instinct is unconscious and determining. We are at least dimly aware of our obligations; and we are (quite obviously) perfectly capable of acting contrary to them, though most do not do so most of the time—or our species would not have come this far.

One source of morality then is as life's defense against its own most flexible (but dangerous) tool. Felt obligation is "virtual instinct" in organisms mainly equipped with intelligence. But one limitation of this first sort of morality needs to be noted: its dedication to the survival of the group against external threats means it is always oriented to one in-group as over-against other groups and dangers. It is by its very nature a "closed" morality, in which obligation is felt to *our* family as opposed to your (and every other) family, *our* ethnic clan against yours; *our* nation against all others. In this, there is both safety for life and quite obviously still further dangers. When the ingenuity of intelligence is coupled with the ecstatic self-forgetfulness of group-selfish nationalisms, it can be an extremely explosive mix.

Life provides a second source of morality, however; one that if heeded can counter even this great danger to life. It is what Bergson calls "open morality." This morality represents a difference in kind, not just in scope. It does not consist in a feeling of pressure to conform to group norms. It is not a sense of heavy obligation that outweighs the urgencies of self-interest. Instead, it consists in the attraction to the good, the better, the best. Not dully impersonal, like moral obligation, it is kindled by admiration of some morally charismatic person, leader, or hero. Lives touched by this attraction are made open to Life itself, everywhere manifest. Thus, this second source is quite different from the first. It does not depend on having an external enemy or danger—not even "aliens from outer space" to unify earthlings—instead, it wells up from interior emotion kindled by the warmth of life itself.

Eventually, even open morality will doubtless "cool" into the structures of a new group morality, new rules, new obligations—until the next pioneer dares to transcend the rules and open souls again to the direct emotion of goodness. Eventually new doctrines, new metaphysics, crystallize at the same time. Neither the morality nor the ideas has priority.

Antecedent to the new morality, and also the new metaphysics, there is the emotion, which develops as an impetus in the realm of the will, and as an explicative representation in that of intelligence. Take, for example, the emotion introduced by Christianity under the name of charity: if it wins over souls, a certain behaviour ensues and a certain doctrine is disseminated. But neither has its metaphysics enforced the moral practice, nor the moral practice induced a disposition to its metaphysics. Metaphysics and morality express here the self-same thing, one in terms of intelligence, the other in terms of will; and the two expressions of the thing are accepted together, as soon as the thing is there to be expressed (Bergson 1935: 49).

Talk of doctrine and Christianity moves the discussion to religion. Here, too, Bergson sees two sources. Both come from life but in different ways.

The first source of religion is as life's pseudo-intellectual counterweight to the life-threatening tendencies of intelligence. This is what Bergson calls "static religion," so named not merely because it is life's way of keeping the status quo, but especially because it is made up of static images, myths, and doctrines—it is the secret thumb that life uses to depress the scales of calculation against life-destructive fears. The intelligence of the human race is a notorious factory of myths. Why?

If intelligence now threatens to break up social cohesion at certain points—assuming that society is to go on—there must be a counterpoise, at these points, to intelligence. If this counterpoise cannot be instinct itself, for the very reason that its place has been taken by intelligence, the same effect must be produced by a virtuality of instinct, or, if you prefer it, by the residue of instinct which survives on the fringe of intelligence: it cannot exercise direct action, but, since intelligence works on representations, it will call up "imaginary" ones, which will hold their own against the representation of reality and will succeed, through the agency of intelligence itself, in counteracting the work of intelligence. This would be the explanation of the myth-making faculty (Bergson 1935: 119).

The first defensive function of static religion is just the same as closed morality. "The truth is that intelligence would counsel egoism first," Bergson warns. "The intelligent being will rush in that direction if there is nothing to stop him" (Bergson 1935: 122).

But nature is on the watch. Just now, before the open gate a guardian appeared, to bar the way and drive back the trespasser. So now some protective deity of the city will be there to forbid, threaten, punish (Bergson 1935: 122).

The second defensive bulwark is against the paralyzing fear of personal death, which may make everything seem worthless. Our capacity to foresee our own mortality can be a potent threat, tingeing everything with absurdity.

Nature, then, looks as if she is going to stumble over the obstacle which she has placed on her own path. But she recovers herself at once. To the idea of inevitable death she opposes the image of a continuation of life after death; this image, flung by her into the field of intelligence, where the idea of death has just become installed, straightens everything out again (Bergson 1935: 131).

A third defense of myth is against discouragement by the realization of how much can go wrong between aim and achievement. The intelligence works by analysis, and analysis (as we saw) is most at home in mathematics, where infinite divisibilities loom between any two points. Folk wisdom warns we should expect "many a slip" betwixt the cup and the lip. Analytical intelligence insists there are infinitely many! But at this point friendly gods step in to assist. Even the only partially personal myth of "lady luck" can encourage us to go on. More than this, prayer, incantation, and belief in special providence can nudge us to move forward with our plans despite the irrationality (from Zeno's highly abstract intellectual perspective) of ever moving at all. As Bergson puts it, these myths are *"defensive reactions of nature against the representation, by the intelligence, of a depressing margin of the unexpected between the initiative taken and the effect desired"* (Bergson 1935: 140, emphasis in original). In sum, static religion *"is a defensive reaction of nature against what might be depressing for the individual, and dissolvent for society, in the exercise of intelligence"* (Bergson 1935: 205, emphasis in original).

But this is only one kind of religion welling up from only one source. Bergson concludes his last major publication with a paean to what he calls "dynamic religion": something as different in kind from static religion as open morality is from closed. Indeed, all four are related. Just as the flame of open morality rises directly from the kindling of life itself, so dynamic religion sweeps through history as the Élan Vital itself makes itself directly known. In dynamic religion, myth is peeled away as unnecessary distraction. Life is supported and encouraged by love and joy in those who feel for themselves the warmth at the heart of the universe. This means, above all, that we need to heed the mystics who are our best witnesses to Life's radiant power to transform and motivate. The best of the mystics are not only filled with the transcendent peace reported by Eastern seers; in Bergson's philosophy, the best will have this peace *plus* a sense of personal love for what they call God *plus* a dynamic capacity to change the world. Since Christian mystics have been both full of love and empowered to action, these are the best vehicles for revealing Life itself.

Alas, all things cool. Even Christianity, which (as we noted) Bergson considered the "fulfillment" of Judaism and all higher religion, cannot keep inspiration hot and fluid. As mystic intensity suffers detension, Christianity inevitably develops an external crust of doctrine and cultus—the matter-like deposits of once-molten spirituality. But this frozen surface can point our attention toward the possibilities of first-hand intuition and, thus, has its heuristic place in the service of the ultimate dynamic of our evolving universe. Cooling—though it always happens—is always only temporary. Every frozen surface will be broken through again and again by the white-hot magma of fresh inspiration, since the principle of the kosmos itself is warmth, life, and love.

In this way, the arthritic Bergson affirms the values of fluidity, easy motion, health; and in the face of the gathering darkness of Europe's most dangerous oppression, supported by the keenest weapons of technological intelligence in modern history, he announces his commitment to the ultimate resiliency of freedom. Many of his deepest values can be seen to run throughout his work from youth to old age. Above all, he treasures immediate experience, as opposed to the tyranny of abstract concepts. Despite its excesses of analysis, he obviously cares for science all his life, devoting himself to years of study of the empirical findings of psychology and evolutionary biology—so that they can be re-understood in metaphysically more adequate ways. His profound valuation of mystical religion, especially in its Christian form, grew slowly, but at the end of his life he cares very much that science and religion both be reconciled. He finds this reconciliation not in specific ideas the two generate; ideas, after all, are on the surface; rather, the reunion of science and religion is found in the direction in which they both point, though standing on different ground. He calls this the "method of intersection." Bergson realizes his arguments are not deductively certain; his whole case, at best, rests only on probabilities.

> Yet probabilities may accumulate, and the sum-total be practically equivalent to certainty. We have alluded elsewhere to those "lines of fact" each one indicating but the direction of truth, because it does not go far enough: truth itself, however, will be reached if two of them can be prolonged to the point where they intersect. A surveyor measures the distance to an unattainable point by taking a line on it, now from one, now from the other of two points which he *can* reach. In our opinion this method of intersection is the only one that can bring about a decisive advance in metaphysics (Bergson 1935: 248).

One of the attainable points has been biology. The living world evolves, is on the way toward greater and greater complexity, including human society; it requires that we acknowledge, somewhere behind the visible facts, an impetus capable of accounting for this vast dynamism. The other attainable point is in the direct experience of exceptional selves—exceptional in their openness to life but not beyond our intuitive resonance with them. Sighting from these two points we see where they meet: at God, the God whose very nature is love and whose creative outflow is found in the wonderful story of life.

Bergson, with his high valuation on life and mind and change, opposed all attempts to reduce accounts of reality to what mathematics can handle; and, in this, he reminds us of George Berkeley, who also insisted on the values of immediate experience as against the fictions of mathematical convenience. Berkeley, however, had no such sense of the pervasiveness of change as the post-Hegelian, post-Darwinian era encourages. And Berkeley's understanding of "idea" was far different from Bergson's fluid, often vague, interpenetrating, memory-based account of first-hand experience. Berkeley's fundamental *percipio* was crisp and cool, where Bergson's was molten and warm. Interestingly, the French philosopher's treatment of Descartes' "clear and distinct" ideas was to locate them on the surface, that is, to consider them superficial, while the Briton's empiricism concentrated precisely on this surface, relegating the actively perceiving "spirit" to a realm in which we can have no ideas, only "notions."

F. H. Bradley, no less interestingly, would find himself both comfortable and uncomfortable in this discussion. In the account he gives of "feeling," Bradley points to something too deep for explicit "qualities" and "relations" to describe. Diversity without multiplicity, a Bradleyan phrase, sounds much like a Bergsonian intuition into the unity of duration. In neither case can ordinary "thought" (Bradley) or "analysis" (Bergson) or "ideas" (Berkeley) cope with what is there first-hand, in our primary, preabstracted, living experience. Bradley's discomfort, of course, would be with Bergson's enthusiastic embrace of change and time. Bergson trusts intuition to reveal change as fundamental reality; Bradley instead trusts the Law of Noncontradiction to rule time only an appearance. Bradley would have denounced Bergson as an irrationalist, not "playing the game" of metaphysics. Bergson would have retorted that Bradley's "game" is the wrong one to play—if reality is at issue.

Again, the clash of fundamental values is obvious here. Bergson was often chided (though also praised by some, like William James) as an anti-intellectual. It is certainly true that he had harsh things to say about the intellect. Must all concepts distort when we try to think about the real? At times, Bergson clearly says this is necessarily so. And yet he works with many concepts, images, metaphors, and analogies to make his case. There seems to be a dualism: *either* intelligence *or* intuition. Bergson was uncomfortable with dualisms. His deep commitment to unity—unity in lived experience of duration, unity between science and religion—pulls against irreconcilable dualism. He worked to overcome Descartes' dualism of matter and mind with an ingenious suggestion that at bottom matter is "relaxed" mentality expended through the creativity of the Élan Vital. Could he rest content with a final dualism within mentality between conceptual thought and immediate feeling?

This question was never fully resolved in Bergson's work. It must remain an issue on our agenda, however. The problem is too crucial for metaphysical theory itself to be passed over. Whitehead will offer a direct answer; but before him we shall hear from yet another philosopher who urges us to "take time seriously."

ALEXANDER

Samuel Alexander, who coined the above phrase to express his high appreciation for the early philosophy of Bergson, was born in Bergson's birth year, 1859, in Sydney, Australia. His undergraduate studies at Wesley College, Melbourne, and then at the University of Melbourne, showed outstanding strengths of mind, leading to a scholarship from Balliol College, Oxford, to which he travelled at the age of nineteen. After graduation, at twenty-two, he was appointed a Fellow at Lincoln College, Oxford, and remained in that post for a dozen years. During this time, he travelled to Germany to study with the brilliant experimental psychologist Hugo Münsterberg (1863–1916), just prior to the latter's move to Harvard University, where Münsterberg pioneered construction of the experimental psychology laboratories and overlapped in tenure with psychologist-philosopher William James (1842–1910).

During his Lincoln College years, Alexander also published his first book, *Moral Order and Progress* (1888), based on a prize-winning essay he had written while at Balliol. The book established his credentials as a major light on the British horizon and before long led to his appointment, in 1843, at age thirty-four, as Professor of Philosophy at Owens College of Manchester Victoria University. When Alexander arrived in Manchester, Friedrich Engels was still living and his spinning machines were still humming. Manchester was a factory town, bustling with technology and energy, transforming raw materials from around the world into finished goods with value added. A large part of the mission of the University of Manchester was technological: to its founding institutions, Owens College and the Manchester School of Medicine, the Manchester Institute of Science and Technology as an associate college was added. Growth and change were in the air. Alexander's earlier interests in progress found a suitable home.

This setting remained his home for the rest of his life. During the years 1916–1918 he visited Glasgow to present his distinguished Gifford Lectures. In 1920, at age sixty-one, Alexander published these reworked lectures as *Space, Time and Deity*, in two volumes, his life's major work. In the next year he published *Spinoza and His Time* and retired in 1924, at age sixty-five, from his professorship. He remained hard at work after retirement, focusing on his aesthetics. In 1925 and 1933, respectively, he published *Art and Material Beauty* and *Beauty and Other Forms of Value*. He died in 1938, two and one-half years before Bergson.

Samuel Alexander developed a metaphysics that was organized around his commitment to development: to change, to progress, and to the manufacture of new value from the churning of material forces. It was a suitable metaphysics for the industrial age; the factories of Manchester could be its model. Unlike Bergson, who was equally committed to change, Alexander did not consider life the center of the dynamic universe. Life, as we shall see, is for him a more lately arrived property, spun like a new product, with new characteristics, uses, and value added to its raw materials from the spinning machines of matter. Life, for Alexander, is nothing but matter in its make-up; but simultaneously it is something—when it arises—genuinely distinct that emerges out of its humble ingredients when they are put together in just the right way.

Democracy was another characteristic preference of this Australian immigrant, who taught at one of England's "red brick universities" (in invidious comparison to the "ancients" of Oxford and Cambridge). Alexander used this value-laden word to oppose any "aristocratic" pretensions of mind, as somehow metaphysically above and naturally ruling over all else, as proposed by Berkeley, Kant, or Bradley. Mind, like life, is nothing more (or less) than an emergent property of life, manufactured out of particularly complex organisms, and, as such, has the same ontological ancestors as everything else. There is nothing unique, he argues, about the cognitive relation (we shall return to this in a moment), but even if there were,

> there is no warrant for the assumption, still less for the dogma that, because all experience implies a mind, that which is experienced owes its being and its qualities to mind. Minds are but the most gifted members known to us in a democracy of things. In respect of being or reality all existences are on an equal footing. They vary in eminence; as in a democracy, where talent has an open career, the most gifted rise to influence and authority. . . . [T]he real greatness and value of mind is more likely to be established on a firm and permanent basis by a method which allows to other existences than mind an equally real place in the scheme of being (Alexander 1920: Vol. I, 6–7).

As we noted earlier, Alexander began his schooling with a special interest in psychology and epistemology, studying during his Lincoln College years with Hugo Münsterberg in Germany. But unlike most British philosophers, he gradually came to set epistemology within metaphysics, not the reverse. His "democratic" metaphysics identifies life and mind as latecomers, though especially talented latecomers, in the evolving universe. And, if this is so,

> It follows that for the empirical method the problem of knowledge, the subject-matter of epistemology, is nothing but a chapter, though an important one, in the wider science of metaphysics, and not its indispensable foundation (Alexander 1920: Vol. I, 7).

Alexander offers a hypothesis of extreme epistemological realism, to be judged later by the success of the whole metaphysical vision. Mind is special because it is aware, and nothing else is. Cognition is the peculiar property of organisms in which minds have emerged. Cognizing is just what minds do. When an apple hangs on a tree, there is an important biological "compresence" between tree and apple. The tree nourishes the apple in its development; the apple offers the possibility of fresh trees in the future. When a living person with operative sense organs and a wide-awake mind stands before the tree with its apples, another important relationship is added: the "compresence" of mind with the tree-with-apple. This is the cognitive relation, namely, the "compresence" of a functioning mind with an objective something to know.

Minds cognize only objects. As cognizing they are only subjects. That means that minds cannot, strictly speaking, cognize other minds (directly) or even themselves. Minds are not objects; only brains or bodies are. But Alexander makes an important distinction here between *contemplating* and *enjoying*. The cognitive relationship, strictly speaking, is between a mind "compresent" with an object it contemplates. At the same time, every mind is directly aware of the ongoing contemplation while it cognizes its object. That awareness is *enjoyment* of its own mentality. In this technical sense, even a painful experience is "enjoyed" (paradoxically, perhaps, since mental awareness of awareness has nothing to do with pleasure), but Alexander is willing to risk misunderstanding for the sake of having a word that suggests immediacy without objectification.

To underline and illustrate this thoroughgoing realism in epistemology, set in metaphysical terms, Alexander offers a memorable image. Suppose for a moment there is something in reality higher than mind. Suppose there is an angel, who can look down on and contemplate minds in the way minds contemplate other objects of all kinds. From this "angelic point of view," (on Alexander's hypothesis) the tree-and-apple in "compresence" with the living-person-with-mind could be contemplated. The angel could even compare the contemplative contents of mind with the objective world it contemplates. This is impossible for us, of course (as Kant made much of); but it is not impossible in principle if there are—or might be—higher orders of material reality than mind.

Might there be? Let us now go to the heart of the matter—to matter. What is it, for Alexander, and what might be possible for it? How high, in this democracy of things, might material things hope to rise?

The place to start in answering such questions is at the beginning of things, and at the most general and pervasive level of reality. Metaphysics, Alexander believes, is an empirical study, but differs from the special sciences in having as its subject matter what is *always* present for experience, what is absolutely pervasive (thus a priori) throughout the character of all things. If we peel away all the merely contingent features sometimes present, sometimes absent, we come at last to space and time. Kant was right in holding these "a priori," but wrong in attributing them to the mind. They are indeed universal and necessary features of experience, because they are never missing and never can be missing. They *are* the fundamental reality. The reason they are never missing is that everything that exists—to the extent it exists—must inevitably share these features of reality. Why? Because everything more particular is *made up of* and is *generated by* this most general space-time. Space-time is both ultimate raw material and fundamental spinning machine; and the machine spins on.

Space and time are so pervasive that there are no sense organs specifically devoted to either of them. And yet everything experienced is spatial and temporal. Further, they need one another. Time, if taken alone, would be wholly successive and thereby discontinuous. In a total discontinuum of separate instants there would be no way even to recognize the flow of temporality.

Something must bind the instants together. Therefore, time, even to be tempo-ral, requires another principle providing continuity—space. Space, if taken alone, would be wholly continuous. It would in itself offer no way of distin-guishing "here" from "there," since its "all-togetherness" would fail to allow for its own multiplicity of parts. To be space as we know it, space requires an opposite principle providing discontinuity, that is, time. Since neither space nor time can exist apart from each other, it is best for most contexts to refer not to space and time but to space-time.

Still, for Alexander, there is a point, while dwelling in these ultimate gen-eralities, to distinguishing a certain metaphysical priority for time over space. Order in the universe cannot be provided by space, which is completely homo-geneous and has no intrinsic order; but order can be and is provided by time through its inherent irreversibility. Even space derives whatever order it has from being constantly regenerated in time. All spatial order, including (going from) left (to) right, is temporal. The mistake made by Einstein in following Hermann Minkowski's (1864–1909) mathematics of four-dimensional "time lines" for his depiction of space-time is time is not literally the fourth dimension of space but is, rather, the constant repetition of the three-dimensional spatial continuum. Like Bergson, Alexander objects strongly to the loss of becoming, stolen from the real universe by means of this mathematical abstraction. Indeed, if anything is most fundamental to the universe as a whole it is the becoming of time, since space is constantly *generated* in time. Time could not be generated by space which does nothing. "Space, even to be space, must be temporal" (Alexander 1920: Vol. I, 59).

Out of this dynamic space-time mix, time (as leading partner) drives the universe to motion. Motion is not yet the motion of any *thing*—things have not yet emerged—but space-time alone, even in Plato's vision of the Receptacle, we recall, is not without its constant shiver. This is hard for us to picture, as we are mainly adapted to perceive distinct things in motion. Alexander gives us a number of images to help:

> We may choose a disturbed ant-heap or the less pleasing instance of a rotten cheese seen under the microscope. But a severer and more useful picture is that of a gas in a closed vessel, conceived according to the kinetic theory of gases. The molecules of the gas dash against the sides of the vessel and each other in all manner of lines of advance, whether straight lines or not is for us indifferent. The molecules stand for instants of Time with their dates, some being earlier and some later, in various degrees of remoteness, than the point-instant which is the centre of ref-erence; some simultaneous with it, that is, possessing the same date. The gas is not considered as it is at any moment but as it exists over a lapse of time. . . . For us it is perfectly easy to contemplate the motions of the

gas over such a lapse of time, for we have memory to help us and expectation, and we can keep in our minds at once a limited piece of the history of the gas (Alexander 1920: Vol. I, 63).

Perhaps these images help, perhaps not. They are only imaginative aids to conception of the fundamental dynamic reality from which all else rises in a still-unfinished story of progress.

The upward trend of the universe, from the earliest infusion of motion into space through time, is portrayed by Alexander as a series of analogous emergents. The analogy is based on the dynamic power of time to bring into being something importantly new. This new is not made out of any material that was not there before; all that is can claim no more than a common ancestry in space-time. But the complexity of order, and, therefore, the temporal dynamism of the new is such that real new properties and powers are present where none such were present before.

Alexander's key model is the relationship between the brain and the mind. Both the brain and the mind, on his metaphysics, can at bottom be nothing else but space-time. To that extent, they are the same thing: looked at from the outside as organic life, from the inside as consciousness. Not all brains, however, are conscious all the time! Therefore, being a brain is not a sufficient condition for having a mind. Still, there are no minds without brains. Therefore, having a brain is a necessary condition for being a mind. They are one, but not the same, and not at the same level of priority. Minds are *emergents* from brains, or, more generally, from living bodies. They constitute a higher order. This is the key: *Minds are to bodies as time is to space.* Or, putting it the other way, more dramatically (as Alexander prefers): *Time is the mind of Space.*

> The formula may be received as a hypothesis to be judged by its success in unifying the different forms of empirical existence. . . . It is, that Time as a whole and in its parts bears to Space as a whole and in its corresponding parts a relation analogous to the relation of mind to its equivalent bodily or nervous basis; or to put the matter shortly that Time is the mind of Space and Space the body of Time (Alexander 1920: Vol. II, 38).

Alexander chooses this body-mind relationship as his key model for illumination of every level of the universe, because it is of all things the most familiar. We experience our body-mind identity-in-difference constantly and first-hand. What we should realize is that we are simply experiencing, at our level in the progressive kosmos, what is everywhere the case. But to forestall anthropocentrism, that is, the "misapprehension that we are the standard and exemplar of things," Alexander cautions, "the statement is better made in the reverse and truer form that we are examples of a pattern which is universal and is followed not only by things but by Space-Time itself" (Alexander 1920: Vol. II, 39).

We have already dealt with fundamental space-time, the dynamic priority of time, and the emergence of motion. Now, Alexander suggests we simply go on to note the repeated playings of this pattern. After motion, and from it, emerge finite material things. Time, in its guise of emergent motion, is the restless urge that pushes first to mere motion and then beyond into material qualities. Material things are to motion as time is to space, or as mind is to body. At this primitive level, we can apply our formula, thus: "Matter is the Mind of Motion."

Material things, however, are further driven by the temporal *nisus* toward further complexity, and in due time there emerge chemical properties that were never there before. The next-lower level from which they emerge is their necessary but not sufficient condition. They are nothing but matter, which is nothing but motion, which is nothing but space-time, but each stage has its own distinct character. At each level, "the quality and the constellation to which it belongs are at once new and expressible without residue in terms of the processes proper to the level from which they emerge . . ." (Alexander 1920: Vol. II, 45); thus, in Alexander's way of speaking, "Chemistry is the Mind of Matter."

Chemical substances and processes are in turn driven by time, the ever active "cosmic *gendarme* who makes stagnation impossible, and at once creates the movements which constitute things and keeps things in movement. *Circulez, Messieurs*" (Alexander 1920: Vol. II, 48). Thus, from the level of chemistry, at some point life emerges. Chemistry is not the sufficient condition for life, but it is life's necessary condition. They are ultimately of one "stuff," namely, space-time; but they behave with different laws and possess radically different powers. "Life is the Mind of Chemistry."

In the long organic progress of evolution, life is hurried on by the universe's restless gendarme, until at last mind as we know it leaps from the indescribably complex biological entities we call human brains-in-bodies. Minds, like all the other newly emergent orders, are nothing but their prior level in a new more complex arrangement, and so on, "all the way down" to space-time. But minds are different and new in what they can do. They can know and remember and decide. They can lead the body, discipline it, defend it. Bodies are not sufficient conditions for minds but are necessary conditions. Odd though it sounds, "Mind is the Mind of Life." Clearly, in each case the pivotal phrase, ". . . the Mind of . . . ," is used analogically. Here the analogy returns to where it began, its long trip completed from its earliest application to space-time until the present era.

Completed? Does time, the cosmic gendarme urging everything to "move along," now retire from the force? Impossible! Therefore, we must expect, Alexander says, that out of what we now know as mind will emerge—

someday, somewhere—another level of reality as different from and higher than mind as mind is different from and higher than mindless organic life. This next emergent in the progress of the universe can hardly be conceived by us, but we know it must be on its way, and we know at least something about what it will be like. It will have at least all the powers (though transformed, no doubt) that minds have; and minds will be necessary (though not sufficient) conditions for its emergence. Relative to us, this next higher stage in the cosmic progress is deity. As body is to mind a step back in the cosmic emergent order, so deity is to mind a step ahead. Looking upstream toward the origins of everything, mind is the "deity" of living body; living body is the "deity" of chemistry; chemistry is the "deity" of mere physical matter; and so on. Looking downstream toward the flow of the future, deity is the mind of mind, and after that will emerge a deity of deity, and so on again.

Alexander realizes this manner of speaking commits him to a metaphysical form of polytheism, but he is prepared to follow the argument where it leads. There will be many deities in the future of the universe, and they will have wondrous powers we can now hardly conceive; but they will all be finite. They will be like the "angel" he imagined earlier, to give illustration for his realistic theory of knowledge. There is much here that cannot even be imagined of course; but the one thing he is sure of is that the universe will never cease to progress and create new emergents in its infinite course toward the future.

This brings us to one last sense in which Alexander will use the word "Deity." "Deity" in this final sense, reflects his assurance of endless progress and is in sharp contrast with his use of the uncapitalized word to refer to the finite deities we have discussed. The infinite Deity is, for him, the constant nisus in the universe that drives every achieved level beyond itself. In this sense, Deity is the uncompleted universe, infinite space-time itself, ever full of promise but never finally actual. It is the never-attained Omega toward which the Alpha strains.

Here, however, we encounter a problem for Alexander's progressive metaphysical vision. Somehow it makes more sense to look *forward* to endless levels of greater complexity for the infinite domain of space-time, than to look *backward* at what must be both a starting point and yet no starting point. In Alexander's vision, space-time unadorned is clearly a starting point, which after a finite period of time gave birth to motion; after another finite period, bore physical things; then, after still other finite periods, bore chemical properties, then life, then mind—and now is great with deity. Since becoming is real for the universe, there is a clear point to saying "now." *Now* is the point the universe of space-time has reached in its progress to date. Yet adding together finite periods of becoming, however long they may be, will still reach only to a finite starting point. The universe-process may have no ending, but it clearly must have had a start, to account for our being just *here* in the process. We are here and now because there has not been enough time to get further along. For Alexander's world picture to work, past time at least must be finite.

On the other hand, it is quite clear that for Alexander, past time is not finite. Its finitude would be literally unthinkable. It would count as the beginning of existence, since existence is defined as space-time.

> But a beginning of existence is itself an event in Space-Time which is the system of point-instants or pure events, and it is clear therefore that Space-Time as a whole begins either everywhere or nowhere (Alexander 1920: Vol. I, 62).

Thus, space-time both requires a beginning (if a finite progress to this "now" point is to be conceivable) and defies any beginning (if existence itself is to be defined in spatio-temporal terms). Both of these conditionals, both "ifs," are essential to Alexander. Therefore, he seems caught on the horns of a hopeless dilemma. To give up the infinitude of space-time would allow him a cosmic "now." But that would destroy his postulation of space-time as the original and only stuff of existence. To give up the idea that the universe has a finite temporal location would allow him the infinitude of space-time, but it would make our having a particular place in the great progress of things unintelligible.

A second profound problem for Alexander's scheme is raised by the central notion of "emergence" itself. What does it explain? Since Descartes, the modern agenda has been to understand the possibility of mental qualities in a realm of mindless matter. These realms are completely different. They remain completely different too for Alexander, though he has the sheer boldness to take the greatest unsolved problem of modernity as the model for "explaining" all the rest of the universe. The question of how matter can account for the properties of mind would seem essential for any modern metaphysics. But Alexander rides the tiger of this question. He simply rejects the idea of getting off to search for illumination on the "how."

> The higher quality emerges from the lower level of existence and has its roots therein, but it emerges therefrom, and it does not belong to that lower level, but constitutes its possessor a new order of existent with its special laws of behaviour. The existence of emergent qualities thus described is something to be noted, as some would say, under the compulsion of brute empirical fact, or, as I should prefer to say in less harsh terms, to be accepted with the "natural piety" of the investigator. It admits no explanation (Alexander 1920: Vol. II, 46–47).

No explanation! What is our enterprise? Clearly, for Alexander, there is no value in working at the minute level to understand relations between great emergent orders. The greatness of their sweep from level to level is where he has invested his concern; and here he has painted dramatically, using broad brush strokes dipped in multicolored pigments of space-time, flung against the mobile canvas of a universe in pervasive positive change.

Alexander's values are expressed through his world picture. They are shown also by what he did *not* deem important to achieve. With this in mind, we turn to the last philosopher in our narrative, who attempts to maintain a macroscopic picture worthy of an Alexander or a Bergson. While so doing he presents an account of the microscopic as well as the intermediate levels of human life.

WHITEHEAD

Alfred North Whitehead was born in February 1861 into an Anglican clergyman's family, the youngest child of the Reverend Alfred and Maria Whitehead. He was reared where he was born, on the coast of Kent just north of Dover in Ramsgate, Isle of Thanet. His father, who, in addition to clerical duties, headed the Chatham House Academy for boys, founded by his own father Thomas Whitehead, chose to tutor this youngest child at home. Eventually, at fourteen, young Whitehead was judged robust enough to go to school in Dorset, where he attended the Sherborne School. Besides absorbing a fine classical education, he turned out tough enough to play rugby and to show leadership skills which led to his selection as Captain of Games and Head Prefect in 1879, the year James Clerk Maxwell died and Albert Einstein was born. He completed these studies in 1880.

Obtaining a mathematics scholarship to Trinity College, Cambridge, in the same year, he joined a brilliant mathematical tradition and entered a program that allowed him to feast exclusively on mathematics, in which he excelled. All other subjects were learned informally. His honors examinations in 1884 were so good that at the end of his studies he was selected for a fellowship at Trinity College and was admitted to Trinity's mathematics faculty at age twenty-three. Especially interesting for this narrative is the fact that he chose for the topic of his fellowship dissertation the mathematical theories of James Clerk Maxwell (another Trinity College alumnus) on electricity and magnetism—the very theories that were to fascinate young Albert Einstein a decade later in Zürich.

The year 1890 was of great personal importance to Whitehead for two reasons. First, he met Bertrand Russell (1872–1970), when he served as Russell's examiner for an entrance scholarship to Trinity College and soon became his teacher. Second, he married Evelyn Willoughby Wade, a life companion who not only bore him three children and managed his household, but maintained in him a strong, undeviating magnetism toward literature and the arts.

There is no doubt Mrs. Whitehead exerted a major influence on her mathematical husband's human values—values that were to make a crucial difference, as we shall see, to his theories about reality.

After publication of his first book, *Universal Algebra* (1898), Whitehead was honored by election to the Royal Society in 1903. In the same year, he was promoted to Senior Lecturer at Trinity College and was provided a ten-year contract. The contract would have provided employment at Trinity until 1913 (exceeding the maximum of twenty-five years, counting from 1884, normally permitted by College statute); but, at forty-nine years of age, with Mrs. Whitehead's encouragement, Whitehead did a bold thing. In 1910, the year of publication of the first volume of *Principia Mathematica*, on which he had been collaborating with Bertrand Russell since 1901, Whitehead resigned from Trinity College, which had never paid very well (Russell, who had sometimes lived with the Whiteheads during the collaboration, was accustomed to slipping Mrs. Whitehead significant secret sums to keep the household afloat). He then moved with his family to London to seek advancement outside Cambridge University. The gamble succeeded. After a year, when his popular *Introduction to Mathematics* (1911) was published, Whitehead was appointed to the faculty of University College, London; and three years later in 1914, after the completion of the third and final volume of *Principia Mathematica* in 1913, he was named Professor of Applied Mathematics at the Imperial College of Science and Technology.

The year 1914 marked the beginning of World War I, a tragic time for many families on both sides of that agonizingly protracted slaughter. Whitehead's older son North served unscathed; but in 1918 his younger son Eric was killed in action. This was a profound sorrow to the Whiteheads, who had supported the war as a cruel necessity. It was not made easier by Bertrand Russell's righteous preachments on pacifism. In the year of Eric's death, Russell was convicted of libel for an article opposing the war and was imprisoned for six months. His former associates at Cambridge, including the philosopher John McTaggart (1866–1925), Russell's teacher and friend at Trinity College, turned fiercely against him, working to oust him. But Whitehead, despite the heaviness of the recent loss of his son which weighed his spirits, took the opposite course and visited Russell in jail.

After the war, Whitehead was much involved in the education of teachers. His keen mind, kind disposition, and firmly reformist views combined to make him a sought-after administrator. During this period he served as Dean of the Faculty of Science at the University of London; as the lone mathematician on the British government's commission on status of the classics in higher education; and as chairman of the board of governors of one of London's leading colleges of education, Goldsmith's College. Earlier, in 1916, he called for educational reform in "The Aims of Education," delivering his presidential address before the Mathematics Association. Now he had the opportunity to implement his ideals.

His ideals for theories about the universe were also coming into focus in the same years through three books that appeared in quick succession. The first of these, *Principles of Natural Knowledge* (1919), stressed, against the cold abstractions of mathematical physics, the importance of retaining, in scientific theories of space and time, a ground in warm human perception. The second, *The Concept of Nature* (1920), was less technical, required no mathematics, but stressed similar themes, introducing the Bergsonian idea of creative advance as fundamental to nature—creativity manifest in events requiring temporal thickness, that is, durations. The third, *The Principle of Relativity* (1922), published when Whitehead was sixty-one, offered an alternative to Einstein's general theory of relativity, based on a completely reformed worldview in which human experience has a place, temporal becoming is fundamental, space and time are differently defined, and yet the measurable data are accounted for. By contrast, it showed Einstein, for all his revolutionary departures from Newton, as fundamentally conservative of the scientific materialist framework, tinkering as little as possible with those metaphysical fundamentals despite the counterintuitive price of curved space and contracted time set in frozen linearity.

Nearing retirement, Whitehead (on the strength of his post-war work in the philosophy of science) received an invitation to make another bold step—one that made the risky move from Cambridge to London in 1910 look positively cautious by comparison. Harvard University challenged him to leave his native land for America and to leave his familiar status as a mathematician for a position—the first in his life—as a professor of philosophy. With Mrs. Whitehead's cheerful consent, he accepted the challenge, moving to the "other" Cambridge (Massachusetts) in 1924. He was sixty-three.

Whitehead's Harvard years were not limited to philosophy of science, though that is where they began. Early in 1925 he delivered the distinguished Lowell Lectures in Boston. They were published later that year, with the addition of more material (his first dealing with the topic of God) as *Science and the Modern World*. In the following year, he gave another series of Lowell Lectures expanding his views on religion, published as *Religion in the Making* (1926). The year after, age sixty-six, he published an original theory of knowledge, which provided a new interpretation of human experience suitable to support his theories of science and religion in *Symbolism: Its Meaning and Effect* (1927).

Now the dynamo was further accelerated by an invitation from the University of Edinburgh to prepare a set of Gifford Lectures for delivery the following year. In response, Whitehead wrote the foundations of his theory of fundamental reality (which he called the "philosophy of organism"), later published in his greatest single work, *Process and Reality* (1929). The lectures, delivered in 1927 and 1928, were extremely hard to follow, but the profundity of the book, as we shall see, lasted longer than the bafflement of the audience.

Also in 1929 Whitehead published a much easier book (much deeper than it seems), *The Function of Reason*, and still another book of essays including the title essay from many years before, *The Aims of Education*. At seventy-two Whitehead published his last book before retirement from Harvard. It was *Adventures of Ideas* (1933), which contained an application of his metaphysical views to the history of the fight against slavery (among other things) and his difficult presidential address as presented to the Eastern Division of the American Philosophical Association.

At this point I, as author of this narrative, have the happy opportunity to report that during the next two years (Whitehead's last in active duty at Harvard) my father, Nels F. S. Ferré (1908–1971), served as a graduate assistant for Whitehead, arguing eagerly with the benevolent old philosopher every step of the way. It was from my father, who introduced me to Whitehead's thought, that I eventually gleaned many first-hand stories about the great man of the frail, stooped body and the gentle, high-pitched voice. In 1937, Whitehead retired at last, full of years and honors. In retirement, he published one more book, *Modes of Thought* (1938), but his principal interests turned more toward informal teaching through his famous Sunday evening open houses with Mrs. Whitehead in their home on Brattle Street in Cambridge. He died there at age eighty-six, in December 1947. His remains were cremated. There was no ceremony, there is no grave. His only lasting monument is his work.

That work can usefully be grouped into three levels. These are the microcosmic level, the macrocosmic level, and the middle level of human experience, institutions, and history. Whitehead, at best, is not easy to follow. But since one of the main obstacles to understanding Whitehead has been the special-purpose technical jargon he developed, my presentation will refrain—as I have throughout this entire narrative—from much reliance on these handy (but often impenetrable) terms. There is nothing intrinsically wrong with using special vocabulary. Every specialized community, from garage mechanics to international bankers, invents a shorthand to make communication quick in special, pre-understood contexts. Whitehead himself deliberately made up new terms to break the hold of old conceptions on familiar words. He had a good point. It is hard to make wheels go in new directions when deep ruts have been worn in old paths. Minds confronted with old words tend to fall into hidden associations and to make faulty assumptions. At least when confronted with a new word, there is no immediate presumption of premature understanding.

Unfortunately, when there are too many new words and not enough motivation to learn a new vocabulary, the result will be no understanding at all. Many philosophers have gone to the trouble of mastering Whitehead's special lexicon. There are technical journals and specialized scholarly societies where these terms fly happily about; in my father's (and now my own) metaphysics seminars on Whitehead, this was and is a necessary condition for success. But, in fact, most professional philosophers, not to mention the educated reading public, have not so equipped themselves. The neologisms once designed for precision of meaning have become an impenetrable barrier against understanding or even attempted understanding.

This is a pity, since in what follows I hope to show that Whitehead has an extremely important theoretical proposal to make: one that goes far toward completing the modern agenda of reuniting physics with mentality, objectivity with subjectivity, efficient causality with purpose, stability with change. And I hope simultaneously to show that the essentials of his proposal can be understood with only modest use of the special vocabulary associated with Whiteheadian scholasticism.

To begin at the microlevel, we find that Whitehead, who formed his theory of reality after Einstein's key publications, is first of all a quantum thinker. By this, I do not mean that he subscribed to one or another of the specific theories of quantum *mechanics* that were debated in the early years of the twentieth century. All these were mired in traditional assumptions of which Whitehead was leery from the start. Rather, Whitehead's starting point for the microcosmic is with tiny units of energy, each of which come in indivisible packets. Each minimum quantum of energy (of which there are many kinds) endures long enough (and only long enough) to achieve its own definite character, which physicists tend to consider a specific wave-pattern.

Whitehead wisely does not attempt to identify which "wavicles" are fundamental. That is a matter to be left to the empirical investigators. Finite actualities are fundamental. In this, the Atomists were right; and to this extent Whitehead's theory is atomistic. But classical atomism is no longer credible. Whatever its more specific properties, this fundamental minimum quantum of energy-in-pattern is not inert or long lasting. As physics has discovered concerning every "particle," it is also a wave. It needs enough time to complete one full energy pulse in order to be anything at all. Then, when its pulse is spent, another minimum quantum of energy replaces it and—for a split second—throbs its own pattern into actuality. In the electromagnetic microworld, this pattern tends to be replicated in reverse, from positive to negative, negative to positive, the successor quanta similar in all but polarity of field.

This is what Whitehead calls our "vibratory" universe. Everything that is actual is made up of vibrations or pulsations of energy. But any wave-pattern takes a minimum amount of time to complete. When producing a musical tone, an instrument must be given time to vibrate the air, by which it makes its characteristic sound waves. It makes sense to think of the music as lasting for a very short time, but not for a duration shorter than its shortest sound wave. In an instant, with no duration at all, there can be no music—no sound—at all. For the same reason, it is nonsense literally to consider the world existing at an "instant."

The quanta of energy that make up the world during any short period of time are not so much "things" as events; that is, they are the actualizing of energetic patterns which at first (for them) were only possible, then were happening, and finally were completed and done with—succeeded by another and yet another. Each event is the occasion of something's becoming actual and then perishing, passing on its achieved pattern to its successors as a fresh possibility for them. To distinguish these dynamic units of becoming from the inert atoms of classical mechanism, Whitehead calls these minimum quanta of reality "actual occasions." This much jargon should pose no problem.

It is obvious from the stability of things that actual occasions somehow detect their immediate past environments; moment after moment (and for aeons in the physical universe) they pick up and repeat the achieved energy patterns of their predecessors. The more complicated the environment, even for a very simple occasion, the more the possibilities for new patterns. The typical patterns of pulsation that constitute a calcium atom over time, for example, will be more limited in a test tube than in the context of a living bone. Observably, the range of events open to the calcium atom is enlarged when it is in a more complex setting. It must somehow be influenced by its surroundings.

Whitehead calls basic causal influence from the immediate environment "physical feeling." This does not imply consciousness. It simply rests on the empirically grounded requirement that somehow every new event of energy must detect what is in its immediate past if it is to become actual in the rhythmic way that nature actually propagates itself. Still, Whitehead's choice of the word "feeling" here (he also uses the more technical "prehension," to suggest a kind of grasping without "apprehension") is of immense theoretical significance. The one first-hand model we have for being generally linked to our surroundings is through a dim awareness of "something there." Bradley wrote of "feelings" of the same preconscious sort, and though he drew a different lesson from it, Whitehead still makes specific acknowledgment of his debt. Thus, when we ask the question posed earlier by Leibniz—what must it like to be a fundamental unit of reality *from the inside?*—the language of feeling (once stripped of association with conscious awareness) is apt.

It has been characteristic of most modern theories of reality to refuse Leibniz's question. The majority commitment has been to a kind of methodological behaviorism in which questions of "interiority" (such as those vital to Bergson) are simply ruled out from the start. The entities of physics have no insides. They are only what they do. But insisting on this a priori preference has led to the dilemmas of the modern agenda. If we hope that any adequate theory of reality will provide some coherent account of the place of mind in nature, the readiness to take the model of experience as a heuristic clue will be important.

Whitehead adopts the language of feeling for the basic actualities of the universe. He insists each actual occasion feels its entire prior universe, though primarily it is influenced by its immediate surroundings. In this first phase of physical feeling, the universe is received as efficient cause. Every actual occasion begins with this phase. The new quantum of actuality is thus in large part constituted by its felt relations with its past. Sharply departing from Leibniz, Whitehead rejected the notion that the fundamental units of reality are "windowless"; rather, the primary facts about these tiny pulses of actuality—at least at the start of the self-actualizing process—are their relations. In contrast to Bradley, Whitehead affirms relations as internal to whatever becomes real; but another significant difference—these relations are not themselves thought as entities requiring still further relations, ad infinitum. The relations, positive and negative, are what make up the new occasion as each one's indivisible moment for actualization begins.

Every occasion, however brief, however uninteresting, has a flicker of possible originality as part of its make-up. For electromagnetic occasions, as I noted earlier, a tendency to sheer field reversal—toggling between positive and negative—is well established, providing, for the vast numbers of trains of occasions that continue this tendency, a maximum in variety with a maximum in order too. The stability of the physical universe that we know, Whitehead believes, rests on this pattern of vivid contrast with regular repetition.

There are other actual occasions set in more complex circumstances and thereby more highly empowered for which the phase of possible originality is far more important. This is another empirically grounded requirement. If it were not so our universe would lack higher orders of structure, nothing would evolve, and there would be no writing or reading of books about theories of reality. Novelty occurs, however, and sometimes is preserved. Therefore, besides a physical pole for each quantum of energy, that is, the occasion as *inheriting from its past*, there must be postulated a mental pole, that is, the occasion as *evaluating its present possibilities and contributing to its future*.

All this is on a continuum. We know there is a tiny degree of spontaneity even at the most elementary levels of actuality, resulting in random atomic decay. We know some human minds are enormously creative. In most of nature, from what we can observe, physical poles of actual entities are primary and mental poles are almost negligible, except to cover marginal issues like spontaneous decay or random mutations (and the needs of a coherent theory of reality); but in at least some parts of nature there are events in which the attainment of novelty is important. This occurs, Whitehead explains, thanks to the capacity of a more complex occasion to *abstract* the characteristics that have been given to it in its physically felt relations with the immediate environment, to *compare* those abstracted characteristics with relevant alternative possibilities not present in the immediately felt environment, and to *opt* for or against incorporating any of the new alternatives into the pattern being achieved in that moment for the future. Human mentality is our capacity to take account of the physically absent, to deal symbolically with possibilities. The capacity of anything to innovate, to introduce new possibilities at whatever level of awareness, can on this basis be called its "mental" capacity. Mind in this sense is in nature wherever there is relevant novelty. Whenever something new appears, enriching what was physically there before, mental poles of actual occasions have been active.

At this point, it will be useful to consider Whitehead's theory from the macrocosmic level. Stated most generally, what are the theoretical elements presupposed for such a world as this? There are four that require each other: the actualities; the possibilities; the remorseless thrust of change; and something that can give locus and limitation to possibilities while urging the thrust of change toward growing harmony.

First, there is no world without actualities. As firmly as Aristotle, Whitehead insists on the priority of the actual. Everything rests in the end on actual entities and without them there is "nothing, nothing, nothing, bare nothingness" (Whitehead 1978: 167). These actual entities are all occasions or events as described above. Thus, Whitehead promulgates a rule which he calls the "ontological principle," to reinforce his emphasis on the priority of actualities. "The ontological principle can be summarized as: no actual entity, then no reason" (Whitehead 1978: 19). Every metaphysical explanation, that is, must ultimately root in the character of actualities. This follows from the understanding that "the actual world is built up of actual occasions, and by the ontological principle whatever things there are in any sense of 'existence,' are derived by abstraction from actual occasions" (Whitehead 1978: 73).

Second, however, these actual occasions would not be anything at all without characters, qualities, or patterns to make concrete. Sometimes, as we saw, new characters are woven into actuality where they were not before. Once they were just possibilities. Then they were actual. Actualities are fundamental but they require abstract possibilities, "forms of definiteness," in order to become concretely something rather than nothing in particular. Plato called these the Forms; Aristotle and virtually all premodern metaphysics recognized their necessity as well, though many followed Aristotle in rejecting the idea of universal qualities as somehow subsisting by themselves in a Platonic Realm of Forms. Yet most can agree that abstract possibilities as such are different from the time-bound actual entities that manifest them here and there, now and then. Unlike actualities, they are eternal. The objects of pure mathematical manipulations, for example, are irrelevant to the temporal comings and goings of the things that may illustrate them. They are "eternal objects." So are qualities like shades of color that can be instanced in indefinitely many places at the same time and at indefinitely many times in the same place.

Third, we must reckon with just this implacable fact of "indefinitely many times." The universe never rests. As soon as one pulse of actuality occurs it is replaced by another. Each occasion is finite; each occasion perishes. Something (serving the function of Bergson's cosmic gendarme) pushes the universal process on and on. This "something" never appears except in units of actuality, just as energy never appears without some quantum state or other; but it is not in itself another actuality. Rather, it is the creative advance of the universe or what Whitehead calls "creativity." It may be compared to Spinoza's infinite Substance, since it is what everything actual comes from; but it is quite different, since it represents everlasting change rather than timeless eternality. Looked at in one way, it is the principle of tragedy, since it makes all achievements of actual value merely temporary. In other ways, it holds the principle of ultimate promise, since it allows for another moment, and another, for new and still richer achievements.

Fourth, there needs to be something else, Whitehead adds, that can perform several needed functions if there is to be a world at all. One function is to provide a locus in actuality for the whole infinite range of pure possibilities. Siding with Aristotle against Plato, Whitehead rejects the idea of a Realm of Forms somehow suspended apart from actualities. His commitment to the ontological principle makes it essential that all possibility be grounded in actuality. But of course there are far more possibilities than can conceivably be actual even in the largest universe. Many abstract possibilities are mutually incompatible in actuality though quite clearly mutually entertainable in concept. Some actual entity must do the entertaining and the conceptual ordering of the whole infinite set. Drawing on tradition, this actual entity Whitehead calls God.

In addition to simply holding the eternal objects in conceptual envisionment, God must do more if there is to be any definite world. There are too many possibilities, as we have seen, for mutual actualization; yet the world exists with definite structures. It did not need, in pure theory, to be just so. Infinitely many other possible worlds could be conceived; yet here is a world, a huge brute fact arbitrarily thrust on us, with no good reason for its being in this rather than in some other way. Some principle of arbitrariness, sheer choice, needs to be postulated by any metaphysical theory. Theory, no matter how coherent and adequate, cannot explain forever. "God" is whatever accounts for this logically necessary silencing of the theoretical "why?" The best we can hope for is that the coherences provided by our basic concepts continue to hold as far as we can dimly discern.

Still, the source of definiteness in our universe seems to have "chosen" an order that allows for the evolution of more complexity, at least in our immediately observable world, including the complex self-consciousness of human beings and with it our greatest expressions of poetry, art, philosophy, and religion. From this fact we can infer that God, already recognized as the font of all possibilities and the arbiter of the world's original structuring, must somehow also be helping the process become richer. God needs to be considered an actual entity on the ontological principle; and since coherence is our goal "all the way out to dim discernment," we must not introduce a theoretical incoherence at this point. This means that God is a manifestation of creativity just as all lesser actualities are. God is not a "creator out of nothing," for Whitehead, but a "fellow-sufferer who understands" (Whitehead 1978: 351). God's actuality, from within, must be subjectivity, since there is no other kind of actuality. It will be a growing subjectivity, "feeling" the achievements of all lesser subjects (comprising "the world") and harmonizing them into a cosmic unity where all finite achievements are retained and fulfilled.

For God's own enrichment, as well as for the stimulus to novel richness of harmonies in finite actual entities, God—who is in intimate touch with every finite occasion, as it feels its immediate past and determines its future—offers, out of the infinite store of eternal objects preserved abstractly in the divine nature, relevant novel possibilities for each situation. God, that is, is the "lure" to enriching novelty. It is God who can account for the conceptual availability of possibilities that are not obtainable from the objective past environment. God is unable to decide whether this novel possibility will be accepted or rejected in the actualizing moment. Only the finite actual occasion determines that. God's lure can be frustrated by the world. There is no guarantee of automatic progress. But God works for the best in all situations and preserves the results of all achievements in an experienced harmonizing of otherwise discordant elements from the world that reminds us of Bradley's description of the Absolute's ultimate sentience.

This sketch of Whitehead's macrocosmic thinking should suffice for the purposes of this book's narrative, although there are many issues of detail that my treatment has deliberately avoided. Can God even in principle, for example, be no exception to the categories that cover all other actual entities? God is held by Whitehead to be the one nontemporal entity, meaning not that there is no duration in God's experience but that there is no perishing, no closure, no "epochal" character in the divine subjectivity. This is hard to credit if, concurrently, Whitehead wants to hold that actuality itself is only attained in "subjective satisfaction," that is, a closure in which everything merely possible becomes finally determinate. How can God feed back to the world the fruit of harmonized satisfaction if there is never a satisfaction for God? Further, how can God interact with the world, as Whitehead suggests, if God (as everlasting) is a contemporary of every actuality? Contemporaries cannot feel one another once they have entered the unified process of becoming actual. Some have responded by arguing that God should be conceived as having an "epochal" character, pulsing from subjective satisfaction to subjective satisfaction like any normal train of occasions. But this raises the question of God's fundamental unity over endless time. Others ask the question whether Whitehead even needs a concept of God at all in his metaphysical theory. It can be proposed that the possibilities of the universe do not need a central depository—that they can adequately be related to actuality (conforming to the ontological principle) through the infinitely many pulsations of finite actual occasions that make up the world.

These and similar problems need not be addressed here, where sharing a general vision of reality is what matters. Instead, it is time to move from the macrocosm down to the middle levels of human life and values.

Given the four fundamental metaphysical elements: *actual entities*, *abstract possibilities*, *creativity*, and *God* as limit and lure for the creative nurturing of fresh possibility into actuality, it still is not settled in any detail what kind of a world there should be. Whitehead grasps this nettle firmly: this world is very likely not the only world that has ever been or that will be or (in some divine sense of "now") might now be in God's experience. The observable universe is simply our "cosmic epoch," and it has simply the general empirical characteristics that we find. Thus, it makes sense for Whitehead, unlike Alexander, to postulate a long but finite time for this cosmic epoch to have existed. God does not "create" the epochs but at some point there is an initial choice of fundamental traits. Ours is a social epoch. That is, the actual occasions of our universe, as we observe, relate to one another in complex ways, building larger structures from substructures.

The ultimate substructures are the actual occasions already discussed. Gradually, through a kind of natural selection at the level of basic physical swarms of entities, regular habits of social interaction develop. These reflect the way in which entities distribute themselves, approach each other, and propagate influences to one another. Such habits are hard to resist, not only because at low levels actual occasions are mainly characterized by conformity, but also because survival depends on going along with them. These great habits of self ordering groups of actual occasions are what scientists call the laws of nature. "Laws" do not legislate or coerce; "they" are nothing and can "do" nothing. Only actualities are agencies. Laws, evolved long ago, simply describe how regularities in actual agents can be fitted to curves and described by the abstract concepts discovered by mathematical physicists. Some might be disconcerted at the entailed consequence that fundamental natural laws such as the gravitational constant or the speed of light may have evolved from something different and may still be evolving. Whitehead would caution that the massive stability attained in our electromagnetic epoch would make any such evolution extremely slow; but he would finally accept the entailment. Laws are not actualities, therefore, they cannot ultimately explain. Only actual entities can be the reasons for things; actual entities account for laws, not vice versa.

When new properties appear, as they often have in the course of the evolution of this universe, they are not (as Alexander said) simply "emergents" that need to be accepted without explanation and in attitudes of "natural piety." Experience (though not high-level conscious experience) has been present all along. The new possibilities for realization in experience have been abstractly available as eternal objects. As societies, and societies of societies, gradually grow more and more complex, higher grades of actual occasions stimulated within all this potentially fruitful complexity become more and more capable of opting for novel possibilities. If these novelties once actualized can be protected and passed on, societies with novelties can survive and nurture still more novelty when it fits. Usually novelties will be eliminated but sometimes there will be a fortunate innovation. Societies characterized by these novel traits will develop their own regularities of behavior, their own "habits," and a new set of natural laws will be born. These are not mysterious. "They" simply describe how societies actualizing distinct possibilities settle down to multiply and survive.

"Life" for Whitehead is a good example of something that has laws of its own but is not absolutely new and unprecedented. Every actual occasion has the capacity to feel its physical environment, to evaluate new possibilities, and to opt for a future it shares in making. There is a continuum between quanta of energy with only the barest flicker of capacity to evaluate a novelty (low grade physical occasions) at one end, and quanta of energy set in such complexity, at the other end, that the capacity for recognizing and opting for novelty is much enhanced. There is no "line" between the living and the nonliving. Life is characterized by a great deal of capacity for novelty; nonlife, much less capable, is perhaps located (roughly speaking) somewhere between viruses and crystals.

Most of the observable universe is not alive for Whitehead. Even most living organisms are not "entirely living," since they are made up of inorganic structures (societies of molecules, atoms, subatomic particles, quarks, etc.) that are not famous for their capacities of innovation. The more living parts of an organism, especially when they direct the activities of the unified organism, justify our calling the organism as a whole "alive." But the question is always one of degrees. A body does not necessarily die all at once; in the same way there are many stages of being alive.

Exactly similar things can be said about being conscious. Mind is not normally or mainly conscious as Whitehead understands it. Mind extends all the way to the most insignificant puff of actuality constituting a volume of empty space. It is not important there since it does nothing interesting. But it is important in principle that it be recognized as being there, since nothing comes from nothing, and mind is no exception to this rule. It is through the functioning of mind (by definition) that new possibilities, not present in the immediate environment, can be accorded a foothold in actuality. It appears this is not a conscious process, usually. But when the mind-function has worked long and well enough to achieve a world containing living organisms, and when some of these living organisms develop great enough neural complexity to direct motion on the basis of felt sensation (highly useful for natural selection), there comes a point at which a living body, with its great symphony of sense organs set in parallel to amplify and focus feelings of the world, can become at least dimly aware.

Awareness is usually dim, Whitehead maintains. It takes special capacities and special circumstances to become sharply conscious, especially to become sharply conscious of abstract possibilities, whether mathematical ones or sensory ones (like hues or tones) and their mutual relationships. This is the power of human thought. Wherever and whenever it occurs, however, it is of immense value. On the aesthetic side, it makes for the creation and appreciation of poetry and art; on the practical side, it allows significantly free deliberation of moral alternatives. Freedom is of course never complete. We are always limited by our circumstances, and those circumstances include past habits, even addictions, that can limit from within as well as without. But normally to a appreciable degree (and always, in principle, to some degree) there is in mentality the release from determination by efficient causality alone. This grounds real moral responsibility by providing a theory to make sense of limited freedom for self-determining agency. It makes room too for purpose—the envisioning of yet-unrealized possibilities for future actualization—in human life (obviously) and to some degree in nature at large.

Mentality, representing the capacity of actualities to take account of the merely possible, apart from the physically given, is the principle of advance in the universe; by the same token it is inherently anarchical. Firm, predictable order is represented by causal transmission by physical feeling. By itself, unchecked mentality can work the undoing of precious, hard-won orders of every sort. To protect against this tendency to wildness in mentality, mentality itself develops method. A method, a general way of doing, is a type of abstraction; therefore, it falls into the domain of possibility, thus falls to the mental pole. But at its simplest, method is simply the formal aspect of a successful strategy for survival. It is the primitive appearance of reason, whose basic function, as Whitehead puts it, is *"to promote the art of life"* (Whitehead 1929: 4, emphasis in original).

One of the roles of mentality, then, as it helps to restrain mentality's own tendency toward anarchy, is what we call practical reason. Successful methods can save energy, prevent the need to reinvent the wheel (quite literally), and help organisms equipped with methods "(i) to live, (ii) to live well, (iii) to live better" (Whitehead 1929: 8).

At the same time, there is a negative side to method, namely, that one tends to get stuck in presently available methods, although better methods might promote the art of life (i.e., effective innovation) even more usefully. Good methods become the enemy of better ones. Those who deny the need for better ones (and decry even the search for improvement) Whitehead calls "obscurantists." Every success of practical reason generates its own community of faithful obscurantists; that is to be expected; but if the art of life is to be advanced, obscurantism needs to be broken through. This is also the function of mentality freed from practical incentives and reappearing as high-flying, unfettered speculative reason. Speculation is not done for the sake of its practical payoff—that is why it can be so free—but sometimes speculation does in fact pay dividends, often when it is least expected.

Still, speculative reason by itself has inside it the same tendency to sheer anarchy that mentality in general shares. For defense against this tendency, speculative reason itself invents method, conceptual method, to give itself discipline. This is the fundamental character of logic. Logic is the methodological control of mind in its speculative role. Logic is to speculative thinking as practical method is to anarchical mind.

And in the same way, a particular logic, such as the logic of Aristotle or the logic of Giuseppe Peano (1858–1932) or Gotlob Frege (1848–1925)—or Whitehead and Russell!—can as a method (like any method) develop its faithful band of obscurantists, who cling to the method and deny the need to look for ways of improving it. A particular method, including the method of modern science—and the more successful, the more attractive it is to obscurantist defenses—can become a trap, preventing its own criticism and blocking the way forward to better ways of thinking. Whitehead urges that speculation, including his own, beyond present achievements should never cease; the anarchical principle of mind should always eat away at theoretical achievements to get beyond them. In this way he answers Bergson's despair of conceptual thought: by agreeing that our given theories can never be fully satisfactory at any level of refinement, but by denying that abstractions on that account need to be abandoned. They need to be criticized, improved, made more richly adequate to the subtle nuances of human experience and especially guarded against the frequent delusion that abstractions can be substituted for the reality intended, the ever-dangerous "fallacy of misplaced concreteness" (Whitehead 1925: 51).

In the end, theory must be responsive to fact. "The basis of all authority is the supremacy of fact over thought" (Whitehead 1929: 80). Logic of whatever kind will demand confirmation of theory, after the highest flights of speculation, by return to the ground of experience. Experience itself of course is saturated with thought. Thus, confirmation is not a simple matter of "seeing is believing." Instead, the fundamental confirmation of a general way of thinking is through its capacity to organize effective life over the long run. This means that a general scheme of ideas must be able to support and sustain the institutions through which we express our practical and cultural lives. By this, Whitehead means the economic and political, educational and artistic, technological and religious institutions of a civilization. Fundamental ideas about what can be expected of nature, of human beings in economic and political circumstances and the like, are what lead to the building and maintaining of the market system, constitutions, armies, factories, highway systems, hospitals, schools, museums, churches, and prisons. "Thus the study of the ideas which underlie the sociological structure is an appeal to the supreme authority." (Whitehead 1929: 81).

This "supreme authority" fact is, however, never at a standstill. The complex sociological facts are confused and changing. Simply because institutions can be built on a set of methods and fundamental beliefs does not mean they are perfect or without need for improvement. On the contrary, everything Whitehead says leans to the opposite. Institutions embody largely successful methodologies and widely confirmable ideas or they could not have been created and sustained; but every method craves criticism and so do the institutions of society at any given moment. To the extent that our market system works, the general ideas behind it are partially confirmed, though confirmation is a logically tricky business and is much less clear than disconfirmation. But everyone realizes there are also serious failures in our present institutions, embodying general modern ideas on nature and values. These issues can be noted here, but must wait for the third volume of this series for adequate treatment.

The point is that history is the realm of institutional change. Insofar as human institutions embody deep ideas and beliefs, as these change, so do institutions. This does not mean that some dialectic of abstract ideas à la Hegel determines historical change by itself. Not at all. Whitehead examines the slow-grinding processes that led from the classical world's slave culture to the abolition of the institution of slavery in modern times and finds many factors at work. At the start, the Stoics offered the "impossible dream" of human dignity, implying freedom from chattel-bondage as the natural right for all. But within the institutions of that day, this was in fact unattainable without the destruction of civilization itself, and all of the values represented in the art, literature, philosophy, and delicacy of human feeling of that great era. Still, the ideal survived as an ideal, and as other forces worked to change the institutional realities—forces like the barbarian invaders that finally toppled ancient Rome and the steam technologies that revolutionized modern economic life—the ideal could grow and gradually shape the institutional realities themselves. History, Whitehead argues, is mainly changed by the interplay of physical and mental poles of influence. On the physical side, in this example, were the barbarians and steam; on the mental side, keeping possibilities bright and beckoning, were Christianity and the great luring ideal of Democracy. Both the latter were pulls toward the freeing of every human, because it is right. Both the former were (relatively) blind pushes toward breaking up the old and making the situation malleable to purpose. Of course, neither the barbarians nor the Industrial Revolution were literally without mentality; the Goths and Visigoths and Vandals were drawn by their own hopes and purposes; the technologies of the age of steam were highly reflective of intelligence disciplined by the science we call modern. And so the bipolar character of the actual occasion is reflected in various ways and on various levels in the fabric of the cosmos. Mind is ingredient, with physical causality, in nature, society, and the course of history itself.

Whitehead, by accepting the implication that his own scheme itself will need to be constructively overcome, opens the door gladly to the future. History is change; but it is not just blind change. Institutions are powerful; but they are neither everlasting nor omnipotent. Mathematics fits much of nature; but it does not exhaust it. Modern scientific method is highly successful; but it is not beyond challenge and improvement. Modern thinking is brilliant; but it is at the end of its creative curve.

Whitehead's values, expressed through his wide-ranging exercise in speculative reason tempered by discipline of logic, include many we have come to call modern. He is much impressed with the findings of science and builds his scheme with these in mind. He loves mathematics and, with Russell, is one of the founders of modern symbolic logic. He is deeply empiricist and anti-authoritarian to the core: not only did he live and die outside any religious institution, he would not accept the authority even of David Hume and his British followers on the character of experience. At the same time, Whitehead clearly embraced many of the values we have called premodern. He respects subjective qualities and possibilities beyond formal mathematical ones as eternal objects, resembling the Forms, especially as understood by Aristotle, that is, located always in prior actuality. He respects the fainter, dimmer aspects of human experience and value including the moral and religious. His theory has a place for God. He insists on the presence from the ground up of mind and purpose and freedom in nature. And he is fully committed to unity and coherence for any conceptual scheme worthy of the kosmos.

In Whitehead, we find a blending of the premodern with the modern, which, with his stress on welcoming a better future, opens the door to something postmodern. This is not an easy agenda. Ever-powerful obscurantist tendencies warn against rocking the boat by any deep criticisms of the modern; ever-present anarchical tendencies aim at deconstructing everything modern. There is no agreement on a postmodern agenda. It is a time that has not fully been born, an era lacking a proper name. Should we seek stability in simply repairing the present, or should we venture toward a still-undefined postmodern world of metaphysical speculation? Whitehead's answer follows:

> What looks like stability is a relatively slow process of atrophied decay. The stable universe is slipping away from under us. Our aim is upwards (Whitehead 1929: 82).

Part 3

POSTMODERN METAPHYSICS

9

DEFINING THE POSTMODERN

Giving definition to the postmodern is imagining a profoundly different future. This is at best an uncertain exercise, but one vitally needed in our present age of felt transition. The modern is in our bones and blood. How then can we think clearly about an era that is not yet, one that requires definition by contrast to what has dominated thought and institutions for three hundred years?

This is not the first time in our history that an age, seemingly solid as rock, has turned out porous to intimations of radical change. When modernity rose and shattered centuries-strong assumptions and institutions of premodernity, some felt the early vectors with apprehension, others with exhilaration. Many, like Leonardo da Vinci or Francis Bacon, had the sense of a new day dawning—something post-medieval, something drawn by new values or at least strikingly new configurations of values, something not yet clear but portentous, something seeking a name.

It is ironic (but fitting) that the most general name to become associated with the new mechanistic, progressive age was simply "modern," from the late Latin *modernus*. Initially, the English word "modern" (first recorded in the sixteenth century) meant "just now, contemporary." It was an indexical expression, related linguistically to the "mode" or current "manner" and merely pointed to whatever was present or recent. As such, though the things it indexed could quickly become outdated, the modern itself—having no content of its own—must move on to denote whatever is new and fresh. In this way, the epoch following the medieval could not be conceived easily, by those within it, to have the characteristics of an epoch, that is, to be one of many *periods* of time.

It would have been different if the Modern Age had been known instead as the Age of Clockwork or the Age of Mechanism. Then, as resonating quartz crystals began to replace cogs and wheels in clocks, and as pulsating information feedback systems started to transform the very idea of machinery, our coming to recognize the end of an old epoch and the opening of a new might not have been so hard.

In my judgment, nothing will become outmoded so surely as the name "postmodern." It is a stopgap. It is a place marker used to point to something once again in search of a name. When I first used the term in print in 1966 (Ferré 1966: 624), it seemed exciting, a potential way (in Whitehead's word) "upwards." It meant to me that the modern age, with its distinctive methods and commitments, triumphs and insoluble despairs, need not dominate forever. Something else, something as different from the modern as the modern was from the premodern could be on its way. Three decades later I continue to feel the excitement of the coming new with even greater assurance; but I am bored with fighting for the name. The name itself is paradoxical. Of course it is—if "modern" is taken to mean, merely, "up to the minute." But the paradox is just the point: to shake awake the many who use "modern" both consciously in its neutral sense of "current" and also unconsciously in the other sense that privileges the assumptions, commitments, and institutions characteristic of the "modern" period in (mostly Western) history between the seventeenth century and our recent past. Some periods can be long. Yet all periods are open in principle to endings; and certainly our modern period cannot make itself immune to mortality by drinking at a merely linguistic fountain of youth.

Additionally, when I first used "postmodern" roughly thirty years ago and during some of the subequent years (Ferré 1976, 1982), I was blissfully unconcerned about the other senses that could be and were given the term. In art history, "modernism" designates something specific in nineteenth- and twentieth-century literature, theater, music, and the visual arts. When that style faded, its successor was termed "postmodernism." "Postmodern" architecture is set apart by yet another set of signifiers and has a distinctive recent history of its own. In recent years, the term "postmodern" most prominently has been made the banner for advancing troops with deconstructionist intent, mainly found among literary critics in America, but firmly grounded in French philosophy, as I shortly shall explore at greater length. My own use was directly influenced by none of these, but was inspired instead by Whitehead's treatment of the "modern" in his *Science and the Modern World* (1925). It seemed to me Whitehead showed both the need for and the possibility of moving beyond the once-triumphant (but now atrophying) conceptual commitments of the modern world, and that a step in that direction would be . . . "post modern." To emphasize the on-beyond-the-modern character of the possible new conceptual synthesis, I tended in the early days to use a hyphen between "post" and "modern," but editors (always more alert to current literary "modes") prevailed against such old-fashioned orthography; and now the accepted word is spelled "postmodern"—without hyphens or spaces—as though there were somewhere a solid concept with a unified meaning to support it.

Sympathetic readers of Whitehead, such as John B. Cobb, Jr., and David Ray Griffin, make an identifiable speech-community with me and others in which the "philosophy of organism" (as Whitehead labelled his own work) is centrally ingredient in our reasonably unified concept of the postmodern. This is another matter to which I shall return in later chapters. Still, whatever the more specific content of the new that is envisaged, "postmodern" functions to express a widely shared sense of significant transition for all its varied users. A once enormously vigorous era is approaching its end. Dying, as noted in the previous chapter, need not be accomplished all at once. In some ways, in some aspects, the modern age has already ended. Something very different, something not merely a regression to what existed before it, is on its way.

In other ways the modern era, though not "entirely living," is still very much alive. It surrounds us on every side and literally becomes part of us as we eat, breathe, and perceive. The institutions of modernity, for example, the nation-state, the departmentalized multiversity, the economic market, the military-industrial complex, the specialized sciences, the information and advertising media, the hospitals, the great corporations, and—intimately woven through these institutions—the modern-science-led technologies in which we live (dwell, dress, ride, work, read, relax), everywhere press us to take for granted the implicit values and associated worldview inherited through them from our immediate past. Those who would think other possibilities or live in other ways must overcome mentally the entrenched power of the status quo, the actual world, which in many ways holds what Ivan Illich calls a "radical monopoly" on the readily available choices: that is, many alternatives are eagerly offered for ready adoption, but none is provided to the *whole menu*— on which all the proffered items fit snugly within the modern framework (Illich 1973: 64–71). One may major in a dizzying variety of departments in our modern multiversities, for example, but attempting synoptic depth in interdisciplinary studies goes against the grain of institutional support, faculty interest, and academic reward. It is even taken for granted that interdisciplinarity, in principle, cannot be "deep"—thus, must be "shallow" and not worthy of respect. Research support for faculty is governed by similar values embodied in analogous grant-controlling institutions, and the system is perpetuated from generation to generation. The refusal of a dominant methodology to recognize its general limitations or to acknowledge the need to advance beyond its familiar, mainly successful techniques is what Whitehead calls "obscurantism." Even now the winds of modern obscurantism seem steady and strong.

A postmodern metaphysics will need to be worked out while buffeted by these modern winds. But other winds are also blowing, often fiercely, in this turbulent present. Nationalism is a modern phenomenon; but what sometimes goes by the name of nationalism in the latter years of the twentieth century is not nationalism; rather, it is premodern tribalism. Ethnic savagery, now observed in various parts of the world after the loosening of external constraints imposed by the Cold War between the United States and the former Soviet Union, is a murderous way of asserting the values of particularity. The clan, the family, the religious in-group are precious to the point of torture, rape, and slaughter of any nearby who are different. These values of particularity will need to be safeguarded in any viable postmodern worldview, but slaughter and "ethnic cleansing" do not represent the appearance of the postmodern in the present. Rather, they are fearful regressions to savagery after the breakup of the modern nation-state.

Likewise, the many appearances of religious ultra-conservatism in the late twentieth century are no harbingers of the postmodern. Rising from nearly every major faith around the world, they represent reactionary counterrevolutions aimed against modernity, whose religious emptiness in these latter days has become all too evident. In some cases they are populist movements, fueled by disgust with the hyper-rational, hypo-spiritual character of modern civilization's materialistic plunge into unlimited crassness. In other cases, there are great premodern institutions involved, such as the Vatican (in contradistinction from the living faith of many Catholic Christians, worldwide), which deliberately steers a reverse course in values and might be more at home in the Ptolemaic universe than in our own.

Despite acknowledged pressures from the actual to conform within the institutions of modernity, and despite various atavisms urging retreat from the modern, it is my thesis that the present age is one strongly drawn toward yet-unnamed but urgent novelties that will demand their own theories of reality, led by and grounded in their own fundamental priorities. In support of this thesis I adduce not simply the widely shared private intimations of fundamental changes in the making. In addition to these, toward the end of the twentieth century striking new public movements embodying radical challenges to the value structures of modernity have appeared. These are what I shall call the movements of poststructuralism, liberationism, feminism, and environmentalism. Perhaps, if we attend to them, they may indicate the openness of the future to significant change, heralding the possibility of new institutions and new theories of reality. It is by no means certain that any of these, alone or in some combination with others, will mark the path into the next millennium that will eventually give the postmodern its substantial character and its positive title. Still, it is certain that in this study, we had better be alert to what these value-phenomena may mean for the future of metaphysics.

POSTSTRUCTURALISM

What I call poststructuralism goes by many names and speaks in many tongues here. The only thing more foolish than attempting to group the positions and deal with them together—in a section of a book on metaphysics, no less—would be presuming to ignore them.

One trait that all the thinkers of this quirky lot share is (paradoxically) the aversion to being grouped by such common traits. They will not applaud, therefore, even when I express my appreciation for their vivid animosities. But since they applaud very little and are highly unlikely to be swayed by anything this book contains, I shall not be deterred by such a prospect. My best strategy will be to keep this section as fair as I can and as brief as possible.

The poststructuralists of this discussion are those who have largely succeeded in monopolizing the name of "postmodernist" in the academic professions and the public press. For reasons already given, I am reluctant to forfeit the label, wary though I am of it, without at least a small fight. In Chapter 12, I shall provide still more reasons in a new context. For now, quite apart from the issue of the title to postmodernity, I shall limit myself to noting the principal values these "postmodern," "neopragmatic," "deconstructionist," "hermeneutical," poststructuralists bring to philosophy in the waning days of the present millennium.

It is easier to say what the poststructuralists are against than what they are for. Each has a different way of expressing (often even of spelling, in nonstandard ways) the positive ends to be sought. But all are opposed to a cluster of crimes, alleged to have been perpetrated by classical metaphysics and modernity. Many attack philosophical "hegemony" as a bad thing, that is, one set of ideas gaining predominant influence among many; others complain of "totalizing," which resonates with echoes of totalitarianism. Jacques Derrida opposes "logocentrism," the attempted imposition of hegemonic control of a single, totalizing idea foisted on others by a philosopher's subjective presence through speech. (Writing, in contrast, provides a text that cannot be controlled by the writer against playful deconstruction.) Poststructuralists are especially averse to anything unchanging or "ahistorical." Such ahistoricity might suggest dreaded "absolutism," which might inflict "grand unifying perspectives" or "theories" (which totalize and lead to hegemony).

From these aversions we may correctly infer that poststructuralists tend to value "pluralism," "change," "incommensurability," "flexibility", "playfulness," and the "uniqueness" secured by finding "differences" ("différance," Jacques Derrida; "différend," Jean-François Lyotard) everywhere.

We are instantly reminded of Henri Bergson. In many ways, all these values were championed by his vitalistic philosophy, which, as we saw, attacked any metaphysics based on timelessness, "ready-made" concepts, or the rigidities of abstract analysis. Another early preoccupation of Bergson, after his immersion in mathematics and mechanical science, was his polemic against the inadequacies of abstract, nondurational concepts in modern science, particularly in physics. An important member of the poststructuralist movement, Gilles Deleuze, advances the same critique. The concepts of modern science are taken as "sovereign," he complains. This leads to the hegemonic excesses of "State science," which oppresses all alternatives. (At this point one can almost hear a cheer from Whitehead, whose critique of modern obscurantism makes the same case.) A "nomad science" is needed to stress movement, becoming, multiplicity, and differences. Unfortunately, the apparatus of State science "continually imposes its forms of sovereignty on the inventions of nomad science" (Deleuze 1987: 362).

Science has even more to answer for. Deleuze points out that all laws of science are based on repeated events, observations, and experiments. From these repetitions, sovereign science attempts to unpack timeless laws. But there are no perfect repetitions, he declares (reminding us again of Bergson). No two events are ever exactly the same in all respects. With every repetition there comes a vital difference (Deleuze 1968). Therefore, the icy laws of "royal" science are based on what Nietzsche called "lies (in a nonmoral sense)." There are no shared qualities, no eternal forms (Nietzsche 1954: 45). The Logos of modern science, already reduced in fortune from the rich, multivalent concept of the premoderns to mere logic, has finally gone bankrupt.

This supposed eternal Logos is the prime target also for Jacques Derrida, whose attack is focused against the "logocentrism" that fraudulently (he says) offers the goal of self-presenting truth, radiating meaning to the mind of a reasoning subject. It was the lure of this impossible goal, Derrida argues, that made Plato prefer speech (for which the thinker must be present and in control) to mere writing. Texts, unlike speech, allow infinite commentary and "displacement" to illustrate the hopeless gap between the written words and any single, totalizing idea behind the text.

But even in living speech, there is no getting beyond language to pure meanings or to absolute references. Terms cannot be nonlinguistically compared to their referents, as though (in Kant's vocabulary) the phenomena of our thought and experience could be checked against noumena in the absence of thought and experience. There is no reference outside of linguisticality. Therefore, there is no reality beyond language. Reference is dead. The linguistic or "mimetic" situation must be completely accepted.

> Any attempt to reverse mimetologism or escape it in one fell swoop by leaping out of it *with both feet* would only amount to an inevitable and immediate fall back into its system: in suppressing the double or making it dialectical, one is back in the perception of the thing itself, the produc-

tion of its presence, its truth, as idea, form, or matter (Derrida 1981: 207, emphasis in original).

To Derrida's deconstruction of text and dereferencing of language, Jean-François Lyotard adds a stern rebuff to narrative—at least to narrative controlled by an overarching idea or point of view. "Little narratives" are allowed, *petits récits*; but "metanarratives"—especially such philosophic epics as Hegel's grand narrative of the dialectic of the Spirit—are ruled out as the designs of a totalizing logos (Lyotard 1984; and Schrag 1992: 20).

It is not clear to me whether, on the one hand, the various narratives I chose to tell in the first two parts of this book would count as petits récits, since each is limited to a human situation and explicitly recounted in terms of the values operative in the shaping of some human account (though a grand account) of what reality should be, or on the other hand, whether the very scope and sweep of these accounts together would taint them for Lyotard as "metanarrative." I suspect the latter and expect a lashing, since there is a steady philosophical purpose guiding the choice of my lesser narratives into the grand narrative. Granting this and accepting Lyotard's disapproval, it is still not clear to me why such an exercise should be vicious. The very existence of plurality among my subnarratives seems defense against totalizing; and the presence of a purpose behind my overall presentation is hardly likely to inflict lasting hegemonic control over my readers. Still, it is hard to please everyone, and the happy truth is that it is not necessary, either.

In this spirit of chastened pluralism, we may conclude this section with a reflection on Richard Rorty's dictum that our current age of troubled transition has finally come to the "end of philosophy" (Baynes 1987). The effort to reconstruct philosophy is futile, he argues, since the correspondence of thought with reality is untestable and coherence unattainable. The wise neopragmatic attitude would be to accept the incommensurability of problems, affirm pluralism, and live without the "rage to order" the universe in all-embracing perspectives. Life is too precious to be wasted on fool's gold at the end of metaphysical rainbows.

It is hard to refute a shrug. The question really comes down to a matter of judgment, whether it is worthwhile to keep trying—persisting in the old human quest for a conceptual dwelling place at the outermost limits. Rorty, after thoughtfully reviewing the frustrations of the search, judges in the negative. But of course it is equally hard to prove a negative; and just because there have been many disappointments, there is no hard evidence the game is no longer worth the challenge.

Here we are faced with a classical case of value-judgment. In fields that are organized around what Thomas Kuhn calls "paradigms" and Imre Lakatos terms "research programs," there comes notoriously the time for struggle between those who are ready to give up on the project and those who are prepared to stay the course. Sometimes it is wise to give up; sometimes it is premature. There is no algorithm by which the decision can be settled.

Philosophy is "pre-paradigmatic" on Kuhn's standards (Kuhn 1970: 20), but the logic or illogic of the matter is at certain points the same. We need to make the decision without firm handholds. In the end, what we decide will be based on a constellation of qualitative considerations: How serious were past failures? How important do we judge the rewards of success? How steep, to ourselves and others, would be the cost of continued failure? What other avenues look open? What else might we do with our finite energies? What are *their* chances of success? What are *their* rewards, costs, etc.?

In one respect, the pre-paradigmatic character of metaphysics makes the situation even more open to private decision than in paradigmatic sciences. Everyone reinvents the field. Institutional givens and constraints are loose or nonexistent. There are precious few research teams depending on the largesse of continued grants or competing for laboratories and equipment that would be released by abandoning a purported dead end. To pronounce "the end of philosophy" may mean no more than that one is personally jaded. If others feel so too it will become apparent as fewer articles and books are written and traditional philosophical topics, when broached, rouse no interest. As a pronouncement it is not so much descriptive as prescriptive: "I have become tired of seeking coherent and adequate perspectives on the kosmos; please become so too!" To this only a personal response is appropriate.

Reflecting on the horror with which the poststructuralists tend to gaze on traditional metaphysical efforts, one must wonder whether the reaction is exaggerated. Hegel was no doubt a "totalizer," a teller of "metanarratives." So was Marx. Much of the actual revulsion within the poststructuralist community is in fact expressed against Hegel, who is often explicitly named, and much of the rise of poststructuralism may have been due to disappointment with the failure of the Marxist "metanarrative." Other theories of reality also became hegemonic. The Newtonian mechanical world picture ruled with sovereign imperiousness for many years. Einstein's holds sway today with hardly any audible challenge. And yet the *enterprise* of theorizing allows for great variety. As my own narratives show, there has been abundant historical pluralism. For every Newton there has been a Leibniz or a Berkeley at work on the conceptual foundations, challenging, asking key questions, offering other, perhaps better alternatives. All are working on comprehensive issues, since that is the relevant framework; but the enterprise of thinking about totality need not be "totalitarian," in the sense of "tyrannical" or "dictatorial." Indeed, it is interesting to recall how frequently materialistic "totalizing" was put to use as a weapon of radical opposition to the ancien régime of oppressive Church and State. The same spirit of "écrasez l'infâme" that animates today's poststructural opponents of metaphysics was expressed by yesterday's metaphysicians of matter.

Is there anything inherently bad or wicked in trying to think at the boundaries of comprehensiveness? Perhaps it is a waste of time, though that has not been rigorously proven (and more will be said on this in Chapter 12); but is it somehow *wrong*? Hegel's vast totalities seem to draw indignation from all sides. The Logical Positivists of the Vienna Circle detested Hegel for their own reasons (but no less hotly) before the poststructuralists began to lay on. There is even a side of Hegel emphasizing his *Logic* (and developed further by Bradley) which is "ahistorical," despite his earlier stress on the historical dialectic. This granted, the ahistorical is not the whole story. There is also Bergson, for a contrasting example, whose fluid vision of the whole, friendly to change and qualitative richness and differences, rests on the same bed of values and intuitions motivating the poststructuralists. Is blanket condemnation of visions of the whole fair to the actual varied history of metaphysical thinking? Some theories of the whole may deserve vigorous opposition (though not, one hopes, without attempting also to understand the values these are attempting to defend), but undiscriminating condemnation of the activity itself seems inappropriate. Modesty, even while thinking about totalities, seems no contradiction in terms. Whitehead's theorizing, for example, calls for its own surpassing.

It seems possible then to affirm much of what the poststructuralists value without simultaneously embracing their aversions. Pluralism, change, flexibility, playfulness, uniqueness, respect for differences—these are values worth accenting. Even valuing incommensurability is important if we are to do justly by the criterion of adequacy. It is too easy to dissolve evidence, explain it away, ignore it, if we have no tolerance for incommensurability. Judgments may differ in different circumstances, but it is probably a good rule to side with adequacy and incommensurability over premature coherences. This is especially true in times of change and information overload. In those times it is especially tempting to take refuge in familiar theories to defend ourselves against the disturbing new. This much agreed, there is no need to abandon hope—and (for some at least) the active search—for larger coherences that eventually can make sense of the currently incommensurable (and make way for new incommensurabilities that drive us forward).

The poststructuralists represent an important movement in our time because they shout the urgency of radical change. They insist something is deeply wrong with the modern framework as such. Metaphysical "business as usual" is bankrupt. We must brace ourselves to proceed to something profoundly postmodern. For all the posturing and exaggeration, this is a needed message.

LIBERATIONISM

Another vital development of the late twentieth century, pointing toward the postmodern, is liberation theology. Philosophers of the so-called First World—

or the global North, as I prefer—tend not to pay much attention to this phenomenon. This is because the modern institutions of specialization have taught us that we are philosophers, not theologians; and it is also because we are securely situated in the global North, where the writings of Latin American priests tend not to be heard with any deep resonance. This is not the case for black theologians in the United States, however, whose religious roots, though very different in origin (Protestant instead of Catholic, African instead of Latin American) have fed a common cause. Perhaps those interested in listening for revolutionary trends in value should give more heed.

David Tracy, a distinguished Roman Catholic theologian at the University of Chicago, opens his introduction to a recent book offering various viewpoints on liberation theology with the following declaration:

> It is now clear that the major breakthrough in Christian theology in the last decade has been the explosive emergence of political and liberation theologies. From Latin American, African, and Asian liberation theologies through Euro-American political theologies to North American black theologies and feminist theologies, the theological landscape has been irretrievably changed (Mahan 1981: 1).

The principal reason for the "explosive" character of liberation theology is its source. It is not a phenomenon of the intellectuals (like the hyper-modern "death of God" fad of the 1960s), nor even of the working clergy in the prosperous middle classes of Europe and America.

In fact, its source is one of the most striking points of differentiation from the nineteenth century "social gospel," which also preached political and economic justice from Christian premises. Walter Rauschenbusch (1861–1918), a Baptist minister serving a working-class German Baptist congregation in New York, concluded that Jesus' teachings on the Kingdom of God included all the circumstances of life, not just the "spiritual." As one who had profited from the upward mobility of the Industrial Revolution, and as one whose father (a Westphalian immigrant Lutheran minister) had gained an excellent education and was able to provide even better opportunities for his son, Rauschenbusch found himself a winner in the modern capitalist system and from this position of strengh wanted to create a new postcapitalist order for the sake of the less advantaged.

Liberation theology, by contrast, rises from below. It is a voice from people conscious of having been left out of—or worse, victimized by—the promise of modernity. Its voice, even when coming from middle-class, educated spokespersons, is heavy with the sense of oppression. As James H. Cone, a leading black liberation theologian puts it:

When the meaning of Christianity is derived from the bottom and not from the top of the socio-economic ladder, from people who are engaged in the fight for justice and not from those who seek to maintain the status quo, then something radical and revolutionary happens to the function of the "holy" in the context of the "secular." Viewed from the perspective of oppressed peoples' struggle for freedom, the holy becomes a radical challenge to the legitimacy of the secular structures of power by creating eschatological images about a realm of experience that is not confined to the values of this world. . . . For inherent in the Christian gospel is the refusal to accept the things that are as the things that *ought* to be. This "great refusal" is what makes Christianity what it is, and thus infuses in its very nature a radicality that can never accept the world as it is (Cone 1981: 53).

And Gustavo Gutiérrez, one of the most prominent voices for Latin American liberation theology, insists on the difference between generous sharing and radical restructuring of the modern world.

The poor person is the by-product of the system in which we live and for which we are responsible. He is the oppressed, the exploited, the proletarian, the one deprived of the fruit of his labor and despoiled of being a person. For that reason, the poverty of the poor person is not a call for a generous act which will alleviate his misery, but rather a demand for building a different social order (Gutiérrez 1976: 25).

The modern social order gains its strength from high technology resting on mechanistic modern science developed in Europe and America since the seventeenth century. Both the technology and the science are heartless; both are exploitative to the core. And both tend, as a combined cultural phenomenon, to undermine the seriousness of spiritual value. During Gutiérrez's dissertation defense in 1985 at Lyon, France, his dissertation director Christian Ducoque asked the already-prominent priest why he thought Christianity from "below" could liberate when "technoscience has produced what might be called a form of religious indifference. As a result, Christianity is viewed as one opinion among others and as having no more content than the others" (Gutiérrez 1990: 25). Gutiérrez replied:

The point you raise is one that we have discussed a great deal in Latin America. I think that science and technology do have a secularizing effect, as has been seen in Europe. But I also think that historical phenomena do not repeat themselves in precisely the same form. . . . In the final analysis, history is not a matter of inevitable fate but depends in large part on our initiatives and actions. I think that we in Latin America can learn a lesson from the European experience of secularization and its consequences, and will be able to confront our greatest present problem: poverty. It is my own conviction that if we are able to be present to this poverty as Christians, the consequences that secularization has had in Europe will not be repeated (Gutiérrez 1990: 25–26).

Poverty, presented as the central Christian issue, will keep spirituality alive and values potent, Gutiérrez believes. Even the secularizing force of the materialist worldview will not be able to extinguish the passion for social and economic justice if oppressed Christians make achieving it their enlivening gospel.

Technoscience is an enemy in another sense as well, according to liberation theology. We in the global North may not see it, since (for the upwardly mobile majorities) science and technology have been our servants; but the impoverished masses experience science and technology as alien invaders. This was sharply drilled into my consciousness and the awareness of many other comfortable Northern academics at the World Council of Churches meeting on science and religion held at the Massachusetts Institute of Technology in July 1979. I came to deliver my invited paper on epistemological issues in science and religion (Ferré 1980: 97–111), but found to my dismay that these issues were perceived as irrelevant by the delegates from poorer lands. Their emphasis was on Francis Bacon's original understanding: that knowledge is power. But power in our world today is not well distributed. Science, declared our colleagues from the South, is the ideology of the ruling classes in the modern world, reaching out through multinational corporations, banks, and often through direct military influence, to oppress and exploit. Technoscience has created a worldview, we were told, that functions as a weapon in the service of injustice. For many present, it was a sobering message.

The language of ideology and exploitation of the lower classes, of revolution and restructuring of society, echoes—at least at crucial stages in its development—tones made familiar by Karl Marx and his followers, tones we have already heard in our narrative. Marxism was explicitly utilized in liberation theology. José Miguez Bonino explicitly affirms that "the thought of these men is characterized by a strict scientific ideological analysis, avowedly Marxist" (Bonino 1975: 87); though he also warns that "the Marxist scheme cannot be taken as a dogma, but rather as a method" (Bonino 1975: 87).

Needless to say, a great deal of hostility to liberation theology was generated by the simple fact of its formative Marxist slant. Ronald H. Nash, for example, writes a passionate defense of the ethics of capitalism in "The Christian Choice Between Capitalism and Socialism" (Nash 1984: 49–67). He maintains that real liberation requires the firm rejection of socialism in "a *new* liberation theology that will recognize the irrelevance and falseness of socialist attacks on capitalism, that will unmask the threats that socialism poses to liberty and economic recovery, and that will act to move existing economic institutions and practices closer to the principles of a free market system that alone offers the hope of economic progress" (Nash 1984: 49). Similarly, Michael Novak rejects the attitude of blame that liberationism takes toward the inventive, scientific North. The poverty of the Latin Americans is due to their failure to modernize their thinking. They should blame themselves.

> Nothing prevented Brazilians from inventing the combustion engine, the radio, the airplane, penicillin, and other technologies which give resources their utility. Although Brazil is apparently one of the most richly endowed of all nations in material resources, neither Brazil nor other Latin American nations have so far provided a system favorable to invention and discovery. . . . Those cultures which value the intelligent and inventive use of God's creation are far better off than those which do not. . . . Latin America is responsible for its own condition (Nash 1984: 30).

Blaming the poor for their poverty comforts the wealthy—and illustrates the chasm between the viewpoint from "above" and "below." The anger and explosive rejection of the whole modern system felt by the afflicted (whoever rightly is to blame) is likely to be stoked still further by what Marxist theory would diagnose as the ideological blindness of such guilt-free Northern explanations for the extreme maldistribution of wealth in the global society of the late twentieth century.

At the same time, the weapon of ideological analysis is double-edged. Used by the poor to afflict the comfortable rationalizations of the rich, it may indeed comfort the afflicted. But the question hovers: To what extent is liberation theology itself an ideology, a mere mental filter through which the poor, because of their economic desperation, see the world and themselves? Religion for liberation theology is far from an opiate, as Marx claimed; but in it has an ideological inversion become simply a stimulant for action, a weapon in a class war now broadened to international—intercultural—battlefronts? To what extent does liberationism remain a *theology*, primarily aiming at truths about ultimate realities, and to what extent have its words and images been reduced to tools of praxis in redistributing wealth?

Liberation theologians are nearly as impatient with theoretical issues concerning the kosmos as are the poststructuralists. If we are looking for hints about postmodern metaphysics, we will not find them directly in doctrines of God or nature constructed by these passion-filled speakers for social justice. Undoubtedly, as Schubert Ogden (a major contemporary Protestant theologian who was one of the earliest to pay serious attention to liberation theology) maintains, new constructive theorizing is demanded by liberation theology. A God who is somehow especially concerned about and participates in the misery of human masses around the globe will not be symbolized easily by the imperial religious images of the premodern or modern eras. The problem of evil represented by social injustice may need to be approached in a new way. Redemption may need to be distinguished from emancipation and grounded in different aspects of God's nature (Ogden 1979: 69–95).

Science, too, will need to be rethought in light of its history of easily lending itself to applications of social oppression. Are the "value-free" objective attitudes inculcated by modern science themselves contributors to alienation between the researcher and the subject matter studied? Are modern science's cold experimental techniques—with the emphasis on analysis and drive to specialization—capable of being reformed into a new configuration as postmodern science? Can a new sort of technology—a way of achieving intelligent purpose—that is more sensitive to users and to its social consequences arise out of this? As Michael Novak points out, there will be no long-term liberation without technology to lift and science to lead. The tendency among liberationists has been to reject science and technology, since from "below" they have seen its inhumane face turned against their interests. To them "science" simply means *modern* science with all its power, its associated culture, its implicit worldview, and all its noted problems in relating to quality and value. Perhaps this can be challenged. Perhaps the values of liberation theology can motivate deep rethinking that will forge a new kind of science and technology, as different from modern science as modern science was different from premodern. If so, then the anguished cry that is liberation theology today may nudge the world toward postmodern theology, postmodern science, and postmodern technology.

FEMINISM

An ironic joke among workers in various liberation movements is that the women of the movement still make the coffee and do the dishes. This is no laughing matter for feminist thinkers who see in such patterns—reminding us of women's near-universal subordination to "helper" roles—another evidence of an underlying oppressive hierarchical order that is the fundamental enemy of human liberation.

Since many diverse voices speak for feminism, no single "doctrine" or party line should be expected. My treatment will follow what the level-headed feminist philosopher Victoria Davion calls the "approach" approach: that is, simply noting the differences made to various major areas of life and thought when they are approached with a clear concern for the specific interests of women.

Valuing both justice and women, simultaneously and intensely, is the key to law professor Catharine MacKinnon's approach to politics, the domain of power and its distribution (MacKinnon 1987). MacKinnon proposes that since sexuality is even more fundamentally significant to the human condition than work, Marx's analysis can be put to deeper use if transposed into a feminist key. Sexuality is a presocial, universal impetus; but it never appears apart from historically conditioned specific forms. Therefore, sexuality both creates society and, in its particular manifestations, is socially created. This is a theory (like Marx's) of the totality of social life, including not only the "differences" between men and women (matters of historically conditioned "gender" attributes), but also the way we think and feel about ourselves, each other, and the universe.

Male power, MacKinnon argues, is what has constructed the modern world of life, thought, and feeling. Women who live in this male-constructed world think and feel about gender differences as though contingent, historical, male-valued constructions were necessary biological givens. Actually, most of the "differences" (MacKinnon specifically includes *"différance"* as well) between men and women are artificial gender-constructs. This does not mean that there is no real difference between men and women:

> Of course there is; the difference is that men have power and women do not. I mean simply that men are not socially supreme and women subordinate by nature; the fact that socially they are, constructs the sex-difference as we know it (Arthur 1993: 471).

In this constructed social world (no less real for being constructed), women are the objects of male definition. Men, on the approved epistemology of modernity, are encouraged to take an "objective" point of view on women; which means, MacKinnon adds, that women are made objects, since only subjects are granted the privilege of taking an objective viewpoint. Given the power to define, men create women's reality. This, MacKinnon tells us, is the philosophical significance of pornography, through which women are defined as sexual beings, in which rape is defined as intercourse, and in which women are defined as desiring degradation.

Mere power, self-perpetuating and unjustly distributed, has no necessity and no justification. There is no "higher reason" why males happen to be subjects who define and females the objects defined. As MacKinnon reflects on the pure contingency of female subordination it becomes clear that in the very contingency of male power lies its status as a challenge for change:

> Of course it [the arbitrary fact that males define females] could be in any way at all. That it could be and isn't, should be and isn't, is what makes it a political problem (Arthur 1993: 474).

As a "total" theory MacKinnon's feminism calls for a radical change in political realities. Heterosexuality itself needs to be redefined. The nuclear family resting on marriage, child care, and all that strikes many as familiar (and therefore acceptable) "family values" is finally—to eyes opened by adequate commitment to justice and to the value of women—seen as a crass form of prostitution, that is, the exchange of sexual favors for material compensations like room, board, and clothing. The fantasy of romantic love is a male political construction. Thus, this feminist approach to politics calls for a wholly new world to replace the modern.

> We cannot address aesthetics without considering pornography. We cannot think about sexuality and desire without considering the normalization of rape, and I do not mean rape as surplus repression. We cannot do or criticize sciences without talking about the masculinity of its premises. We cannot talk about everyday life without understanding its division by gender, or about hegemony without understanding male dominance as a form of it. We cannot talk about production without pointing out that its sex division, as well as sexual harassment and prostitution (and housework), underpins and constitutes the labor market (Arthur 1993: 478).

This new world MacKinnon foresees is far removed from the actual economic and political realities that surround us; but what Whitehead calls the "lure" of novel possibilities may challenge and eventually change the actual. To this end, alternative possibilities need to be kept visible by those like MacKinnon who sense this as a major transition-time in history, a wrenching time between worlds.

A similarly thoroughgoing critique can be expected for the domain of ethics and religion when feminists such as Mary Daly or Elizabeth Dodson Gray approach what Daly calls "phallic morality" (Daly 1973: 98–131). Ample warning that something is deeply wrong with both ethics and religion is given by recognition that there exists today a "planetary sexual caste system" (Daly 1973: 2), demeaning to half the world's human population, but somehow supported by the religions and ethical systems that shape our values and guide our behavior.

Daly and Dodson Gray take individual positions, in tone and in detail, but both break sharply with what they call "patriarchy," rule by the "fathers" in the widest possible sense. Dodson Gray defines the term with classic directness: "By patriarchy I mean a culture that is slanted so that men are valued a lot and women are valued less; or in which men's prestige is up and women's prestige is down" (Gray 1982: 19). The key problem for both is (as Dodson Gray puts it) that "men are always in control of the myth system" (Gray 1982: 22).

Religiously, this means there is nothing more vital than to challenge the dominant masculinity of theological images in modern culture's religions. Mary Daly depicts the traditional Father God of Christianity as a fallen, or at least failing, idol of our time.

> The method of liberation, then, involves a *castrating* of language and images that reflect and perpetuate the structures of a sexist world. It castrates precisely in the sense of cutting away the phallocentric value system imposed by patriarchy, in its subtle as well as in its more manifest expressions. As aliens in a man's world who are now rising up to name— that is, to create—our own world, women are beginning to recognize that the value system that has been thrust upon us by the various cultural institutions of patriarchy has amounted to a kind of gang rape of minds as well as of bodies (Daly 1973: 9, emphasis in original).

Speaking of God as "He" reinforces the masculine tendency to arrogate authority. Dodson Gray explains: "Since God does not have genitals, it seems to me obviously inappropriate to describe God as either male or female." She continues:

> I also have little sympathy for adding "She" to "He" or "Mother" to "Father" when describing God. Both uses are too anthropomorphic for me to take seriously as religious concepts. I think these are steps backward rather than forward (Gray 1982: 75).

Dodson Gray accepts the premise (hotly disputed by some feminists like MacKinnon) that there are distinctively different modes of perception typical of males and females, as such. Males, she argues, tend to be more adventuresome, risk-taking, and aggressive; females tend to be more security-minded, nurturing, and irenic. Citing Carol Gilligan (Gilligan 1982), she also posits a significantly different path of moral development for boys and for girls. What is needed for adequacy, she concludes, is balance between these, not the subordination of either. The goal is diversity without hierarchy.

Daly also emphasizes the uniqueness of women's contribution to the future of civilization. Nothing less than a new revelation of the nature of being can be expected to come from what Daly calls the "mysticism of sorority" (Daly 1973: 34).

> What I am proposing is that the emergence of the communal vocational self-awareness of women is a *creative political ontophany*. It is a manifestation of the sacred (*hierophany*) precisely because it is an experience of participation in being, and therefore a manifestation of being

(*ontophany*). . . . In other words, women conscious of the vocation to raise up this half of humanity to the stature of acting subjects in history constitute an ontological locus of history. In the very process of becoming actual persons, of confronting the non-being of our situation, women are bearers of history (Daly 1973: 34–35).

Ultimately, "What is at stake is a real leap in human evolution, initiated by women" (Daly 1973: 35–36). But this leap, as Dodson Gray also insists, is not simply to some alternate hierarchical system controlled by females instead of males. That would be in essence a return to patriarchy merely spelled with an 'm' (Gray 1982: 94).

This is an important point, since many who are antagonistic to women's liberation ignorantly and unimaginatively insist that the result will be the same kind of society with women "on top." "On top" thinking, imagining, and acting is essentially patriarchal (Gray 1982: 94).

The answer Daly gives is "androgyny," in the sense of wholeness of personhood, no longer split between the dualisms of male-female, up-down, strong-weak, and the rest. This androgynous healing of dualisms and hierarchies will heal men as well as women and alone will provide genuine liberation for all.

Only radical feminism can act as "the final cause," because of all revolutionary causes it alone opens up human consciousness adequately to the desire for nonhierarchical, nonoppressive society, revealing sexism as the basic model and source of oppression. Without the power of this vision to attract women and men so that we can will to transcend the whole array of false dualisms, there will be no real change. The liberation "movements" that leave sexism unchallenged can, of themselves, only spin delusions of progress, bringing about endless, arbitrary variation within the same senescent system (Daly 1973: 190).

The one philosophical resource that makes the most sense to Mary Daly, given feminism's strong requirement to move beyond the bifurcations and dualisms that patriarchy has until now foisted on civilization, is Whitehead's organismic process thinking. "The process philosophy of Whitehead and some of his intellectual progeny comes closer to anticipating the dawn of the rising woman-consciousness," she writes (Daly 1973: 188). Specifically, this is seen in Whitehead's persistent determination to overcome all the basic dualisms: including mind-body, freedom-necessity, and final-efficient causality splits. Whitehead's future is fully open to innovation. Whitehead's God is not the Patriarch but the "fellow sufferer who understands." Whitehead is neither an anti-intellectualist nor a shallow objectivizer. In all these ways and more, his philosophy may be considered a useful vehicle toward a radically androgynous future, Daly says, but only if used with caution.

> The fact that philosophers of the future do not speak directly to the problem of sexism is a warning. "Whiteheadians" can be oblivious to the "process" of the female half of the species in our struggle to become. The essential thing is to hear our *own* words, always giving prior attention to our *own* experience, never letting prefabricated theory have *authority* over us. Then we can be free to listen to the old philosophical language (and all philosophy that does not explicitly repudiate sexism is old, no matter how novel it may seem). If some of this language, when heard in the context of female becoming, is still worth hearing, we need not close our ears. But if we choose to speak the same sounds they will be formally and existentially new words, for the new context constitutes them as such. Our process is *our* process (Daly 1973: 189).

This vigorously sounds a sentiment that Whitehead himself would certainly have applauded.

Approaches to politics and power, to religion and ethics, are all influenced by our approach to science, from which our modern age draws its authoritative understanding of the world around us. An influential feminist approach to science (as well as to "ecofeminism" as we shall see in the next section) is offered by Carolyn Merchant in her respected book, *The Death of Nature: Women, Ecology and the Scientific Revolution* (Merchant 1990).

Merchant is primarily interested in giving due notice to alternative visions of nature. Most histories of science take for granted the victorious mechanization of the modern world picture. These standard histories tend to ignore or derogate other conceptions of nature. Writing from the unchallenged viewpoint of the victors in the long struggle that led to the modern mechanical worldview, they waste little ink on organic conceptions of nature or on alternative scientific traditions that prospered in the centuries prior to the powerful hegemony of modern science and modern metaphysics.

This is unfortunate, Merchant points out, since important alternatives once flourished, drawing lively attention to aspects of nature that are sorely missed in the dessicated masculinist sciences of our day. In earliest conceptions nature was female. On the one hand, "she" was seen as reasonable and nurturing; on the other, raging and destructive. The former aspect of "mother" nature was eventually replaced by the orderly, impersonal imagery of mechanical principles; the latter aspect demanded strategies of control. "An organically oriented mentality in which female principles played an important role was undermined and replaced by a mechanically oriented mentality that either eliminated or used female principles in an exploitative manner" (Merchant 1990: 2).

The effort to control nature by modern science was inherently anti-feminine, intimately associated with the control of witches, Merchant shows. In the grinding tension between the vision of the world as feminine organism, leading to such great utopian works as Tomasso Campanella's *The City of the Sun* (1602) and Johann Valentin Andreä's *Christianopolis* (1619), on one side, and the rising vision of the world as dead material waiting to be exploited for human consumption, on the other, old or unpopular women by the thousands were destroyed as witches.

> The witch, symbol of the violence of nature, raised storms, caused illness, destroyed crops, obstructed generation, and killed infants. Disorderly woman, like chaotic nature, needed to be controlled (Merchant 1990: 127).

The victory, as we saw in the narrative of Part Two, went to the metaphysics of mechanical matter; and modern science has to this day shied from what might be called the "feminine" in nature: that is, the softer, living, qualitative aspects of the subjects it studies. Its analytic methods chop off aspects that are important both for understanding nature and (increasingly) for environmental health and human survival.

Science today needs fundamental reform in the direction of holism in method and respectfulness in attitude toward its objects. Here, Merchant states, feminism and ecology join forces.

> The most important example of holism today is provided by the science of ecology. Although ecology is a relatively new science, its philosophy of nature, holism, is not. Historically, holistic presuppositions about nature have been assumed by communities of people who have succeeded in living in equilibrium with their environment. The idea of cyclical processes, of the interconnectedness of all things, and the assumption that nature is active and alive are fundamental to the history of human thought. No element of an interlocking cycle can be removed without the collapse of the cycle. The parts themselves thus take their meaning from the whole. Each particular part is defined by and dependent on the total context (Merchant 1990: 293).

The link between women and ecology is important. "The conjunction of conservation and ecology movements with women's rights and liberation has moved in the direction of reversing both the subjugation of nature and women" (Merchant 1990: 294). In this way, a new-old idea of organic reality can link forces with the power of feminist ideals to transform both our polluted modern landscape and our over-abstract modern sciences.

A new scientific revolution is needed and may well be in progress. A feminist approach to science will emphasize the *relatedness* of things to one another and will accept the possibility of *intrinsic values* in subject matters to be studied—thus, readmitting the relevance of *subjectivity* for approaching what is to be understood. It will be a science of *appreciation* including tenderness, not simply manipulation. Given such a science, it would be less difficult to imagine a postmodern world like MacKinnon's based on radically altered power-relations, no longer based on attitudes of patriarchal domination but with other gender definitions making for fuller expression of human potential in all humans. It is also easier to imagine the spread of alternative religious expressions and ethical attitudes, once they are not forced to cut against the grain of what the culture understands to be its most reliable resource for an accurate grasp of nature. In all of these "approaches," feminism in all of its variety is united in search of nothing short of a new world.

ENVIRONMENTALISM

This new, postmodern world—of poststructuralists and liberationists, but with the exception of some of the environmentally oriented feminists discussed above—tends, on the whole so far, to be a predominantly *human*-centered world. The exception is significant: There are strong inclusivist, holistic, and organismic currents in basic feminist values that lead toward a rising concern for "nature," as we heard especially from Merchant and Dodson Gray. An important strand in feminist thought has defined itself as ecological feminism, or "ecofeminism" (Griffin 1978; Salleh 1984; Diamond 1990; Warren 1990; Plumwood 1991). Still, poststructuralism, liberation theology, and much of political and economic feminism are mainly seeking value-revolutions on behalf of the domain of civilization. In the traditional duel between "history" and "nature" they tend to second the claims of history.

In contrast, a fourth contemporary movement pulling hard toward a significantly postmodern framework of life and thought is environmentalism. There are many different stripes of environmentalism of course—from Saturday morning pick-up-litter clubs to the advocates of deadly "ecotage." As a sorting device, I shall focus here on the environmentalism that most deeply challenges modernity in principle by challenging ingrained modern values of anthropocentrism.

To most modern thinkers, whether minority idealists or majority materialists, anthropocentrism has been the only thinkable option. The primacy of "mind," for those who have attempted to defend it, has in most cases, with the notable exception of Leibniz, been understood in terms of human minds. From

Berkeley to Kant, human valuers held center stage, while God provided the necessary conditions for the stage itself. For Hegel, if there is to be any dialectical movement beyond anthropocentrism, it will be "upward," ever more removed from the lower orders of nature. For the mechanist majority, "matter" excluded all value—along with all nonmathematical qualities—and forced whatever could be salvaged of value into dependence on human minds. It is hard to overstate the challenge to modern thinking, therefore, that is represented by nonanthropocentric environmentalism. Although I shall limit myself, as in the other sections of this chapter, to only a few examples, the movement itself is well-advanced and could be exemplified by many other voices.

One of the first important voices to oppose the philosophical presumptions of anthropocentrism in modern civilization was that of a forester meditating alone in the wild. Aldo Leopold composed his essay "The Land Ethic" in 1949. It is perhaps the most stirring and influential statement ever made on postmodern environmental responsibility (Leopold 1966). Leopold is in many ways the founder-patron of environmentalism as I am defining it here. His influence has been immensely constructive. His evocation of the morally appalling image of Odysseus hanging "all on one rope a dozen slave-girls of his household whom he suspected of misbehavior during his absence" (Leopold 1966: 237) required many people to think for the first time about the rightness of doing "whatever they wish with their property," even when that property is land rather than ladies.

In this way, he forced the issue of "moral considerability" for nature and required us to notice that the range of recipients of our moral attention has slowly but steadily grown. To members of other tribes or language groups, to prisoners of war, to men with different-colored skins, to women—the circle of those to whom moral obligations are due has expanded; and nothing but habit, Leopold implies, prevents us from making the evolutionary move toward incorporating in our ethics the land and animals and plants that live on it. He writes, "The extension of ethics to this . . . element in human environments is, if I read the evidence correctly, an evolutionary possibility and an ecological necessity" (Leopold 1966: 239).

But Leopold was actually urging more than a simple "extension" of ethics; he was proposing a genuine revolution. In the same essay, he formulated a new *standard* for ethics. In judging the very meaning of *right* and *wrong*, he said, we should put the living land at the center: "A thing is right when it tends to preserve the integrity, stability, and beauty of the biotic community. It is wrong when it tends otherwise" (Leopold 1966: 262).

J. Baird Callicott, a primary interpreter and advocate for Leopold, is right, therefore, when he maintains that this is not evolutionary at all, but rather a revolutionary contribution of the land ethic (Callicott 1980: 318–24). The land ethic shifts concern from collections of human individuals, as was the central consideration for both main branches of modern philosophy, and places attention squarely on the health of the *biotic system*. Thus, Leopold seeks holistic, bio-centric values in contrast to the mainly atomistic, anthropocentric values characteristic of all the modern traditions. The human species is one among throngs of species; it should live in its proper place, not as conqueror of the land-community, but as "plain member and citizen" within it (Leopold 1966: 219–20).

Another pioneer, the Norwegian philosopher-naturalist Arne Naess, strongly supports these values in the brief but influential article in which he founded the concept of "deep ecology" (Naess 1973: 95–100). If we human beings are to play our proper democratic parts as "plain citizens" in nature, we must weed out from our policies those prejudices which automatically favor our own kind. "To the ecological field-worker, *the equal right to live and blossom* is an intuitively clear and obvious value axiom" (Naess 1973: 96, emphasis in original).

Naess, even as he wrote this, acknowledged that "biospherical egalitarianism" could be affirmed only "in principle." "The 'in principle' clause is inserted," he noted, "because any realistic praxis necessitates some killing, exploitation, and suppression" (Naess 1973: 95). Naess and his followers have taken this principle, nevertheless, as a necessary condition for "deep" ecological thinking. George Sessions, for example, excludes Whitehead's organismic theories from alliance with "deep ecology" solely on the ground that it allows for gradations of value, depending on the quality of experience enjoyed by different forms of life. "The point," he writes, "is not whether humans in fact do have the greatest degree of sentience on this planet . . . deep ecologists argue that the degree of sentience is *irrelevant* in terms of how humans relate to the rest of Nature. And so, contemporary Whiteheadian ecological ethics does not meet the deep ecology insistence on 'ecological egalitarianism in principle'" (Sessions 1979: 18).

This insistence, affirmed not only as standard for "depth" but also as criterion for virtue, motivates the sometimes bitter charges of "speciesism" against those who do not adopt it. Arguing from the analogy of racism, sexism, and other such groundless prejudices against victims of exploitation, some vigorously condemn any who cling to the view that the human species is special in any morally relevant way. And from such condemnation of systematically *pro*-human outlooks it is a short step to systematic *anti*-human attitudes. Our species has done vast, irreparable damage. Humans have much to answer for. A misanthropic cast is frequently found in the rhetoric from deep ecologists. As Baird Callicott observes, "The extent of misanthropy in modern environmentalism . . . may be taken as a measure of the degree to which it is biocentric" (Callicott 1980: 326).

The very conviction, however, that our species has done much that is wicked, deplorably selfish, heedless of our larger moral responsibilities to the earth, makes it impossible to maintain in any simple way that the human species is in every respect just a "plain member and citizen" of the biotic community. Our species is distinguished from all others by standing under moral obligations *not* to be wicked, selfish, and heedless. There is no known species other than the human to which it makes sense to preach self-restraint, sacrifice of species-advantage, or limitation of growth. Literal adoption of species-egalitarianism for humanity would seem to imply a "let 'er rip" policy quite the opposite of what deep ecologists approve.

Richard Watson develops these implications with fine irony. Unless we appeal to the uniquely personal capacities of the human species, we have no leverage for self-restraint, no basis for an ecological ethics. Taking a purely biocentric view of nature, including the human as literally no more than one more "plain citizen," our species should be allowed to live out its "destiny" without any more moral censure than is applied to other species that trample and consume.

> Human beings do alter things. They cause the extinction of many species, and they change the Earth's ecology. This is what humans do. This is their destiny. If they destroy many other species and themselves in the process, they do no more than has been done by many another species. The human species should be allowed—if any species can be said to have a right—to live out its evolutionary potential, to its own destruction if that is the end result. It is nature's way (Watson 1983: 253).

The opposite conviction, that *more* should be expected of the human race, is a form of anthropocentrism, Watson points out. Thus, if "the posing of man against nature in any way is anthropocentric" (Watson 1983: 252), then "deep" ecological thinking, which seeks deliberate moral controls on organic human urges to multiply and consume, has not escaped anthropocentrism.

> If man is a part of nature, if he is a "plain citizen," if he is just one nonprivileged member of a "biospherical egalitarianism," then the human species should be treated in no way different from any other species. However, the entire tone of [deep ecological thinking] is to set man apart from nature and above all other living species. Naess says that nonhuman animals should be "cared for in part for their own good." Sessions says that humans should curb their technological enthusiasms to preserve ecological equilibrium. Rodman says flatly that man should let nature be (Watson: 1983: 251–52).

Another important approach within the nonanthropocentric environmentalist movement is offered by Holmes Rolston, III, who defends a "deep" and demanding environmental ethic while avoiding the contradictions generated by deep ecology's ill-considered postulate of species egalitarianism (Rolston 1988). This he does by sharply distinguishing ethical principles appropriate for application to human society, on one side, and to the nonhuman environment, on the other. Rolston sees very clearly that the tenderheartedness we cultivate for dealings among human beings is unsupported and unsupportable in nature. He is, however, keenly aware that the predacious standards of biotic health in nature are morally outrageous when imported into human culture. He states the contrast very clearly:

> Nature proceeds with a recklessness that is indifferent to life; this results in senseless cruelty and is repugnant to our moral sensitivities. Life is wrested from her creatures by continual struggle, usually soon lost; those few who survive to maturity only face eventual collapse in disease and death. With what indifference nature casts forth her creatures to slaughter! Everything is condemned to live by attacking or competing with other life. There is no altruistic consideration of others, no justice (Rolston 1988: 39).

Since this is so, "right" and its opposite cannot be simply equated with what enhances or hinders biotic flourishing. Thus, drawing on widely shared ethical intuitions, Rolston concludes that there are "elements in nature which, if we were to transfer them to interhuman conduct in culture, would be immoral and therefore ought not to be imitated" (Rolston 1988: 39).

Rolston's realism about what actually goes on in ecosystems forms the foundation of his environmental ethics. Despite our tender human sympathies for an innocent fawn, for example, we must accept that a hungry cougar will make a meal of it, if it can; and even if we have a chance to intervene to save the fawn, we *should* not. This follows from one of Rolston's major principles: "There is no human duty to eradicate the sufferings of creation" (Rolston 1988: 56). Here, we catch a familiar echo from Leopold's Land Ethic, as when Rolston writes that "environmental ethics has no duty to deny ecology but rather to affirm it" (Rolston 1988: 56). But this ethic, Rolston insists, should not be used for interhuman guidance. On the basis of sheerly biological principles, there would be little or no difference whether a hungry predator were to eat a wandering fawn or a lost child. We *should not*, on Rolston's principles, save the fawn; but our ethical intuitions strongly urge us that we *should* save the child. Rolston accepts this difference and explains:

> The fawn lives only in an ecosystem, in nature; the child lives also in culture. Environmental ethics is not social ethics. . . . We would not want to take predation out of the system if we could (though we take humans out

of the predation system), because pain and pleasure are not the only criteria of value, not even the principal ones (Rolston 1988: 57).

The more important criterion for Rolston is "satisfactory fitness" in nature. Fitness rests on predation, which makes for suffering; and since animals are morally innocent, this results in enormous quantities of innocent suffering. Is this a problem? Yes and no, for Rolston:

> It may seem unsatisfactory that innocent life has to suffer, and we may first wish for an ethical principle that protects innocent life. This principle is persuasive in culture, and we do all we can to eliminate human suffering. But ought suffering to continue when humans do or can intervene in nature? That it ought not to continue is a tender sentiment but so remote from the way the world *is* that we must ask whether this is the way the world *ought* to be in a tougher, realistic environmental ethic. A morally satisfactory fit must be a biologically satisfactory fit. What *ought to be* is derived from what *is*. . . . Nature is not a moral agent; we do not imitate nature for interhuman conduct. But nature is a place of satisfactory fitness, and we take that as a criterion for some moral judgments. We endorse a painful good (Rolston 1988: 58–59).

Behind this sharp dualism between what is appropriate for human ethics and what is right in our dealings with nonhuman nature is Rolston's carefully articulated defense of drawing environmental "ought" from environmental "is." He knows perfectly well that an elementary principle in logic rules out allowing more in one's conclusion than is present in one's premises. This is the main basis for the hoary truism that one cannot derive prescriptive from purely descriptive statements. But Rolston is not making such an elementary mistake: on the contrary, his key thesis is that the environmental "is" *contains* value. When he writes of "satisfactory" fitness, he has already taken the first step toward a *normative description* of nature.

This step is followed by many others, as Rolston goes on to maintain that there are intrinsic values not only in *individual organisms* but also in such collectivities as *species* and *ecosystems* and, indeed, in *nature itself*, the evolving rush toward complex order and diversity that finally equals "systemic beauty" (Rolston 1988: 241). If one adds the nearly tautological principle "that one ought to protect values" (Rolston 1988: 231), then the basis for environmental duties is grounded in the ontology of the environment itself. These will be duties that human beings, as moral agents, will often find jarring and contrary to *prima facie* species interests. This will be hard to deal with, so accustomed have we become in the modern thought-world to assume anthropocentric priority in all matters. But in the postmodern world, if there is to be a healthy future for human beings at all, we must become accustomed to finding human interests trumped by other considerations in which "liberation" reaches out beyond culture and includes nature as well.

These are some of the value-movements that indicate, if we give heed, that our moment in history is a transition time between more radically new attitudes toward—and understandings of—ourselves, our civilization, and our environment, than have arisen in hundreds of years. Those I have chosen to describe are not the only ones, of course. Another is the "animal liberation" movement, which has been gaining strength in the latter years of the twentieth century. This is not properly to be included under the environmentalist movement, as is sometimes supposed. It is no less nonanthropocentric in its values (and often misanthropic as well) and therefore counts as a radical challenge to the modern worldview; but it does not share with environmentalism the central valuation of flourishing ecosystems and general biotic health. Instead, it focuses its value concerns on individual animals, confined in scientific laboratories or raised for fur or food. These are important value questions (Ferré 1986: 391–406), but they are not the same questions raised by environmentalists. Indeed, the preachments of the animal liberation movement may sometimes conflict with the preachments of environmentalists, as when Rolston argues that humans have no duties to relieve the sufferings of nature, or when he and other environmentalists support the practice of hunting when animal populations grow unhealthily large.

Such conflicts hint that the value-movements toward a postmodern world are not all leading in the same direction. There are problems and conflicts within as well as between the movements. I refer not just to the obvious abrasions between male-generated liberation theologies and feminism, or between the theorizing trends in both movements and poststructuralism's disdain for "totalizing" theories, or between the anthropocentric tendencies in all three and the vigorous nonanthropocentrism of environmental and animal rights movements. I refer also to the internal problem of *consistency* within deep ecology's self-defeating species egalitarianism and the internal problem of *coherence* within Rolston's unresolved ethical dualism between "human" and "environmental" ethics. How shall we understand and move to resolve matters when these merely different principles conflict? They inevitably will clash whenever legitimate duties to the well-being of the environment must be weighed against equally legitimate duties to the well-being of humans, for example, when the poor in developing nations denude endangered forests to meet minimal subsistence needs for human dignity.

Inconsistency and incoherence are challenges for theory. This chapter has been a propaedeutic to theory. In it, I have given some definition to the elusive notion of the postmodern, mainly in terms of current revolutions in value that call for fresh thinking about reality. This will provide context for my suggestions on metaphysical ideas adequate for a future world shaped by these values.

10

TOWARD AN ECOLOGICAL
WORLD MODEL

Suggesting the outlines of a theory of reality adequate for a postmodern sensibility is no simple task; but it may be given initial focus by reviewing the agenda of concerns rising from the previous chapter. The trajectory of each of those postmodern movements, whether considered separately or in combination, is toward a deeply different world, not merely toward a fixed-up version of the modern. Profoundly different requirements for theory than those sought by the modern materialists and even by most of their opponents are now laid down.

One key change is stressed by the poststructuralists. However it may be spelled—"*différance*," or "*différend*," or merely "difference"—the modern age of homogenization under lifeless abstractions (particularly though not exclusively drawn from the sciences) is passionately challenged on behalf of a postmodern sensibility that will revel in the subtleties of particularity. Non-quantifiable qualities should be noticed and affirmed in all their variety. Pluralism and respect for otherness should be honored over hegemonic consensus, particularly over the tyranny of quantifying modes of thought.

In company with this healthy revolt against much that is central to modern materialism, there came what I consider an unfortunate overreaction against "totalizing" theories *in general*. Besides this reaction itself being a "totalizing" judgment, and therefore problematic on its own terms if adopted, it is not clear that such wholesale negative reaction is necessary or appropriate. It generalizes too unguardedly from the application (or misapplication) of *some* general theories of reality to what *all* theories of reality must be like. It similarly generalizes from what modern science, genesis of the dominant modern worldview, *has* been like to what all science *must* be like.

But this issue can hardly be debated in the abstract (especially on post-structuralist principles), which means the proof of this pudding can only come later, with its eating. In Chapter 12, I shall raise again the question whether theories aimed at providing conceptual wholeness, while remaining open to experiential evidence in its rich fullness, are more "oppressive" or more "liberating" to human beings who construct them as finite dwelling places for thought and life. But first we shall need to look at an example, soon to be suggested in this chapter and the next.

Liberation theologians, though themselves not much interested in theory, remind us that when we turn to our theorizing, we had better not forget to make a significant place for social justice and injustice on the human scale of reality. Liberationists focus on people in poverty and on the margins of history. In this, they challenge us in our theorizing not to lose sight of persons, those beings in our kosmos capable of the most exquisite suffering no less than of unparalleled feats of creativity. I accept this as an important reminder to "do justly" by persons in any adequate postmodern metaphysics.

Feminist thinkers require us, in any postmodern theory of reality, to pay adequate heed to the importance of relationships, community, cooperation, and networks of interdependence among entities. These, feminists argue, are more fundamental than the atomistic individualism, competition, and hierarchy that have been primary components of the modern (patriarchal) worldview. If the modern worldview has provided a version of reality hospitable to analysis, the postmodern should be capable of supporting holism.

No less holistic in outlook, environmentalists (in concert with all ecofeminists and most animal liberationists) insist that the web of connections must go far beyond the human situation and fully involve the natural order. The human, personal dimension must be shown intimately related to and continuous with at least the biosphere, of which we are a functioning part, and preferably the entire natural environment, living and nonliving.

These postmodern value-preferences—for *qualitative uniqueness, personal integrity, moral responsibility, social justice, essential relatedness,* and *holistic attitudes toward nature*—need not be affirmed at the expense of the classical metaphysical values—*conceptual unity* (coherence) and *honesty before the evidence* (adequacy)—that we have found implicit in theories of reality from the earliest Greek pioneering days. Indeed, embracing these values does not even logically require rejecting help from mathematical abstractions, as long as such help is given without dominating the explanatory process. Likewise, none of these values, alone or together, rules out the use of analytical methods, as long as such analysis is maintained as a tool in the service of larger coherent understanding. I am aware that the contrary is often maintained. "Essential relatedness," some think, is the mortal enemy of conceptual analysis. Some who consider themselves "holists" make a special point of denouncing and excluding analytical methods in principle. But this is an unfortunate mistake, perhaps born of excess zeal or party spirit. It simply sets up a new dichotomy between "analysis" and "holism" while aiming to get beyond all such dichotomies. This is self-defeating. "Holistic" thinking, as it will be used here, is not "anti-" analytical, but is no more (nor less) than the expression of the ancient quest for coherence. As such, it should be large enough to include analysis in its appropriate clarifying place rather than excluding it.

But with these remarks I am getting ahead of my argument itself, in which I aim to show how new paradigms of scientific thinking may serve to help metaphysical theorizing avoid premature either/or conflicts like this one. In the latter part of this chapter and in the next, I shall outline a metaphysical position that I believe is capable of grounding a postmodern worldview which is attuned to and makes sense of the urgent values of many who are in search of a postmodern world.

POSTMODERN ECOLOGICAL SCIENCE

Theories of reality ignore science at their peril. Science of course changes; this is one of the most important facts about science. I am referring not only to the constant stream of novel ideas, fresh discoveries, revised hypotheses, and the like that constitutes the lifeblood of the sciences we see around us at any given time. Nor am I referring only to those occasional revolutions (Kuhn 1970) that set a given science in unexpected new directions or into changed frameworks, as in the revolution from phlogiston chemistry to oxygen chemistry, or in the revolution from Newton's to Einstein's concepts of space and time. I am referring to even larger changes in *what science itself is taken to be*, as in the epoch-making shift from premodern admiration for modes of understanding, grounded in the qualitative categories of Plato and Aristotle, to modern quantitative mechanism.

As we saw in Part Two of this book, the megarevolution that brought out this earlier realignment of viewpoint and values did not happen all at once. In the thinking of Copernicus (surprisingly for those who take him as the "first of the modern" scientists), it did not happen at all. Even in Newton, if we recall his esoteric reflections, the full shift to the so-called "Newtonian worldview" had not occurred.

We should not be taken aback, recalling the messiness of that previous historical transition, by the conflicting currents in our own period of change. Instead, we should expect to see old and new mixed together—sometimes even in the same person (as in Copernicus and Newton). What I am about to suggest should be read in that context. The situation in the sciences today is extremely complex. My treatment of it is a great simplification—deliberately. I want to try a thought-experiment that may throw an interesting anticipation of order on a domain where order is still not clearly formed.

What if astronomy and physics—Copernicus and Newton—had not been such early, triumphant sciences? Consider astronomy. What if Earth's atmosphere had been a bit more moist and warm, so that our skies were constantly overcast with thick layers, miles deep, of cloud? Then there would never have been a chance to watch and ponder the great, remote regularities of the fixed stars or to have been goaded into curiosity by the slight irregularities of the planets or by the phases of the moon. Observational astronomy is, after all, immensely *simple* in its noble cycles. It is a domain of negligible friction. We cannot interfere; nothing seems able to interfere. It is perfectly insulated from earthly life. It is a domain of vast *order*, with only rare, tantalizing exceptions. But there are *changes*, night to night, month to month, season to season, year to year. Even amid these stately changes, order can be found after long inspection and reflection. What more perfect subject matter for the first attempt at a science? But what if we had never been able to see the stars and planets? In a world with billowing clouds above and buzzing bees below, would anyone have had the inspiration to see order within the constant flux?

Without astronomy to lead the way, would the regularities of falling objects have drawn us into a physics of dynamics? Leaves and sticks and stones and snowflakes fall with such apparent diversity of manner, perhaps a young Galileo unversed in the friction-free motions of celestial objects would have had a much harder time even searching for laws of terrestrial motion. Perhaps the swinging chandelier would still have inspired him. It is as close to an isolated system of extremely *simple* but highly *regular* visible *change* as one is likely to get in the interconnected world of everyday life. The pendulum is attached to the rest of the world at only one point. A heavy chandelier indoors is not likely to be affected by strong gusts of wind. The pendulum is ideally hung in a vacuum. But by what right do we skip back and forth between a real chandelier, hanging on a heavy chain, bedecked with candles, set in motion by an acolyte, on the one hand, and an ideal pendulum, on the other? Without the *habit* of simplification, of ideal abstraction, of mental games and thought-experiments, Galileo might well have missed his chance with the pendulum; and without the pendulum ("seen" as constrained falling motion) the prospects of thinking abstractly about falling motion, with or without control by inclined planes and in the absence of all interfering forces, such as air resistance—how likely are they to have occurred?

Astronomy and physics triumphed interdependently, as we recall from the narrative of Part Two. Perhaps the reason for their triumph, we may now consider, was that they were comparatively *easy* fields to conquer. Physics scraped away most of the complexities of the world of everyday life—mere "secondary qualities" were to be systematically ignored and so were "interfering forces"—after which it posed its problems and framed its answers in admiring imitation of the serenely isolated regularities found in astronomy. This is not to say that the real physical world is simple, only that the methods and explanatory ideals adopted by physicists made the conceptual world of physics (comparatively) simple, (comparatively) easy to fit into whole numbers and regular geometrical structures. It should also be added that the entities of the physical world are more patient of being simplified in this way than the far more unruly entities of the bio-psycho-social world.

The atmosphere of Earth is (fortunately) not opaque like that of Venus, and the stars and planets have been allowed to fascinate human observers since time out of mind. What is more, the modern megarevolution actually occurred; unsurprisingly, we late moderns find now that the most admired (and imitated) science is physics. It is "basic" we are told, because it tells us what things are like once their complexities have been scraped away. (The complexities are thus assumed to be negligible.) It is also held to be basic because it is the most mathematical of the sciences, the rest of which yearn, as a result, to quantify and abstract as much as possible.

Now for the next step on this thought-experiment: consider a world of thought and values in which the leading science is not physics but ecology. Suppose once more that astronomy and physics had not risen first. The path of great simplification, we shall imagine, was blocked. What then? If we imagine human curiosity and intelligence are such that science still rises, but if we are forced to suppose a wholly different route to scientific understanding—through complexity rather than simplicity—we come to something distinctly resembling ecological thinking.

This is, of course, not how ecology really began. It rose out of modern science. Even before the name was coined in 1869 by Ernst Haeckel (1834–1919) in Germany, Antoni van Leeuwenhoek (1632–1723), the early microscopist, had done pioneering work on the food chain and on population regulators (Odum 1971: 3). Still, in many ways, the "soul" of ecology is not comfortable and has never been comfortable in the "household" of modern scientific values. It need not be "anti-" modern science, since it can make use of many of its tools and techniques. But it is the antithesis of modern physics in a number of ways.

One of these ways I have indicated already in a playful way, by my cloudy thought-experiment: Physics seeks the great simplicities and gives itself license to treat as negligible all the infinite swarm of complexities that surround us in real life. Quite the opposite, ecology must *deal with complexities*, on pain of not doing its fundamental job which is, as ecologist Eugene Odum puts it, to "study the relation of organisms or groups of organisms to their environment . . ." (Odum 1971: 3). Plainly, the notion of *relationship* is at the heart of the ecological task. Relations are sought and valued (are *not* to be scraped away) among organisms and between living forms and inorganic environment. Odum, a seminal figure in twentieth-century ecology, finally wraps everything together, defining ecology as "the study of the structure and function of nature, it being understood that mankind is a part of nature" (Odum 1971: 3).

Another difference is observed by Odum's last proviso: *humankind, for ecology, is properly part of nature.* Physics excludes human activity from its essential subject matter. It studies nature as though there were no humans or as though humans had never evolved; ecology takes the human species as among its problems, as part of the nature it seeks to understand. Physics, therefore, can rest satisfied with the great impersonalities praised by Einstein, as we saw, content to give no account of the place of mind (or purpose or selfishness or nobility) in the highly abstract scheme over which it presides. That is much too simple for ecology, which needs to consider the pollution-prone heedlessness of the human animal (and also the morally responsive conserver) as one part of its essential subject-matter, linking organisms with environments.

To those familiar firsthand with ecological science, it will have been evident for some time that I am using a normative definition of "ecology." At the present time, when evidence is mixed about trends to the future and when new and old coexist in the same faculty, in the same field project, even in the same person, it is impossible to give a single meaning to a protean word like "ecology" without adopting a norm. This is ably shown in histories of ecology like Donald Worster's engaging *Nature's Economy: The Roots of Ecology* (Worster 1977) and the penetrating study, *A History of the Ecosystem Concept in Ecology: More Than the Sum of its Parts*, by Frank B. Golley (Golley 1993). Those who know the field are aware of the enormous pressures exerted on ecologists by the institutions of the modern world—especially university structures, including departmental interests, promotions criteria, curriculum requirements, etc.—to aim for short-term results that can be published and rewarded in our "normal" ways. Equal or even greater pressures are more subtle: the pressures to conform to modern reductionist/specialist ideals of scientific method, prestige, and "excellence." These pressures are hard to resist. In Europe, except during the International Biological Program (1966–1974) funded generously through the United States National Science Foundation, there has never been much enthusiasm for the holistic, ecosystematic definition of ecology. The rigid university structures of France and the United Kingdom militate against interdisciplinarity even more powerfully than in the United States. In Russia, shortly after the Revolution, promising early developments toward ecosystem ecology were destroyed later by anthropocentric party-liners allied with T. D. Lysenko (1898–1976), who could not tolerate the idea of natural limits to human exploitation. In Germany, the echoes of Nazi abuses of the "organismic" concepts implicit in ecosystem ecology made postwar ecologists wary of anything that might be taken even mistakenly as allied to the Third Reich (Golley 1993: 169–84).

My understanding of "ecology," therefore, is at present mainly exemplified in American settings; and it must be admitted that in the United States it stands far from unchallenged. Still, it is my choice for definition of the field. It may be beset and harried in the present by the powers that be, but for all this it may yet be the harbinger of powers of civilization that *will* be. This ecosystematic understanding of ecology was largely inspired by Eugene Odum's epoch-making text in 1953. Thanks to this book, *Fundamentals of Ecology*, Odum has routinely been identified as "the father of modern ecology." In the usage of this book, I would prefer to amend that intended compliment to "the father of *postmodern* ecology." There is little of the characteristically "modern" in Odum's portrayal of his field, and much that can be recognized as "postmodern."

The key to ecological science, on this definition, is relationship. Systems are networks of relations. Ecosystems are domains of relationships among plants and animals and between these biota and the inorganic environment: chemicals, energy, atmosphere, water, soils, etc. The proper study for ecology defined ecosystematically is the totality of these relationships. This involves not only subfields in biology of every sort (bacteriology, ornithology, botany, entomology, etc., plus genetics, developmental biology, molecular biology, etc.) but also the knowledge brought by geology, geography, oceanography, limnology, biochemistry, chemistry, meteorology, soil science, etc.; and, to deal with the large units represented by many ecosystems, it requires high technologies like "tracer methodology, mass chemistry (spectrometry, colorimetry, chromatography, etc.) remote sensing, automatic monitoring, mathematical modeling, and computer technology . . ." (Odum 1971: 6).

Here is no cry to return to something premodern. Fully state-of-the-art research is called for, but it requires ecologists to go far beyond the specialist, linear modes of thinking characteristic of the modern worldview and its off-spring/defender, the modern university. In this, ecosystem ecology is neither premodern nor modern but fully postmodern: ecology so defined will use the latest, refined discoveries and instruments of modern approaches, including mathematics and computers, but will use them in integrative ways worthy of premodern ideals, emphasizing the working together of domains of knowledge to match the working together of biological and physical relationships in nature.

Studying such large complexities is immensely difficult of course. For one thing, no single individual, however talented and energetic, can possibly bring enough knowledge to bear on such research. Appropriate to its own mission to study relations in nature, ecosystem ecology is essentially bound to the reality of human relations: in teamwork, sharing, and mutual assistance. This sounds (and can be) a wonderful opportunity for development of trust and personal growth in a community; but in a competitive culture of individual rewards for individual work, this is an initial burden. Moreover, the practical problem of harnessing short-term graduate assistants to long-term, large-scale projects is acute. As Golley wryly observes, "doctoral students, the work horses of university research, could not easily undertake the study of an ecosystem as a thesis topic" (Golley 1993: 6).

Interestingly, the problem of long-term research required for any serious study of units as large and slow as ecosystems was nervously understood in the United States by the Atomic Energy Commission, saddled with radiation products with half-lives measured in millennia, far better than by most universities, whose promotion and tenure committees demand regular published results not easily obtained while "thinking like a mountain." Odum was able to tap this understanding with successful long-term grant proposals suitable for ecosystematic ecological studies of large, protected areas for long periods of time. Perhaps, ironically, these threatening products of modern science's paradigmatic technologies have stimulated some of the most important and fruitful ongoing activities of postmodern ecological science. In addition, following the completion of the International Biological Program with its many important results, the American National Science Foundation established regular avenues of funding for ecosystematic ecology. Thus, through its agencies, the AEC and the NSF, the United States' government—bastion of modernity—may yet turn out to have played the crucial role in nurturing postmodern science through the present transition era.

Stressing *complexities of relationships* rather than simplicities in isolation, studying *significant wholes* rather than concentrating on parts, requiring *long timespans* rather than quick payoffs, necessitating *interdisciplinarity and teamwork* rather than specialization and competition, involving the human phenomenon (values and all) rather than isolating the knower from the known—these are some of the key features of ecology that mark it postmodern and continue to make it vulnerable institutionally and ideologically in the modern setting. Two more features I shall note here constitute fundamental conceptual issues, leading us back to metaphysics. Both are highly problematic from the modern point of view.

The first raises again the old problem of determinism. Can ecology (in principle at least) make firm, confident predictions based on deterministic laws? An early attempt in 1916 to give an affirmative answer to this crucial question was made by the American ecologist Frederic Clements (1874–1945), who described the succession of plant species in a given area (e.g., a forest recovering from a fire) as fully determined by biological processes, modifying the environment and progressing invariably toward one and only one end state that is stable and self-perpetuating, a so-called "climax" state (Clements 1916). In an important sense, Clements' influential "climax theory" of succession superimposed the Newtonian world-machine image on the biological world. In this respect, it could be comfortably included within the modern household of sciences.

Postmodern ecology, however, can find no such comfort. On closer examination of the real complexities of ecosystems, machine-inspired images of inevitable progressions and deterministic equilibrium states are not required and indeed seem forced or artificial. Golley notes:

> For example, Bormann and Likens . . . described the variation in chemical export from the Hubbard Brook watershed over many years and have shown how the system tracks the environment but is influenced by its history, its physical-chemical character, and the internal dynamics of its populations. David Schindler and his associates . . . have shown through experimental manipulation of whole lakes how properties of the lake, such as productivity, remain within limits of variation while the species populations that dominate the producers and consumers change (Golley 1993: 202).

The conclusion is that the overall states of ecosystems can be forecast within probabilistic ranges of outcomes but are not uniquely deterministic in the cleanly mechanistic, modern sense at issue. The more that environmental constraints, such as shortages of essential resources, simplify matters, the fewer the probable outcomes. But where narrow restrictions on alternatives are lifted, ecologists should beware of categorical predictions.

> Thus, it is not true that the ecosystem approach requires that ecosystems function deterministically. Rather, it is likely that ecosystems evidence probabilistic behavior over space and time, although this is less true where physical or chemical constraints tightly shape the possible biological responses. For example, on tundra or in deserts cold temperature or lack of water may permit only a few biological strategies to be employed, so that there is something of an either-or situation. Further, processes tightly coupled to energy from the sun tend to be more tightly constrained. Where the biota can be active and diverse, the individual genetic differences and the potential variety of adaptive responses to environment create a probabilistic situation, and the variation in response is as important as the modal response. Stochasticity can be programmed into an ecosystem model, so this insight can influence the forms of potential predictions as well (Golley 1993: 202–3).

This means that instead of the notion of a fixed and unique "climax" state for a given ecosystem, we should anticipate a sort of rolling responsiveness to perturbations. Species dominance may change in ways quite different from Clements' early expectations, though other properties of the ecosystem itself may remain quite robust. More fitting for ecosystems than the mechanical abstraction "equilibrium," Golley proposes, is the more biological term "response."

> Rather than equilibrium, this system is better described as a response system, that is in a dynamic relation with its environment. That state at any particular time is contingent upon its history and the environment. . . . Ecosystems are loose systems, we could call them weak wholes, as compared to a strong whole such as an individual or a city. The changing environment in which the ecosystem is placed (that is, its landscape or biome) creates a dynamic response of the system as a whole. If the environment is changing in a consistent way, then the ecosystem will track that pattern. Further, the ecosystem may have damping and controlling influence on the environment; it has a reciprocal relation to its environment and is not merely responding to it (Golley 1993: 195–96).

Postmodern science will be careful about making categorical statements regarding subject matter capable of responding in a variety of ways to given conditions. Since responsiveness may be wide, but is never infinite in its potential variety, there are many things that can be predicted reliably, especially as circumstances constrain response strategies in special ways, simplifying the predictable future. This position of what might be called "limited determinism" or "qualified indeterminism" makes postmodern ecology less useful than some would like for engineering the environmental future. Others would respond that it teaches human would-be engineers to be more humble about what can be known and more cautious about how they should intervene—and that this is all to the good. I shall return to this debate in *Living and Value*, Volume Three of this trilogy.

The final contentious conceptual issue, besides those that have already occupied us, is already implicit in Golley's last quotation. What sorts of "entities" are ecosystems? Are they entities at all? If everything is related to everything else as ecosystem ecology insists, then can ecosystems be distinguished from their larger environments, that is, can they have boundaries—even permeable ones—that can make them identifiable subjects for study? How strong an internal principle of unity is required to make them a genuine "something" rather than just a collection? Are they superorganisms? Or, rather, are they mere fictions of their investigators' minds?

Ecosystems are constituted by "physical environment" and "biota." Already, these two terms are collective nouns. The "physical environment" is the phrase we use to refer to mineral, chemical, atmospheric components in a so-called ecosystem. The "biota" are all the species of living things that live and interact with each other and with the physical environment in the area of interest. But what of species? Are "they" anything, that is, entities in any primary sense? Do they have properties of their own? Can they "do" anything, or is it only individual organisms that actually do and suffer? Evolutionary theory holds that selection is only on the level of the individual organism, which either propagates its offspring or does not. The modern mindset, as we saw in Part Two, has become deeply suspicious of theories that rely on "forms" and "natures" as something real, over and above particular individuals. Will ecosystem ecology need to battle on this front, too, to overcome the vein of nominalism and individualism that seems inseparable from modern thought?

I plan to return to these questions, attempting a systematic answer for them, before the end of this chapter; but first it is worthwhile to note briefly the sort of response made by ecosystem ecologists prior to explicit metaphysical argument. The assumption is made that anything that can have properties of its own is, thus far, an entity in some legitimate sense of the word. Species can have properties. They can be endangered, for example. This has a significance greater than anything one might be able to say about individual organisms, imperilled in the wild or safe alone in zoos. Species can evolve. Individual organisms do not evolve. To this extent, it seems worthwhile talking about "them" as entities. Ecosystems, too, have properties that belong to them rather than to their component species or environmental features. They can manifest succession, they can be productive or nonproductive of chemicals or other output. They can be robust in their responses to perturbations or not. They can be healthy or ailing.

This does not mean that ecosystems warrant being considered superorganisms, as some suggest. As Golley says, ecosystems make up "weak wholes." They have no organs of sensation or reproduction. They have no nervous system, though chemical and other information paths can be traced, often involving feedback loops of great importance. They have no equivalent of skins to make a neat boundary. This does not mean that boundaries are impossible to draw. Often lakes are chosen as examples of ecosystems since boundaries are always more problematic to draw on dry land. But major successes have been scored as well by delimiting ecosystems through watershed areas which can be measured with some precision, especially when low-lying regions of the system are relatively impermeable geologically. Swamps constitute well-demarcated ecosystems and so do large tracts set aside for atomic energy sites.

Drawing boundaries is necessary but dangerous. In principle, for ecology, everything ought to be studied in relation to everything with no boundaries at all. No systems are fully impermeable. Meteorites crash onto the earth from outer space and cause mass extinctions. Watersheds may be ravaged by fire from outside. At the same time, human cognitive finitude is a fact. Post-modern science leans toward omnivorousness but must control its appetite. Ecosystem studies, as we have noted, are difficult enough. Therefore, ecosystem ecologists recognize that their delimited systems contain smaller systems worthy of study in their own right (species, individual organisms, sub-organs, tissues, molecules, etc.) and are contained in larger systems (landscapes, the biosphere), also worthy of study as research funds allow.

How we might interpret metaphysically this pluralistic response from ecology will engage us shortly. But first, to conclude this meditation on shifting ideals of science, I should return to physics and acknowledge that the shift from modern to postmodern ideals and models has not (as I may have suggested) passed it by. It would be a mistake, I think, to portray Albert Einstein as a postmodern thinker. His aims in science were modern to the core. But his genius threw physics into a turmoil it is still experiencing, setting modern ideals of perfect determinism into conflict with seemingly irreducible stochastic behavior in the very small, setting ideals of remote objectivity, at loggerheads with unavoidable disturbing influences from the observer, leading toward theories of chaos and fields of self-ordering energy that deserve recognition as postmodern. Physics, like ecology, has internal stresses pulling in different directions. But if ecology were to become the lead science in the postmodern world, it would not be hard to imagine an ecological physics and an ecological chemistry as well as an already largely ecological geology—and so on through the curriculum, which would look very different in a university where the highest prestige and most resources went with interdisciplinary, holistic studies in large teams of cooperative colleagues. But here we start to dream. The time has come to look more closely at some metaphysical fundamentals.

Understanding Relations

The question of relations is crucial. What are relations? Are they fundamental or derivative? Do they make a difference to what they relate? How are they possible at all? As I have portrayed the leading vectors toward the postmodern, relations are central. This is certainly the case with ecosystem ecology, which I have nominated as the leading postmodern science. Its primary subject matter turns out to be—in a word—relations: relations between organisms and other organisms, relations between organisms and the entire inorganic environment. The stress on relations is no less emphatic in feminist thought. In place of individuals in competition we are invited to see networks in community. The same is true for robust environmentalism, for which the adage "everything is related to everything else" becomes the baseline for adequate seriousness toward the natural world and the role of the human species in it.

Relations in general, however, pose an old problem for metaphysical thinking. When commitment to the values of conceptual unity overwhelm all other considerations (as we saw in Chapter 2 in the case of Parmenides and the other Eleatics, but also, variously, in Chapter 4 throughout the long Neoplatonic tradition, especially when treated by religious visionaries like Philo or Plotinus or Maimonides), the very notion of relations becomes an unthinkable stain on the seamless coherence of the One.

At this depth of commitment, the issue between those who would take the problem of relations as sufficiently significant to debate, versus those who would simply dismiss the question, is virtually impossible to adjudicate. Parmenides, and after him a long tradition, assures purity for Being by fixing total concern on the urge toward oneness. Relations imply multiplicity, that is, the relativity of *one* relatum to *another*. But if plurality is unthinkable (since even allowing two relata would distinguish *this* as *not-that*, and such thinking, involving negatives, is alleged to be impossible), then relativity lacks any possible location on this conceptual map. The rebuttal that all life and experience is shot through with multiplicity, relations, and change is simply disqualified—ruled out in advance as without standing—therefore, offering nothing of evidential weight. For those who revile experience on religious grounds, perhaps, or because of a single-minded commitment to rational order alone, any appeal to the demands of adequacy is wasted.

Faced with impasse at this depth, there is no choice but to choose. This is not quite a choice between adequacy and coherence, since the concept of coherence itself is predicated on the presence of *parts* or *elements* that must be tied effectively together. The choice at this depth, rather, is between a commitment to *unity*—so total that it offers no conceptual place even for coherence, much less coherence in dynamic balance with adequate openness to experience—and, in contrast, a commitment to *making the most unified sense possible* out of many given elements. Parmenidean unity fails to account for even the possibility of this necessary choice, since it fails to suggest how Being, devoid of every sort of relativity, could allow for a *second* realm of apparent plurality, alongside itself. If, *p*, Being were as perfectly unified and without relation as the theory requires, then, *q*, our experiential world would be impossible. But, not-*q*, the experiential world, is not impossible, since we experience it. Therefore . . . ? Logic would seem to require, by simple *modus tollens*, that the antecedent premise be deemed false, not-*p*, since its consequent, a necessary condition for its truth, has been found false in direct experience; but manifesting what in Chapter 6 I began to call "theoretical commitment," resolute Eleatics may simply rule out *any* premises based on experience to save the theory. Such a tactic strikes me as absurd, especially if the *relativities and pluralities of discourse* are used in the domain of experience to convince *another* of the nonevidentiary status of the domain of experience. But absurdity cannot be proven; it is the dead end of argument; it must simply be displayed and recognized for what it is. If commitment to the value of ontological unity is overriding, to the point where recognition of this outcome as an absurdity will not be allowed, there likely is no further mode of argument left. I move therefore that we decide to admit experience as evidence—and move that we move on!

A decision like this reflects basic values but is not irrational. It gives substance to what "rational" is to mean. My position is that it is less than fully rational to base theories of reality on rational abstractions alone, released from the checks and balances of the empirical upwelling of data. At the same time, we should not suppose our data come uninfluenced by our theoretical predispositions or by our mental and physical capacities, or that these data should be exempt from being reworked by theory responsive to them. Just as it is rational for theory to remain open to experience, so it is rational for experience to be put into illuminating context and thus altered in significance by theory.

Making the decision to admit experience—relations and all—is therefore by no means the way to determine the significance of relations. It may still be argued that for all their pervasiveness in experience, relations are not possible candidates for inclusion in any acceptable theory of reality. As we briefly saw in Chapter 7, F. H. Bradley is one who urges this position with great force. Bradley is far from an Eleatic. He insists that whatever appears to be must be included in the one, all-encompassing Absolute. Where else, he asks, could Appearance be but in Reality? Therefore, all experience is to be included in the Real, emphatically involving all experience of plurality and relations.

Whatever cannot be consistently thought, however, cannot be included *as such* in a satisfactory theory of reality. Relations, for Bradley, fail in intelligibility. They may be "data" at the level of naive experience, but they are "data" in need of complete reworking for any coherent theory.

On the one hand, relations do not exist without something to relate; terms are essential if there are to be relations at all. These terms may be individuals (as "Don is a brother of Harry") or properties (as "five is half of ten"), but in general Bradley rests his critical case on properties or "qualities." Individuals are related, if they are related, because of having certain qualities. If Don is the brother of Harry, it is because Don truly has the property of having the same father and mother as Harry. Without the prior admission of some properties, it seems, there could be no relations. Relations depend on the properties of the terms related.

On the other hand, terms in a relation do not exist apart from their relations: Relations are essential for the terms to be just what they are. If Don and Harry were not the sons of the same parents, they would not be the very persons they are. If five were not half of ten, it would not be what we mean by five. The relation makes an essential difference to what its terms are. But here Bradley finds a contradiction. Relations are *both prior and not prior* to their terms.

Where there is contradiction, there is no meaningful possibility for a theory of reality. Relations must be reconsidered as belonging to appearance only.

On a second line of attack, it is vital to know, Bradley insists, just how any relation is related to the qualities in its terms. It must be related, or it would make no difference to these qualities.

> But how the relation can stand to the qualities is . . . unintelligible. If it is nothing to the qualities, then they are not related at all; and, if so, as we saw, they have ceased to be qualities, and their relation is a nonentity. But if it is to be something to them, then clearly we now shall require a *new* connecting relation (Bradley 1893: 27, emphasis in original).

Unfortunately, once we start looking for relations between the terms and their relations, the process will never end, since as relations are identified, they will themselves need to be related to *their* terms by new relations, and so on forever. Relating relations to what they relate is necessary, Bradley says, but the infinite interior webwork revealed will forever baffle theory. Relations must make a difference to the things or properties related; but once allowed to do so, the theoretical frustrations are endless.

On these grounds, Bradley concludes that the very concept of relations is flawed when it comes to describing reality. It may be practically required for daily life, he admits, but it is unsuitable for metaphysical thinking.

> The conclusion to which I am brought is that a relational way of thought—any one that moves by the machinery of terms and relations—must give appearance, and not truth. It is a makeshift, a device, a mere practical compromise, most necessary, but in the end most indefensible (Bradley 1893: 28).

As we have seen, this would be a most unwelcome conclusion for a postmodern metaphysical understanding of the world. Are relations in general really "indefensible" against Bradley's broadside? Two comments at the outset might be helpful. First, if we take seriously the criterion of adequacy to experience, as we have determined to do, we may be encouraged at least that the burden of proof is not on the defenders of relations. The very fact that Bradley himself recognizes that thinking relationally is a "most necessary" device (albeit for "mere" practical life) is an important concession to the pervasive pressure of experience. An extremely heavy burden rests on those who would, in the name of theory, deny us the use of relationality in constructing an adequate understanding of reality. Second, we must insist that our burden is simply a matter of turning back specific charges of unintelligibility. If a "not proven" verdict can be achieved, this is all (at this point) we need. Consequently, if relations can be rescued from the twin charges of self-contradiction and entrapment in infinite regress, there is no further Bradleyan obstacle to our making the concept as central as we like.

Is there a genuine contradiction implicit in the fact that relations presuppose terms and terms presuppose relations? Bradley thinks so, but it seems more fitting to hold that such a mutuality of presupposing is exactly what *constitutes* the relational situation. If terms-in-relation constitute a single complex fact, then it is no less true to say the relations depend on the terms than it is to say the terms depend on the relations. The genetic history of Don and Harry determines their relation as brothers, and their relation as brothers determines that they must share common parental origin. Contradiction would arise if and only if this reciprocity were *not* the case. Bradley's finding some theoretical "discrepancy" in this inevitable mutuality of dependence between terms and relations seems to have begged the question in advance against the very character of relationality. There is no contradiction here.

Second, is there implicit in the concept of relation, as Bradley says, a hidden abyss of infinite regress? If so, even though this would not count strictly as logical contradiction, it would raise a fatal impediment against the use of such a concept in theories designed to offer human understanding. Infinite regress may not be technically absurd, but neither does the never-ending chase provide intelligibility. This worry seems unnecessary. If one is careful (as Bradley is not) to take relations as *relations* between terms rather than as *entities* in their own right, there exists no basis for fear of infinite regress. Bradley, we recall, posed his problem with, "how the relation can stand" to its terms. If "it" has no relation to its terms, then "it" is nothing to them; there is no relation. But if "it" has a relation to the terms, then this represents some new relation, relating the relation to its terms, which (in turn) will call for new relations ad infinitum. Bradley's error we see is in treating the first relation as something other than a relation. By reifying "it" he verbally has turned what exists only in and through the relational situation into something that sounds suspiciously independent of and additional to that situation—something that can "stand," something that can "be something" to its terms, and something that must at all costs avoid being "a nonentity." Yet relations can be (and are) important without being "entities."

What an entity can be will occupy us in the next section of this chapter, but even prior to that discussion, it seems clear that if my pencil is to the left of my pen, the "to the left of" relation does not consist in being an additional item, over and above the pen and pencil, needing to be related somehow to them by new relations at each term. It consists in the pen and pencil entities "standing" in spatial connectedness relative to a framework defining "left" and "right." The relation might be real, therefore, and even important (in some imaginable contexts), without being real as an entity. If the relation is not an entity, then it does not need to be further related to its terms—it *is* the relation of its terms—and the infinite regress Bradley envisions never starts to yawn beneath us. It seems the Bradleyan reconception of relations as necessarily restricted to the domain of appearance has failed. Can something more positive be said?

Relations are not only conceptually legitimate, they are essential for any description of the world of experience. But is that all they are, that is, *our* descriptions, *our* way of making a world of independent things hang together? A first reaction may be to answer in the affirmative. Let us imagine a pen and pencil lying near each other, with the pen on the right. What counts as "near"? This is an adjective that we must supply in terms of human spatial scale and human interests. The pencil is to the left of the pen. What counts as "left"? We are the ones who set up the framework that defines left and right.

Further, it seems to make no difference to the pen or pencil if their places are switched. The pen is just as much itself—it writes just as well or badly—whether it is to the left or to the right of the pencil. The spatial relation between these two objects seems entirely *external* to the terms. By this, I mean (to use an Aristotelian expression) that the relationship between the two terms seems completely *accidental* to their natures. The pencil in itself is not detectably changed by being placed first on the left and then on the right of the pen. Even when we broaden the network of relations, the desktop on which they lie seems indifferent to whether they are there or not. The desk remains the same desk, it appears, whether they are laid out left and right on its top or tossed into its drawer. If I take one and start to write with it, I do not seem significantly a different person, nor are the words I write essentially different because I use one or the other. The pen will lose some ink as I write; but it seems to remain the same pen despite this. The pencil will wear down and need sharpening; its eraser will become smaller from use. Even these relations, though descriptive of parts of the pencil itself, seem safely accidental, at least within a broad range of acceptable variations.

It is worthwhile beginning with recognition of the many ways in which relations can rest lightly on the terms related. Consider the alternative. If we considered all relations somehow *internal* or *essential* to their terms, then our world would be so viscous with the sticky syrup of connectivity that it would be impenetrable for conceptual understanding. In such a world, the pen to the left of the pencil would no longer be the same pen if placed to the right of the pencil; the desk would not be the same desk with the pen and pencil on its top or in its drawer; I would not be the same person if I were to write with the pencil instead of the pen; the world itself would not be the same world with the pencil dull as with the pencil sharp.

Freedom from the cloying atmosphere of internal relations gives breathing room for thought. At the same time, the liberating doctrine of external relations pushed to extremes creates a vacuum in which it is impossible to breathe at all. If terms are not in the slightest affected in what they are by their relations, what can affect them? Spatial relations seem ideally suited to illustrate external relatedness, but this is usually because we simplify our context, assuming (for example) the surface of the earth and a highly restricted range of masses. If our pencil were imagined on the surface of the sun instead, it would be obvious it would not long remain our pencil in any meaningful sense. And if our pen were imagined to have a mass equivalent to the moon's, then gravitational phenomena, normally negligible, would make a large difference to the direction of the pencil's movement, whether it is located on one side of it or the other. We need not rush to say the pencil is a "different pencil" because of its gravitational attraction toward the pen (this is a decision about entities to be discussed later), but spatial relation is no longer a matter of indifference under such dramatically changed circumstances. If we now think about it again, even without such imagined changes, we must realize that reciprocal gravitational pulls are present (even though negligible for most of our purposes) even in normal desktop settings. Could this be metaphysically significant?

I believe it is. It gives a useful hint as to how external relations can be attributed even while the full ontological context, pressed beyond the normal limits of observable differences and the normal range of human purposes (both theoretical and practical), may still provide relatedness. If external relations were the whole story, then no relational properties could be essential to anything. But in the world of experience all properties are relational. This holds not just for spatial properties ("to the left of," "near," "fifty meters above," etc.) but also for all color properties, which are defined in terms of relations of similarity to exemplar hues, and indeed for all intersubjectively identifiable properties whatever. If all relations are external and accidental, then all terms are shorn of essential (defining) traits and in consequence become "bare particulars," completely undetermined by any of the relations in which they may happen to stand or by any of the properties they may happen to possess. This leads to a perfect conceptual vacuum, in which thought about the real world can no more breathe than when stifled in the perfect connectional plenum of unrelieved internal relations.

Somehow we need both. We need to have the conceptual freedom, the "looseness in the joints," represented by the external relations of the pen and pencil to one another, but also the tighter family relationships represented by the brotherhood of Don and Harry. Let us look more closely at what this requires.

What allows the externality of the relations between the pen and pencil? In part, as we noticed, it is a function of our own simplifications—our abstracting from the full connectedness of physical objects through at least the common gravitational field. This is not the whole story. We are licensed to make our simplifications by the further facts that the pen and pencil do not stand in genetic relation to each other, and they are nonliving. That is, they were produced in causal isolation from one another; and now they are contemporary lifeless objects. They are not the sort of things that respond to their environments. Their internal elements are locked into self-replicating patterns with extremely little probability of spontaneity. Their internal geometrical structure is tight; the repetitive energetic pulses of their constituent atoms now need no external feeding; and although the wood cells of the pencil once had an active metabolism, this has ceased. Similarly, the complex petrochemical molecules of the plastic pen have not been alive, responsive in tendrils of Jurassic fern to the energy of the sun, for millions of years.

The wooden desk beneath them is equally unresponsive, which is no doubt why we prefer to make our furniture from nonliving material. We do not want too much active internal relatedness between our furniture and writing implements, for obvious reasons. But when I enter the scene and pick up a pencil, it may not be so clear that I am not at all influenced—or my writing changed in detectable ways—by the ways in which I as a living, responding being relate to my tools. Had I picked up the pen, for example, I might well have written more slowly and cautiously, since ink is not so easily erasable. I might have thought through my sentences with more care. My style might have been more formal, definitive, perhaps even ponderous. With the pencil, I can be messier in my scribble and more undisciplined in my mind. But, by the same token, I can erase and erase and get it right in the end. Suppose I had decided to use neither of these writing tools, but my electronic word processor instead. Would this have made a further difference in my style and in the character of my thought? Speed of expression and ease of revision are vastly increased. It would be most surprising if there were found no internal relatedness between our writing processes and our literary products.

This counts as only a one-way internal relatedness, however. My use of the pencil (or the computer) may influence me and my writing in essential ways, but my writing only influences my tools in accidental or trivial ways, too negligible in importance to be considered "internal." When do we have cases of genuine mutual internal relatedness?

Do Don and Harry, sons of the same parents, count for this? There are common genetic sources for these relatives. The relationship "brother" certainly goes deeper into who they are than the relationship "to the left of" enters the character of the pen or pencil. Their very flesh and blood are similar in vital ways because of the biological relationship. They are, however, contemporaries. They may well have drifted far apart. However similar their noses or blood types or hairlines, these two brothers may have little that would constitute a relationship of mutual internal relatedness. Being the offspring of the same parents is by itself not enough.

Suppose, however, the brothers come to live together, making a household. Then the biological relation is supplemented with a social relation of daily interactions. Don and Harry are not like the pen and pencil: they are living, responsive beings subject to irritations from their environment. After a while, it may be true to say Don and Harry would not have been the persons they are today without the mutual influences—both positive and negative— they have presented to one another. If this is indeed true it is an interesting kind of truth that is neither accidental (it deals with their characters in profound ways) nor analytic (it is not guaranteed by any definitions). It is contingently the fact that these brothers have become essentially what they are through internally transforming social interactions.

This is not so strange. It probably happened to their parents before them. Good marriages are grounded in positive internal relations. We each become individually what we are because of the presence of the other in us, our rough edges are smoothed through repeated interactions, some of which may take the form of irritations, others endearments. In this way, we sometimes say we have become (are becoming) "one." But, continuing the parallel, good marriages had better leave plenty of scope for external relations as well. If unity completely swallows diversity, one or both partners risks loss of identity. "Total togetherness" sounds cozy but it is cloying. "Open marriage" sounds free, but it is disintegrative. Postmodern metaphysics needs a conception of reality in which relations can be real, sometimes strongly internal, sometimes less strong to varying degrees, and sometimes external. With such a conception, we may be able to construct a satisfactory theory of entities.

UNDERSTANDING ENTITIES

"Entities" are defined by the *Oxford English Dictionary* as what have "a real existence . . . as distinguished from a mere function, attribute, relation, etc."; and this may be a good place to start. What old notion lies behind the word "mere" when it modifies "function, attribute, relation, etc."? A "mere" attribute or relation, I suggest, is one that is not essential to the entity in question; it can be disregarded without doing violence to the subject of discussion, which will continue to have whatever real existence it has quite apart from consideration of whatever is set aside as "mere." That is, a "mere" attribute or relation will be (in Aristotelian language, again) *accidental* to the entity.

Arguments over what is essential and what is only accidental for an entity can be of great importance in some contexts; but we should not be misled by our language. These are not typically "deep" questions into the nature of things so much as arguments over how we shall classify something relative to our purposes, and over what sorts of attitudes and actions we should take respecting it. For example, suppose there occurred a storm in which several vessels moored in a harbor were sunk. The harbor authorities have insurance covering all boats in their care. Among the vessels lost was a seaplane. The insurance company refuses to pay in this instance. They claim seaplanes are not covered by the policy. They are not boats; they are essentially airplanes capable of landing on the water. Their hulls and other boatlike attributes are "mere" modifications of their essential aircraft status. In court, the owner and the harbor authorities argue the opposite position: the seaplane is in all essential respects a boat equipped with a hull, a water rudder, an anchor, a keel, etc., and is "merely" also capable of flight between moorings. A seaplane at rest on the water is essentially a boat, they insist; thus, on the night of the storm, wings and propeller were "mere" superstructure.

In this case, no one disputes the fact that the seaplane had a hull, anchor, etc., *and* propellers, wings, ailerons, etc.; what is in question is how this complex entity should be classified. The interests of the insurance company urge that the classification of "essential" and "accidental" properties go one way; the interests of the seaplane's owner and the harbor authorities urge the reverse. No amount of looking more closely at the design of the seaplane will be sufficient to reveal the answer to this dispute. What is called for is a decision. Eventually, the court's (ill-named) "finding" will provide the publicly sanctioned decision that is needed if practical affairs are to proceed. The function of the "finding" is not literally to *find* some new or hidden fact but to *stipulate* with authority what attributes of the entity may be disregarded as "mere" for purposes of reimbursement.

What is "essential" or "accidental" for entities is a matter of interests and purposes interwoven with the facts. The actual attributes, relations, and functions of something are not irrelevant to the decisions we make. They provide the basis for our decisions. Entities "are" the joint product of what we find and what we make.

Is a mountain an entity? It is hard to refuse entity status for such a huge, long-enduring feature of the landscape. It would certainly be odd, for example, to place a mountain—or all mountains—in the class of nonentities. One does not climb, fall off, or photograph nonentities. If having properties qualifies something for "entity" status, as was hinted in the foregoing discussion of ecosystems, then certainly every mountain is an entity. It can (though it need not) have a name; it will have extremely important geographical relations to valleys and other mountains; its summit will have an important relation to sea level, which relation determines its altitude; it will have indefinitely many other attributes relative to its geological makeup, its associated glaciers, its flora and fauna, and relative to human interests like settlement and mining.

Are these properties essential or accidental? Are the mountain's various relations internal or external? Few would claim that its "mere" name, if it has one, is an essential attribute. What geographers (or explorers or legislators) give they can also take away. It makes little sense, for example, to hold that Mount McKinley would be a different mountain if W. A. Dickey, the prospector who named it in 1896 in honor of the future United States President William McKinley, had favored Democrats over Republicans and had left its name as "Densmore's Peak." The enduring entity status of Mount McKinley went unchallenged even in 1912, when much of its south face was sheared off by earthquakes. But what if some unprecedentedly rapid continental drift were to shift the geographical relations by which the great mountain is defined on our maps? Would we not more probably say that the mountain had moved in position than that its prior latitude and longitude had been "really" essential? Suppose, though, Mount McKinley were to emulate Mount St. Helens and blow off entirely its two great peaks. Would it still be the same entity? Probably we would consider this event sad but accidental (in every sense); this is certainly what we have done with Mount St. Helens itself. This means that neither relations of altitude nor relations of geographical location (which we might normally think of as essential) are taken as internal. Is this plausible? Yes, because it is much easier to redescribe the attributes of an enormous entity like a mountain than to suppose it gone and replaced by another. That is a far more desperate expedient when it comes to entities like mountains. It would become a justified expedient, however, if erosion or earthquakes or giant meteor strikes were to lead to the complete levelling of our mountain. It would require quixotic commitment to continue calling a level parkland "Mount" anything. But since this does not happen to the entities we call mountains within the temporal framework suited to human experience, we do not have to confront these decisions.

What kind of an entity is a mountain? I suggest we call such things *aggregate* entities. They are obvious, enduring, made up of many lesser things, capable of supporting many properties of their own, but are for the most part externally related to their components and to their surroundings. Among the myriad components of a mountain may be many boulders and several glaciers. These too are aggregate entities. A glacier may have a name (e.g., the Hubbard Glacier of the Yukon Territory and Alaska), though it is constantly creeping in position and changing its size through accumulation and ablation of ice and snow crystals. One may say many things about it. It may, like the Hubbard, be a valley glacier, about 100 miles long, moving about three feet per day, etc. A boulder too may have a name and, like mountains and glaciers, may support many properties of its own. Among these, in addition to chemical properties, temperature, color, weight, etc., may be value attributes, including aesthetic properties like interest and beauty for humans and practical usefulness for flora and fauna that live in the niche it provides.

Entities like glaciers and boulders are not so hard for human beings to imagine ceasing to be. Just where the essential/accidental line is crossed is a matter for debate and decision. Is a boulder split in half by frost still "the boulder" we began with? If it has possessed importance enough for human interests, practical or aesthetic, perhaps the decision will be to consider it "one boulder in two halves" instead of "two smaller boulders." But if all we have left from a boulder is gravel, we shall no doubt stop referring to a single entity at all. "The boulder" has disappeared. It was an entity but is an entity no more. Its entity status was not fictitious. Like the mountain, it was obvious, enduring (at least while it was an entity), and in possession of many properties and relations of its own. But like the mountain, its status as an entity is largely dependent on human interests, to group the aggregated facts into a unity capable of taking a name or becoming an object of attention. In the mixture of fact and decision, the larger share for aggregate entities comes from decision.

Another sort of entity, one with more claim to internal coherence of its own, I suggest we call *systematic* entities. An ecosystem, to return to the earlier discussion, is more than an aggregate of many parts. What distinguishes an ecosystem from a mountain as such is the presence within the former of many feedback loops which provide the system as a whole relative (stochastic) stability over time. Earthquakes, eruptions, continental drift, erosion, and the like bring change to aggregate entities like mountains, but there is a far weaker sense of the "whole" for the mountain. It is large and prominent but not self-correcting in the way an ecosystem can be, within limits. The south face of Mount McKinley may fall off, Mount St. Helens may explode, and we may consider these "mere" accidental alterations for our purposes and continue to consider them the same entities as before. But this is *our* doing. The "whole" of an aggregate entity is largely attributed in terms of our interests and values within boundaries set by the facts of the matter.

An ecosystem, in contrast, considered within the permeable but relatively self-containing boundaries we choose, has a property of resiliency that is not simply attributed but found. This property is not an absolute, as noted earlier, but is manifested on a number of levels such as energy flow, biological productivity, and species diversity. Negative feedback loops abound in ecosystems. These are the information-flow and control processes through which excess and deficiency are put to work maintaining stability over time. An early mechanical example is James Watt's flyball governor for his steam engine of 1788. Two balls, attached so that they rotated with the engine, moved in and out by centrifugal force and opened and closed the steam valve, allowing more steam when they rotated slowly than when they were pushed farther out by more rapid rotation. The faster the engine rotated, the less steam was available; but as the engine slowed, more steam was provided again to increase speed. The same principle operates in ecosystems. Herbivores, for example, eat green leaves that subsequently are unavailable for producing nourishment from sunlight. The more the herbivores strip the primary producers, the less there is for them to eat, and the population of herbivores falls. But as their numbers diminish, their food supply is allowed to rebound, and with additional food the herbivore population can climb once again for another cycle of self-regulation. Predator-prey relationships have similar intricate systematic relations, though often made more complex because of multiple predator species with alternative prey. Plentiful chipmunks support growing populations of foxes, which can quickly find themselves in difficulty, however, if all they have to eat is chipmunks. If there are mice and squirrels and rabbits, feedback loops become more complicated and therefore more dampened against sharp overshoot and collapse patterns. If we add consideration of owls and hawks as well, to compete with the foxes, even more internal complexity is woven into the total system. And this just scratches the surface of the actual state of affairs.

There are inevitable delays built into the behavior of systematic entities, since the dynamics of systems are manifest only over periods of time. Watt's steam engine takes a little while to get up to speed; closing the steam valves does not translate instantly, because of momentum, into slower rotation; gradually, less steam takes its effect; the slower rotation opens the valves once more, but again there is a lag, though once stabilized it may be small. In an aircraft, the fixed dihedral angle of the wings to one another means that as one wing rolls into a level attitude, its lift against gravity is maximized, while the other wing's aerodynamic lift pulls less directly against gravity. As a result, the high wing rolls down toward the level attitude and the low wing rolls up, tending in this way, by a constant sequence of small overcorrections, to remain as close to level as turbulence (from outside the system) permits. In a heating system regulated by a thermostat, the temperature continues to fall even as the furnace is switched on; and even after it is switched off the temperature continues to rise for a while. Systematic entities are inevitably periodic. Sometimes the periods are short, as in transistor amplifier systems; sometimes the periods may be very long, as in the natural rise and fall of elephant populations. In some systematic entities like complex ecosystems, there can be innumerable simultaneous periodicities at different frequencies.

Describing such lag-times and interacting feedback loops, both negative and positive (e.g., the greater the herbivore population, the greater the stimulus to primary producers from fertilizers, given appropriate delays), and laying out the complex, mutually influencing relations between them all is an ongoing empirical matter beyond the scope of this discussion. What is of great interest to a postmodern theory of reality is noticing and making appropriate conceptual room for the sort of entity represented by ecosystems. They have no overall direction, but are teleological in the same sense that a thermostatically controlled heating system manifests a tendency to continuous self-correction toward the maintenance of a central value. Someone deliberately invented the thermostatic system, of course, and this is not implied in the case of ecosystems. But the striking fact is that stochastically self-determining resilient systematic entities are an important part of our kosmos.

I have written above about owls and chipmunks, foxes and squirrels, as constituting functioning parts of ecosystems. These are common names of species. We often say things about species: for example, that they are plentiful or endangered. Are species entities? If so, what sort do they represent?

Species do seem to be a kind of entity, since they can support properties of their own. Only a species, not its members, can evolve. Likewise, while individual exemplars of a species may be variously endangered (by predators, disease, etc.), they are not endangered in the same way a species is endangered. Animals die. Species go extinct.

Species are not aggregate entities, however. They are not at all like mountains or glaciers or boulders. Species are not like ecosystems, either. Individual animals of the same species may group themselves in herds or flocks or nests, all of which may have systematic properties, but this does not make the species, as such, a system. Species as such are never seen apart from their exemplars. We can observe ecosystems functioning over time; but species, if entities at all, seem more mental than empirical. They can be engaged only indirectly, on the basis of studies made of individual animals. Species constitute a third, distinct, type of entity, which I suggest we call *formal* entities.

Some formal entities are what Whitehead calls "eternal objects," or pure timeless possibilities. Whitehead sometimes (more pleasingly, to my taste) calls these "forms of definiteness." Triangularity, like a species, appears only in specific instances. Sense qualities as well, like green and red, transcend all instances, indifferent to time or space. Species of living things, however, differ importantly. They are not merely forms of definiteness, they are more profoundly forms of life with a history. They are what we may call *temporal* formal entities in contrast to *eternal* ones.

Species appear only in their instances, true, but, as Holmes Rolston reminds us, they (the species) may have not simply *different* properties from their concrete exemplifications, they may have downright *conflicting* goods.

> Predation on individual elk conserves and improves the species *Cervus canadensis*. The species survives by its individual elk being eaten! When a wolf is tearing up an elk, the individual elk is in distress, but the species is in no distress. The species is being improved, as is shown by the fact that wolves will subsequently find elk harder to catch. . . . A forest fire harms individual aspen trees, but it helps *Populus tremuloides* by restarting forest succession, without which the species would go extinct (Rolston 1988: 147).

Likewise, all individuals carry more genetic "load" (more possibilities for genetic expression) than is needed for the individual—often more than is good for the particular individual. But this genetic excess is good for the species. Moreover, many species produce offspring far in excess of what the environment can sustain. These organisms must starve or be eaten. Not a happy fate for individuals, but good for the species.

> Without the "flawed" reproduction that incorporates mutation and permits variation, without the surplus of young, without predation and death, which all harm individuals, the species would soon go extinct in a changing environment, as all environments eventually are. The individual is a receptacle of the form, and the receptacles are broken while the form survives, but the form cannot otherwise survive (Rolston 1988: 148).

The species is not an individual thing but it is real: it goes beyond the simpler formal entities, it is a complex formal entity but also a historical process. At some point in time it evolves from pure potentiality into second-order actuality through the successful replication at the individual level of a specific vital form in many instances over significant expanses of time. Something about its specific form suits it to the larger environment to which it owes its particularity as a form of definiteness and to which it contributes, reciprocally, in sorting out which other living forms can remain actualized in the ongoing process. When we seek to protect an endangered species, it is not simply the current individuals of that vital form we value; it is the long, improbable, and unrepeatable historical process we honor, too; and, more particularly, it is the indefinitely large possibility of more actual individuals manifesting that species' form, and what this will mean both for these future individuals themselves and for the interlocking network of internal relations with other species-processes that every actual species-process mutually influences.

Species, however, have no "selves" and thus no interests of their own. They seek no goals, are not alive, enjoy no satisfactions. Formal entities, including even temporal ones, are not of that ilk. Many other things, however, including ourselves, do have these properties. Therefore, we need to distinguish a fourth type of entity, *organic* entities.

First, to avoid confusion, it is best to make some simple stipulations. "Organic," as I shall be using it, is not a synonym for "systematic." Sometimes the former term is used merely to refer to things made up of systematically related parts. In my meaning, that is not enough. An airplane is a carefully designed system of parts working together. For me, this does not make it an *organic* entity, though it is a *systematic* entity. Being a systematic entity is a necessary but not a sufficient condition for being an organic entity. Further, "organic," as I intend it, is not essentially linked to the chemistry of carbon compounds. As an empirical matter, on this planet organic entities in my sense are constantly conjoined with compounds involving long chains of carbon atoms. This seems not logically necessary, however, and many have speculated on the possibility of silicon-based organic entities under different environmental and evolutionary circumstances. Manifesting a carbon-based chemistry then is not a necessary condition, and certainly not a sufficient condition for being an organic entity. It does tend, however, to be the case for all the organic entities we know.

The sufficient condition for being an organic entity, in my sense, is that it is or has been a *living* system. A "system" as we have seen is a whole with internally related parts. That is, some parts are what they are or in the state they are because of feedback from other parts, which in turn are what they are or in the state they are because of the first parts. By such coordination of parts, the system as a whole is enabled to carry out some function. What then is added by the problematic word "living"? All living organisms are made up of parts that are internally related; all are governed by holistic feedback systems that allow homeostasis. In manifesting these two traits, *holism* and *homeostasis*, they are no more than systematic entities. But living systems have one more essential characteristic that sets them apart from nonliving systems: they are capable of novelty, improvisation, evolution, growth—in a word, *creativity*. This is their defining characteristic.

It is this characteristic more than any other that differentiates viruses from crystals. Both can grow, replicating themselves. But viruses can undergo mutation and genetic recombination—often to the dismay of research scientists seeking a vaccine—which capacity marks them firmly as living parasites rather than inorganic systems. Still, we must beware of positing a firm "line" between the organic and the inorganic. "Improvisation" comes in degrees; "creativity" is on a sliding scale of importance ranging downward into sheer randomness and upward to the heights of genius. Where we decide to draw our "line" (or "smudge") between "significant" novelty and "mere" unpredictability is, as always, up to us—in conversation with the facts of the case. I am content to join a popular consensus in settling on the virus as the entity for which sheerly systematic existence passes the threshold of organic life. Future explorations of other planets or unexpected findings on our own, perhaps locked in the ice of Antarctica or at the bottom of some ocean trench, may open the topic again by giving us new facts with which to converse.

The role of internal and external relations in organic entities is worth reflection. At one level, it is clear that some very strong internal relations must hold between the coordinated parts that determine one another and the state of the whole entity. In higher organisms, the nonfunctioning or faulty functioning of some key organs will quickly cause death. Fortunately, however, not all organs are "vital." My childhood relation to my tonsils was weakly internal before they were removed. Now I have no relation to them at all. Many organisms are capable of regenerating whole organs, showing the usefulness of internal relations established by chemical messengers, hormonal systems, and the like; the fact that limbs and organs can be lost without complete destruction to the organism—the "simple" fact of healing and the not so simple functioning of the immune system—show the usefulness of external relations as well. We remain ourselves, an integral entity, even when invaded by pathogens, wounded, or amputated (something permitted by external or very weak internal relations to toxins and to some body parts); but we do heal ourselves (made possible by effective internal relations).

Organisms are not only related importantly to their own parts. Changes outside organic entities regularly enter into nonreciprocal internal relation with organisms, altering their states. Positively phototropic stems of plants grow so as to bend toward light; negatively phototropic roots turn away. Positively gravitropic organs grow toward the force of gravity, negatively gravitropic organs grow upward instead. Thigmotropism is manifest in the tendrils of many climbing vines, such as pea seedlings, which wrap around whatever they contact, giving the whole plant needed support. Even protozoans respond to orienting influences in their environments, showing phototaxis, thigmotaxis, geotaxis, and chemotaxis even without sense organs. Organism-and-environment form a simple system, often with reciprocal internal relations, as when amoebae detect, pursue, and engulf food particles.

Mention of food reminds me to add a cautionary word on the distinction within the class of organic entities between plants and animals. From a metaphysical point of view, the distinction between them is far less interesting than the great similarities that unite them as innovative, responsive, creative systems. The principal difference between pigmented plants and animals is found in their food: animals cannot nourish themselves on simple inorganic compounds, while green plants with energy from the sun can manufacture their own food from such compounds. Whitehead put weight on a further distinction, arguing that plants are "democracies" in organization, having less central control over their functions than most animals. This seems generally plausible. Certainly we fail to observe animal-like nervous systems in plants. But these are empirical questions, and new facts are entering the dialogue with possibly surprising consequences. Some plants are capable of defending themselves as a whole, receiving stimuli when attacked and responding with toxins or other defenses in appropriate ways. The tomato plant, for example, uses an electric signal to alert its defense system against grazing caterpillars. Attack on one leaf results in chemical antidigestants being produced in others, slowing the grazing process, thereby longer exposing the caterpillars to predators of their own (Wildon 1992). These electrical signals are not well understood at this writing (and the whole area of investigation has been slowed by what might be termed "metaphysical scorn" from theoretically committed modern botanists), but non-neural electrical signalling is known to occur also in jellyfish and hydra. Plants may turn out to have more tightly organized internal relations than traditional botany has suggested.

Whatever may be the case among plants, it is clear that within the animal kingdom central controls over living systems have become highly developed in organic entities. A human body is composed of inorganic (e.g., water) and organic materials (e.g., proteins, lipids, carbohydrates, and nucleic acids) constituting cells and tissues. There are about 100 trillion cells in the average human body making up many different tissues with different functions. The four main types of tissue are the epithelial tissues, constituting an interface with the surrounding world, including the surfaces of sensory organs; muscle tissues, highly elastic and making movement possible; nerve tissues, allowing the transmission and processing of information; and connective tissues, containing large amounts of extracellular materials. These tissues are organized in multiple systems with interacting parts capable of maintaining their specific functions. The musculoskeletal system made of 206 bones and 700 muscles connected with ligaments provides for motion in the surrounding world. The circulatory system, the heart, arteries, veins, and capillaries, conveys essential nutrients to living cell-systems throughout the body. The cleansing lymphatic system, the respiratory system, the digestive system, the excretory system, and the reproductive system—all function in subtle and interconnected ways, mutually regulating and being regulated in their respective domains. Integrating all these processes are the endocrine and nervous systems. In particular, in vertebrates with significantly developed brains, the nervous system provides both necessary coordinating control over these various other systems; and, through a variety of specialized sense organs capable of receiving, organizing, and transmitting influences from the surrounding world to the brain, also provides vital centralized control for the entire organism in response to conditions in the environment. Through this capacity for organism-environment interactivity, the organism itself becomes a functioning part of the interlocking larger systems that eventually return us to the level of ecosystem, where we began.

This is simply a sketch of some of the facts with which an adequate postmodern theory of reality needs to be informed, but even at this level it is noteworthy that the concept of "individuality" needs considerable loosening from its normal modern fixation on an organism's outer boundary, the skin. Under the skin are many systems with their own claims to individuality of a sort based on strong internal relations between functioning parts. But through the epithelial tissues, which allow excretions and absorptions, exit wastes (nutrition for other organic entities in larger systematic relations), and enter nourishment and oxygen and water and information (sound waves, light waves, chemical presences, heat, pressures), which make the lines between "inside" and "outside" porous. The literal flow of material and information among as well as within bundled organic systems should put us on guard against epidermal definitions of individuality, although many important practical reasons (of tracking, for example) make the skin (or chitin) an important criterion for identifying entities. Above all, the central coordination of entities made up of parts should lead the definition of individuality. In cats, which characteristically prowl alone, central coordination is very largely a matter of what is bundled under the skin. In bees, however, the situation may be very different. Perhaps the unit of organic entity should not in this case be epidermally defined. The hive rather than individual bees may be the appropriate unit of organic individuality. What provides the evident central coordination for a hive of bees is a matter for speculation. Perhaps it rests a complex signal-system; perhaps there are extrasensory influences from the queen to her workers of which we have yet to gain empirical knowledge (Ferré 1994: 147–66). At any rate, in this as in many other possible cases, we do well to be on our guard against oversimple models—"atomic" models drawn from modern followers of Democritus in the old "billiard ball" style—for what counts as an individual organic entity.

Such an opening reminds me to discuss, though briefly, the sorts of things represented by such items as molecules (and atoms). Molecules are not simply *aggregates* although whether they represent chemical compounds or elements, they are comprised of many smaller parts. Since concrete, they are not *formal* processes. They are not in any obvious way *systems* made up of differentiated interactive parts and are certainly therefore not living *organic* systems. For molecules, then, I suggest the term *compound* entities.

Compounds differ from mixtures (and from aggregates) in having some characteristic or characteristics that rest on the combination itself. Strong internal relations are present though without the apparent dynamics of system. This type of entity includes a great deal of the world we experience. Water is a compound entity as is common table salt. Both are chemical compounds. The chemical elements of salt are the poisonous gas chlorine and the metal sodium. The compound entity we use on our food, the chemical compound sodium chloride, is neither gaseous nor metallic but white and crystalline and nonpoisonous.

Compound entities can be microscopic or highly prominent in our experience on the human scale. Water is a good example. Water remains water all the way down to a single molecule of it. Dividing such compounds mechanically will not get rid of the special compound character. Water is a compound of gases, one gas highly flammable and the other essential to combustion. Water's own properties, being liquid, inflammable, etc., will not be lost by simple physical methods of cutting, squeezing, or filtering. Molecules of water need a special chemical process, electrolysis, to break them down into atoms of oxygen and of hydrogen, their chemical elements.

If atoms themselves were simple substances, à la Democritus or Epicurus, that is, pure bits of unitary Parmenidean Being essentially uncomposed and without parts, they would not qualify for the present category of compound entities; but twentieth-century science has taught us that this is not the case. We are accustomed to contrasting "compounds" with atomic "elements" and to defining the latter as samples of matter that "cannot be broken down." Since 1911, however, when Ernest Rutherford (1871–1937) demonstrated central structure in the atom, the ancient idea that atoms are by definition "indivisible" (from the Greek *a-tomos*, not-cuttable) has given way to the general realization that atoms, too, are entities compounded from parts. Later, thanks to Einstein, the phenomenon of nuclear fission offered the most dramatic public demonstration of the inadequacy of Democritean metaphysical theory. We now know that the internal relations between the parts of atoms can be much stronger even than the strong internal relations between the parts of chemical elements, requiring the processes for separating these parts from one another be of different orders, nuclear and chemical. Still, there is no doubt that there are parts involved. And in all probability these parts will be found to have parts, until we arrive at the most basic parts of all.

What are these parts? Science cannot now—perhaps may never—tell us in precise quantitative terms about what I shall call *fundamental* entities. Metaphysics needs this category (for reasons I shall elaborate in the next chapter) and needs to be in conversation with—but must avoid becoming the captive of—current scientific theories. Ideally, theories of reality should converge. Working with the most general requirements for what must be necessary for a coherent and adequate theory, metaphysics can tell us *that* we need fundamental entities in general, and even *what* general characteristics they must have to make theoretical sense. Working with quantitative methods of maximal formal simplification and within the artificial purity of laboratory controls, physics can tell us *how* very simple entities—approaching fundamental status—behave in their most uncomplicated environments. Specifically, they behave dynamically, in finite units of duration, with extremely rapid replications of energetic patterns and with many interactions. Hadrons (the entities capable of the strongest internal relations known as the strong nuclear force) may indeed be nothing more than the interactions of component quarks, which themselves cannot exist in isolation from one another. Electrons are periodic bundles of energetic pattern. Photons oscillate sinusoidally in fields across space and time. Are any of these fundamental? If not, what must be postulated as fundamental to understand their behavior, not in detail but in general? Theorists of reality have

immense amounts to learn from attention to all this; so (as the best of the theoretical physicists will testify) do the physicists themselves.

What postmodern metaphysicians need to address are two aspects of fundamental entities that modern physics (led by its alliance with modern metaphysics) has systematically neglected. The first aspect involves the application
of an ecological model of thinking; that is, we must ponder what fundamental
entities must be like in order to function as they do in full *complexity*. How can
what behaves simply in simple surroundings be thought also the basis for the
vast universe of different sorts of entities, including even the creative domain
of organic life, even sentient life—and life, like ours, capable of pondering the
ecology of fundamental entities? The second, related aspect requires speculation about the character of fundamental entities not simply as they appear externally, leaving marks on photographic plates or producing meter readings;
more, we need to ask what fundamental entities must be like when also considered *from within*. What, in other words, must it be like to be a fundamental
entity? What, from its own perspective, would the world of an electron or a
photon be like?

These two questions will occupy us in the next chapter; before we turn to
them, it may be useful to reflect briefly on where this chapter has progressed. I
began by nominating ecosystem ecology as the appropriate model for a postmodern science. It offers a way of thinking rigorously about nature, of using
the tools of modern science, but in a way markedly different from the standard
ways of abstraction, analysis, and specialization that have dominated and
defined modern science. Ecosystem ecology is above all a relational way of
approaching concrete subject matter; that is, it is a way of respecting (rather
than pruning) relations among the items it studies and of accepting (rather than
recoiling from) relations between investigated and investigator. In so doing, it
incorporates in its approach many of the highly relational values we identified
in the previous chapter as clamoring for recognition in a postmodern era.

Relations, therefore, become a critical issue for discussion in their own
right. Are they conceptually tainted, as Parmenides, Bradley, and others argue?
I defend the concept against such charges and go on to defend the conceptual
legitimacy—and importance—of both internal and external relations. Modern
metaphysics may have tended to overemphasize external relations, but the
postmodern theory of reality needs to avoid swinging to the other extreme.

Finally, I show the role that relations play in distinguishing various sorts
of entities which any adequate theory of reality needs to acknowledge. All five
of the prefundamental entities I discuss are relational, but in different ways.

Aggregate entities are characterized principally by external relations
among their parts. That is, they are such that their parts are only loosely related
to what we take to be their essential identities. They are not fictitious but their

unity and identity as entities are significantly dependent on our interests and definitions. Also, their relations to their larger surroundings tend to be external or only weakly internal. Where a boulder lies on the side of a mountain is not normally taken as a defining characteristic of the boulder. It probably rolled there from somewhere else; it may roll on. Even a mountain may change in its external coordinates as well as in many of its major internal features without ceasing to be what it is.

Systematic entities, in contrast, are characterized by at least some strong internal relations between parts that vary with one another and together perform a common function. The entity as a whole is what it is because of the interplay of these parts, and without them it would cease to be an entity of that kind. A heap of airplane parts on a hangar floor—even a complete set of parts—is not an airplane.

Formal entities are constituted entirely by internal relations to specified possibilities. Those possibilities—forms of definiteness—together with our linguistic activities, make formal entities what they are. Some formal entities are constituted entirely by relation to "eternal objects" alone; some, however, like species, are constituted by relation to concrete historical entities bearing the defining characteristics. Formal entities like animal or plant species are also not fictitious; rather, they are historical processes to which we give a name, in which identifiable patterns of characteristics are replicated across time through internal relations with many individuals who relate to one another. They are not, however, in any meaningful sense "agents." And, like aggregate entities, they are highly dependent on our interests and definitions for their delimitation.

Organic entities are systematic entities that show significant degrees of spontaneity. This means that as systematic entities they will have at least some strongly internal relations to their parts, but also strong relations to future and past entities of similar kinds and to their surroundings. But, importantly, if they are to be identifiable entities, they will bear some significant external relations both to (some of) their parts and to (some of) their environments. They must have a character that is not simply the product of their surroundings if they are to be "trackable" in ways denied to, say, electrons. Since all organic entities are porous to their environment, this means that much of the decision on what is to count as essential to the individual organism—and what are to count as "individuals"—will be matters for our interests to determine. There will be far less room for arbitrary decision on these matters, however, than is allowed for either aggregate or formal entities. Some decisions remain up to us. To determine the locus of individuality in a beehive or a colony of mushrooms, for example, may take careful decision-making as well as close observation. But a rattlesnake in our path has a strong claim to recognition as an entity largely independent of our theoretical categories to make it so.

Compound entities are nonliving, nonsystematic entities constituted by strong internal relations. They are what they are and have the properties they have due to at least some very strong relations between their parts. The relations are so strong indeed that they cannot be broken without special chemical or nuclear methods. With them we approach the end of the line. This is not to say that there may not be a point to distinguishing many more types of entities. Postmodern metaphysics is not likely to reject claims for recognition of entity status for whatever exhibits "difference" enough to attract sustained attention: for example, families (social entities), markets (economic entities), tools (technological entities), or the like. But entities, though open to addition for cause, cannot be multiplied from nothingness. At some point, the postmodern theorist of reality must come to terms with what needs to be acknowledged as fundamental to all these relations and relations of relations. To this we next turn.

11

TOWARD A KALOGENIC UNIVERSE

One basic theoretical commitment that has been encountered earlier in these pages—from Aristotle's insistence that "actuality is prior to potentiality" to Whitehead's "ontological principle"—now deserves my own endorsement. I take it that logical coherence and experiential adequacy both require that any theory of reality needs grounding finally in actuality rather than in possibilities alone.

From the point of view of logical coherence, the reason for anything to happen cannot rest on the simple possibility that it *could* happen. Many things could happen, many—perhaps infinitely many—states of affairs could obtain. There are, for example, indefinitely many possibilities for the outcome of my upcoming airplane flight, but only actual circumstances will sort out which of these possibilities become concrete facts.

There may be no strict self-contradiction in holding that pure possibility is the ultimate basis for this kosmos. An explicit logical contradiction would result only if one were first to assume as a premise something like the ancient *nihil ex nihilo fit*, "nothing comes from nothing." But such a principle implicitly affirming the priority of the actual would be just the issue for those who might deny it. Therefore, assuming it would be question-begging. Negating Whitehead's ontological principle is not ruled out by the rules of pure consistency.

Coherence, however, as noted in Chapter 1, requires more. It ties ideas together, allowing intelligible passage from one to the other. There is a radical conceptual gulf between the idea of what is taken as actual and what is taken as nonactual. The actual is often defined as the "not merely possible." The purely possible, reciprocally, may be understood as "the nonactual" (though actualizable under some circumstances). Only reference to something itself already actual can serve as a reason for the actualization of what was hitherto only possible. The alternative would be complete explanatory incoherence—a mental leap without connection. This helps explain the form of Whitehead's previously quoted dictum: "The ontological principle can be summarized as: no actual entity, then no reason" (Whitehead 1978: 19). The circumstances that can account for the actualization of just *this* possibility, in contrast to the infinite set of others left unactualized, need to be actual themselves or they could account for nothing. Perhaps actuality itself is just the power to affect other actualities and to effect possibilities. This will be argued below.

The standard of adequacy too demands the ontological principle. It may be possible to deny the "reality" of experience in some theoretical sense as F. H. Bradley does; but it is not possible without excluding the whole domain of data to deny that "mere appearance" too is *actually* presented. True, actual experience may be misleading as we all know from experiences of illusion or hallucination; we often need to make corrections for perceptual error. But the demonstration of defectiveness in our data comes from additional or more carefully treated actual data organized into larger coherences.

As we look into the question of fundamental entities, therefore, we can reasonably insist that whatever they are, they must be actual. I plan to argue, in addition, that in the process of becoming actual they also give rise to beauty; that is, that actuality is inherently *kalogenic* (from the Greek *kalós*, "beauty," added to the familiar "birth or coming to be" stem, *genesis*). This is obviously a much more ambitious metaphysical proposal, to which I shall return later in this chapter. But at a minimum, something must be fundamentally actual. Other sorts of entities, such as those distinguished in the previous chapter, may also be derivatively actual; but only fundamental entities—being actual in themselves—are "actual entities" in the primary sense, since the actuality of all other types of entities depends on the fundamental entities' actuality.

FUNDAMENTAL ENTITIES: IN GENERAL

Do we need "fundamental" entities at all? If we think about reality at a sufficiently abstract level, may we not simply consider the kosmos on the principle of an infinite set of Russian dolls, a smaller doll nesting inside each larger one "all the way down"? The story of atomic theory is one of discovery of finer and finer structure within every supposed "ultimate" particle. At first, even into the twentieth century, atoms themselves were supposed to be unstructured wholes of pure being whose essential characteristic was indivisibility. Then, after publication of Sir Ernest Rutherford's work in 1911, structure was admitted even in the previously supposed "uncuttables" of the universe. After this, electrons and the nucleus were supposed "fundamental" until complex structures were required of the nucleus itself and "subatomic particles" multiplied in dizzying profusion. Quark theory gives a coherent account for most of the nuclear elements, but quarks are supposed to come in three irreducible kinds. Why not assume that this process of disintegration will continue forever? Why not simply do without any supposedly "fundamental" building blocks?

It is doubtless wise to recall the elusiveness of fundamental entities, especially when the language of "particles" and "building blocks"—the true mark of the modern—still comes so easily to would-be postmodern theorists. It could even be that the profusion of subatomic elements is a function of our instruments for investigating the atom's nucleus. In a way analogous to the demand for more and more "epicycles" forced on premodern astronomical theory by the arrival of the telescope, which provided increasingly more precise data on the motions of the planets, so our ever larger and more powerful accelerators may be creating increasingly subtle meter readings in need of explanation by "entities" that are in fact far from real things. Wave-particle duality makes every "particle" a wave-function, every "bit" of matter a complex packet of energy. Looked at this way, perhaps there is a conceptual confusion involved in supposing that there is one and only one "simplest" and "shortest" wave-frequency corresponding to one and only one "smallest" particle of "stuff."

The reminder is welcome, but Russian dolls still do not make a good model for a postmodern theory of reality. For one thing, the dolls stand to one another in the relation of containing and being contained. There is no suggestion that larger dolls are *made from* the smaller dolls inside. All the dolls, large and small, are made from the same materials. Only the shape and size are different. By the time the size-scale comes down to a few molecules of doll-stuff, shaping a doll from them becomes physically impossible; by the time the scale reaches down to a single molecule, the concept itself becomes absurd.

Abandoning the image of Russian dolls, then, what is to prevent an infinite regress of lesser and lesser parts of whatever anything is made from? This question is not about "nesting" but about composition. Is there any argument that can make us sure that there must be fundamental entities at all?

The answer lies in the ontological principle. Infinite regresses are not ruled out in abstract mathematics where they are frequently encountered without dismay. The series of integers, for example, is infinite. There can even be many infinite series; the series of odd numbers constitutes a different series but is infinite too (and paradoxically half as large as the infinite series made up of *all* numbers, the even as well as the odd). In dealing with fundamental entities, however, we find ourselves not in the realm of abstract possibilities but in the domain of the actual. By the ontological principle, only something actual can account for actuality. Dividing for a *long time* before coming to a stop with something that can account for what is actual makes sense; but never—really *never*—coming to a stop does not make sense. It postpones giving an account, not just for a while but permanently.

The apparent intelligibility of the suggestion of infinite series comes from the familiar experience of having to continue searching, of being forced by the evidence to revise expectations that we have at last reached the bottom level. There is nothing logically peculiar about this. What is peculiar would be the notion that there is no bottom.

Infinite regress, taken as a theory of reality rather than as a mathematical abstraction, implies that actualities are made up of nothing fundamental, that is, of nothing. The ontology of infinite regress crumbles beneath every footing. As an "account" it is simply the tantalizing method of snatching away every account. Since it is the job of a theory of reality to give an account, not to defer one, such theory must draw back from the vertiginous attraction of this abyss and attempt to determine what fundamental entities need to be like.

Still at this preliminary level of theory, a postmodern metaphysics needs to ponder whether, in this quest for the fundamental, the proper term should be "entities" (plural) or "entity" (singular). On what grounds have I been using the plural, in the foregoing, after the mode of the physical sciences? Could it not be the case that there is only one fundamental actual entity, like Plotinus' One or Spinoza's Substance or Hegel's Spirit or Bradley's Absolute? Such a singular entity would provide the needed stopping place against infinite regress. Is it mere atomistic prejudice, some precipitate of modern atmosphere, that privileges plurality?

The question should give pause. I have no special affection for classical atomism. I hope I have shown in Part Two of this book its many theoretical defects. I plan to show in the third and final volume of this trilogy the many ethical problems it has raised for modern society. But lurching to monism is no solution.

Why not? My response, frankly, is a mixture of theoretical motives strengthened by valuational revulsion from the implications of ultimate monism. Given a strong theory of relations, I can understand how from *many* entities there can be woven unity strong enough to satisfy the demands of theoretical coherence and ethical harmony. But given only a *single* entity, I find it impossible to understand how genuine differentiation can arise. Differentiation, otherness, is required for adequacy to experience of the changing, varied world, as well as for the experience of irreducible moral accountability. Historically, Plotinus' notion of emanation, for example (see Chapter 4), seems language without clear content. Is the kosmos merely "attenuated One"? What can it mean to "attenuate" the fundamental entity? Similarly, Spinoza's "modal appearances" of infinite attributes belonging to a single Substance are not grounded in anything inherent in Substance as he defines it. They remain a surd, simply given. In just the same way for Bradley, the appearances of the many are not accounted for, they are simply asserted necessarily to belong to (and mysteriously to be resolved within) the Absolute. In no case do we find an intelligible path from One to Many.

In the end, the requirement that multiplicity, variety, otherness be taken with the ultimate seriousness implied in postulating *many* fundamental entities, rather than *one*, may rest on a judgment of the importance of particularity—and on an ethical intuition into the stubborn value of personal existence not swallowed up by the All. If so, this intuition will need to be supplemented and balanced by a theory of relations that can withstand the disintegrative effect of sheer atomism.

If this is accepted, there is still one more preliminary question to be considered: Must all the fundamental entities be *alike*, or may there be many irreducible types? The postmodern quest for "difference" may suggest the latter. Why should all the basic elements of the universe be just alike when life is full of such variety? Just because something is fundamental, it does not follow that it must be fundamental *in the same way* as its neighbor. If the value of particularity is invoked in arguing against monism, it may seem that a commitment has already been made for variety in kinds of fundamental entities.

I agree with this judgment—to a point. There seems no good reason, a priori, to demand that every fundamental entity be indistinguishable (in duration, in internal complexity, etc.) from every other. There may well be good reasons, as we shall see for the opposite view. It would be oddly arrogant for human thinkers cogitating on planet Earth to demand that all the fundamental entities in this vast kosmos be exactly uniform.

And, yet, there is a good reason to keep this welcome variety within a few basic parameters of variability. Metaphysics at a minimum requires underlying conceptual coherence in order to accomplish its mission of constructing intelligible theory. Coherence does not demand identity among the elements of things, but it does require the rejection of sheer unrelation. If the fundamental entities of our universe are simply different, irreducibly so, with nothing in common in structure or function, then we would lose hope of a common conceptual framework in which to link these elements *together*, as making up an ordered universe. We would find ourselves in a situation analogous to Descartes' mind/matter dichotomy, postulating irreducibly different fundamental types of entity, denying ourselves any way of relating them. That mistake led directly to the frustrations of the modern agenda we traced in Part Two of this book. Postmodern metaphysics—for all its appreciation of differences and pluralism—must take care not to repeat or even compound this mistake.

The answer, I propose, is to affirm variety in development—to greater and lesser degrees—within a few coherence-making categories of variability. Then dull sameness can be avoided without introducing complete conceptual disconnection as the price of differences. The outcome of this proposal would be a theory of reality in which the indefinitely many fundamental entities are sometimes strikingly different from one another, but in which all the basic units of reality share certain constants. These are the structural constants that allow the kosmos to be both a *uni*verse, "well ordered," as well as the realm of diversity and newness we experience.

FUNDAMENTAL ENTITIES: IN BASIC STRUCTURE

What are these structural constants? For one, as a necessary condition of any world, there must be available *possibilities*: that is, those "forms of definiteness" that each fundamental entity rescues from remaining merely possible by actively realizing them in the energy of actualization. Affirming this condition at the outset does not in the least imply, in contravention of the ontological principle, that possibility is somehow "prior" to actuality. My order of exposition here is entirely independent of ontological priority. In considering the basic ingredients in a theory of reality, each is a necessary condition for a thinkable world. Remove one and all are removed. Unless fundamental entities are permitted to be *definite* "somethings," there can be nothing actual. A source of definiteness of character—from sensory qualities like blueness to mathematical properties like triangularity—is therefore an essential ingredient in our kosmos.

Where do these timeless characters "reside" prior to their actualization by a given fundamental entity? The ontological principle rules out a Platonic answer. The reason for the availability of pure possibilities for actualization must finally invoke something already actual. A "form of definiteness" in its purity is a universal, indifferent to time and place—and, therefore, by definition not actual in the sense required here. Combining these forms in a "realm" with other forms does nothing to solve the problem. Naming it a "realm" evokes the language of actuality—realms, that is, kingdoms, are political entities that are either recognized as actual or at least made up of actual things— but this language is (misleadingly) applied, in this case, to what is nonactual.

Two answers, both compatible with the ontological principle, then remain: Either formal possibilities are available because they are all present in pure abstraction in some *single* actual entity which provides a standing reserve for all of them; or, these possibilities are available because they are variously actualized in the indefinitely *many* actual entities that constitute the concrete universe. Additionally, the two answers can be combined, as in the philosophy of Alfred North Whitehead, who, as we recall from Chapter 8, located forms of definiteness *both* concretely in the constitution of the world of many things *and* (as "eternal objects") in the "mental pole" of a single actual entity he called God. I shall speculate later in this chapter about what answer might be best for a postmodern metaphysics. For the present, it is enough to notice that both a "centralized" and a "decentralized" approach seem to be open in addressing the question of the actual grounding of the forms of definiteness required for our world.

Beside available possibilities, there needs to be the *energy* that allows the actual bundling of such formal elements into particular unities in time and space. "Energy," at the moment, remains an undefined term, simply designating the process that actualizes what is not yet realized and turns it for at least a fleeting moment into fact. Energy is another necessary condition of a thinkable world, since without the power of activity, nothing could be transformed from potentiality to concrete reality. Whitehead was inclined to call this energy "creativity." From an ultimate perspective, this is perhaps not ill-named; but the word may carry excessively cheery initial connotations for postmoderns too keenly aware of the destruction that energy can also cause. In a post-Auschwitz, post-Hiroshima world, the connotations of "creativity" need to be earned, not stipulated at the start.

In addition to (1) available pure *possibility* (somehow grounded in actuality) and (2) *energy* to bring at least some possibilities to concrete realization, postmodern vision sees (3) *particularity* in the world—all inseparably intertwined and requiring each other. Therefore, I propose we adopt the basically Whiteheadian speculative hypothesis that all the varied fundamental entities admitted in the previous section of this chapter are alike in being occasions of energy that achieve momentary patterns of possibility and then perish—leaving only their concrete patterns as data for successive similar pulsations of actualization in the future. This way, qualitative differences among fundamental entities may be great, as acknowledged, but these differences reside in the *patterns* achieved, not in the *process* that achieves the patterns.

Let us take a closer look at what must be the constants that vary in any such process. If we imagine the "decentralized" view of the status of possibilities (ignoring for now the question of God), we can outline the basic phases of this process in three steps.

Step one: The newly concrete environment contains within it a number of completely determinate characteristics, including (for example) a particular shade of green, even as the energy of the universe begins a new pulsation in some particular spatio-temporal locus contiguous to this environment. In this moment, while the actual occasions of the immediate past are freshly concrete and the new occasion is still mainly indeterminate (except for its location), the new occasion needs to be able to grasp somehow its determinate environment. If there is to be any account of enduring continuity of properties in a world made up of brief pulsations of energy, this continuity must be grounded in every actual entity by the presence of strong *internal relations* between new occasions and immediate environments. The energetic grasping of the determinate characters in an environment in fact constitutes what the new occasion of fundamental actuality will be. There is nothing until there are the new energetic graspings. There is no entity that first exists and then grasps its environment. In these localized graspings—a vector of characteristics from the immediate past to the near future—the new actuality becomes itself.

At the same time, a new energetic pulse need not (probably cannot) positively grasp *all* the multiplicity of characters that are presented in the determinate environment. Some will be (must be) excluded from the start. The new entity will arise not only in continuity but also in contradistinction. Exclusion of some characters lays the foundation for *external relations* between any entity and its environment. Something is as much to be defined by what it *is not* as by what it is. The vectors of possibility are sometimes present—perhaps primarily—by negation. This fact underlies the independence of externality.

External relations are also assured to every fundamental entity by the causal irrelevance that must hold between any two contemporary occasions. Two contemporary events are defined by their lack of involvement in each other's pasts. This does not mean that the *trains* of events of which these contemporaries may be part do not have causal bearing on one another. If, while I am lifting a book in Boston, a friend in Tokyo boards a bus toward a temple, the two contemporary events are externally related; but (it may be) in the past I have read to my friend from this book about temples in Tokyo; and thus, indirectly, through causal contacts in the past, there may be extended influences between us. What is important, however, is that *enduring* personal entities who are related over time are made up of *momentary* contemporary events. The former are each composed of many fundamental entities and may exchange many mutual influences in their extended careers as time goes by; the latter, while individually occurring, are out of causal touch with each other. In contemporaneity, as well as in negative grasping, we find the basis for freedom and individuality.

Step two: The new pulse of energy swells toward achieving its pattern, the possibilities for which are largely drawn from its environment. During this brief process of self-patterning there can be surprises. With statistical regularity, but no fine-grain predictability, even physical events sometimes startle normal expectations, particularly among the larger, complex radioactive elements. Mutations are common among biological events. Defiance of the environmentally given is frequent among psychological events. For example, even while sitting in a wholly green-painted room, one can dream of orange-flowered wallpaper. During the short duration of this process, from initial indeterminateness to full achievement of pattern, an outside observer must simply wait to see what comes from the blending of present with absent possibilities. While this process continues, since it is contemporary with any observer, there is no chance (for reasons just given) of causal interference or internal inspection.

Step three: The pattern is complete. The last vague spots of indeterminateness are filled in. The energetic moment of determination is over. Actuality is achieved. We can inspect the outcome of the process, as it starts to influence our organs of observation, sinking rapidly into our causal past. From the pattern newly made concrete, a possible future starts to rise. Fresh pulsations of energy, on the way to determination, grow out of vectors of realized possibility flowing from the new actual, to form a new step one.

Even from this quick sketch it is important to notice that the earlier question (Chapter 10) of priority between relations and things related is answered here with a rejection of priority. Relations of possibilities, energized by fresh actualization in the immediately prior moment and grasped in a new pulsation of energy are all that fundamental entities are "made from." There is no "entity" before there are energetic relations. Conversely, however, there are no relations without actual entities which have drawn or are drawing abstract possibilities into concrete achievements of character. To the query, "Which comes first?" we can offer the principled reply, "Neither!"

It is also important to notice that while internal relations provide the essential binding among fundamental entities, there is also plenty of scope allowed for external relations. "Community" between entities, though strongly grounded, is not total. Both solidarity of essential connection and freedom from essential connection are the case. Exclusion, contemporaneity, and indeterminateness of the future make it possible to shield entities ontologically from total absorption in one another, while positive grasping of the immediate causal past serves to tie them together. The latter, internal relations, are more fundamental since exclusion and contemporaneity can occur only against a field of positive relations. This assures against the radical disconnectedness of classical atomism. Disconnection in my view is always limited in principle by the prior fact of fundamental connections. But in some contexts and for some purposes the more compelling fact is disconnection and individual integrity. Earlier events are externally related to their not-yet-actual successors; as they actualize, events are internally related to their actual predecessors. The social and ethical importance of this metaphysical situation will become apparent in Volume Three.

To this point, the fundamental entity has appeared as a pulsation of energy, essentially relational, essentially dynamic, essentially ephemeral. I have looked at it from the outside. I have even argued that there is no direct way of prying into the crucial moment of energetic determination of achieved character, since during the process it must be the contemporary of any observer and therefore out of causal interaction, neither vulnerable to interference from outside nor open to the outflow of information. It will be interesting, however, to speculate next about what is going on within and during the energetic pulse that leads from possibility to determinacy. Such speculations could have important consequences for a postmodern worldview. What might be guessed then in keeping with adequacy and coherence about the "inside" of fundamental entities in general?

FUNDAMENTAL ENTITIES: IN THEMSELVES

If we take the principle of adequacy first, gathering and assessing our evidence before attempting to unify it, we must realize with some dismay that our direct evidence concerning the "inside" of any existing things is extremely limited. We observe the changes of things, their outward behavior, but we never—or almost never—have any clue beyond that level. This is certainly true for energetic events in cloud chambers, where we see the trace but never the tracemaker, much less the interior (if there is one) of what is pulsing into actuality in that laboratory environment. Perhaps we imagine something different when it comes to higher animals, when we look into their eyes and seem to see recognizable interior states of fear or anger or playful affection. But do we really have *data* about what it is like to be even our closest pet—or are we just speculating? When the topic turns to other people, faithfulness to the principle of adequacy seems to limit our claims. We may be able to empathize with our "significant other" if we have one, but can we literally see the world through eyes other than our own? Some behaviorist thinkers simply deny that there is any meaningful interiority in other persons; Gilbert Ryle went so far as to deny the availability of "privileged access" to *our own* more important interior states, motives, purposes, and the like. (Ryle 1949).

Even Ryle, however, did not go so far with his form of behaviorism as to deny personal—even private—experience altogether. Tickles and itches, pricks and burns, he acknowledges, are felt. We are aware of these in a uniquely intimate and vivid way not shared by others. It would indeed have been paradoxical for an author to discuss the phenomenology of experience while denying the fact of experience. But the problem leading to the thorny modern issue of Other Minds and how to establish their reality is this: that somehow we know (or just grant) that others like us have tickles, itches, etc. (and most of us further admit intentions, worries, hopes, and the like); but our ordinary experience seems to fail to include direct information about any of these.

There is one way around this paucity of data. We *almost* never have conclusive access into the interior of existing reality; but one enormous exception—our own experience of ourselves as existing beings situated in a world—provides a wealth of data. This has proven for many modern thinkers (already made uncomfortable, after Descartes, with the place of mind in reality) a true embarrassment of riches. There seems (barring telepathy) no way to gather data from others' subjectivities directly, for example, by reliably experiencing the experience of other human beings; and yet outright *denial* of this unverifiable subjectivity would be preposterous. It would make one's own field of experience—so subtle, rich, multifarious, and *important*—the only one of its kind in the universe, a cosmic singularity of the most implausible sort. Such denial (solipsism) is usually taken to be a *reductio ad absurdum* of which no disproof is possible—or needed.

We must settle, therefore, for indirect evidence of some sort, even to check up on claims of telepathic communication. First, with regard to other human beings, we can cite above all linguistic evidence. People *tell* us they are having experiences; they *describe* them to us with subtlety, force, and in ways that often resonate with our own directly presented states. Further, they *behave* in ways we can observe to reflect well on the assumption that they are receiving information from their world and acting with awareness of it. Still further, if we want to get technical, we can explore data on the human nervous system, particularly data on the brain as observable, for example, by positron emission tomography (PET) scans. We can treat ourselves to a PET scan while performing subjective tasks and see which areas of our brain light up; then we can give PET scans to our friends and watch analogous areas light up in their brains. We are sure, by first-hand acquaintance, of *our own* experienced subjectivity; we can see our own test results as well and hear our own verbal reports. Then—when we see highly similar PET scan results and hear equally similar verbal reports from *others* on their own subjective experience—while it may be possible to remain a committed behaviorist (despite all these data), it would be a severe strain. The overwhelming evidence points to lively experience going on within other human beings, despite the total absence of direct data of their subjectivity.

It is somewhat easier to be a behaviorist in the teeth of widespread evidence for animal subjectivity, but it still takes effort. Ethologists continue ingenious testing among a wide range of species: sea lions and parrots, dolphins and apes, and many more. At an important conference (in 1992 at Georgia State University) for ethologists, psychologists, and philosophers, the consensus among the animal researchers was profound: animals feel, think, plan strategies, and even dissemble. The absence of clear linguistic data (for the most part, but here, too, evidence is increasing rapidly) and the presence of significant differences in brain structure and associated systems attenuates the evidence, but the evidence nevertheless is very strong. We are not just emoting when we look into our dog's eyes and find a fellow center of subjectivity—one that can feel and plan as well as defy and yearn. The question of animal "thought" is not in play at the moment; this requires much careful definition (and relating to symbolic capacities) before it can be discussed fruitfully. The question rather is of subjectivity. Evidence of experience—some level of interiority, quite apart from the more dubious issue of self-consciousness and other higher functions—is hard to deny for higher animals (Linden 1993: 54–61).

Considering the data, how much farther down into the animal kingdom do we go to find evidence of some degree of subjectivity? All animals, even single-celled ones, show some sensitivity to their surroundings, if we judge by their behavior in pursuit of food or in escape routines. Is this strong evidence for experience at some primitive level of awareness? This question is difficult to answer. What the evidence *means* (how "strong" it is) can hardly be supplied by considerations of adequacy alone.

If sensitivity ("irritability") is the standard, then even tomato plants—or parts of them—can be credited with some low level of subjectivity when they defend themselves against caterpillars grazing on their leaves (Chapter 10). There are few analogies between tomatoes and humans or even higher animals. But here in the vegetable kingdom is behavior that might be considered indicative of "awareness" of the state of the world.

This seems clearly not the case when it comes to rocks or water. A rock does not "behave" the way a tomato plant (or even moss) may. There is no data to support the notion that a rock or a volume of water or similar inanimate things experience the world *as* rock or *as* unit of liquid. A metaphysical theory would be hard pushed to claim warrant on the adequacy principle for any such attribution.

Rocks and volumes of water, however, are not the sorts of entities in which we are currently interested. They are aggregate entities—a volume of water being even more obviously an "entity" only by grace of our definitions and interests. A rock, as we saw in the previous chapter, is to a large extent the same sort of thing (i.e., an aggregate entity) as a unit of frozen water, though its parts tend to hang together more tightly than liquids do and to persist longer than most blocks of ice. A rock can crumble; it can split; it can wear away gradually to sand. Since it is not a unified system, not an independent "whole" in any important sense, there is only a prima facie "it" there. We should no more look for some central experience in a rock qua rock (or a mountain or a glacier) than in a species. These examples represent different sorts of entities—the former represent aggregate entities, the latter formal ones—but, in addition to the absence of linguistic, neurological, and behavioral evidence, neither sort of entity is appropriate for attributions of subjectivity.

If there are smaller wholes that make up aggregate (and formal) entities, then might *these* be centers of subjectivity in some sense? The data show that living cells and even different chemical elements can "recognize" each other in making combinations and reactions. Without some sort of mutual recognition such reactions would not occur; chemicals would come together and nothing would happen. Such evidence, however, is of the most indirect sort. All we directly observe is chemical *behavior* watched from the "outside."

Does this then oblige us to conclude that this is all there is? In other words, must we be behaviorists concerning chemicals (and the even more fundamental entities on which the behavior of chemicals rest), but not concerning entities more obviously like us? Our evidence is certainly indirect in all cases, from the human level "all the way down," but it becomes more attenuated and more speculative as one gets away from the familiar analogies that unite people and animals.

Thus, the adequacy principle cannot answer this alone. It is time to add considerations of coherence. What sorts of speculations about the fundamental character of things are best supported by the theoretical requirement to make unified sense of the diverse evidence at hand?

Postmodern theory builders should learn one thing above all from the long, unsatisfied modern quest for a coherent account of mind and value in nature: namely, the unbearable cost of exceptionalism. The dualistic Cartesian heritage, still strongly influential even today in modern assumptions (and institutions) requires that human experience be considered the huge, unbridgeable exception to the character of everything else. The historical parts of this volume were provided to teach one lesson above all: if we begin with this great bifurcation, there is no way back to coherence in our overall theory of reality.

Coherence would strongly suggest that the one precious sample of reality to which we have intimate access should be taken instead as our best clue to whatever else is real and effective in itself. It is our *only example* of the interiority of an existing being; and it provides the *inescapable context* for every bit of data we receive.

When I say our subjective experience provides the best clue for thought about what other things are like internally, the immediate (modern) tendency is to mock the idea that other things have "interiority" at all. Is even entertaining the question a throwback to premodern animism? Is calling our immediate experience a "clue" just a way of begging the question whether we should suppose the issue itself legitimate?

We have travelled part of this terrain before in this chapter. Mocking the idea that other realities besides oneself have subjective states (at all) is, at its strongest, solipsism. Solipsism, really believed, is a pathological condition associated with serious psychoses. It is a tragic condition. The sound of hospitalized solipsists doubting the genuine subjectivity of the persons trying to tend them does not ring solidly as a philosophical argument. Let us assume most modern scoffers are not solipsists. They admit (though it cannot be conclusively proven) the reality of subjective interiority for other human beings; and they may admit it for a range of higher animals. The question, then, becomes: How far does subjectivity extend?

The speculation here is that subjective interiority—of some sort—is pervasive. This does not mean *self-conscious* subjectivity is supposed to be widespread beyond the human species. Even within the human species, self-consciousness is not a constant condition. Infants, daydreamers, drunks at certain levels of inebriation, persons falling asleep, or gradually waking, or under hypnosis, or experiencing mob frenzy—or in states of spiritual exaltation or ecstacy from religion or art or sex—these examples and many more varieties of human experience fall outside (below or above) the boundaries of self-consciousness. Thus, experience, to be experience, need not be self-conscious. We know from our experience that there are many different sorts and degrees of it. In a fully conscious state we may remember our dreams (or frenzies or ecstacies); wakeful, again, we can even recall various stages of diminishing consciousness as we sank through them toward sleep—and to the much-craved period of unconscious experience everyone needs. There is nothing paradoxical about the phrase "unconscious experience." It occurs normally and regularly in humans, and not only during actual sleep periods. We know it happens during our sleep, no matter how deep, when we reflect on the ease with which a crying baby can wake a parent whom even thunderstorms fail to disturb. Perception goes on, is evaluated and processed, even in deep unconsciousness. We know it happens during wakeful hours, too, when we are focusing our attention on other things. While reading, for example, one might not be consciously aware of events—a car backfiring, a clock striking—that can be later accurately recalled.

To say that experience is pervasive, then, does not imply premodern animism, if by that is meant the attribution of conscious thoughts, intentions, and preferences to everything around us. A baby who scolds a wooden block for tripping toddling steps, a pilot who gratefully pats an aircraft's propeller after a safe flight—these are harmless examples of the sorts of animism to which our anthropomorphizing tendencies are prone. (Not all anthropomorphism may be equally harmless; but that is an ethical matter to be saved for the third volume of this trilogy.) At any rate, the present speculation is not animistic. First, mere experience or subjectivity does not entail anything remotely close to personality; second, the entities on this theory that are nominated as centers of subjectivity are not wooden blocks or airplanes. A child's block is not a system. An airplane is made up of many systems but is not a living system. Even living systems (e.g., plants) may not be unified by a single center of experience. Living systems unified by centralized neural networks (e.g., lobsters) may experience as wholes but still "understand" very little. Worry about animism is only a red herring; it should not be allowed to distract us.

Perhaps it may be granted then that human experience is the sole clue we have for speculation about the interior of fundamental entities, and that it is neither absurd nor childish to consider seriously this clue for the construction of our theory. It may even be granted that there is a potential advantage in coherence if we reject the temptation to exceptionalism that frustrated the modern agenda. A single clue with pervasive application is well-positioned, in principle, to provide a model offering theoretical wholeness. Just what, though, does this specific model do for theory? What theoretical benefits accrue from taking experience—diluted, simplified, unconscious as it may be—for our unifying model of basic reality?

A three-part answer is that human experience, the inescapable context for whatever data we receive, is such that it illuminates our understanding of the status of *relations* in reality, the *dynamic* character of the pulsating world we find ourselves inhabiting, and the place of *value* in the nature of things in general.

1. *Relations*. In our earlier discussion of relations, we found ourselves in need of some way of understanding degrees of relatedness. Internal relations are primary, but they must be seen as subject to variations of stronger and weaker, allowing also for the freedom and integrity of external relations. This is exactly what experience helps us understand, since it consists in just these relational characteristics.

Experience is what it is because of its contents; it *is* what is *grasped together*. In human conscious experience, we speak about what is "apprehended." This word simply means what is "taken hold of" mentally; it rests on the Latin *prehendere*, "to take or grasp," which also gives us such words as "prehensile," as in the gripping tails of monkeys or the grasp of human thumbs. Whitehead, as we saw earlier, coins the general verb "prehend" and the noun "prehension" to refer to experiential grasping in general, without any implication of conscious thought. In my own discussion, I have settled thus far for the simple word "grasp," also in a use neutral to the issue of consciousness; but for those interested in comparative jargon, I mean by "grasp" what Whitehead stipulates for "prehension." Whitehead also sometimes substitutes the simpler word "feeling," which—perhaps because of its vagueness—suggests depths of emotion at the heart of experience. I accept the affective basis of experience and may use the term "feeling" especially in contexts that highlight the relatively passive side of experience; but experience is active no less than passive, for which "grasp" may carry the more suitable connotations.

What we experience becomes part of us in a most fundamental way. The contents of our experience, whether the abstract contents of free possibility we entertain in reading novels or daydreaming, or whether the concretely embodied contents of our environment forcing themselves on us, *are* our experience, together with the affective tone with which we feel what we grasp. In the realm of experience, internal relations rule. In the structural language used earlier, experience unites *possibilities*, either free or embodied, into *particularity* by the *energy* of grasping. Without some forms of definiteness, some "whatnesses" related, experience would not be at all. But without some energy for grasping the felt "whatnesses" into local contexts, particularity could not be at all.

Experience is what it is because of its internal relatedness to its contents, but we well know that actual experience does not include "everything," not even everything within the immediate environment. The energy that grasps also excludes. I can fend off from my distinct apprehension the rumble of the furnace and (temporarily at least) the rumble of my hungry stomach when I am otherwise absorbed. What Whitehead calls "negative prehensions" are essential to experience. While the barriers are up, I am not utterly out of relation to the rumbling furnace, but my experience is externally related to it.

The "line" (or smudge) between internal and external is not absolute or permanent. What we find is that experience is fundamentally a field of internal relations in which some elements may have stronger or weaker levels of internal relatedness. The degrees are often temporary, surging from urgent to negligible and back. What we call external relations are relations so weak as to be negligible for the purposes at hand. As purposes and circumstances change, so will our ratings on the sliding scale of "strong" and "weak." At one time, my hunger is irrelevant to what I am focussed on; it is barely present to me (though I may be able to recall it later, if prompted); at another time, my hunger may invade my experience enough to prompt a complete change in focus and activity. I may drop my work to find a snack. Such variability is a familiar part of the dynamics of experiential feeling and grasping.

2. *Dynamics*. Turning more specifically to the dynamics of experience, it is vital to realize just how essentially restless it is. Experience never stands still. Even if nothing in the content of experience changes over time, its affective tone becomes different as duration extends. This is, for example, what makes it so challenging to "stare someone down," deliberately refusing to shift visual focus from another person's eyes for a prolonged duration. Nothing changes except for the amount of time that has passed—and the feeling tone that swells and alters quality with the experience of this passage. But this can be an enormous change.

Human experience is normally a flitting matter, episodic and punctuated. Sustained experiential focus is fatiguing. This accounts for at least some of the discomfort in staring fixedly at another person's eyes—attentively, insistently, for a long period of time. Even staring fixedly at a teapot, however, is tiring. With the best of intentions, our attention to lectures and to concert performances comes in pulses. These pulses vary in duration. Usually, in normal waking states, our grasp can hold together whole sentences (or musical phrases) across several seconds of passing time. Sometimes, in attending to an unusually inspiring lecturer, we may grasp still longer units of meaning, lasting for a minute or more, with hardly a flicker. In the other direction, experience can become fragmented, the pulses of attention shorter and more scattered in content. With the onset of sleep, sentences we hear (losing internal relatedness among their words) may no longer make sense as unities; and even words may fall apart into sounds bereft of significance. As intensity of experience weakens, the frequency of discrete pulses of experience increases.

3. *Values.* The longer unities of experience are more fatiguing, but, by the same token, are more rewarding. Whether or not Wolfgang Amadeus Mozart was literally capable of experiencing whole movements of his symphonies in single, unbroken pulsations of attention (Chapter 8), we can (almost) imagine such a feat and admire it. Its intensity, its richness of detail, grasped all at once in intricate wholeness, mark the experience as of extremely high *intrinsic value.* Our own achieved moments of sustained rich-textured unities of experience may not be up to Mozart's standard, but they glow with an intensity of worth in themselves—beyond the need of justification by anything else. They are, instead, what justify. Other things are justified as leading to them. They are satisfying simply as and when they occur.

Peak experiences may occur seldom for some, never for others, but experiences need not be Mozartian or near-Mozartian to be valuable in themselves. Modestly satisfying moments of experience, succeeding one another for several hours, may make for a very good morning—a morning worthwhile in itself for the experiencer, though perhaps nothing special on the human scale of values.

If experience extends beyond the human species, at least to the higher animals and—as required for coherence—is found pervasively in nature, then the human scale of values represents just one small segment on a spectrum. At the upper end, intense, complex human realizations of experiential elements— what I call Mozartian moments—are at or near the top of the known scale, though, for all we know, even now there may be entities capable of still more remarkable experiences somewhere in the universe, and such entities may perhaps evolve here on earth in time. The human range, though only part of the full spectrum, is wide. The capacity to manipulate symbols vastly enlarges human potential for subtle satisfactions of all sorts. At the end of the spectrum shared with many other species, experiences like eating and mating are open to huge enhancement through the awakening of symbolic meaning, through linguistically aided anticipation, through conscious memory, comparison, and the like. All animals feed; only humans dine.

Nevertheless, there are doubtless many areas of overlap between the human continuum of intrinsically satisfying experience and other experiencing entities. Not all human experiences need to be richer in complexity and intensity than those of other large-brained animals. The joy my dog and I feel when we play may be quite comparable. She may, indeed, outdo me in sheer intensity. More generally—considering humans from infancy to senility and animals both domestic and wild, all under varying conditions of health and alertness— the overlap may often give the advantage to the nonhuman experiencer. There is no single, ordinally arranged, mutually exclusive "ladder" on which the human is always conveniently on top. Betty Jean Craige is right when she urges us to "lay the ladder down" so as to recognize diversity without invidiousness and anthropocentric pride (Craige 1992).

Still, it is hard not to acknowledge that greatly different degrees of complexity and intensity of experience are distinguishable, not only within the human range but also between the human range as a whole and other ranges. Ethnologists sometimes compare chimpanzee mentality with that of human children. To a point, when neonates of both species are experimentally brought up together as though they were siblings, the chimpanzees may forge ahead of the human in discrimination and complexity of experience; but, after a while, the human normally surpasses the chimp. This does not make the human being "better" in any absolute sense, but it does mean the intrinsic values achievable in the human's experience are richer, on the whole, than in its simian playmate's.

Similarly, we may acknowledge that birds experience their environment and that earthworms do too. But we do not need to equate the complexity, intensity, and (therefore) the degree of value to the entities involved of the respective experiences. Bird brains may be small, but they surpass the ganglia of earthworms. We must surmise that an alert bird is far more intensely something for itself, more in focussed possession of a life of its own, than a somnolent worm with its much more diffuse nervous system.

If the living cells of animals and plants are also something for themselves with a dim grasp of their organic environments, we should suppose their level of experience makes an earthworm seem a Mozart by comparison. Intra- and intercellular organic processes are environmentally responsive. They grasp what is going on and participate in it. Their quality of experience, however, is something we humans can postulate but not imagine. The same would be true for electrons and for the yet more fundamental entities that make up the inanimate universe. Even if the category of experience is to be used (for coherence's sake) to describe their mode of relating to their environment, most fundamental entities in this great universe of physical stability must be considered wholly unconscious. The regular, rapid achievement of definiteness by energies pulsing at the level of the ultra-small and ultra-simple produces its tiny share of value for itself. Intrinsic value, of whatever degree of simplicity or complexity, *is* this enjoyed achievement of definiteness from a moment of indeterminate possibility. Yet this is the "blind" end of the continuum, where feeling exists but novelty and subtlety figure least.

THE KALOGENIC UNIVERSE: IN THE MAKING

What follows from the foregoing speculation about the interiority of fundamental entities for our key questions of being and value? At the start of this final section we may harvest a few important results.

First, it follows that values are firmly—indissolubly—grounded in being, since on this theory the process of an entity's *coming to be something definite* can be equated with the *generation of intrinsic value* for the entity concerned. Considered externally, that process represents the entity's achievement of concrete actuality from a larger range of possibilities in the moment of its energetic pulse. Considered internally, it is the triumph of specific character over mere prospect; it is also the satisfaction of contributing some definite inheritance to the future.

Second, by acknowledging that every actuality, in its own moment of actualizing, has a subjective aspect, we break free from the incoherence of exceptionalism. We reject the modern myth of inert, passive substances at the bottom of things. Instead, we build wholeheartedly on a vision of an energetic universe in which every fully actual entity is dynamic, vibratory, and momentarily something for itself.

Third, to realize definite character, an occasion of actuality needs to achieve the sort of subjective satisfaction in which every positive element is related to every other, in some way permitting mutual coexistence. To be something specific depends on acquiring a noncontradictory character; thus, actualization implies that at least a simple harmony of elements is achieved by every fundamental actuality. Harmony does not exclude dissonance, of course; tension overcome in unity adds vividness and interest. The more disparate the elements that need to be unified, the more complex and interesting the harmonies, and the more challenging it will be to achieve them. The greater the challenge, the more valuable the achievement.

Finally, without some trace of subjective satisfaction (at however low an order), there is no value in being. In the absence of a valuer, the concept of value is as empty as the idea of pain without a perceiver, thought without a thinker, love without a lover. If it were not for satisfactory subjectivity, the universe would contain no value. This is true both for intrinsic and for instrumental value, since instrumental values are defined simply in terms of their usefulness in contributing eventually to bringing about some state of intrinsic value. If there were no intrinsic values to be achieved, there could be instruments but no instrumental values. Thermostats could work (for a while) in a world without valuers; but absent some experiencing subject to enjoy the equable warmth provided, thermal stability in itself would have no intrinsic justification. It is for the sake of intrinsically valued experiences that our instruments are valued as means. Even the most finely wrought violin is not valuable in itself. It may (by the way) be financially valuable; but if so, such market value is only instrumental to the owner's ability to exchange it for alternative means to intrinsically satisfactory experience. It may (by the way) be also visually pleasing; but if so, the subjective satisfaction found in its visual form is the intrinsic value rendered. Even its primary function—to produce when in the hands of a skilled player highly enjoyable tones and overtones for listening satisfaction—is sheerly instrumental, dependent for its status as valuable on its constant ability to contribute to producing harmonies in direct experience that need no further justification.

To achieve subjective harmony is to generate beauty. "Beauty," as I intend it here, is the most general term for satisfactory experience. As such, it includes such other expressions as "lovely," "pleasing," "pretty," "attractive," "handsome," "fair," "comely," and even "sublime." I shall treat all of these as distinctions within beauty.

There are many degrees of beauty. In the spectrum of human experience, we know that some subjective harmonies may be much more satisfactory than others. We may be reminded of Socrates' conversation (Chapter 3) with Diotima in the *Symposium*, in which higher and higher modes of beauty are distinguished as lures on the ladder of love. Beauty is what is sought for itself, but there are lesser and greater beauties. Achieving one level is rewarding in itself; but since becoming actual can be only momentary, even for a Mozart, the achievement provides no resting place. Even to repeat the achievement takes further energy; without more investment there is deterioration; against this danger of loss there seems also to be something that makes us restless for increasingly complex and interesting harmonies—an urge upward in the generation of beauty.

Since it is so fundamental for this theory of reality, we need a name for the generation of beauty. As indicated earlier, I shall call it kalogenesis. As we have seen, in its process of becoming actual every fundamental entity must result in a unified harmony of definite elements held together in experience. In this way, every pulse of actualizing energy represents in itself an act of kalogenesis. The universe comprised of kalogenic entities and their combinations is therefore, strictly speaking, the by-product of beauty.

It is impossible to picture what this means at the most primitive, inanimate levels of actuality. Just as the "interiority" of fundamental occasions is too dim for our visualization, so the kind of harmonies achieved in those dark subjectivities are open only to speculative discussion. We need to think where we cannot imagine. Whitehead's suggestion may be as far as we can go. He proposed that the complete contrast between vibratory phases in wave propagation—the sheer "flip/flop" represented in James Maxwell's equations by reversal of sign from plus to minus, minus to plus—provides a maximum of aesthetic vividness of feeling together with a maximum of stability in wave characteristics when these are repeated over unimaginable numbers of generations of inheritances, reversals, and further inheritances (Whitehead 1978: 279).

These extremely brief but reliably repetitive events of kalogenesis represent the vast bulk of the actualities in the (known!) universe. They are inanimate, showing no significant capacity for novelty in responding to their immediate environments. Their main mode is mirroring patterns with the vividness of contrast provided by sheer reversal of field. Yet, over incomprehensibly large numbers of generations, types of occasions have found mutually supportive social arrangements with other types through linking up in the (mainly) stable processes of interaction we call atoms and molecules. The characters of any rogue entities that fail to conform to these socially established patterns are not passed on. Their legacies are eliminated. Such social intolerance is what we describe in our laws of physics. The laws of nature are thus only the habits of actualities contingently self-organized into regular societies, but they are *deeply ingrained* habits. At the atomic and molecular levels of social organization, one should not bet on exceptions. Laws of nature may evolve as the societies change into which actual events group themselves, but the process will be an immensely slow one. Nature at this level is as implacable as it is blind.

"Slow" or "fast," if meaningful, are terms measured by some metronome. Does this theory provide one? In principle, the duration of the simplest and most primitive actual occasions, whatever this duration might be, could offer the needed "beat." Its length is a contingent question open to empirical investigation. It cannot be longer than the shortest discoverable frequency of physical vibration. Is this one trillionth of a second? Is it less? Metaphysically, this does not matter very much. There will be some minimum duration for any universe, for the same reasons that there must be some fundamental entity. These briefest pulsations of actuality constitute the minimum units of time. There is then no such *entity* as time, which is simply a collective noun for many rapid and overlapping durational events; there are only entities actualizing. This actualizing comes in pulses of temporality, shorter or longer depending on complexity of elements and intensity of contrasts. Each achievement of actuality represents a subjective satisfaction, however low the grade; and each subjective satisfaction is an instance of kalogenesis. Time, like the universe at large, is consequently also a by-product of beauty.

Every pulsing element of our kosmos is beautiful to some degree in itself and for itself. Ugliness and loss are real but relative matters. Fuller discussion of evil must await the third volume of this trilogy, but a few words on the subject limited to the metaphysical fundamentals may be in order here. Loss is an essential part of the metaphysical situation in a dynamic universe. Every achievement of subjective harmony is valuable in itself but ephemeral. Finally attaining full determinacy is the achievement that ends process. There is nothing more to do. The actual moment must perish as it succeeds. Further, unless the character of beauty achieved is taken up by successor moments of actualization, it too will vanish. Mephistopheles knows Faust is fooling himself in thinking he can freeze any moment. "Hold, thou art so fair!" is always a fool's command. Loss must follow achievement. It is real, unavoidable, and tragic—

but not in itself evil or ugly. Loss of subjective immediacy is the transition to objectivity. Objective achievement of some harmony, if affirmed by a new present, is the building material for future beauty that may equal or surpass the past.

Ugliness is either destruction of past objective achievements of beauty or interposition of lesser achievements in place of greater possibilities. Vandalism is the type of the former; it depends parasitically on the slashing or obliteration of what past moments of subjective satisfaction have left to the future. Destruction of higher achievements, whether by accident (a person falling off a cliff), by malevolence (murder), or simply by processes of nature, fall in this category. Philistinism is the type of the latter; it depends relativistically on the smug rejection of fuller possibilities on behalf of inferior achievement (it is to aesthetic feeling what Whitehead's "obscurantism" is to thought). Vandalism and philistinism both involve diminution of quality in subjective immediacy, either by forcing discordant elements on subjectivity or by negating elements of potential richness. In either case, we can speak only in comparison to what might have been. Ugliness exists only against some assumed field of subjective harmony with some degree of beauty.

In the inanimate universe of relatively uncomplicated physical entities like electrons, atoms, or molecules, we must recognize that the degree of beauty internalized probably must be trivial. In saying this I am not suggesting that human beings *thinking* about the wonderful formal properties evolved by the societies composed of these entities have less than sublime experiences of mathematical beauty. Physicists and mathematicians often report that these are among the highest beauties humans ever experience, and there is no reason to doubt them. I am referring instead to the extremely simple internal states of the physical entities *themselves*. But even these may not be the simplest degrees of harmony conceivable. The achievement of stable social orders as complex as atoms and molecules by more primitive entities is in itself a remarkable feat. It may indeed be that only a small fraction of the universe has reached this degree of social organization and regularity. Astronomers are still looking for 90 percent of the mass of the universe, the so-called "dark matter." These are empirical questions, but it would accord well with this theory if the bulk of actuality is preatomic.

Out of atomically organized actual entities, in any case, vastly more complex societies, formed through natural selection over long periods of time, can push the concept of kalogenesis closer to levels we are able to imagine. These are the living systems we have previously discussed. Because they are systems, internally related, they are capable of focussing complex information on nodal points within themselves. The actual entities located at those points of concentration have the opportunity for grasping together much richer experience drawn from throughout the system than is available to entities situated in less complex environments. There is nothing essentially different about these actual entities except their locations at the intersection of hugely enhanced streams of possibilities for harmonization based on information flowing within the systems of which they are parts. Given this richness of possibility, the nodal actual entities are in a position to achieve complex patterns, including elements of spontaneous novelty, in the energetic pulses through which they acquire determinateness of character.

All living organisms show this capacity for spontaneity to a significant degree, some more than others. Those with internal pathways specialized for receiving, transmitting, and even processing and amplifying information—like central nervous systems and brains—have the most impressive capacities of this sort; and with these centralized capacities they can become engaged *as whole organisms* with degrees of beauty that humans can also recognize as beautiful.

All the entities that make up the physical body of a living organism are to some extent kalogenic; to the extent cells and organs within the organism are centrally directed in their functions (by some actual entity located at a nodal point for them), these subordinate organs may generate their own richer harmonies and act to pass on their achievements to still more central locations; if such organs are further related by limbic and central nervous systems, these subordinate organs may transmit their own achieved harmonies to key moments of experience—Whitehead calls them "regnant occasions"—that can both enjoy and direct the whole organism from moment to moment. Each regnant occasion's advantage and the well-being of its many direct successors will be found in the continuing health and flourishing of the organism as a whole; reciprocally, the whole organism functions best in its environment when coordinated as a systematic entity effectively unifying its many constitutive entities in sub-systems and sub-subsystems.

Butterflies and bees, though simple by mammalian or primate standards, are wonderful complexes of this sort, with sense organs, neurotransmitters, and central direction of movement. On this theory, it is no coincidence that they are attracted to flowers that are beautiful to them in hue and fragrance. The living world is kalogenic at a much higher order than is the world of physics. The possibilities extended to complex entities at this mesocosmic level include sensory elements like colors and odors and are grasped everywhere (with what could only quasi-metaphorically be termed enthusiasm) by organisms dwelling in trenches below the sea and on peaks above the clouds, wherever living systems venture. Sexual reproduction makes the search for beauty even more intense and gives advantage to decorations, iridescent fins and fine feathers, prowess at dance, attractive odors, and the like, throughout the sexually animated kingdoms, botanical as well as zoological. The universal quest for satisfactory experience, for subjectively enjoyed beauty, draws organisms whether or not their experience (compared to ours) is dim and unselfconscious. At the biological level, we find ourselves within an intensely kalogenic universe.

Just as there is no sharp line between life and nonlife (because the difference rests on degrees of spontaneity)—there are however, clear cases of one (puppies at play) and of the other (stones at rest)—so we should expect no sharp line between conscious and unconscious life. There is nevertheless an obvious difference between the sort of life enjoyed by an oyster and that of a poet, a composer, or a saint. This difference I shall summarize by the phrase, the "capacity for taking thought." Thought in this sense does not rule out feeling; it rests on it and is normally pervaded by it. But thought entails a significant ability to take account of the absent: that is, that which either is out of direct causal contact or is merely possible. An interesting empirical question is posed as to distribution of these abilities beyond the human species. Ethologists, as noted above, are pushing back supposed boundaries in dramatic fashion. Still, it is generally accepted that the human species is outstandingly gifted in this capacity. With no invidiousness toward other species or inappropriate sense of prideful exclusiveness, we can recognize and rejoice in the astounding enhancement to immediate subjective satisfaction made by consciousness as we know it.

Consciousness rises gradually out of complexity of experienced contrasts. The most basic contrast is between what is actual in a given situation and what is possible. When sharply posed, this is the experienced contrast that makes deliberation about the future a significant option for humans but not for oysters. Deliberation over alternative possibilities in turn opens consciousness to moral categories—which future possibilities "ought" to be made actual?

The human brain, with its at least ten billion neurons capable of almost infinite interconnections, is the most complex system in the known universe. High-grade occasions of actualizing energy, located at nodal points in this immensely intricate structure, one after the other, rapidly grasp together the brain's vast inflow of multifariously organized information from outside and inside the body to form its unified sequence of conscious moments. These moments are greatly enhanced in their capacity to take account of the absent by creating symbols to name forms of definiteness, both those causally transmitted from the environment and those made relevant by contrast to the environment. Such regnant moments are contiguous to each other in temporal sequence, each inheriting the particular harmony attained by its predecessor, though spatially they may jump rapidly from node to node among the fields of information generated by the normal waking brain.

These regnant occasions of conscious experience are the locus of the most complex and prolonged subjective satisfactions—the most intense beauties—in the known universe. The subharmonies of elements drawn from the actual world—sensory qualities gathered, simplified, and intensified by specialized organs—grasped in balance together with elements of pure possibility, held in multiple contrasts and further transfused with comprehensive symbolic meanings, can reach levels of sublimity. Beauty in classical music, for example, is physically grounded in sensory elements exquisitely formed by experts playing well-crafted instruments, these elements further combined in harmonies of tone and timbre (including dissonances, adding further intensity) which require time for development and resolution. Immediate sensuous harmonies are heightened by still more contrasts: for example, with past and future moments by the listener's capacity to recall and anticipate identifiable musical phrases, sometimes to be delighted by welcome repetitions, sometimes by musical surprises. To these contrasts are added memories of other performances, alternative possible interpretations, as well as nonmusical associations of all sorts. Contrasts and contrasts of contrasts, sensuous and ideal, are in this way the stuff of musical beauty. The same might be said for poetry or painting or dance or any of the fine arts.

Kalogenesis in human experience is of course not limited to the explicit arts. Its dynamic is present, at lower or higher intensities, in all conscious experience. A good meal is productive of one sort of beauty; a saintly life is productive of another. Love, morality, religion, the pursuit of knowledge—all rise from and resolve in complex experiential contrasts of actual and ideal. In this process, human experience remains continuous with the kalogenesis of our universe in general; but such human phenomena are raised to an intensity of intrinsic value almost beyond comparison with other centers of subjectivity. Why should a startling, highly localized increase in quality of this sort have come about? Should a postmodern theory of reality attempt an answer?

Arguments abound in premodern and modern metaphysics on this topic. They are usually couched in terms of "God's existence," though sometimes, as we saw, the question may be posed in other language: for example, "the Absolute" or an "Élan Vital." I am not happy with any of this language. "Absolute" language rings alarm bells for postmoderns who value the importance of change and relations and feel the unacceptability of hegemonic or tyrannical concepts at the heart of reality. "Élan Vital" language is linked to a form of quasi-scientific vitalism suggesting the existence of a mysterious life-stuff that has no support in late twentieth-century biological understanding or in the speculative theory advanced in this chapter. "God" language on its metaphysical (distinct from religious) uses appears both in premodern (e.g., Aristotle) and modern (e.g., Descartes) theories of reality. Perhaps this language is least objectionable, therefore, though the initial capital on the word "God" so strongly suggests a proper name that personal pronouns are almost automatically used. (Such pronouns have been consciously avoided throughout this book, not only to remain innocent of gender-specific offense but also to hold clear of implicit commitment to personal categories.) If theory supports postulating an entity to perform the functions of a god, there need be no objection later to finding religious comfort in this outcome. In Volume Three, we shall return to these matters and to the great value-drenched images of various religious communities as they relate to metaphysical theories of god. For now, however, it will be more in keeping with the spirit of this project if we avoid the appearance of dealing with the traditional concept of God, the all-powerful creator and moral legislator, by omitting the honorific capital that turns the theoretical entity god into Maker of Heaven and Earth.

A. N. Whitehead, whose vision inspired my approach to postmodern metaphysics, proffered four principal reasons for including a single remarkable actual entity—a god—in an adequate and coherent theory of reality. I am not sure any of these reasons or the combination of them is sufficient for postmodern metaphysics. Still, all are worth considering. It may be that a complete postmodern worldview needs the concept of a god and that a theoretical basis can be argued. If so, a postmodern god will differ immensely from both modern and premodern conceptions. It will not be properly imagined as a mighty King but as a barely detectable bias toward kalogenesis in the universe.

One reason for postulating a god-entity within a theory of reality constructed on the ontological principle (that actuality is more fundamental than possibility) is that some single actual entity is required to provide a general locus in reality for all the basic possibilities—the forms of definiteness—of which our detectable universe manifests only a selection. Whitehead called this locus the "Primordial Nature" of his bipolar conception of deity. In keeping with his general description of actual entities, he depicts the god-entity as having both a mental and a physical aspect (or "pole"), of which the former holds all the "eternal objects" in perpetual conceptual envisagement. This establishes a "place" for pure possibilities without falling foul of the objection to the Platonic "realm" of Forms as somehow unintelligibly subsisting independent of and even prior to any actuality in which they participate.

At the start of this chapter, I declared my endorsement of the ontological principle. Therefore, a mysterious realm of pure characteristics without anything characterized is ruled out for me too. But the question remains whether all the fundamental forms of definiteness need to be located in a *single* great actual entity, as a god would provide, or whether they might be distributed through the infinitely many finite entities—known and unknown—of the kosmos itself. The latter would satisfy the ontological principle. It would lack the neatness of a central repository graded and maintained by a single cosmic mind; but in a universe conceived as a "bottom up" process of evolving complexity, perhaps a central locus is neither logically required nor valuationally supported. All that would be needed is that fundamental possibilities be widely enough distributed so that in any given cosmic epoch the evolving background regularities ("laws of nature") can provide hospitable contexts for all the more specialized societies within them. It is not even necessary to suppose that *all* forms of definiteness need to be present in that region (spatial or temporal) of the everlasting universal process. Those missing would simply not be possibilities for any given region of the total kosmos. The natural laws of that region would not include them, and they would not be missed. Nor is it easy to say how many really fundamental possibilities are required for a cosmic epoch to evolve. There are innumerable possibilities that are clearly not fundamental: the generic possibility of the helicopter, for example, or the detailed possibility of this particular squirrel playing outside my window on a particular November day are complex possibilities. Complex entities not yet invented or evolved cannot be supposed to be required from all eternity in the central repository, on pain of simply replicating the actual world in an absurd tangle of possibilities of possibilities ad infinitum. Perhaps a decentralized conception of the locations in actuality of basic possibilities—ranges of sensory qualities, patterns of energetic pulsation, frequencies, etc.—is in fact more intelligible after all.

A second Whiteheadian reason for postulating a god in a metaphysical account of the kosmos is the vast surplus in our (or any) universe of unrealized possibilities over actualized ones. Somehow the infinite range has been narrowed. Reality must contain what Whitehead calls a "principle of limitation" or a "principle of determination." He writes:

> According to this argument the fact that there is a process of actual occasions, and the fact that the occasions are the emergence of values which require such limitation, both require that the course of events should have developed amid an antecedent limitation composed of conditions, particularisation, and standards of value (Whitehead 1925: 178).

At some point this antecedent limitation must appear simply arbitrary, even irrational. It is a metaphysical requirement that reality have the attribute of somehow making this initial limitation from the superabundance of pure possibilities.

> This attribute provides the limitation for which no reason can be given: for all reason flows from it. God is the ultimate limitation, and His existence is the ultimate irrationality. . . . No reason can be given for the nature of God, because that nature is the ground of rationality (Whitehead 1925: 178).

We should note, however, that on this point Whitehead did not at that time of writing intend his concept of God to refer to an actual entity. "God is not concrete, but He is the ground for concrete actuality" (Whitehead 1925: 178). For Whitehead, it was enough that the process of the universe (what he then called "the substantial activity" (Whitehead 1925: 178) *itself* contains this attribute of arbitrary determination. The invocation of a god as agent for this necessary limitation is suggested faintly by Whitehead's traditional language (including gender-specific personal pronouns), but the suggestion is uncompelling. The fundamental experience of ultimate limits beyond explanation is widespread among cultures; only some choose personal entity-language to interpret it.

> In respect to the interpretation of these experiences, mankind have differed profoundly. [The principle of limitation] has been named respectively, Jehovah, Allah, Brahma, Father in Heaven, Order of Heaven, First Cause, Supreme Being, Chance. Each name corresponds to a system of thought derived from the experiences of those who have used it (Whitehead 1925: 179).

The concept of chance, in this respect the logical equivalent of arbitrary choice by a god, functions equally well to block attempts to get behind that concept in search of prior reasons. Thus, we may acknowledge, with Whitehead of 1925, a metaphysical need for some principle of ultimate limitation without being drawn into a decision on what further character its source might have. While Whitehead himself went on in *Process and Reality* to affirm the need for a single divine agent, fuller discussion of the warrant for this will be reserved for Volume Three of this trilogy.

A third major Whiteheadian reason for urging incorporation of a concept of god in our dynamic postmodern theory of reality would be to account for the availability—for each actualizing entity at each moment of actualization—of relevant possibilities for its achieving novelty. One function of a god conceived as present in the immediate environment of each actual occasion would be to account for the capacity of entities to incorporate new possibilities not otherwise nearby for grasping. Such an omnipresent god envisaging for the benefit of each occasion appropriate alternatives to the physically given—alternatives that might enrich the pattern of the actual and enhance the level of kalogenesis—would account for their rising as new possibilities in an environment otherwise devoid of them. They must have some source in actuality. Not only are they new, they are relevant to the situation. An occasion dominated by a musical tone, for example, would feel the possibility of an alternative musical tone when grasping the conceptual feeling provided through the presence of god, not a color or a taste or a geometrical shape. This hypothesis of god as ingredient in every immediate environment allows the principle that all conceptual feelings, even of physically absent possibilities, are grounded in physical feelings. Whitehead explains:

A "physical feeling" is here defined to be the feeling of another actuality. If the other actuality be objectified by its conceptual feelings, the physical feeling of the other in question is termed "hybrid." Thus the primary phase is a hybrid physical feeling of God, in respect to God's conceptual feeling which is immediately relevant to the universe "given" for that concrescence (Whitehead 1978: 225).

Such a theoretical construct, involving god in the immediate environment of every moment of actualization, further preserves epistemological simplicity by grounding the view of Aristotle and Hume, that whatever can be present in concept must first be physically felt.

The objectification of God in a temporal subject is effected by the hybrid feelings with God's conceptual feelings as data. Those of God's feeling which are positively prehended are those with some compatibility of contrast, or of identity, with physical feelings transmitted from the temporal world. But when we take God into account, then we can assert without any qualification Hume's principle, that all conceptual feelings are derived from physical feelings (Whitehead 1978: 247).

Even more important, postulating such a god makes evolution intelligible. Without the postulate of a god as the ubiquitous supplier of physically absent possibilities, Whitehead argues, the world's increase in complexity—what I have called its kalogenic character—would be without any ontological grounding.

Apart from the intervention of God, there could be nothing new in the world, and no order in the world. The course of creation would be a dead level of ineffectiveness, with all balance and intensity progressively excluded by the cross currents of incompatibility. The novel hybrid feelings derived from God, with the derivative sympathetic conceptual valuations, are the foundations of progress (Whitehead 1978: 247).

I wonder, though, whether such an elaborate theoretical construct as a god in immediate contact with each actual entity is genuinely necessary to account for the universe as we experience it. The concept itself brings many unresolved problems into the overall theory. As we noted briefly in Chapter 8, these are far from resolution among Whitehead scholars. How can a god be spatially present for every actual occasion and physically felt by each, even by a "hybrid" physical feeling, if contemporary occasions are causally irrelevant to one another? To avoid irrelevance, must god's present experience be considered briefer than the briefest moment of actuality? This would allow god to be in the immediate causally relevant past of each moment of actuality, but it would make god's experience less prolonged and presumably therefore less intense than average low-grade occasions and briefer than most normal human moments, much less Mozartian ones. God's experience should ideally be more rich and extensive than any conceivable human ones, but this conception would make such a "vibratory" god the most fleeting of all the temporal occasions rather than the one "nontemporal" entity with no past that Whitehead postulates (Whitehead 1978: 87–88). It raises, therefore, serious questions about the quality of experience of such an ephemeral god, especially when combined with the need to account for the possibility of god's simultaneous spatial omnipresence for every occasion, even to the farthest galaxy of this universe and, perhaps, to other cosmic orderings beyond.

Can the rising of relevant novel possibilities not be accounted for in some other, less elaborate way? For most of the universe, we can observe there is not much need for a theory of novelty since, as we earlier observed, most of the physical universe seems stable or gradually degrading in its order. The stability of alternating energetic fields hardly requires a god to suggest "plus" when the environment presents "minus," and vice versa. Such "novelty" is not particularly subtle; the restlessness of the energetic process itself might be sufficient to account for the entire vibratory, inanimate domain in which mentality is presumed to be at a rudimentary level. For the rest of the universe of living things, in which more subtle and interesting novelty plays a significant part, we are (on this theory) dealing with vastly enlarged powers of mentality in actual occasions enriched by the complexity of their organic social settings. May not mentality simply be granted the capacity to deal with possibilities in absence—in genuine absence, not the pseudo-absence represented by god's invisible involvement at every place and every moment? Whitehead's god provides a "where" for all abstract possibilities, but is it logically necessary—logically appropriate—to require a "where" for characteristics which are admittedly devoid of a "when"? Simple levels of mentality do not stray far from the possibilities embodied in their present situation; but variability happens, new characteristics are tried out, and sometimes they are selected in the winnowing process of natural selection. Still more impressive feats of mental freedom from the actual environment are found in human life. Must this apparent power of creative thought be discounted and turned into a hybrid physical feeling obtained from god? Creativity is a precious value for a postmodern theory of reality. Reducing the "real" ontological status of biological and human creativity to dependence on subtle promptings from some other source—even from god introduced as a "lure to novelty"—threatens to undermine this value. The empiricist respectability that comes from conformity to Hume's epistemological bar against genuine mental creativity (as I shall argue further in Volume Two), may not be worth the cost.

A fourth Whiteheadian reason for postulating god in a kalogenic universe is to account for the amazing advance of life on our planet in an otherwise wasting universe. Relative to the likelihood provided by pure chance in the time available since the cooling of the earth, there has been an explosion of improbabilities culminating (as far as we are concerned) in our own immensely unlikely species as conscious, purposive, morally responsible, aesthetically sensitive, worshipping animals. Something behind the scenes, Whitehead argues, must be postulated to account for this counter-entropic trajectory of exponentially increasing kalogenesis.

> The material universe has contained in itself, and perhaps still contains, some mysterious impulse for its energy to run upwards. This impulse is veiled from our observation, so far as concerns its general operation. But there must have been some epoch in which the dominant trend was the formation of protons, electrons, molecules, and stars. Today, so far as our observations go, they are decaying (Whitehead 1929: 24).

Without some "impulse" to account for the pressure toward increased order and complexity, the present universe is unintelligible. Interestingly, here Whitehead does not rule out in principle our capacity eventually to detect such an impulse at work, perhaps with better scientific instruments.

> The moral to be drawn from the general survey of the physical universe with its operations viewed in terms of purely physical laws, and neglected so far as they are inexpressible in such terms, is that we have omitted some general counter-agency. This counter-agency in its operation throughout the physical universe is too vast and diffusive for our direct observation. We may acquire such power as the result of some advance. But at present, as we survey the physical cosmos, there is no direct intuition of the counter-agency to which it owes its possibility of existence as a wasting finite organism (Whitehead 1929: 25–26).

Is this an argument for god? The concept of an "agency" suggests a single entity at work. That suggestion, together with Whitehead's clear affirmation of the concept for other theoretical purposes, as we have seen, makes it possible that he is offering here a modified teleological argument in which his concept of god is somewhere between an omnipresent lure for novelty and Henri Bergson's Élan Vital. Contrariwise, the stress on the "diffusive" character of the "impulse" may be read to suggest that one should postulate in the nature of all things some restlessness (a primitive mental pole) that is not taken into consideration by the physicalist categories of modern scientific thought.

I do not know whether Whitehead in *The Function of Reason* was backing away from his more centralized conception of god's place in the universe, at its maximum in *Process and Reality*. But Whitehead's own intentions are not my main interest. Is the universe more coherently thinkable when unified by a master-entity, god? Or is the evidence more adequately acknowledged in a decentralized theory?

My inclination is toward decentralization—toward locating the "diffusive" impulse toward kalogenesis in every energetic pulse and thus toward local modes of self-evolved order with different rates and different outcomes. But this could be wrong. We still know too little about the great kosmos of which we inhabit one ecologically vital but tiny corner. It is a pity that the United States government dropped one scientific program that would have had major metaphysical implications, namely, the program of listening systematically to radio signals from other parts of the universe in search of evidences of ongoing intelligent communications. At the moment, we have nothing to compare against the kalogenic processes of the earth. We know that symbolic thought has evolved here, along with much else of great intrinsic value. Just how local a phenomenon is this? If our minds are unique in the universe, discovering this would reinforce the presumption of a decentralized impulse to kalogenesis. But if other symbol-using mentalities have independently evolved, vastly compounding the initial improbabilities still further, we would have more reasonable ground to consider postulating some coordinating entity—a god—with a strong bias toward novelty, including purpose, freedom, and responsibility in its trajectory toward increasing degrees of beauty.

These are matters beyond present knowledge. They strain even the powers of speculation that draw us in the first place to construct theories of reality. Nevertheless, from the viewpoint of a kalogenic theory of reality, what we can observe on earth should make us even more appreciative of varieties of beauty that are both achievable and, alas, also extinguishable within the local pocket of reality in which we find ourselves. Just as Earth is our home planet, so our metaphysical outlook provides us a spiritual dwelling place. Theory is finally for the sake of life. Thus, no matter how far we roam in our speculations about being, we always come home again to deal with lives and values. This has been true from the beginnings of metaphysics. It will be no less true in the postmodern world.

12

TOWARD A RECONSTRUCTED METAPHYSICS

I began this book by remarking that metaphysics is a miserable word. The field, nevertheless, is endlessly fascinating. Succeeding chapters followed its hopes and frustrations through premodern and modern eras; and now I have added my own prescriptions for a theory of reality appropriate to the values of a postmodern world. Throughout, I have grounded doctrines in persons, emphasized historical contexts, and shown the interweaving of fundamental values with fundamental visions.

In this concluding chapter, I want to explore what playfully might be called a "meta-metaphysical" perspective. That is, I want to think not *in* but *about* metaphysics—to consider from the viewpoint of postmodern values what we ought to expect of the discipline of metaphysics in general and how we should assess its efforts and accomplishments. This reflection is not a matter of substantive metaphysical positioning; but, coming as it does immediately after the two preceding chapters, it cannot be divorced in fact from my own substantive point of view and my own values.

To pin those down it might be useful to add certain qualifying words to the "miserable" one. My metaphysical stance is *panexperiential*. That means I value the categories of experience and find them illuminating in principle throughout the full range of theory of reality. I locate the highest intrinsic values in experiential terms, and I understand the most primitive physical relations among actual entities in those terms as well. I do not believe that being or value exist apart from some quantum of experience, however minor. I do not believe that there can be greater being or value than experience at its fullest.

Since in my view only one domain of reality exists, within which qualitative variation depends on evolutionary achievements of social complexity, my stance is *panexperientialist evolutionary naturalism*. The question of an evolving super-entity, a god, is not settled for me, as the concluding portion of Chapter 11 makes clear; but even if further evidence should tilt metaphysics toward a "centralized" agency favoring more complex and beautiful forms of experience, the god in question would not be outside the processes of nature. Such a god would be one of the pervasive activities in nature.

From god, if there be a god, to the most trivial actual occasion of experience, the momentary achievement of actuality out of possibility is the winning of a value, great or small. That value, the integration of disparate parts into a unified experience, is beauty. This qualifies my evolutionary naturalist metaphysical position as *kalogenic panexperientialism*. I believe the universe constantly rejustifies its being by continuously achieving beauty for itself in all its disparate parts. Some of its parts are living systems of lesser parts, all of which exist both for themselves and for the enhancement of regnant occasions of experience which can rise to harmonies of symphonic proportions.

As in a great symphony, individual parts can be valued both for their own sakes and for their contributions to the single towering and mounting effect made on appreciative centers of conscious experience by the whole orchestra. The "good of the strings" and the "good of the brass" may clash in the tensions of developing themes, but they are both values in themselves, the parts can be played well or badly, and they deserve appreciation for their own accomplishments as well as for the essential contributions made by each to the complex satisfactions provided in the whole. In nature, the real achievements of unconscious centers of value deserve respect by those conscious centers capable of awarding respect. The latter are what we call persons; the former are organisms—in my sense as not simply biological organisms but as self-integrating entities "all the way down." Organisms and persons are not to be confused. They are different in repertoire of behavior, different in kalogenic capacity, different in proportion of intrinsic to instrumental value. But organisms and persons are not to be separated. Without the good of organisms there can be no good of persons. Without the good of persons there can be no conscious respect for or nurture of the good of organisms. This means my metaphysics can be further described as *personalistic organicism*, resting on a foundation of *evolutionary panexperientialist kalogenic naturalism*.

These qualifiers soon become comic. This is part of the reason that metaphysics is such a miserable word. It endlessly demands too much qualification. But through this it pushes us to define our views and admit our values. My motive for all this fun with labels is to prepare for a final look at the place and function of such a theory in a postmodern future.

Personalistic Organicism

The metaphysics of personalistic organicism is well-situated to respond to the concerns of environmentalists, feminists, and liberationists in a postmodern age in which their values resonate. This is not the place to deal in any extended way with social or ethical topics. That must await the third volume (*Living and Values*) in the present trilogy. In the present volume the metaphysical resources available for later deployment need to remain center stage.

As we saw in Chapter 10, ecology is the supreme science of real relatedness. Everything is connected to everything else. Context matters. The environmentalist movement, though not identical to scientific ecology, shares this profound intuition into the connectedness of things and takes inspiration from ecologists who show in detailed ways how inescapable these connections are in nature. Beneath and supporting these intuitions and empirical findings, an organismic metaphysics—in which every entity, great and small, is in largest part what it is because of its relations to the entities in its environment—is exactly the right vehicle for interpreting this vision in a completely general fashion. The findings of ecologists are parallel, on the ecosystematic level, with the findings of sociologists, psychologists, geologists, biologists, chemists, and physicists on their respective levels of subject matter. The world is one of dynamic social orders.

Another intuition of many environmentalists (not necessarily but often encountered also in field ecologists) is a sense of community between human and nonhuman members of the large interactive social orders comprising the earth's biosphere. Human beings may not boast a monopoly on value in the world. Anthropocentrism is aberration. And so it must be considered within kalogenic organicism as well. The whole domain of actuality is a pulsing field of achieved and achieving value. At the evolved level of living organisms these achievements are awe-inspiring. Value, intrinsic to actualization in general, clearly becomes evident on a panexperientialist organic worldview when living things pursue interests of their own. There is plenty of room in this worldview for *appreciative using* of nature's achievements. This is a universal given for all living forms, a fundamental fact of dynamic interconnection. But, at the same time, there is no room for *heedless exploitation*, as though nature's achievements were nothing but resources for one species. A basic axiom for entities capable of understanding, the obligation of respect for value wherever found, would rule out anthropocentric exploitation of nonhuman achievement. Ruthless oppression of nature is incompatible with the spirit of panexperientialist organicism.

Feminists, no less than environmentalists, stress the profound importance of relatedness and particularity. Among ecofeminists in particular, the language of connections is pervasive. At the same time, feminists reach out to liberationists—constitute a form of liberationists—in their strong condemnation of oppressions of all sorts. Oppression is indivisible. Oppression of nature, of animals, of the earth, is intimately related to human oppressions of all sorts. Here, theory of reality that is not simply *organistic*, in which the flourishing of communities is grounded, but is also *personalistic*, in which are recognized the special values attained by entities who can be conscious, free, and morally responsible, is called for especially. There is a prima facie conflict, as we noted in Chapter 9, between the legitimate claims of *collective wholes* and the special status of *individual persons*. Exclusive focus on organic models, correctly emphasizing the well-being of wholes, can easily obscure the importance of unique centers of personal value. Liberationists and feminists stress the inviolable demands of justice toward persons. Postmodern metaphysics must respond to the need to elucidate *both* the intuitions of value intrinsic to the great social wholes that constitute unconscious nature *and* the requirement that personal centers of conscious value not be trampled in some ill-considered rush to biocentric egalitarianism. This it does by providing a multidimensional continuum of value running from trivial to immense. The continuum is complex, made up both of intrinsic and instrumental value. What may be of relatively low-grade intrinsic value, such as grass, may be of extremely high instrumental (ecological) value in the interdependent community of things. And what may be of low instrumental value, such as the appreciation of a magnificent sunrise, may be of high intrinsic value. Working out the ethical implications of this continuum is not our present task. What is important here is to note that a metaphysics of personalistic organicism holds together—in polar tension, no doubt, but necessarily together—the groundwork for both an ethic of communal flourishing and an ethic of individual justice. Neither the temptations of ecofascism nor the arrogance of anthropocentrism can be warranted on this theory of reality.

CONSTRUCTIVE POSTMODERNISM

But is it arrogant and oppressive in principle to offer "metanarratives" and "global unities" of perspective such as the one here prescribed? Some of the poststructuralist claimants to the title of postmodern assert this, as we saw in Chapter 9. I promised there to return to these attacks on comprehensive theorizing as such, asking whether unities need to be oppressive.

Surely there is a special anguish in feeling trapped in someone else's worldview. Metaphysical theory can be inimical to all that one holds dear. Students who have never examined their religious convictions sometimes writhe silently before the clever arguments of professors intent on stripping away ill-founded faith. Many others in all walks of life have felt unable to answer when the value-excluding metaphysics of modern materialism drums on its themes: that reality holds no better, no worse, and that all qualities—moral, aesthetic, religious—are figments of minds which themselves lack secure status in what is real.

One understandable reaction against mental tyranny by such imposed unities—what I might call premature coherences, and what Whitehead fought as "misplaced concreteness"—is to rage against basic unity in thought itself, as though this were an inevitable source of anguish. This may be understandable but is not in the end wise for two reasons: (1) seeking coherence at the outermost limits need not be done oppressively; and (2) disdain for coherence may bring even greater anguish from disintegration.

First, philosophers who attempt metaphysical visions of the whole are indeed likely to have a deep commitment to the value of unity in thought. This much we have seen from the outset. It is a commitment shared from pre-Socratics to the present. Perhaps we should recognize it as the basic motivating commitment of metaphysical theorizing. Still, other values may inhibit the temptation to impose unities on others. In the picture we gain from Plato's writings, Socrates is profoundly antidogmatic in attitude and method. Though he would like to find unity in understanding all the great values—justice, piety, beauty, truth—and their status in ultimate reality, he is reluctant to lecture. In principle, dialogue requires partnership in seeking, however much one seeker may lead. Only when all partners personally see the necessary conclusions, independent of the leader, can the journey be complete. Until then, premature closure must be interrupted, obstructed, forestalled. Aristotle's writing, though interpreted oppressively in later years, is full of "mulling" of issues and provides many chances to consider alternative possibilities. Indeed, the whole long narrative of metaphysical theory, premodern and modern, so obviously highlights the clash of mutually exclusive unities that the best antidote to oppression by any single scheme is more knowledge of their profusion. Another complementary antidote is cultivation of the attitude of tentativeness we found in Whitehead's approach and which, by intention at least, has been embodied in my own pages. On matters of this sort, pretensions of certainty are ill-fitting. On this, the deconstructionists and poststructuralists are quite right.

Second, however, the poststructuralists are quite wrong to derogate metaphysics as such. Abandonment of the attempt to think about reality with as much coherence as possible is no guaranteed escape from oppression. On the contrary, it exposes persons without coherent worldviews to the oppressions of unchecked partial perspectives and the frustrations of fragmentation in mind and action. The longing for wholeness is simply the imperative toward health in thought and policy. Perfect wholeness is no doubt out of reach for human thinkers—at least if associated with proper respect for adequacy to all the evidence. But to court fragmentation is a dangerous practice. Further, to suggest by using the name "postmodern" that sheer fragmentation is normative for the future is to toss away compass and charts at the start of the voyage. For this reason above all, I find it worthwhile to continue struggling against forfeiting the postmodern title to the poststructuralist camp.

For the most part, the deconstructive postmodernists are welcome to the postmodern title. Many of the preferences they articulate are shared in the philosophy of this book. They criticize static visions. I wholly agree, since evolutionary panexperientialism exults in the values of change. They emphasize variety. Again I applaud, because particularity of achievement is the ground of value itself. Particularity, however, does not entail sheer incommensurability when conceptual measure is available at a deeper level. They deconstruct the value-free emptiness of the modern worldview. Once more I rejoice, since deep critique is a useful and necessary task for our transitional time. But stopping here is the problem. This age is not only in need of deconstruction, it begs for reconstruction as well. For this endeavor, it is not oppressive but liberating to seek a constructive postmodern metaphysics by which to sort through the rubble of the old and help build for the mind a dwelling worthy of the new.

ADEQUACY: THE MATERIAL FOR CONSTRUCTION

Theories are conceptual constructions. As we have repeatedly seen in the course of this book, theories of reality—built by human beings with human concerns—are no exception. Materials used in this construction are various. Different eras and people with different temperaments within the same era tend to draw on different resources for the building of their metaphysical visions of the kosmos.

In premodern times, social and religious images served frequently as models for reality. The value-drenched conception of the well-disciplined military formation, from which the word kosmos originally sprang, is itself one of the lasting resources for metaphysical thinking. As noted at the outset, the cosmetic, reflecting concern for beauty and "decency," has been entangled with the cosmic from the start. The well-run society was clearly a prime inspiration for Anaximander's theory that the world is held in place by "Justice." Fairness, retribution for overstepping boundaries, restitution after theft—all these were conceptual materials for theory-construction before neutral terms like "equilibrium" had been abstracted from their social matrix.

Later in the premodern era, with the rise of great monotheistic religions, other great unifying images became available to builders of theory. Theory typically was constructed by the same persons whose deepest values were expressed in worship through liturgies, hymns, stained glass, parables, rites, and prayer organized through such symbols. Theology is not identical to metaphysics. Theology is explicitly the language of a community of religious belief; metaphysics is in principle independent of such communities. It is not in principle beholden to the rewards or subject to the sanctions of these communities. The story of Spinoza is a case in point.

Despite such claims to quasi-independence, metaphysical theory, like all theory, is expressed in language that is social, is constructed by people who are members of institutional structures, and is reflective of the beliefs and values of persons whose sense of what is real and important is pretheoretically informed by commitments and presumptions pervasive in their civilization. Metaphysical arguments and established conclusions work themselves into theological positions—on ways of demonstrating God's existence, on ways of articulating doctrines of life after death, on understanding the ontological status of angels, and the like. And religious commitments draw theory to issues of keen valuational focus, for example, the absolute perfection (omnipotence, etc.) of the One and associated problems: the status of the many, the finitude of time, the uniqueness of the world, the character of evil, and so on. Religious interests, linked to powerful institutions and weighty with near universal acceptance, functioned for premodern metaphysical theory as a kind of "data," exerting strong pressures on the adequacy pole of theory builders. This does not mean that religious "data" so received was somehow theory-neutral. It involved experience of a world extended by imagination and richly laced with concepts—usually with earlier metaphysical concepts used by religious thinkers seeking coherent ways to articulate the symbols most intensely and comprehensively important to their communities of faith. This should not alarm; data for theory can never be completely theory-neutral.

This involvement of concept with data is illustrated further in the modern era by the interplay between science and metaphysics. Science plays the role vis à vis theory of reality in the modern era that religion played in the premodern. Religion then and science now cannot be ignored safely by metaphysics. Like religion in premodern times, science in modern times is widely understood to be making reliable claims about reality. In either context it would be foolish of metaphysical theory-builders to ignore what is being said. The findings of science press on the adequacy pole of metaphysical theory-builders, demanding inclusion as data. But religion then and science now are not sources of "pure" data. Like religion in premodern times, science in modern times provides an experienced world extended by imagination and interwoven with concepts—often with earlier metaphysical concepts and assumptions employed by scientists seeking coherent ways to articulate findings important to the scientific community.

To make matters even more complex, scientists themselves are human beings with preferences and fears, commitments and aversions, who work in community with other persons sharing similar inventories of beliefs, hopes, prejudices, community pressures, habits, and hunches. Thus, on the one hand, metaphysical theory-builders need to be fully open, on the principle of adequacy, to what scientists say about the universe. To exclude such information when both metaphysicians and scientists are hoping to understand the same world would be folly. On the other hand, metaphysicians need to be on guard. Some of what scientists say—without necessarily being aware of it—may reflect metaphysical conclusions from another era, that is, metaphysical constructions as open to question as any other competing metaphysical theory.

It is difficult at the moment to sort out what aspects of scientific pronouncements in a given era may be mainly metaphysics in disguise. Retrospectively, it is easier. In Chapter 5 we could see with relative clarity the influence of Platonic commitments in the adoration of the sun and the perfect circles that pervaded Copernicus' findings; of Pythagorean theories in the mathematical exuberance of Galileo; of the great abstract leaps of Democritus and Epicurus on Being and Void in Gassendi and Boyle, and then in Newton's atomism. Darwinism, we now can see clearly, is shot through with a mechanical metaphysics excluding in principle final causation from the universe. Closer to our time it is possible perhaps to untangle the metaphysics of Spinoza from the rest of Einstein's work; but this would be futile without having an alternative framework—possibly something like Whitehead's—in which to fit the less theory-laden empirical data drawn from our pulsating quantum universe into new contexts of significance.

The materials with which metaphysical construction can be done are not to be lifted directly from science or from religion, though both are intimately related to the project. These quests for reality are of great importance. They each rest on and thematize immense foundations of experience of different sorts. Each demands respect: science for its explicitness and precision, religion for its qualitative depth and pervasive power. Both, however, come to metaphysics no longer metaphysically innocent. Metaphysical construction needs to include their evidence and rework it. In addition, metaphysical construction needs to be open to other forms of experience of all kinds. Moral experience with its great intuitions of obligation, responsibility, good, and right, needs to be included with respect. Other personal experiences such as freedom, purpose, love, limits, aspiration, possibility, and creativity are resources as well. Equally crucial for a kalogenic philosophy, aesthetic experience—the satisfactions of beauty as well as the irritations of ugliness, disharmony, and failure—will make still more vital material for metaphysical development. All of these and more of their like, when properly included as they should be on the adequacy principle, provide inoculation against premature coherences (e.g., from theology or science) that might have been smuggled into seemingly neutral data-claims, hidden viruses weakening prospects of fresh growth.

COHERENCE: THE MANNER OF CONSTRUCTION

The *matter* of metaphysical reconstruction is experience—of all sorts—in accord with the principle of adequacy. What shall be the *manner* of our reconstruction? In general principle, the answer is easy. We should apply the standard of coherence to the jumbled data of experience, showing how everything relates to everything else. But, alas, in practice matters are not so simple.

First, we have to realize (as we have reflected several times in this book) that a human choice lies behind taking experience seriously at all in the construction of metaphysical theory. Some theories of reality, from Parmenides to Bradley, have inveighed against the choice. I believe, for reasons given earlier, they are wrong; but even after that crucial choice is made there are still more choices waiting. Are some forms of experience considered more significant than others? If so, what should they be? Evidence does not come with its own labels of relevance neatly attached. Many thinkers in the premodern era considered quantitatively precise sense experience irrelevant and found the symbolic meaning of perception—the holly's red berries, the ant's persistent labors—far more significant. Many others in the modern era dismiss experience of the sacred or of moral obligation as nonevidential for reality. The postmodern theory-construction I advocate will remain open to all varieties of experience as potentially relevant, but this is a choice to be made. It is in many ways not a convenient choice, since it makes the job of finding coherence even harder than it would be if some whole ranges of experience could be excluded at the outset as tainted, illusory, or irrelevant.

Second, despite every determination to remain open, experience simply left in its enormous variety would be overwhelming. Experience needs initial interpretation and classification if we are to cope at all. This is not just a need for theory; it is a fact of human life. Data does not come to us raw but processed. Some of this is no doubt the outcome of evolutionary selection, allowing us to perceive a world of objects posing opportunity and threat; but, some is the product of social preference for certain modes of classification over others. These preferences are for models of reality on the basis of which some features of experience are drawn into the foreground for notice and others are pushed into the background. Makers of metaphysical constructions are not exempt from these commonsense models by which experience is sorted out and initially interpreted. As human beings socialized in one setting rather than another, we too have our initial biases. A medieval Islamic philosopher reared to acknowledge several times a day the inscrutable governance of Allah over every detailed occurrence may not be expected to have the same appreciation of intuitions of personal creative freedom as may a late twentieth-century philosopher from a liberal democratic home. Even set in the same era, models of reality picked up in large urban settings where all is technology may differ in important ways from models suited to rural life in a mixed community with many animals and plants. Fortunately, the initial preference for a model of reality is not fate—travel, education, religious conversion, sustained reflection, are all potential avenues to the modification of initial presumptions—but it would be foolish to underestimate the power of early models of reality in constraining (by influencing what "feels right") the range of fresh coherences for theory.

Third, even assuming every readiness to be open to wide ranges of data and to give fair hearing to unfamiliar models of reality, fallible human decisions need to be made when problems rise in the process of theory-building. There are always problems, even when one has worked oneself free from the presumptions of childhood and taken pains to think through the implications of one's theoretical preferences. Thinking now critically with a chosen model rather than reacting simply in terms of an inherited one, the normative question inevitably arises as to when one ought to give up in the face of recalcitrant incoherences or even apparent contradictions. The manner of construction of a theory of reality cannot avoid hunch, hope, and all the issues of individual temperament and social pressure. A promising theory in the making is a precious thing. It should not be discarded too lightly. But what counts as "too" lightly? How soon should failure be admitted? No algorithm can be applied. Even after centuries of frustrating work on what I have called the modern agenda, that is, the quest for coherent relations between mind and matter defined as radically different substances, the hopes of some dualists are not extinguished. The coherences supplied by modern materialism hold such attractions to many that there remains widespread reluctance to let go of them and admit that the modern agenda has failed. Perhaps it is the case that the mind-body problem still has no coherent solution. Is that so bad? Perhaps there is no way of understanding the universal experience of temporal becoming within the framework of Einstein's world-model. Is that a fatal defect? Perhaps qualities cannot be acknowledged as significantly grounded in reality. Is that enough to abandon ship? In my own judgment, as is evident from this book, the answers are yes to all these questions. But such admissions cannot be wrung by force from unwilling lips. These are matters of judgment on which various factors play a part. Important among these factors is one's prior investment of hope and work—perhaps including publications and professional reputation—with implications for some general worldview. The opinions of one's friends and colleagues matter, too. Group solidarity even in philosophy makes a difference. Scorn is not an argument, but it can be an effective sanction. Fear and fashion can be sanctions as well. Fear of losing promotions or of being a laughingstock can inhibit exploration of new coherences. Moreover, building something new involves much work. Why exert the effort if loyalty to familiar paths is the prudent policy? But this is unfair to the young. The pleasures of adventuring should not be left to people safely nearing the ends of their careers.

Fourth, if a postmodern metaphysics is to be constructed despite these social and temperamental obstacles, we need to ask about the appropriate standards of rigor. "Rigor," in modern philosophy, is both a descriptive and a highly evaluative term. On its descriptive side, it generally means minute analysis of terms and extensive development of argument upon argument, leaving nothing undefended, making everything explicit, plugging all loopholes. On its prescriptive side, this is taken to be "good philosophy," as contrasted with reflections treated with less detailed texture—these often denigrated as "hand-waving," which (of course) is "bad." Postmodern theorists, however, are relieved from using these definitions of rigor since expectations must be adjusted to the noncoercive character of our discipline at every level. If human judgment must be employed at each step, from the *choice* to affirm (or not) experience as the ground of authority for thought, to *preferences* for models aiding the organization of experience, and even to *decisions* about what counts as disproven (or proven), then the realm of philosophical discourse should be considered more like a Mandelbrot fractal mathematical universe. There is no "bottom" level at which everything is completely explicit and coercively shown to be so. Instead, there are delights in contemplating formations at the present level—whatever that might be—while recognizing that towering struc-tures rise indefinitely above, and fascinating textures sink indefinitely below, one's present standpoint. In such a fractal universe it does not matter what level one might occupy. Rigor lies in the appreciation of the whole picture rather than in shrinking scale. There is nothing wrong with moving downward to smaller questions. It is always interesting and rewarding to shift scale. Moving to smaller dimensions provides the fascination of unpacking a part of the pic-ture and seeing its hitherto invisible structure more clearly. This is the justifica-tion of analysis, which is indeed a wonderful tool highly developed in modern thinking, both scientific and philosophical—a tool that has both its useful and its intrinsically delightful role to play. Moving upward to larger dimensions is also an option. *No* scale can be the *whole* scale. To move upward to see the larger structures of which one's former universe was just an atom can be as use-ful and intrinsically satisfying as plunging down toward the small. For post-modern rigor, synthesis is just as important as analysis. The rigor lies precisely in their being smoothly joined.

Fifth, and finally, human judgment is needed to assess the worth of this enterprise itself. Constructive postmodern metaphysics does not claim to be coercive as a system. It is surely not compulsory as an activity. Is it then impor-tant enough to spend time on? Each person needs to give a personal answer to this question. I strongly believe the answer should be positive, but I have not yet come close to expressing all my reasons. I am not yet in a position to do so. Before I get there, I shall need to weigh the question whether there are other cognitive pursuits that might be in a different situation, for example, indepen-dent of personal values, more capable of generating coercive knowledge. In other words, I need to develop a constructive postmodern epistemology. This will follow in the sequel volume, *Knowing and Value*.

Still, the question as to what is *worth* doing within a limited span of years will still not be answered fully, even by the end of the next volume. Issues of that sort require reflections on ethics and the even wider contexts of religion and the future of society. Such issues call for a final volume, *Living and Value*, in which present questions of *what is* are put to work on future questions of *what ought to be*.

WORKS CITED

ALEXANDER, SAMUEL. 1920. *Space, Time and Deity.* In two volumes. New York: Humanities Press.

ALLEN, REGINALD E. 1985. *Greek Philosophy: Thales to Aristotle.* Revised and expanded edition. New York & London: Free Press & Collier Macmillan Publishers. First edition, 1966.

ANSELM, SAINT. 1903. *Proslogium.* Translated by Sidney Norton Deane. La Salle, Ill.: Open Court.

ARISTOTLE. 1935a. *Metaphysics.* Translated by Hugh Tredennick. Cambridge, Mass.: Harvard University Press.

———. 1935b. *Physics.* Translated by F. M. Cornford & F. Wicksteed. Cambridge, Mass.: Harvard University Press.

———. 1946. *Nicomachean Ethics.* Translated by H. Rackham. Cambridge, Mass.: Harvard University Press.

———. 1967. *Politics.* Translated by H. Rackham. Cambridge, Mass.: Harvard University Press.

ARTHUR, JOHN, ed. 1993. *Morality and Moral Controversies,* 3d ed. Englewood Cliffs, N.J.: Prentice-Hall.

AUGUSTINE, SAINT. 1950. *The City of God.* Translated by Marcus Dods. New York: Random House.

———. 1961. *The Confessions of St. Augustine.* Translated by Edward B. Pusey. New York: Washington Square Press.

———. 1964. *On Free Choice of the Will.* Translated by Anna S. Benjamin & L. H. Hackstaff. Indianapolis: Bobbs-Merrill.

BACON, SIR FRANCIS. 1960. *The New Organon.* Edited by Fulton H. Anderson. Indianapolis: Bobbs-Merrill.

BAYNES, KENNETH, JAMES BOHMAN, & THOMAS McCARTHY, eds. 1987. *After Philosophy: End or Transformation?* Cambridge, Mass.: MIT Press.

BERGSON, HENRI. 1935. *The Two Sources of Morality and Religion.* Translated by R. Ashley Andra & Cloudesley Bereton. Garden City, N.Y.: Doubleday. First French edition, 1932.

———. 1944. *Creative Evolution.* Translated by Arthur Mitchell. New York: Random House. First French edition, 1907.

———. 1955. *Introduction to Metaphysics,* 2d ed. Translated by T. E. Hulme. New York: The Liberal Arts Press. First French edition, 1903.

BIRD, OTTO ALLEN & ALBERT THIBAUDET. 1974. Henri Bergson. In *Encyclopedia Britannica*, 15th ed., vol. 2. Chicago, London, Toronto, etc.: University of Chicago Press, 843–5.

BONINO, J. M. 1975. *Doing Theology in a Revolutionary Situation.* Philadelphia: Fortress Press.

BRADLEY, F. H. 1893. *Appearance and Reality.* Oxford: Clarendon Press.

BURTT, EDWIN ARTHUR. 1954. *Metaphysical Foundations of Modern Physical Science.* Rev. ed. Garden City, N.Y.: Doubleday. First edition, 1924.

CALLICOTT, J. BAIRD. 1980. Animal Liberation: A Triangular Affair. In *Environmental Ethics*, vol. 2, no. 4, 318–24.

ClaRKE, DESMOND M. 1982. *Descartes' Philosophy of Science.* University Park: The Pennsylvania State University Press.

CLEANTHES. 1988. Hymn to Zeus. Translated by C. A. Trypanis. In *Penguin Book of Greek Verse.* C. A. Trypanis, editor. New York: Penguin Books.

CLEMENTS, FREDERIC. 1916. *Plant Succession: An Analysis of the Development of Vegetation.* Washington, D.C.: Carnegie Institution.

CLERKE, A. M. 1882. John Kepler. In *Encyclopedia Britannica*, 9th ed., vol. XIV. Edinburgh: Adam and Charles Black, 45–48.

COMTE, AUGUSTE. 1891. *The Catechism of Positive Religion*, 3d ed. Translated by Richard Congreve. London: Kegan Paul, Trench, Trübner. Original French edition, 1852.

CONE, JAMES. 1981. Christian Faith and Political Praxis. In *The Challenge of Liberation Theology: A First World Response.* Edited by Brian Mahan & L. Dale Richesin. Maryknoll, N.Y.: Orbis Books.

COPLESTON, FREDERICK. 1962. *A History of Philosophy*, in seven volumes. Garden City, N.Y.: Doubleday. First edition, 1946.

CRAIGE, BETTY JEAN. 1992. *Laying the Ladder Down: The Emergence of Cultural Holism.* Amherst: University of Massachusetts Press.

DALY, MARY. 1973. *Beyond God the Father: Toward a Philosophy of Women's Liberation.* Boston: Beacon Press.

DELEUZE, GILLES & FÉLIX GUATTARI. 1987. *A Thousand Plateaus: Capitalism and Schizophrenia.* Translated by Brian Massumi. Minneapolis: University of Minnesota Press.

———. 1968. *Différence et répétition.* Paris: Presses Universitaires de France.

DERRIDA, JACQUES. 1981. *Dissemination.* Translated by Barbara Johnson. London: Athlone Press. First French edition, 1972.

DIAMOND, IRENE & GLORIA FEMAN ORENSTEIN, eds. 1990. *Reweaving the World: The Emergence of Ecofeminism.* San Francisco: Sierra Club Books.

DIJKSTERHUIS, E. J. 1961. *The Mechanization of the World Picture.* Translated by C. Dickshoorn. London, Oxford, New York: Oxford University Press.

DODD, C. H. 1953. *The Interpretation of the Fourth Gospel.* Cambridge: Cambridge University Press.

DONNE, JOHN. 1990. An Anatomy of the world: The First Anniversary. In *John Donne.* Edited by John Cary. Oxford: Oxford University Press. Original publication, 1611.

EINSTEIN, ALBERT. 1930. Religion and Science. In *The New York Times Magazine*. November 9.

———. 1949. Autobiographical Notes. In *Albert Einstein: Philosopher-Scientist*, vol. I. Edited by Paul Arthur Schilpp. New York: Harper & Brothers.

FERRÉ, FREDERICK. 1966. Review of *Radical Theology and the Death of God*, by Thomas Altizer and William Hamilton. Indianapolis: Bobbs-Merrill. In *The Christian Century*, vol. LXXXIII, no. 19, May 11, 622–24.

———. 1970. Grünbaum *vs*. Dobbs: The Need for Physical Transiency. In *The British Journal for the Philosophy of Science*, 21, 278–80.

———. 1971. Transiency, Fate and the Future. In *The Philosophical Forum*, vol. II, no. 3, New Series, 384–95.

———. 1972. Grünbaum on Temporal Becoming: A Critique. In *International Philosophical Quarterly*, vol. XII, no. 3, 426–45.

———. 1973. Self-Determinism. In *American Philosophical Quarterly*, vol. 10, no. 3, 165–76.

———. 1976. *Shaping the Future: Resources for the Post-Modern World*. New York: Harper & Row.

———. 1980. Science, Religion, and Experience. In *Experience, Reason and God*. Edited by Eugene Thomas Long. Washington, D.C.: Catholic University of America Press.

———. 1982. Religious World Modelling and Postmodern Science. In *Journal of Religion*, vol. 62, no. 3, 261–71.

———. 1986. Moderation, Morals, and Meat. In *Inquiry*, vol. 29, no. 4, 391–406.

———. 1992. Natural Theology and Positive Predication: Might Maimonides Be a Guide? In *Prospects for Natural Theology*. Edited by Eugene Thomas Long. Washington, D.C.: Catholic University Press.

———. 1994. Whitehead and the Advance beyond Modern Mindlessness. In *Journal of the American Society for Psychical Research*, vol. 88, 147–66.

Genesis. 1952. *The Holy Bible*. Revised Standard Version. New York: Thomas Nelson & Sons.

GILLIGAN, CAROL. 1982. *In a Different Voice: Essays on Psychological Theory and Women's Development*. Cambridge, Mass.: Harvard University Press.

GOLLEY, FRANK B. 1993. *A History of the Ecosystem Concept in Ecology: More than the Sum of its Parts*. New Haven & London: Yale University Press.

Gospel Acc. to John. 1952. *The Holy Bible*. Revised Standard Version. New York: Thomas Nelson & Sons.

Gospel Acc. to Matthew. 1952. *The Holy Bible*. Revised Standard Version. New York: Thomas Nelson & Sons.

GRAY, ELIZABETH DODSON. 1982. *Patriarchy as a Conceptual Trap*. Wellesley, Mass.: Roundtable Press.

GRIFFIN, DAVID RAY, WILLIAM A. BEARDSLEE, & JOE HOLLAND. 1989. *Varieties of Postmodern Theology*. Albany, N.Y.: State University of New York Press.

GRIFFIN, SUSAN. 1978. *Woman and Nature: The Roaring Inside Her*. New York: Harper & Row.

GUTIÉRREZ, GUSTAVO. 1976. Faith as Freedom: Solidarity with the Alienated and

Confidence in the Future. In *Living with Change, Experience, Faith.* Edited by Francis A. Ligo. Villanova, Pa.: Villanova University Press.

———. 1990. *The Truth Shall Make You Free: Confrontations.* Translated from the Spanish by Matthew J. O'Connell. Maryknoll, N.Y.: Orbis Books.

HERBERT, SANDRA. 1977. The Place of Man in the Development of Darwin's Theory of Transmutation, Part II. In *Jounal of the History of Biology,* vol. 10, no. 2, 155–227.

HOBBES, THOMAS. 1969. *Leviathan.* Edited by Michael Oakshott. New York: Macmillan.

HOWARD, WILBER F. 1952. The Gospel according to St. John. In *The Interpreter's Bible,* vol. VIII: 437–63. New York & Nashville: Abingdon-Cokesbury.

ILLICH, IVAN. 1973. *Tools for Conviviality.* New York: Harper & Row.

KANT, IMMANUEL. 1929. *Kritik of Judgment.* Translated by J. H. Bernard. 2d ed., 1914. In *Kant Selections.* Edited by Theodore Meyer Greene. New York: Charles Scribner's Sons. First German edition, 1790.

KERFERD, G. B. 1967. Protagoras of Abdera. In *The Encyclopedia of Philosophy.* Edited by Paul Edwards. New York & London: Macmillan & Free Press/ Collier-Macmillan Limited, vol. 6, 505–6.

KIRK, G. S. & J. E. RAVEN. 1962. *The Presocratic Philosophers: A Critical History with a Selection of Texts.* Cambridge: Cambridge University Press. First printed, 1957.

KUHN, THOMAS S. 1957. *The Copernican Revolution: Planetary Astronomy in the Development of Western Thought.* New York: Random House.

———. 1970. *The Structure of Scientific Revolutions,* 2d ed. *International Encyclopedia of Unified Science,* vol. 2, no. 2. Chicago: University of Chicago Press. First edition, 1962.

LEOPOLD, ALDO. 1966. *A Sand County Almanac: With Essays on Conservation from Round River.* New York: Ballantine Books. First edition, 1949.

LIGO, FRANCIS A., ed. 1976. *Living with Change, Experience, Faith.* Villanova, Pa.: Villanova University Press.

LINDEN, EUGENE. 1993. Can Animals Think? In *Time,* vol. 121, no. 12, March 22: 54–61.

LUCRETIUS. 1957. *On the Nature of Things: A Metrical Analysis.* Translated by William Ellery Leonard. New York: Dutton.

LYOTARD, JEAN-FRANÇOIS. 1984. *The Postmodern Condition: A Report on Knowledge.* Translated by Geoff Bennington and Brian Massumi. Minneapolis: University of Minnesota Press.

MCINNES, NEIL. 1967. Karl Marx. In *The Encyclopedia of Philosophy.* Edited by Paul Edwards. New York & London: Macmillan & Free Press/Collier-Macmillan Limited, vol. 5, 171–3.

MACKINNON, CATHARINE A. 1987. *Feminism Unmodified: Discourses on Life and Law.* Cambridge, Mass.: Harvard University Press.

MAHAN, BRIAN & L. DALE RICHESIN, eds. 1981. *The Challenge of Liberation Theology: A First World Response.* Maryknoll, N.Y.: Orbis Books.

MERCHANT, CAROLYN. 1990. *The Death of Nature: Women, Ecology and the Scientific Revolution,* 2d ed. San Francisco: Harper & Row.

NAESS, ARNE. 1973. The Shallow and the Deep, Long Range Ecology Movement: A Summary. In *Inquiry*, vol. 16, 95–100.

NASH, RONALD H., ed. 1984. *Liberation Theology*. Milford, Mich.: Mott Media.

NIETZSCHE, FRIEDRICH. 1954. On Truth and Lie in an Extra-Moral Sense. In *The Portable Nietzsche*. Translated and edited by Walter Kaufmann. New York: Viking Press.

NORRIS, CHRISTOPHER. 1987. *Derrida*. Cambridge, Mass.: Harvard University Press.

NOVAK, MICHAEL. 1984. A Theology for Development for Latin America. In *Liberation Theology*. Edited by Ronald H. Nash. Milford, Mich.: Mott Media.

ODUM, EUGENE. 1971. *Fundamentals of Ecology*, 3d ed. Philadelphia: W. B. Saunders Company. First edition, 1953.

OGDEN, SCHUBERT. 1979. *Faith and Freedom: Toward a Theology of Liberation*. Nashville: Abingdon Press.

PLATO. 1937a. *Laws*. In *The Dialogues of Plato*, vol. 2. Translated by B. Jowett. New York: Random House. First edition, 1892.

———. 1937b. *Theaetetus*. In *The Dialogues of Plato*, vol. 2. Translated by B. Jowett. New York: Random House. First edition, 1892.

———. 1962. *Cratylus*. Translated by G. S. Kirk & J. E. Raven. In G. S. Kirk & J. E. Raven. *The Presocratic Philosophers: A Critical History with a Selection of Texts*. Cambridge: Cambridge University Press.

———. 1985a *Crito*. Translated by R. E. Allen. In *Greek Philosophy: Thales to Aristotle*. Revised and expanded edition. Edited by R. E. Allen. New York & London: Free Press & Collier Macmillan Publishers.

———. 1985b. *Meno*. Translated by K. C. Guthrie. In *Greek Philosophy: Thales to Aristotle*. Revised and expanded edition. Edited by R. E. Allen. New York & London: Free Press & Collier Macmillan Publishers.

———. 1985c. *Phaedo*. Translated by R. Hackforth. In *Greek Philosophy: Thales to Aristotle*. Revised and expanded edition. Edited by R. E. Allen. New York & London: Free Press & Collier Macmillan Publishers

———. 1985d. *Republic*. Translated by F. M. Cornford. In *Greek Philosophy: Thales to Aristotle*. Revised and expanded edition. Edited by R. E. Allen. New York & London: Free Press & Collier Macmillan Publishers.

———. 1985e. *Symposium*. Translated by R. E. Allen. In *Greek Philosophy: Thales to Aristotle*. Revised and expanded edition. Edited by R. E. Allen. New York & London: Free Press & Collier Macmillan Publishers.

———. 1985f. *Timaeus*. Translated by F. M. Cornford. In *Greek Philosophy: Thales to Aristotle*. Revised and expanded edition. Edited by R. E. Allen. New York & London: Free Press & Collier Macmillan Publishers.

PLUMWOOD, VAL. 1991. Nature, Self, and Gender: Feminism, Environmental Philosophy, and the Critique of Rationalism. In *Hypatia: A Journal of Feminist Philosophy*, vol. 6, no. 1, 3–25.

POPPER, KARL 1963. *The Open Society and its Enemies*. Princeton: Princeton University Press. First German edition, 1957–58.

ROLSTON, HOLMES, III. 1988. *Environmental Ethics: Duties to and Values in the Natural World*. Philadelphia: Temple University Press.

RYLE, GILBERT. 1949. *The Concept of Mind*. New York: Barnes & Noble.

SALLEH, ARIEL KAY. 1984. Deeper Than Deep Ecology: The Eco-feminist Connection. In *Environmental Ethics*, vol. 6, no. 4, 339–45.

SCHRAG, CALVIN. 1992. *The Resources of Rationality: A Response to the Postmodern Challenge*. Bloomington & Indianapolis, Ind.: Indiana University Press.

SESSIONS, GEORGE. 1979. Spinoza, Perennial Philosophy and Deep Ecology. Unpublished paper.

SHAKESPEARE, WILLIAM. 1974. *Hamlet*. In *The Riverside Shakespeare*. Edited by G. B. Evans et al. Boston: Houghton Mifflin.

THORSON, THOMAS L. 1963. *Plato: Totalitarian or Democrat?* Englewood Cliffs, N.J.: Prentice-Hall.

TOULMIN, STEPHEN & JUNE GOODMAN. 1961. *The Fabric of the Heavens: The Development of Astronomy and Dynamics*. New York: Harper & Brothers.

WARREN, KAREN J. 1990. The Power and the Promise of Ecological Feminism. In *Environmental Ethics*, vol. 12, no. 2, 125–46.

WATSON, RICHARD. 1983. A Critique of Anti-anthropocentric Biocentrism. In *Environmental Ethics*, vol. 5, no. 3: 245–56.

WHITEHEAD, ALFRED NORTH. 1925. *Science and the Modern World*. New York: Macmillan.

————. 1929. *The Function of Reason*. Princeton: Princeton University Press.

————. 1933. *Adventures of Ideas*. New York: Macmillan.

————. 1978. *Process and Reality: An Essay in Cosmology*. Corrected edition. Edited by David Ray Griffin & Donald Sherburne. New York & London: Free Press & Collier Macmillan. First edition, 1929.

WILDON, DAVID et al. 1992. Electrical Signaling and Systemic Proteinase-Inhibitor Induction in the Wounded Plant. In *Nature*, vol. 360, no. 6399, November 5, 62–65.

WOLFSON, HARRY A. 1967. Philo Judaeus. In *The Encyclopedia of Philosophy*. Edited by Paul Edwards. New York & London: Macmillan & Free Press/Collier-Macmillan Limited, vol. 6, 151–5.

————. 1970. *The Philosophy of the Church Fathers*. 3d ed. Cambridge, Mass.: Harvard University Press.

WORSTER, DONALD. 1977. *Nature's Economy: The Roots of Ecology*. San Francisco: Sierra Club Books.

NOTE ON CENTERS

This series is published under the auspices of the Center for a Postmodern World and the Center for Process Studies.

The Center for a Postmodern World is an independent nonprofit organization in Santa Barbara, California, founded by David Ray Griffin. It promotes the awareness and exploration of the postmodern worldview and encourages reflection about a postmodern world, from postmodern art, spirituality, and education to a postmodern world order, with all this implies for economics, ecology, and security. One of its major projects is to produce a collaborative study that marshals the numerous facts supportive of a postmodern worldview and provides a portrayal of a postmodern world order toward which we can realistically move. It is located at 6891 Del Playa, Isla Vista, California 93117.

The Center for Process Studies is a research organization affiliated with the School of Theology at Claremont and Claremont University Center and Graduate School. It was founded by John B. Cobb, Jr., Director, and David Ray Griffin, Executive Director; Mary Elizabeth Moore and Marjorie Suchocki are also Co-Directors. It encourages research and reflection upon the process philosophy of Alfred North Whitehead, Charles Hartshorne, and related thinkers, and upon the application and testing of this viewpoint in all areas of thought and practice. This center sponsors conferences, welcomes visiting scholars to use its library, and publishes a scholarly journal, *Process Studies,* and a quarterly *Newsletter.* It is located at 1325 North College, Claremont, California 91711.

Both centers gratefully accept (tax-deductible) contributions to support their work.

NAMES INDEX

Adam, 85, 86, 190
Addison, Joseph, 191, 232
al-Farabi, 91
al-Mansūr, Caliph, 92
Albert the Great, 95, 99
Alexander the Great, 56, 65, 70, 72, 73, 74–75
Alexander, Samuel, 249–258, 268, 269
Ammonius Saccus, 80, 82
Anaxarchus, 72
Anaximander, 21–22, 24–26, 31, 376
Anaximenes, 24–26, 27
Anaxagoras, 34–35, 40, 50, 53, 72
Andreä, Johann Valentin, 296
Anselm (of Cluny), 34, 66, 88–90, 96, 97, 102, 139
Aphrodite, 69
Aquinas, Thomas, 94–99, 100, 102, 133
Archduke Ferdinand of Styria, 121
Archimedes, 108, 172
Aristotle, 1, 9, 35, 39, 55–63, 66, 72, 90–95, 96, 98, 100, 101, 109, 110, 112, 115, 122, 130, 133, 202, 229, 265, 266, 271, 273, 307, 339, 363, 367, 375
Arouet, François-Marie. *See* Voltaire
Augustine, 80, 84–87, 88, 89, 102, 145
Averroës, 90–93, 98
Avicenna, 91–92

Bacon, Sir Nicholas, 117
Bacon, Sir Francis, 117–120, 132, 133, 137, 139, 152, 162, 277, 288
Bakunin, Mikhail, 226

Baron Verulam, Viscount St. Albans. *See* Bacon, Sir Francis
Barrow, Isaac, 152, 153
Bauer, Bruno, 224
Beeckman, Isaac, 136
Bergson, Henri, 234–248, 249, 250, 253, 258, 263, 266, 271, 281, 282, 285, 369
Berkeley, George (bishop), 161, 184, 191, 192–197, 201, 215, 248, 249, 250, 284, 298
Bernoulli, Daniel, 174
Bertocci, Peter A., 220
Bérulle, Pierre de (cardinal), 136, 149
Blanshard, Brand, 220
Boerhaave, Hermann, 162–163
Bonino, José-Miguez, 288
Born, Max, 180
Bowne, Borden Parker, 220
Boyle, Robert, 148–151, 153, 158, 159, 174, 184, 378
Bradley, Francis Herbert, 212–221, 224, 248, 249, 250, 263, 264, 267, 285, 318–321, 336, 340, 342, 343, 379
Brahe, Tycho, 9, 121–122, 126
Brightman, Edgar S., 220
Brown, Robert, 178
Bruno, Giordano, 116–117, 131, 132, 146, 147
Buridan, Jean, 103

Cabanis, Pierre-Jean George, 168–169
Callicott, J. Baird, 293, 299
Calvin, John, 113, 145
Campanella, Tomasso, 296

SUBJECT INDEX